The Culture
of Professionalism

The Culture of Professionalism

The Middle Class and the Development of Higher Education in America

BURTON J. BLEDSTEIN

W · W · Norton & Company · Inc ·
New York

Library of Congress Cataloging in Publication Data

Bledstein, Burton J.
    The culture of professionalism.

    Includes bibliographical references and index.
        1. Education, Higher—United States—History.
2. Middle classes—United States—History.
3. Professional education—United States—History.
4. Educational sociology—United States—History.
I. Title.
LA227.1.B53   1976   301.44′1   76-17031
ISBN 0-393-05574-4

FIRST EDITION

1 2 3 4 5 6 7 8 9 0

To *Noah* and *Hannah*

To Noah and Hannah

Contents

Preface

The culture of professionalism is the neglected theme in American history. Frederick Jackson Turner explored the significance of the frontier in American history, Charles A. Beard described industrial capitalism as a social force, and Perry Miller analyzed the impact of Puritanism. But the significance of the culture of professionalism, its total influence upon American lives, including those of Turner, Beard, and Miller, remains undefined. Indeed, the culture of professionalism has been so basic to middle-class habits of thought and action that a majority of twentieth-century Americans has taken for granted that all intelligent modern persons organize their behavior, both public and private, according to it. This books describes a cultural process by which the middle class in America matured and defined itself.

By the middle of the nineteenth century, social perceptions about the uses of space, time, and words had begun to change dramatically. These perceptions were not wholly mental or imaginary, but corresponded to the reality of how people saw themselves—a reality that affected human lives. The middle class in America appeared as a new class with an unprecedented enthusiasm for its own forms of self-expression, peculiar ideas, and devices for self-discipline. Here was a great opportunity for people to identify themselves without the support of a community and in the absence of the kind of rigid barriers found in Europe.

Ambitious individuals in America were instrumental in structuring society according to a distinct vision—the vertical one of career. The most emphatically middle-class man was the professional, improving his worldly lot as he offered his services to society, expressing his expanding expectations at ascending stages of an occupation. Professionalism emerged as more than an institutional event in American life, more than an outward process by which Americans made life more rational. It was a culture—a set of learned values and habitual responses—by which middle-class individuals shaped their emotional needs and measured their powers of intelligence. As examples in this book demonstrate again and again, when men had to make crucial decisions about the directions of their lives, the culture of professionalism was usually decisive in influencing their future. Though this culture was not totally homogeneous, not the single influence that ordered the events of an age, it did present Americans with a pattern of acceptable options.

Purely economic theories have "explained" the emergence of the midde class, but they have said too little about subsequent consequences for everyday existence and less about the content of the culture of professionalism. Once the economic historian has isolated the cause of the phenomenon, the particulars of its features lose interest for him. The main interest of this book centers not on social causation but on historical outcomes, not on "explanations" of human motivation but on descriptions of individual responses, in the numerous contexts of an unfolding culture, which led to the arrival of the professional man.

With the creation of the university in America, an institution unlike any in Europe, the middle class succeeded in establishing an institutional matrix for its evolving types of behavior. By and large the American university came into existence to serve and promote professional authority in society. More than in any other Western country in the last century, the development of higher education in America made possible a social faith in merit, competence, discipline, and control that were basic to accepted conceptions of achievement and success.

Professional ambition liberated the creativity of the self, thereby encouraging the ego to explore the world and discover knowledge. But regard for professional expertise compelled people to believe the voices of authority unquestioningly, thereby undermining self-confidence and discouraging independent evaluation. Historically speaking, the culture of professionalism in America has been enormously satisfying to the human ego, while it has taken an inestimable toll on the integrity of individuals.

What began as a monograph has moved beyond into a work of synthesis—not definitive but exploratory, probing, and, hopefully, instructive to the student of American life. I do not present the culture of professionalism as an archetype, a model, or the "mind" of an age. Rather, I view it as having provided a context for values that pointed individual Americans in specific directions, Americans who had real decisions to make concerning their lives. Over time, those decisions became established in new habits of thought which were cumulative. Undeniably older habits of thought often continued to persist making for inconsistency. But inconsistency is not the focus of this book. Its purpose is to describe the historical continuity between cultural responses in the nineteenth century and the twentieth. On the one hand, the historian must neither underestimate the wealth of confusion inherent in the complexity of any event, especially as experienced by the participant, nor ignore the methodological danger of telescoping developments in time for the sake of a false clarity. On the other hand, the historian must not overlook the coherent cultural values that an increasing number of Americans relied upon to give meaning—self-importance, status, and dignity—to their lives within the flux and fragmentation of their society.

I have made an effort to attribute ideas, perceptions, and information to the sources, both primary and secondary. The text rests on the extensive notes that appear within the book, notes intended to be useful to the reader who wishes either to examine or pursue a topic.

My debts are numerous. The National Endowment for the Humanities granted a fellowship during a critical period of this study. A sabbatical year from the University of Illinois, Chicago Circle, allowed me to continue the project undisturbed by institutional responsibilities. Libraries throughout the country but especially in the Chicago area, specifically the collections at the University of Chicago, were invaluable for source material. Many people assisted the project with their comments, leads, and interest. Adrien Janis Bledstein generously took time away from her own studies to read copy and clarify many difficulties. I grew to rely upon her intellectual and literary judgment. I owe special thanks to Richard Levy and Peter Stanley whose understanding of the aims of the manuscript as a whole drove me to continue writing through many drafts until the fullness of a thought was expressed. Ira Berlin and Ken Lockridge read chapters critically which led to constructive changes. The lives and friendship of Robert A. Lively and Gilbert Osofsky influenced my development as an historian. James Mairs, my editor, has consistently encouraged the work. For three summer seasons, Olin-Sang-Ruby Union Institute in Oconomowoc, Wisconsin, permitted me to retreat from the city, pursue the writing in their small but impressive library, and discuss ideas with informed individuals in pleasant surroundings.

The Culture
of Professionalism

I

The Advantage of Being Middle Class

AN AMERICAN PORTRAIT

From the 1840s until the present, the idea of the middle class has been central in the history of American social attitudes. No other national history has been so essentially concerned with this one idea. Indeed, one can conclude that the middle class has been the only class in America conscious of itself. Few have doubted that the middle class has made a significant difference in American lives. But what has that difference been?

The term "middle class" appears in a variety of historical contexts. For instance, in a college course surveying nineteenth-century American history, a student today could hear a professor say that a new middle class of farmers, tradesmen, and liberal professionals supported the election of Andrew Jackson in 1828; that a new middle class of nascent capitalists formed the basic constituency of the Republican party in the 1850s; that a new middle class of modernizers who espoused the values of "continuity and predictability in a world of endless change" renovated the political party system after 1895. A student could hear about such middle-class reform movements in the later nineteenth century as the Knights of Labor, the Nationalists, the Populists, and the Christian Socialists. Or he could hear about an American middle class that taught sexual prudery and began practicing birth control in the 1840s; or about an urban middle class that segregated itself in residential neighborhoods and suburbs in the 1870s.

In the professor's lectures about the twentieth century, references to the middle class are even more diffuse. Among fictional personalities, for instance, not only did George Babbitt characterize himself as middle class, but such figures as Jennie Gerhardt, David Levinsky, Martin Arrowsmith, Willy Loman, and the man in the gray flannel suit shared this identity, as do Archie Bunker, Marcus Welby, and the Godfather.[1] Among recent events, the Watergate scandal stunned disbelieving Americans because clean-cut, respect-

[1] The handful of books with "middle class" in the title published in America during the first half of the twentieth century are not very useful to the cultural historian. They tended toward journalistic reaction to contemporary events. The first two books appeared in 1922, and then four more appeared between 1935 and 1940. See John Corbin, *The Return of the Middle Class* (New York: Charles Scribner's Sons, 1922); Ross L. Finney, *Causes and Cures for the Social Unrest: an Appeal to the Middle Class* (New York: The Macmillan Company, 1922); Alfred M. Bingham, *Insurgent America: Revolt of the Middle-Classes* (New York and London: Harper and Brothers Publishers, 1935); Lewis Corey, *The Crisis of the Middle Class* (New York: Covici, Friede Publishers, 1935); Franklin Charles Palm, *The Middle Classes: Then and Now* (New York: The Macmillan Company, 1936); Arthur N. Holcombe, *The Middle Classes in American Politics* (Cambridge, Mass.: Harvard University Press, 1940).

In the early 1950s, some American academics became increasingly concerned with describing and analyzing the attitudes of the middle-class state of mind. See David Riesman, *The Lonely Crowd: a Study of the Changing American Character* (New Haven, Conn.: Yale University Press, 1950); C. Wright Mills, *White Collar: The American Middle Classes* (New York: Oxford University Press, 1951); and Joseph A. Kahl, *The American Class Structure* (New York: Holt, Rinehart and Winston, 1953), pp. 184–220.

In more recent years, see Joseph Bensman and Arthur J. Vidich, *The New American Society: The Revolution of the Middle Class* (Chicago: Quadrangle Books, 1971); Richard Parker, *The Myth of the Middle Class: Notes on Affluence and Equality* (New York: Liveright, 1972).

able-looking men who embodied the best credentials, the good fortune, and the living pieties of the middle class obstructed justice, violated laws, and betrayed the public trust at the highest levels of government. In his farewell address to his staff, the resigning President publicly remembered ". . . my old man. I think they would have called him sort of a little man, common man. He didn't consider himself that way. . . . Streetcar motorman, farmer, grocer . . . he was a great man, because he did his job and every job counts to the hilt regardless of what happens." And Richard Nixon's mother? Nobody would "ever write a book" about her, but "my mother was a saint." In a most difficult moment of his career, Nixon invoked the romantic—the culturally religious—origins of middle-class ambition.[2]

In 1940, *Fortune* magazine published a portrait of the American people which revealed that 79.2 percent of the population considered itself to be middle class, a group that included industrial workers, white-collar service employees, civil servants, technologists, professionals, and small and big businessmen. According to the survey, the category "middle class" in America reflected no economic realities, no distribution of income, no sociological classifications. Attitudinal likenesses among different groups in America were greater than in any other major nation in the world, and the "most universal American traits" were these: "A rejection of the idea that classes, proletarian or plutocratic, exist among us; a sweeping confidence that for the individual the present is better than the past, that the future will be better than the present, and, notwithstanding a faith in material gains, a greater devotion to intangible values as a heritage to be passed on to posterity."[3] Is *Fortune*'s interpretation a working definition of the attitudes of the middle class?

In part, of course, the very looseness of the concept "middle class," its lack of structure in sociological terms and its lack of exclusiveness in financial terms, commends it to

---

2 *Chicago Sun-Times*, August 10, 1974, p. 6.
3 "The Fortune Survey: XXVII, The People of the U.S.A.—a Self-Portrait," *Fortune*, 21 (February 1940), 20, 14.

Americans. They cultivate the image that any prudent, average man may belong to this social state of being. "Middle class" for the American is a broader and more rewarding concept than either Marx's bourgeoisie, which owns the physical means of production and property, or Marx's proletariat, which owns only its labor.[4]

The middle-class person in America owns an acquired skill or cultivated talent by means of which to provide a service. And he does not view his "ability" as a commodity, an external resource, like the means of production or manual labor. His "ability" is a human capacity—an internal resource—as unlimited in its potential expansion and its powers to enrich him financially and spiritually as the enlarging volume of his own intelligence, imagination, aspirations, and acquisitiveness. "A salesman is got to dream, boy. It comes with the territory": the requiem for Willy Loman caught the spirit of men desperate to establish their own importance and respectability.[5]

And middle-class Americans have dreamed about upgrading their occupations: from distributing a commodity to offering a service based on an acquired skill. Only in America, for example, did undertakers in the nineteenth century sever their historical ties with cabinet-makers, manufacturers of funeral furniture, and liverymen. They enhanced their prestige by calling themselves "funeral directors," proposing to provide a full personal service for the bereaved from the moment of a cherished one's death to the maintenance of a grave site. The professional importance of an

[4] For discussions of the class analysis, see "Classes," Karl Marx, *Capital: a Critique of Political Economy*, 3 vols. (New York: International Publishers, 1967), 3, *The Process of Capitalist Production as a Whole*, ed. Frederick Engels, 885–86; H. H. Gerth and C. Wright Mills, eds., *From Max Weber: Essays in Sociology* (New York: Oxford University Press, 1958), pp. 180–95; Schlomo Avineri, *The Social and Political Thought of Karl Marx* (Cambridge: At The University Press, 1971), pp. 22–27; Richard Ashcraft, "Marx and Weber on Liberalism as Bourgeois Ideology," *Comparative Studies in Society and History* 14 (March 1972): 130–68.

[5] Arthur Miller, *Death of a Salesman: Certain Private Conversations in Two Acts and a Requiem* (New York: The Viking Press, 1969), p. 138.

occupation was exaggerated when the ordinary coffin became a "casket," the sealed repository of a precious object; when a decaying corpse became a "patient" prepared in an "operating room" by an "embalming surgeon" and visited in a "funeral home" before being laid to rest in a "memorial park." In the 1890s, the title *mortician* appeared, suggested by the word *physician,* and the subject "mortuary science" soon entered the curriculum of accredited colleges. After all, as one embalming school advertised in the 1880s, "When your fluid fails, who pays the damage?"[6] The American public demanded service and at least the appearance of an acquired skill; middle-class Americans quickly cashed in on this demand, appropriating and inventing the titles that glorified their status. A mortician was a "Doctor of Grief."[7]

Historically, the middle class in America has defined itself in terms of three characteristics: acquired ability, social prestige, and a life style approaching an individual's aspirations. Neither restrictions of income nor even differences between occupations have delimited the scope of the middle class in America. And it has been the breadth of that class which has struck observers who have compared it with middle classes elsewhere.

In nineteenth-century England, for example, the gentry looked condescendingly upon trade and commerce. And the middle class, made very conscious of its social inferiority, was compelled to seek alternatives to elitist institutions such

[6] Robert W. Habenstein and William M. Lamers, *The History of American Funeral Directing* (Milwaukee: Bulfin Printers, Inc., 1955), p. 346; H. L. Mencken, *The American Language: An Inquiry into the Development of English in the United States,* 4th ed. rev. (New York: Alfred A. Knopf, 1946), pp. 287–88; Philippe Aries, *Western Attitudes toward Death from the Middle Ages to the Present* (Baltimore and London: The Johns Hopkins University Press, 1974), pp. 97–103; Stanley French, "The Cemetery as Cultural Institution: the Establishment of Mount Auburn and the 'Rural Cemetery' Movement," *American Quarterly* 26 (March 1974): 37–59; Adolphus Strauch, *Spring Grove Cemetery* (Cincinnati: Robert Clarke & Co., 1869); Jessica Mitford, *The American Way of Death* (New York: Simon and Schuster, 1963); Geoffrey Gorer, "The Pornography of Death," *Death, Grief, and Mourning* (Garden City, N.Y.: Anchor Books, 1967), pp. 192–99.

[7] Mencken, "Honorifics," *American Language,* pp. 271–84.

as Cambridge University, the Inns of Court, and the Royal College of Physicians, where it was only reluctantly made welcome. No comparable institutions developed in America. Class origins in England definitely influenced the prestige of the upper and lower branches of occupations. The average Englishman, for instance, carried the indelible impressions that physicians and barristers were gentlemen and surgeons and solicitors were tradesmen, surgeons originally having been barbers. Few such impressions existed in America. An ambitious middle-class boy in England knew better than to seek entrance into the upper echelons of the army, and especially the navy, where one required a patron, an expensive "liberal" education, the funds to purchase a position, and a private income to maintain appearances.[8]

Before the twentieth century, a man with a Cambridge or an Oxford education seriously considered the harmful effect that entering the common world of business might have upon his status. In contrast, by 1900 commercial pursuits attracted 20 percent of the graduates from the leading American colleges and universities, including about 30 percent of the graduates from such older institutions as Harvard, Yale, Columbia, Princeton, and the University of Pennsylvania. Moreover, the number of American graduates seeking careers in business surpassed the number entering the ministry, law, medicine, and engineering,[9] each field taken separately.

Being middle class in America has referred to a state of mind any person can adopt and make his own. It has not referred to a person's confined position in the social structure, a position delimited by common chances in the market and by preferred occupations. The popular imagination has so closely identified being middle class with pursuing the

8 See W. J. Reader, *Professional Men: The Rise of the Professional Classes in Nineteenth-Century England* (London: Weidenfeld and Nicolson, 1966).

9 Bailey B. Burritt, *Professional Distribution of College and University Graduates,* United States Bureau of Education Bulletin no. 19, whole number 491 (Washington, D.C.: U.S. Government Printing Office, 1912), pp. 74–78.

so-called American dream that "middle class" has come to be equated with a good chance for advancement, an expanding income, education, good citizenship—indeed, with democracy. Most middle-class Americans have convinced themselves that neither communism nor any other social system would, in current slang, give the "average working stiff" as great a "piece of the action" as does American society. No other social system, especially one in which the government makes a habit of distributing free goods, would give the individual the opportunity to "get ahead" on the basis of his personal capacity for enterprise, ambition, and the ability to serve others by winning their trust.

The middle-class American has traditionally rejected the idea that any classes and any permanent forms of privilege divide American society. On the one hand, he has believed that those ambitious individuals who take full advantage of their opportunities will be rewarded by society with a rising material standard of consumption. Stories of success, self-help, and self-confidence have pervaded the popular media; and many accounts have appeared to document the claim that the future holds for the middle-class American with positive attitudes both more fortunate circumstances and a higher standard of living. His opportunities for advancement are better than his parents', and his children's opportunities—especially with higher levels of education—will surpass his own. On the other hand, the middle-class American has believed that society must preserve obedience to the law, order, and conventions necessary for stable civilization. The ambitious individual must present himself as a good citizen, one who defends images of moral probity and ethical integrity, whose character and clean-cut appearance could be held up to youth, who respects religious values and affiliation, who condemns license and intolerance, and who bequeaths democratic freedoms to posterity.

The majority of Americans have aspired to belong to the "fortunate middle class" as the best of all possible alternatives in an imperfect world. Moreover, it has been significant that admission to this group has cut across all lines of social division: black and white, female and male, poor and rich, uneducated and educated, young and old, non-Protestant and Protestant. The enduring capacity of Americans with middle-class biases to ward off threatening values has been more than historical accident and luck. Yet, why middle-class attitudes have persisted in satisfying a basic need in American lives, and what that need is, remain unclear. In order to explain this phenomenon, the American historian must reach into the past and recover the original source of interest.

THE MIDDLE: STATIC AND FLUID

The *Oxford English Dictionary* has cited 1812 as the first occasion upon which the term "middle class" was used, and the circumstances sound familiar: "Such of the Middle Class of Society who have fallen upon evil days." In the previous century writers spoke about persons of middling ranks, the order of commoners, or, more indefinitely, the ordinary people. These writers displayed no awareness of the class rhetoric of "wage-laborers, capitalists, and landowners." In fact, throughout most of the nineteenth century, American reference works preferred to draw upon the broad eighteenth-century terminology. In 1832, *Webster's Dictionary* typically read, "Thus we speak of people of the middling class or sort, neither high nor low," a mean or moderation between the extremes. The definition was general, and the reference was classical. Aristotle's *Treatise on Government* was a familiar work in a colonial American library, and in it was written:

A happy life must arise from an uninterrupted course of virtue; and if virtue consists in a certain medium, the middle life must certainly be the happiest; which medium is attainable by every one. . . . It is plain, then, that the most perfect political Community must be amongst those who are in the middle rank, and those States are best instituted wherein these are a larger and more respectable part, if possible, than both the other. . . . The middle state is therefore best, as being least liable to those seditions and insurrections which disturb the Community.[10]

Different patterns of social organization were to be found in the dispersed, local settlements of eighteenth-century America: inland farm communities, seaboard towns, plantations, and frontier outposts. By no means was colonial life harmonious, a preindustrial patriarchy both oblivious to a market economy and responsive solely to the rhythm of the seasons, an agrarian life free from anxiety, tension, and conflict. By the later eighteenth century, for example, poverty and vagrancy were becoming recognizable problems in American towns, the landless rural population was increasing together with a debtor class, illegitimate births were rising, adding to the high proportion of dependent children in the population who were crowding upon the limited resources, and political factionalism was rife.[11]

Nevertheless, colonial society was not modern by subsequent standards. *Middle* in eighteenth-century America meant rational moderation, the avoidance of extremes. No extreme more threatened the well-being of the community than the excessive accumulation of wealth that drove a man

[10] Aristotle, *A Treatise on Government,* trans. William Ellis (London: T. Payne, B. White, T. Cadell, 1776), pp. 212, 213–14.

[11] See Douglas Lamar Jones, "The Strolling Poor: Transiency in Eighteenth-Century Massachusetts," *Journal of Social History* 8 (Spring 1975): 28–54; Kenneth Lockridge, "Land, Population and the Evolution of New England Society, 1630–1790," *Past and Present* 39 (April 1968): 62–80; Allan Kulikoff, "The Progress of Inequality in Revolutionary Boston," *William and Mary Quarterly,* 3d ser. 28 (July 1971): 375–411; Daniel Scott Smith and Michael S. Hindus, "Premarital Pregnancy in America 1640–1971: An Overview and Interpretation," *Journal of Interdisciplinary History* 4 (Spring 1975): 537–70; Gary B. Nash, "The Transformation of Urban Politics, 1700–1765," *Journal of American History* 60 (December 1973): 605–32; Richard L. Bushman, *From Puritan to Yankee: Character and the Social Order in Connecticut, 1690–1765* (Cambridge, Mass.: Harvard University Press, 1967); Philip G. Greven, *Four Generations: Population, Land, and Family in Colonial Andover, Massachusetts* (Ithaca, N.Y.: Cornell University Press, 1970); James A. Henretta, *The Evolution of American Society, 1700–1815: An Interdisciplinary Analysis* (Lexington, Mass.: D. C. Heath and Company, 1973).

into acts of personal extravagance, luxury, dissipation, idleness, and insensitivity to the shared interests of the community. Self-interest, a powerful human motive for industry, could be an enlightened source of benevolent action for every productive man who identified his particular interest with the general. Selfishness, on the other hand, released by unrestrained competition, exploitation, and a strictly economic view of work, was a social vice that destroyed both public prosperity and public tranquillity. The selfish man indulged his appetites at the expense of his neighbors. Colonists believed that the industrious and frugal man who reconciled his self-interest with the public welfare would receive in a lifetime his due proportion of social recognition, felicity, and affluence—the rewards of a good life.[12]

The official ideology of a literate gentry, seemingly accepted by most Americans, taught that colonial society was characterized by comfortable circumstances and an equitable distribution of property for the majority. Only vague terms such as "better," "middling," and "poorer" sorts of people set apart the life styles of the colonists. Describing the social structure of eighteenth-century America, Jackson Turner Main has identified a property-holding middling class of professionals, entrepreneurs, mechanics, artisans, and farmers—estimated at 70 percent of the white population. Absent were significant numbers of extreme social class types such as beggars and idle landlords. In a local economy, modest opportunity seemed to be widely available to men who worked hard, but who were neither innovative, driving,

12 For various angles of discussion on this viewpoint, see J. E. Crowley, *This Sheba, Self: The Conceptualization of Economic Life in Eighteenth-Century America* (Baltimore and London: The Johns Hopkins University Press, 1974); Gordon S. Wood, *The Creation of the American Republic, 1776–1787* (Chapel Hill: University of North Carolina Press, 1969), especially part 1; Bernard Bailyn, *The Ideological Origins of the American Revolution* (Cambridge, Mass.: Harvard University Press, 1967); Michael Zuckerman, *Peaceable Kingdoms: New England Towns in the Eighteenth Century* (New York: Vintage Books, 1972); Kenneth A. Lockridge, "Social Change and the Meaning of the American Revolution," *Journal of Social History* 6 (Summer 1973), 403–39; Jack P. Greene, "Search for Identity: An Interpretation of the Meaning of Selected Patterns of Social Response in Eighteenth-Century America," *Ibid.* 3 (Spring 1970): 189–224.

nor especially disciplined. America was, as contemporaries referred to southeastern Pennsylvania, "the best poor man's country in the world."[13]

At the local level, men like Benjamin Franklin did respond to the problems of a changing society in pragmatic ways—for instance, by building a "Bettering House" in Philadelphia in which the able-bodied poor would be rehabilitated, cured of the vice of idleness. But the colonial elite, indeed the society in general, was restricted by its outlook. Ben Franklin, for example, somewhat innocently believed that industrious hands prevented social deviancy, contained passions for rebellion, and satisfied the average man's desires for a place in society. Useful work in the community was both morally edifying and materially rewarding. A virtuous materialism, a benign hedonism, an expanding physical well-being—comfort, land, health, old age—served the twin ends of social productivity and public order.[14] The

[13] See Jackson Turner Main, *The Social Structure of Revolutionary America* (Princeton, N.J.: Princeton University Press, 1965), pp. 270–87 *passim;* James T. Lemon, *The Best Poor Man's Country: A Geographical Study of Early Southeastern Pennsylvania* (Baltimore and London: The Johns Hopkins Press, 1972). The contrast between an early market economy in 1790 and a maturing industrial economy in 1840 is graphically described in Allan R. Pred, *Urban Growth and the Circulation of Information: The United States System of Cities, 1790–1840* (Cambridge, Mass.: Harvard University Press, 1973). Kenneth A. Lockridge has suggestively concluded that widespread literacy in colonial New England did not indicate, as is often thought, that literate men had acquired the " 'individualistic, optimistic, and enterprising' personality of modern man": *Literacy in Colonial New England: An Inquiry Into the Social Context of Literacy in the Early Modern West* (New York: W. W. Norton & Company, 1974), p. 6. See also Richard Hofstadter, *America at 1750: A Social Portrait* (New York: Vintage Books, 1973), pp. 131–79; Sidney H. Aaronson, *Status and Kinship in the Higher Civil Service: Standards of Selection in the Administrations of John Adams, Thomas Jefferson, and Andrew Jackson* (Cambridge, Mass.: Harvard University Press, 1964), pp. 47–55.

[14] See Paul W. Connor, *Poor Richard's Politicks: Benjamin Franklin and His New World Order* (New York: Oxford University Press, 1965); Gary B. Nash, "Poverty and Poor Relief in Pre-Revolutionary Philadelphia," in Stanley N. Katz, ed., *Colonial America: Essays in Politics and Social Development,* 2d ed. rev. (Boston, Toronto: Little, Brown and Company, 1976), pp. 389–91; Meyer Reinhold, "The Quest for 'Useful Knowledge' in Eighteenth-Century America," *Proceedings of the American Philosophical Society* 119 (April 1975): 108–32.

republic was founded on the belief, as Ralph Waldo Emerson later put it, "that a shining *social* prosperity was the beatitude of man."[15] The persistence of this social condition so captivated Frederick Grimke that in 1848 he called his era "the golden age of the republic." Americans shared intelligently, compromised their disputes on reasonable grounds, and deferred to each other's talents and station. "The distinguishing feature then of American society," he concluded, "that which differs it from all others either ancient or modern, is that the *tiers état,* or middle class, is not confined to the towns but is diffused over the whole country."[16]

In formal reference works, middling interest or class referred to everyone who was neither aristocracy nor gentry. "Middling interest," John Russell Bartlett wrote in *Dictionary of Americanisms* (1877) was a phrase "peculiar to the United States," and he cited the usage from the *Connecticut Courant* about 1859: "Men of the *middling interest* class are now the best off. . . . They have felt they belonged to the *middling interest,* and have resolved to stay there, and not cope with the rich."[17] Men of the middling interest occupied the great expanse of intermediate territory between a landowning nobility and an indentured peasantry. Editions of Worchester and Webster's dictionaries in the 1860s and 1870s spoke only of the "middle man"

15 "Life and Letters in New England," *The Complete Works of Ralph Waldo Emerson,* 12 vols. (Boston: Houghton Mifflin Company, 1903–4), 10, *Lectures and Biographical Sketches,* 326. "Transcendentalism says, the Man is all," Emerson wrote in his *Journal;* "The world can be reeled off any stick indifferently. Franklin says, the tools: riches, old age, land, health; the tools. . . . A master *and* tools,—is the lesson I read in every shop and farm and library. There must be both." *The Journals of Ralph Waldo Emerson,* ed. Edward Waldo Emerson and Waldo Emerson Forbes, 10 vols. (Boston: Houghton Mifflin Company, 1909–14), 7: 268.

16 Frederick Grimke, *The Nature and Tendency of Free Institutions,* ed. John William Ward (Cambridge, Mass.: Harvard University Press, 1968), pp. 587, 594; especially see Book IV, Chapter IV, "The Classes of Society."

17 John Russell Bartlett, *Dictionary of Americanisms: a Glossary of Words and Phrases Usually Regarded as Peculiar to the United States,* 4th ed. rev. (Boston: Little, Brown and Company, 1877), p. 391.

—"one in the middle rank, a commoner"—and not of the middle class. The latter phrase first appeared in *The Century Dictionary* in 1889, which defined the middle class as "that class of the people which is socially and conventionally intermediate between the aristocratic class, or nobility, and the laboring class; the untitled community of well-born or wealthy people." The editors hastened to add that the common distinction in Britain between upper middle class and lower did not apply to America.

As was so often the case, especially in nineteenth-century America, formal definitions responded slowly to actual changes both in usage and in meaning. In the 1830s, for instance, two Frenchmen visited America, the Saint-Simonian Michael Chevalier and the aristocrat Alexis de Tocqueville. Both found a middle-class state of mind more fully developed in America than elsewhere. Speaking before the backdrop of Western civilization, both Chevalier and Tocqueville commented upon the absence of a proletarian class in America, the absence of an aristocracy, the absence of an idle middle class of landlords. All Americans worked at an occupation, and Chevalier could distinguish only a class of "democrats"—the old-time farmers and mechanics—and the middle class.[18] Historically, the latter was made up of those persons who, in the increasingly popular American phrase, wished to be the "architects of their own fortunes": persons connected with the professions, commerce, the higher branches of the handicraft trades, and clerks in offices.[91]

18 Michael Chevalier, "The Middle Classes," *Society, Manners, and Politics in the United States,* ed. John William Ward (Garden City, N.Y.: Doubleday Anchor Books, 1961), pp. 380–89. On the middle-class characteristics of labor leaders in the era see Edward Pessen, *Most Uncommon Jacksonians: The Radical Labor Leaders of the Early Labor Movement* (Albany, N.Y.: State University of New York Press, 1967), p. 198.

19 The *Oxford English Dictionary* cites an 1873 instance of the phrase "architect . . . ," though it was current in an earlier day. For its usage in America see the references in Lillian B. Miller, "Paintings, Sculpture, and the National Character, 1815–1860," *Journal of American History* 53 (March 1967): 704; Stephan Thernstrom, *Poverty and Progress: Social Mobility in a Nineteenth Century City* (New York: Atheneum, 1969), pp. 64, 71.

The late 1830s and the early 1840s were a watershed in nineteenth-century American history, especially in the North and in the East. Four developments help to establish the scene, and to provide a context—not a cause-effect relationship—for changing word usage.

First, the per-capita rate of American economic growth climbed significantly upward about 1839, establishing the trend of 1.625 percent annually that continued into the twentieth century.[20] During the first four decades of the century many Americans began to identify themselves in terms not used by their fathers: by individual advancement in a career and by the degree of passion for the material symbols of success rather than by social rank, region, and community

[20] The numerical figure is used by George Rogers Taylor, "The National Economy Before and After the Civil War," in David T. Gilchrist and W. David Lewis, eds., *Economic Change in the Civil War Era* (Greenville, Del.: Eleutherian Mills-Hagley Foundation, 1965), p. 1. On the growth of the economy in the nineteenth century, see also George Rogers Taylor, "American Economic Growth Before 1840: an Exploratory Essay," *Journal of Economic History* 24 (December 1964): 427–44; Robert E. Gallman, "[The United States] Commodity Output, 1839–1899," *Trends in the American Economy in the Nineteenth Century*, Studies in Income and Wealth, Vol. 24, by the Conference on Research in Income and Wealth, National Bureau of Economic Research (Princeton, N.J.: Princeton University Press, 1960), pp. 13–72; Gallman, "Gross National Product in the United States, 1834–1909," *Output, Employment, and Productivity in the United States After 1800, Ibid.*, Vol. 30 (New York and London: Columbia University Press, 1966), pp. 3–90. For disagreement with Taylor's figure, see Simon Kuznets, "National Income Estimates for the United States Prior to 1870," *Journal of Economic History* 12 (1952): 115–30; David A. Paul, "The Growth of Real Product in the United States Before 1840: New Evidence, Controlled Conjectures," *Ibid.* 27 (June 1967): 194–95; Donald R. Adams, Jr., "Wage Rates in the Early National Period: Philadelphia, 1785–1830," *ibid.*, 28 (September 1968): 404–17. Relevant to the discussion are the treatments in Stuart Bruchey, *The Roots of American Economic Growth, 1707–1861: an Essay in Social Causation* (New York and Evanston, Ill.: Harper & Row, Publishers, 1965), pp. 160–72; H. J. Habakkuk, *American and British Technology in the Nineteenth Century: The Search for Labour-Saving Inventions* (Cambridge: At the University Press, 1962), pp. 118–28; Douglass C. North, *The Economic Growth of the United States, 1790–1860* (New York: W. W. Norton & Company, 1966), pp. 204–15.

obligation. Chevalier observed that "the American is brought up with the idea that he will have some particular occupation . . . and that if he is active and intelligent he will make his fortune."[21] With the overpopulation of New England and the exodus from unproductive farms, displaced sons were pursuing higher educational opportunities in vocational careers. "Every farmer's son and daughter are in pursuit of some genteel mode of living," one embittered farmer was prompted to remark; "After consuming the farm in the expenses of a fashionable, flashy, fanciful education, they leave the honorable profession of their fathers to become doctors, lawyers, merchants, or ministers or something of the kind."[22]

Second, striking inequalities in the distribution of wealth were manifested in the later Jacksonian era. Property was increasingly concentrated in enduring fortunes that accumulated rather than diminished over time; and by mid-century, the wealthiest 10 percent of the families in America owned about 70 percent of the property. They had owned not more than half the property at the outbreak of the American Revolution.[23] Moreover, the greater an individual's initial stake in riches, the more likely he was to prosper, a fact that has recently caused historians to reassess the

[21] Chevalier, *Society, Manners, Politics*, p. 267.

[22] Cited in Percy W. Bidwell, "The Agricultural Revolution in New England," *American Historical Review* 26 (July 1921): 700. See David F. Allmendinger, Jr., "The Strangeness of the American Education Society: Indigent Students and the New Charity: 1815–1840," *History of Education Quarterly* 11 (Spring 1971): 3–22; Allmendinger, "New England Students and the Revolution in Higher Education, 1800–1900," *ibid.* (Winter 1971): 381–89; Donald M. Scott, "Making It In Ante-Bellum America: Young Men and Their Careers, 1820–1860" (Paper delivered to the Organization of American Historians, April 1971).

[23] Robert E. Gallman, "Trends in the Size Distribution of Wealth in the Nineteenth Century: Some Speculations," in Lee Soltow, ed., *Six Papers on the Size Distribution of Wealth and Income* (New York: National Bureau of Economic Research, 1969), pp. 1–25; Jackson Turner Main, "Note: Trends in Wealth Concentration Before 1860," *Journal of Economic History* 31 (June 1971): 445–47; Lee Soltow, *Men and Wealth in the United States 1850–1870* (New Haven, Conn., and London: Yale University Press, 1975).

actual rather than the imagined social equality and opportunity in the so-called era of the common man.[24]

Third, finding themselves in public competition with
their neighbors, Americans began to segregate themselves
socially, to turn inward voluntarily, and to define their
private lives by associations based upon race, ethnicity, and
religion.[25] In the violence of the Kensington riots of the
early forties, for instance, Protestant weavers fought Catholic weavers in a dramatic American case of fratricidal warfare. Nativism came to the foreground, poisoning the artisan consciousness and the community friendships that had
persisted only a few years earlier.[26] The camaraderie that
survived from the past, the easy recognition of trusting

24 Edward Pessen, "The Egalitarian Myth and the American Social
Reality: Wealth, Mobility, and Equality in the 'Era of the Common
Man,'" *American Historical Review* 76 (October 1971): 989–1034;
Pessen, "Did Fortunes Rise and Fall Mercurially in Antebellum Amer-
ica? The Tale of Two Cities: Boston and New York," *Journal of So-
cial History* 4 (Summer 1971): 339–57; Pessen, *Riches, Class, and Power
Before the Civil War* (Lexington, Mass.: D. C. Heath and Company,
1973).

25 For an example in mid-nineteenth-century America, see Clyde
Griffin, "Workers Divided: The Effect of Craft and Ethnic Differences
in Poughkeepsie, New York, 1850–1880," in Stephan Thernstrom and
Richard Sennett, eds., *Nineteenth-Century Cities: Essays in the New
Urban History* (New Haven, Conn., and London: Yale University Press,
1969), pp. 49–97. David Montgomery has written about the midcentury
period that "ethnic divisions cut diagonally across all the industrial
classes. . . . [T]he deepest line of division within the working classes,
in fact, was that of religion." *Beyond Equality: Labor and the Radical
Republicans, 1862–1872* (New York: Alfred A. Knopf, 1967), p. 42.

On this point see also Howard M. Gitelman, *Workingmen of Wal-
tham: Mobility in American Urban Industrial Development, 1850–
1890* (Baltimore and London: The Johns Hopkins University Press,
1974), pp. 57–62, 158–63, 170–73 *passim.*

26 David Montgomery, "The Shuttle and the Cross: Weavers and
Artisans in the Kensington Riots of 1844," *Journal of Social History* 5
(Summer 1972): 411–46. See also Montgomery, "The Working Classes of
the Pre-Industrial American City, 1780–1830," *Labor History* 9 (Winter
1968): 3–22; Bruce Laurie, "'Nothing on Compulsion': Life Styles of
Philadelphia Artisans, 1820–1850," *Labor History* 15 (Summer 1974):
337–66; Paul Faler, "Cultural Aspects of the Industrial Revolution:
Lynn, Massachusetts, Shoemakers and Industrial Morality, 1826–1860,"
Ibid., 367–94.

peoples, the alliances based on familiarity, the informal and personal approach to organization and affairs—all were now subjected to unprecedented strain.[27]

Fourth, Americans increasingly found themselves lacking in skilled laboring men and without an adequate apprenticeship system. They turned to the use of labor-saving machinery. An "educated intelligence" and knowledge of general principles were more beneficial to the machine operator and inventor than years dedicated to refining specialized craft skills.[28] Foreign observers began remarking on the restlessness of the American workingman, his "go-ahead" spirit, his desire to improve his fortune quickly through the application of his intelligence, ingenuity, and wits.[29]

[27] Michael H. Frisch recounts an instance of this story in "The Community Elite and the Emergence of Urban Politics: Springfield, Massachusetts, 1840–1880," in Thernstrom and Sennett, eds., *Nineteenth-Century Cities*, pp. 277–96. See also Frisch, *Town into City: Springfield, Massachusetts, and the Meaning of Community, 1840–1880* (Cambridge, Mass.: Harvard University Press, 1972).

[28] See as examples of the consciousness of technology in the period, Jacob Bigelow, *Elements of Technology* (Boston: Hilliard, Gray, Little, and Wilkins, 1829); J. A. Etzler, *The Paradise within the Reach of All Men, without Labor, By Power of Nature and Machinery* (Pittsburgh, 1833); Etzler, *The New World or Mechanical System, to Perform the Labours of Man and Beast by Inanimate Powers, that Cost Nothing for Producing and Preparing the Substance of Life* (Philadelphia, 1841); "The Utilities and Pleasures of Science," *Scientific American* 2 (August 21, 1847): 341; the cover illustration of the Singer Sewing Machine patent, *Scientific American* 7 (November 1, 1851): 1; Thomas Ewbank, *The World a Workshop; Or, the Physical Relationship of Man to the Earth* (New York: D. Appleton and Company, 1855). See also Bruce Sinclair, *Philadelphia's Philosopher Mechanics: a History of the Franklin Institute, 1824–1865* (Baltimore and London: The Johns Hopkins University Press, 1974); Nathan Rosenberg, "Technological Change in the Machine Tool Industry, 1840–1910," *Journal of Economic History* 23 (December 1963): 414–43; Hugo A. Meier, "American Technology and the Nineteenth-Century World," *American Quarterly* 10 (1958), 116–30; Merle Curti, "America at the World Fairs, 1851–1893," *American Historical Review*, 55 (July 1950): 833–56.

[29] See Alexis de Tocqueville, "Why the Americans are more Addicted to Practical than to Theoretical Science," *Democracy in America*, 2 vols. (New York: Alfred A. Knopf, 1963), 2: 41–43; Marvin Fisher, *Workshops in the Wilderness: The European Response to American Industrialization, 1830–1860* (New York: Oxford University Press, 1967),

Chevalier observed that "in Massachusetts and Connecticut, there is not a laborer who has not invented a machine or a tool." The inventive American was "devoured with a passion for movement," and he was "fit for all sorts of work except those which require a careful slowness. Those fill him with horror; it is his idea of hell."[30] After 1840, the sentiment of a visiting English engineer was frequently heard in America:

The restless activity of mind and body—the anxiety to improve his own department of industry—the facts constantly before him of ingenious men who have solved economic and mechanical problems to their own profit and elevation, are all stimulative and encouraging; and it may be said that there is not a working boy of average ability in the New England States, at least, who has not an idea of some mechanical invention or improvement in manufacturers, by which, in good time, he hopes to better his position, or rise to fortune and social distinction.[31]

Competitive workingmen were determined not to miss out on what Americans now referred to as a "white man's chance."

In 1840, Tocqueville described the American middle class as made up of those who viewed their lives as sharing a significant range of vertical mobility together with expanding material aspirations. A community no longer circumscribed a man, and identified his style of life by his vocation, rank, and order. Theoretically a man now actively chose his vocation, perhaps more than one vocation in a career. And

pp. 64–75. On the entrepreneurial spirit and the increased flow of information in early nineteenth-century America, see Thomas C. Cochran, "The Business Revolution," *American Historical Review* 79 (December 1974): 1449–66.

30 Chevalier, *Society, Manners, Politics*, pp. 269, 270.

31 Nathan Rosenberg, ed., *The American System of Manufactures: The Report of the Committee on the Machinery of the United States 1855 and the Special Reports of George Wallis and Joseph Whitworth 1854* (Edinburgh: The University Press, 1969), p. 204; *The Industry of the United States in Machinery, Manufactures, and Useful and Ornamental Arts Compiled from the Official Reports of Messrs. Whitworth and Wallis* (London and New York: George Routledge & Co., 1854), pp. iii–xi.

in the world of psychological expectations, an ambitious individual suited his life style to his conception of his life's
chances.[32] To Americans by the late 1830s, the word *ambitious* connoted energetic and industrious drive, full of
animal spirits, aggressive, fiery, mettlesome, and even un-
manageable. An individual could be described as "ambitious as a-wild-cat," a meaning unfamiliar to Americans in
the previous century.[33]

The eighteenth-century citizen had acted on the grounds
of reasonable want and socially sensible material interest.
The nineteenth-century individual required an additional
mental step. In a calculated manner, he actively willed his
action in order to satisfy a drive for self-distinction and self-
assertion. Individual willfulness and desire now upset the
balance of the older eighteenth-century equation.[34] Individual Americans "calculated," a word which now implied

[32] Tocqueville, *Democracy in America,* 2:129.

[33] The examination of nineteenth-century American word usage in
this chapter draws primarily upon the following sources: The 1848,
1860, and 1877 editions of Bartlett's *Dictionary of Americanisms;* editions of the popular nineteenth-century American dictionaries, Web-
ster, Worcester, Century, Funk & Wagnalls; Mitford M. Mathews, ed.,
A Dictionary of Americanisms: On Historical Principles (Chicago: The
University of Chicago Press, 1951); William A. Craigie and James R.
Hulbert, eds., *A Dictionary of American English: On Historical Prin-
ciples,* 4 vols. (Chicago: The University of Chicago Press, 1938);
Mencken, *American Language;* Harold Wentworth and Stuart Berg
Flexner, *Dictionary of American Slang* (New York: Thomas Y. Crowell
Company, 1960); Capt. Marryat, "Language," *A Diary in America:
With Remarks on Its Institutions,* 3 vols. (Longman, Orme, Brown,
Green, & Longmans, 1839), 2: 217–47.

[34] Especially since World War II, many historians have interpreted
the active "will" of many reform-minded mid-nineteenth-century Americans to stand for the madness of an irresponsible individualism, the
tantrums and irrationality of unrealistic evangelical reformers, the
psychology employed by status-deprived persons in order to regain their
positions of power, and the fanaticism of "children of light and children
of darkness." In fact, Romanticism and the particulars of its influence
upon a new middle class in the period remain generally unformulated.
For the best statements to date, see Perry Miller, *The Life of the Mind
in America: From the Revolution to the Civil War* (New York: Harcourt, Brace & World, 1965); James Willard Hurst, "The Release of
Energy," *Law and the Conditions of Freedom in the Nineteenth-
Century United States* (Madison: The University of Wisconsin Press,
1956), pp. 3–32.

more than computing in the counting house. In common life to calculate meant to plan, after thoughtful judgment and due consideration, upon doing something: to esteem, expect, purpose, intend, and believe in doing that something. Self-expectations, individual judgment, and a measure of human uncertainty entered a person's act of "calculating" in the world.

"Middle" no longer referred to an equilibrium between the extreme social orders of the aristocracy and the peasantry. It referred to the individual as "escalator," moving vertically between the floors of the poor and the rich.[35] The middle-class person traversed the widening distance between these floors as he relentlessly maintained his individual identity. He could start out his career at an impoverished level but rise to wealth without changing his vocation, his social attitudes, his ethnic and religious associations. From the European perspective, neither the common mechanic nor the titled aristocrat retained this flexibility. Often they altered their relationship to the community, changed their occupations, and recast their social prejudices as they rose or fell in the social structure.

In mid-century English society, for example, occupations and their honorific titles reflected class origins. Barristers, physicians, and clergymen belonged to the gentry; while solicitors, surgeons, apothecaries, engineers, and most civil servants came from artisan and commercial backgrounds. In contrast, no formal distinction between the upper and lower branches of occupations prevailed in America. General practitioners, surgeons, psychiatrists, osteopaths, chiropodists, dentists, veterinarians all assumed the universal title "Doctor" (surgeons in England were usually plain *Mr.*). Similarly, in the American college all regular faculty members called themselves "Professor"; in England only the select few who held chairs in a university acquired the title, with

[35] The word *escalade-escalader*, according to the *Oxford English Dictionary*, was first widely used in the Victorian era. Literally it meant, "to scale, climb up, or get over a wall, a series of terraces, or a staircase, usually by means of ladders." "Ascent" was an analogous meaning.

lesser faculty known as readers and lecturers. In nineteenth-century America, "Professor" was a grandiose title quickly appropriated by anyone who claimed to make a living at a skill, or according to Bartlett, who pretended to "make a profession of anything." Barbers called themselves "Professor," as did dancing-masters, banjo players, tailors, phrenologists, acrobats, boxers, music-hall piano players, and public teachers of all sorts. By means of their titles, Americans intensified their self-importance. By the twentieth century, for instance, every respectable school superintendent and a good many school principals and clergymen had acquired the title "Doctor." [36]

In America, the middle-class person insisted that individual attainment at a fleeting moment in a career, and not class structure, allowed for the observable diversity in standards of living. Wealth did not indicate class or rank. To the contrary, possessed by his vision of vertical movement, the individual praised the equity of economic inequality; he approved the fairness of hierarchic divisions of material riches. Listen, for instance, to Ralph Waldo Emerson, a spokesman for this new class:

Man was born to be rich, or inevitably grows rich by the use of his faculties; by the union of thought with nature. Property is an intellectual production. The game requires coolness, right reasoning, promptness and patience in the players. . . . A dollar is not value, but representative of value, and, at last, of moral values.[37]

Ideologically, economic restrictions could not confine tenacious persons who were incapable of admitting defeat, possessed "know-how," "knew the ropes," and did not "fool

[36] Mencken, *American Language*, pp. 271–73; *supra*, note 31.

[37] "Wealth," *Emerson Works*, 6, *The Conduct of Life*, 99, 103. Compare Emerson's essay to Ben Franklin's article "The Way of Wealth," written nearly a century earlier: Chester E. Jorgenson and Frank Luther Mott, eds., *Benjamin Franklin: Representative Selections*, rev. ed. (New York: Hill & Wang, 1962), pp. 280–89. In contrast to Emerson's intellectual approach to wealth, Franklin emphasized the habits of industry, frugality, and prudence, and warned against the vices of idleness, sloth, pride, and vanity. *"Early to Bed and early to rise, makes a Man healthy, wealthy and wise"*: Franklin's prescription almost defied mental effort.

around." Self-styled originators and producers, middle-class persons pushed ahead on the basis of energy, enterprise, skill, and service rather than strictly on the basis of wealth. Their language emphasized perseverance, aiming at a goal, and the willingness to take risks. Persons "on the make" sought a "clear swing" or good opportunity to "make a move" and "make one's mark."

Tocqueville observed that ambition in America was not related to the income of a class but to styles of consumption and to patterns of psychological hope, envy, and despair. Of course, such moods were completely relative, originating in the covetous eyes of the beholder. Thrust into public contact with a competitive body of peers, the middle-class American opened his eyes to life's reward and to life's adventure. In the context of the eighteenth century, the person with a "middling interest" reconciled any conflict between social practicality and personal expectations. In the context of the mid-nineteenth century, however, the person with a "middling interest" lived suspended between the facts of his social condition and the promise of his individual future. Now he protected his precious right to play the game of fortune seriously, to wear disguises and assume aliases in the gamble of life, to deceive and to be deceived in the race for success. Such phrases as "skullduggery" and "shenanigan," a dupe or easy victim known as a "sucker," and the "confidence man" or "operator" swindling and "gulling" kind-hearted people with his "confidence game" entered American English.[38] Gullibility was an unwritten amendment to the nineteenth-century middle-class bill of rights. And that gullibility was frequently accompanied by its opposite, cynicism.

[38] "If, next to mistrusting Providence, there be aught that man should pray against, it is against mistrusting his fellowmen" (1857 [Herman Melville, *The Confidence-Man: His Masquerade* (New York: Grove Press, Inc., 1949), p. 26]). See Susan Kuhlmann, *Knave, Fool, and Genius: The Confidence Man As He Appears in Nineteenth-Century American Fiction* (Chapel Hill: University of North Carolina Press, 1973); Neil Harris, *Humbug: The Art of P. T. Barnum* (Boston-Toronto: Little, Brown and Company, 1973). The "prince of professional humbugs," one contemporary dubbed Barnum (p. 191).

As the American inflated his self-esteem, he also took the chance of magnifying his limitations, defects, and inability. A dread of failure, a fear of lost position, a wavering of confidence: all accompanied the middle-class passion for status. In the new social morality, anxiety pushed the American as much as ambition pulled him. An agitated person might now describe himself as being "shook up."[39]

Middle-class expectations of physical comfort and respectability rose with expectations of improving one's condition. Americans were intensely acquisitive and the popular phrenologists attributed the general desire to covet and possess objects apart from their functions to a special organ or region of the brain.[40] The need to exaggerate the state of

[39] However, the anxiety, doubt, and subsequent need for child-like assurance and security can be overemphasized, especially by historians who wish to come down heavily on the bleak, unhappy, dour, taciturn, and repressed side of the Victorian middle-class character. Perhaps the problem has been that American scholars have drawn too extensively upon European examples, such as those found in Walter E. Houghton's, *The Victorian Frame of Mind, 1830–1870* (New Haven, Conn., and London: Yale University Press, 1957). In his recent study, William G. McLoughlin rested part of his case on the anxiety-assurance thesis: *The Meaning of Henry Ward Beecher: An Essay on the Shifting Values of Mid-Victorian America, 1840–1870* (New York: Alfred A. Knopf, 1970). From a different perspective, there is ample evidence to demonstrate that the sanguine middle-class American could associate anxiety and even remorse with emotionally satisfying feelings of boldness, optimism, exhilaration, and thrill. He normally considered the healthy and ambitious person to be nervous, restless, strained, irritable, and even belligerent. Inertia, stagnation, and the loss of anxiety were more to be feared than nervous affliction, insanity, and death. Did this person love to be miserable, or did he not define his condition in such terms? "No men are fonder of their own condition," Tocqueville remarked; "Life would have no relish for them if they were delivered from the anxieties which harass them, and they show more attachment to their cares than aristocratic nations to their pleasures." *Democracy in America*, 2:222.

[40] O. W. Fowler, *Fowler's Practical Phrenology*, 22nd ed., rev. (New York: O. S. and L. N. Fowler, 1845), pp. 89–96. "*Location*—This organ is located just before secret[iveness] and above aliment[ive]; or, upon the sides of the head, and a little farther forward than the fore part of the ears; or, in the middle of a line connecting the organs of cautious-[ness] and calcu[lation]. It seldom causes a protuberance, but, when it is large, the thickness of the head just in front, and a little above the tops of the ears, will be conspicuous, even to the eye."

one's well-being was now located in human anatomy itself, and Americans used superlatives in their speech indiscriminately. "First-rate," an individual might reply to an inquiry about his health and spirits. Or "first-class," "first-swathe," "first-cut," "first-grade," "first-best," "first-rate-and-a-half," he might reply to an inquiry about his possessions. Bartlett observed that formerly "first-rate" was only "said of large and important things. . . . Now we hear of 'first-rate pigs,' 'first-rate liquors,' 'first-rate lawyers.' "[41]

Chevalier noticed that aristocratic luxuries in Europe were pursued as middle-class necessities in America.[42] Even rich men in America, Tocqueville wrote, "do not form a distinct class which may be easily marked out and plundered; and moreover, as they are connected with the mass of their fellow citizens by a thousand secret ties, the people cannot assail them without inflicting an injury upon themselves."[43] In reality, the improvement in an individual's circumstances could be as marginal as the acquisition of a

---

[41] Bartlett, *Dictionary of Americanisms*, p. 219.

[42] Chevalier, *Society, Manners, Politics*, p. 413. On the nature of the middle class in world history, see Alfred Meusel, "Middle Class," in Edwin R. A. Seligman and Alvin Johnson, eds., *Encyclopaedia of the Social Sciences*, 15 vols. (New York: The Macmillan Company, 1933), 10:407–15; Lenore O'Boyle, "The Middle Class in Western Europe, 1815–1848," *American Historical Review* 71 (April 1966): 826–45. In England: Asa Briggs, "Middle-Class Consciousness in English Politics, 1780–1846," *Past and Present* 9 (1956): 65–74; J. D. Y. Peel, *Herbert Spencer: The Evolution of a Sociologist* (New York: Basic Books, Inc., 1971), pp. 56–81, *passim;* F. Musgrove, "Middle–Class Education and Employment in the Nineteenth Century," *Economic History Review*, 2nd ser., 12 (1959–60): 99–111; Roy Lewis and Angus Maude, *The English Middle Classes* (New York: Alfred A. Knopf, 1950); John Raynor, *The Middle Class* (London and Harlow: Longmans, Green and Co., Ltd., 1969). In France: Elinor G. Barber, *The Bourgeoisie in 18th Century France* (Princeton, N.J.: Princeton University Press, 1955). In India and Japan: B. B. Misra, *The Indian Middle Classes: Their Growth in Modern Times* (London, New York, Bombay: Oxford University Press, 1961); Y. P. Chibbar, *From Caste to Class: a Study of the Indian Middle Classes* (New Delhi-5: Associated Publishing House, 1968); Ezra F. Vogel, *Japan's New Middle Class: The Salary Man and His Family in a Tokyo Suburb* (Berkeley and Los Angeles: University of California Press, 1965).

[43] Tocqueville, *Democracy in America*, 2:252.

heavy mortgage on a small, private house.⁴⁴ In a country in which every self-reliant white man increasingly thought he had a little something to lose—if only a financial debt and a nervous investment in dreams of respectability, comfort, and a sense of superiority over others—the image of middle-class society as the most progressive in history animated the Northern imagination.⁴⁵

⁴⁴ "It is not so much the objectively horrible character of a situation that goads men to action," Stephan Thernstrom has written, "as it is a nagging discrepancy between what *is* and what is *expected*. And what one expects is determined by one's reference group—which can be a class, an ethnic or religious subculture, or some other entity which defines people's horizon of expectation." Thernstrom is specific: "Immigration provided an ever renewed stream of men who entered the American economy to fill its least attractive and least well rewarded positions, men who happen to have brought with them very low horizons of expectation fixed in peasant Europe." "Urbanization, Migration, and Social Mobility in Late Nineteenth-Century America," in Barton J. Bernstein, *Towards a New Past: Dissenting Essays in American History* (New York: Vintage Books, 1969), p. 162. Thernstrom is speaking about later nineteenth-century America, but he has made a similar point about the earlier period in *Poverty and Progress,* p. 216. See also Thernstrom, "Notes on the Historical Study of Social Mobility," *Comparative Studies in Society and History* 10 (January 1968): 162–72.

⁴⁵ Tocqueville described the phenomenon as pervasive in American life: "Whatever profession men may embrace and whatever species of property they may possess, one characteristic is common to them all. No one is fully contented with his present fortune; all are perpetually striving, in a thousand ways, to improve it. Consider any one of them at any period of his life and he will be found engaged with some new project for the purpose of increasing what he has. Do not talk to him of the interests and the rights of mankind; this small domestic concern absorbs for the time all his thoughts and inclines him to defer political agitations to some other season. This not only prevents men from making revolutions, but deters men from desiring them." *Democracy in America,* 2:254. On occupational mobility in nineteenth-century America see Clyde Griffen, "Occupational Mobility in Nineteenth-Century America: Problems and Possibilities," *Journal of Social History* 5 (Spring 1972): 310–32; Griffen, "Making It in America: Social Mobility in Mid-Nineteenth Century Poughkeepsie," *New York History* 51 (October 1970): 479–99; Herbert G. Gutman, "The Reality of the Rags-to-Riches 'Myth': The Case of the Paterson, New Jersey, Locomotive, Iron, and Machinery Manufacturers, 1830–1880," in Thernstrom and Sennett, eds., *Nineteenth-Century Cities,* pp. 98–124; Stuart Blumin, "Mobility and Change in Ante-Bellum Philadelphia," *Ibid.,* pp. 165–208; Michael B. Katz, "Occupational Classification in History," *Journal of Interdisciplinary History* 3 (Summer 1972): 63–70.

MIDDLE-CLASS CULTURE

"I saw what I might call the middle-class culture in process of formation," Carl Schurz recalled about his journey on the lyceum circuit in the 1850s.[46] Would-be middle-class Americans were seeking mental guidance on how to upgrade their condition. And they listened to practical ideas with spiritual consequences that fired their interest in moral self-improvement. Lecturers spoke about the relationships among habits of self-discipline, physical fitness, dietary control, temperance, and sexual restraint.[47] They spoke about faith in one's talents, faith in God, faith in the American way, and faith in positive thoughts about worldly prospects.

As a spokesman for the moral management of a calculated life, Ralph Waldo Emerson gained fame on the lecture circuit. Though his logic seldom convinced an audience, his message did inspire it. "All great men come out of the middle classes," he said, " 'T is better for the head; 't is better for the heart."[48] Why? Because the middle-class person was the democrat incarnate. Because unlike the experience of any other class, that of the middle class included the polari-

[46] *The Reminiscences of Carl Schurz*, 2 vols. (New York: The Mc-Clure Company, 1907) 2: 158.

[47] On movements concerned with physical education and physical health see John R. Betts, "Mind and Body in Early American Thought," *Journal of American History* 54 (March 1968): 787–805. On dietary reform and its implications see Richard H. Shryock, "Sylvester Graham and the Popular Health Movement, 1830–1870," *Mississippi Valley Historical Review* 18 (September 1931): 172–83; Stephen Nissenbaum, "Careful Love: Sylvester Graham and the Emergence of Victorian Sexual Theory in America, 1830–1840," (Ph.D. diss., Dept. of History, University of Wisconsin: Madison, 1968). On sex, masturbation, and muscular alternatives see Charles E. Rosenberg, "Sexuality, Class and Role in 19th-Century America," *American Quarterly* 25 (May 1973): 141–53; Ronald W. Hogeland, "Coeducation of the Sexes at Oberlin College: A Study of Social Ideas in Mid-Nineteenth-Century America," *Journal of Social History* 6 (Winter 1972–73): 160–76.

[48] "Considerations By the Way," *Emerson Works*, 6, *The Conduct of Life*, 259–60. Emerson, the spokesman for the middle class, is examined by Newton Arvin, *American Pantheon* (New York: Dell Publishing Co., 1967), pp. 10–14; Daniel Aaron, *Men of Good Hope: a Story of American Progressives* (New York: Oxford University Press, 1951), pp. 3–20.

ties found within human nature. No other class was so comprehensive.

In his heart, the middle-class person was competitive, active, bold, brave, and even reckless. He mercilessly combated those who hated innovation. He agitated against complacency, he destroyed prescription, he invented means, he subverted monopoly, he opened doors of opportunity, and he multiplied the avenues for wholesome rivalry. The middle-class person was not merely self-reliant, he was absorbed in his own egotism. In the need to assert himself, to build his self-esteem, he could behave in a manner both "thoroughly unscrupulous" and "singularly destitute of generous sentiments."[49]

In his head, however, the middle-class person attempted to eliminate wasteful competition and to establish universal standards for moral and civil behavior. He was the world's organizer: punctual, industrious, mathematical, and impersonal. He sharpened his mind into an analytic knife. He sought accurate information, acted with the "coldest prudence," and built a more perfect institutional order than had ever been known, an order that permitted meritorious middle-class persons to realize their inner selves by means of publicly recognized status, power, and wealth.

Emerson spoke for an emerging middle class in the North that forged its consciousness by hammering against what it considered to be the uncontrollable lust and dissipation of the American southerner, toward whom Emerson expressed a special scorn. "The Southerner asks concerning any man, 'How does he fight?' The Northerner asks, 'What can he do?' "[50] Emerson said of this contrast in 1837. "What can he do?" or "What does he do?" were becoming familiar questions among Americans who wished to identify each other.

[49] Emerson perceived that the popularity of Napoleon's image in America in the 1840s was built around the conception of the Frenchman's aggressive middle-class characteristics. The theme served to organize Emerson's successful essay: "Napoleon; Or, the Man of the World," *Emerson Works*, 4, *Representative Men*, 252, 253, 255.

[50] *Emerson Journals*, 4:275.

What could the southerner do? He was an aristocrat gone to seed; he could drink to excess, brag about his sexual conquests, abuse slaves, pick fights, hunt, and duel. "The shooting complexion, like the cobra de capello and scorpion, grows in the South," Emerson wrote contemptuously; the South "has no wisdom, no capacity for improvement: it looks in every landscape, only for partridges; in every society for duels."[51]

In the imagination of the northern middle-class reformer, the South was a backward region that squandered its human and natural resources. Southern provincialism and the exercise of arbitrary power prevented the appearance of a redeemer middle class with its characteristic foresight and lucidity. Because the region failed to develop educational institutions, according to the northern image, the South both stifled the emergence of a class with professional skills and was burdened by the highest illiteracy rate in the nation. An illiterate people, lacking the discipline necessary to avoid promiscuous sex and illicit orgies, was insensitive to the sanctity of the nuclear family with its example of control, planning, and management. Overindulgence of sensual desires depleted the human energy required by an active intellect, and the process of mental degeneration culminated in the feeblemindedness of morons and idiots. Northern observers of the South dwelt on numerous examples of societal retardation. Inadequate transportation and port facilities, for instance, prohibited the South from trading directly with its primary markets, forcing the region to be commercially dependent upon the North. And the many German and Irish immigrants in the 1840s and the 1850s, with their cheap labor, their artisan skills, and their availability for military conscription, avoided the benighted South, preferring to settle in the prospering North and West. In the northerners' minds, southerners acted as if they had no future, whereas faith in the future dwelt at the

51 *Ibid.*, 9:121.

cultural center of the northern middle class with its teachings about delayed gratification and careful calculation.[52]

It was significant that Emerson perceived society from the perspective of "culture," which influenced the entirety of a person's responses, everything that person did, large and small. "It is a measure of culture, the number of things taken for granted," Emerson said, "the whole state of man is a state of culture." Being middle class transcended the mere economics of capitalism; just as being a southern aristocrat transcended the mere economics of slavery. Culture was "all which gives the mind possession of its own powers." It invaded and formed the semiconscious life as well as the conscious one: "culture inspects our dreams also." It was even "a question of Culture," Emerson wrote, "which is best, a fair or a blotted page."[53] In Emerson's view, more than northern armies had triumphed in 1865; the middle-class culture in the North had proved itself both superior to and more durable than the aristocratic culture in the South.

[52] Northern views of the South are examined by Eric Foner, *Free Soil, Free Labor, Free Men: The Ideology of the Republican Party Before the Civil War* (New York: Oxford University Press, 1970), pp. 40–72; Ronald G. Walters, "The Erotic South: Civilization and Sexuality in American Abolitionism," *American Quarterly* 25 (May 1973): 177–201; Ruth Miller Elson, *Guardians of Tradition: American Schoolbooks of the Nineteenth Century* (Lincoln: University of Nebraska Press, 1964), pp. 174–78. See also Carl Degler, "The Two Cultures and The Civil War," in Stanley Coben and Norman Ratner, eds., *The Development of American Culture* (Englewood Cliffs, N.J.: Prentice-Hall, 1970), pp. 92–118; Eugene D. Genovese, *The Political Economy of Slavery: Studies in the Economy and Society of the Slave South* (New York: Pantheon Books, 1965), pp. 13–39. Henry Adams repeated a sentiment prevalent during his youth when he wrote: "Strictly, the Southerner had no mind; he had temperament. He was not a scholar; he had no intellectual training; he could not analyze an idea, and he could not even conceive of admitting two." *The Education of Henry Adams: An Autobiography* (Boston and New York: Houghton Mifflin Company, 1918), pp. 57–58.

[53] "Aristocracy," *Emerson Works*, 10, *Lectures and Biographical Sketches*, 56; "Worship," *Emerson Works*, 6, *The Conduct of Life*, 204; "Progress of Culture," *Emerson Works*, 8, *Letters and Social Aims*, 217; *Emerson Journals*, 4:323; *The Journals and Miscellaneous Notebooks of Ralph Waldo Emerson*, 10 vols. to date, ed. William H. Gilman et al. (Cambridge, Mass.: Harvard University Press, 1960–), 5: 422.

In cultural terms, being middle class referred to the kind of person one was, to the style of life one emulated, not only in vocational pursuits but in recreation, domestic relations, education, politics, war—everything. The middle-class person was relentlessly competitive. He took pride in being "on his own hook." In his own words, he could "go it alone," "go it strong," "put himself into" his work, "see" his opportunity, "skunk" the opposition, "spread" himself, and "shine." The middle-class American artfully tested the limits of the individual ego; he deliberately isolated a segment of experience in order to control it; he shrewdly committed himself to the proposition that educated knowledge was the beginning of power, and power was the source of spiritual and material riches. He attached to himself all the status and honor that an accomplishment would bear; and he needed to be publicly recognized as someone with a special gift and with a decisive influence over others. Generosity, chivalry, and manners disappeared in the middle-class person, who asserted his superior authority over a defeated competitor and who was unyielding in the demand for ceremonial submission.

The North's successful execution of the war itself symbolized the victory of this new culture. "This middle-class country had got a middle-class president, at last," Emerson eulogized Lincoln in 1865. Two years earlier Emerson had clarified his point of view: "War organizes. . . . [M]y interest in my Country is not primary, but professional."[54] Though the middle-class person in the North could behave as violently as the puerile southerner, the violent responses of the former were better disciplined and better organized, more enduring and more impersonal. Lincoln, the middle-class president, fought a total and a sustained war that southerners could neither culturally comprehend nor logis-

[54] "Abraham Lincoln," *Emerson Works*, 11, *Miscellanies*, 334; *Emerson Journals*, 9:493. For the war as a victory for the bourgeoisie in America see Barrington Moore, Jr., "The American Civil War: The Last Capitalist Revolution," in *Social Origins of Dictatorship and Democracy: Lord and Peasant in the Making of the Modern World* (Boston: Beacon Press, 1967), pp. 111–55.

tically prevail against. Indeed, the outcome of the war era, and the devastation of the South, vindicated Emerson's bias against antebellum southern culture. "Slavery is no scholar, no improver," he had lectured to receptive audiences; "it does not love the whistle of the railroad; it does not love the newspaper, the mailbag, a college, a book or a preacher who has the absurd whim of saying what he thinks; it does not increase the white population; it does not improve the soil; everything goes to decay."[55] Emerson depicted southern leaders as the victims of their own intoxicated fantasies, men unaccustomed to placing their dreams of greatness in the service of an analytic intellect that projected long-range purposes, goals, and ideas. Southern culture obstructed the advance of middle-class civilization, and it suffered defeat.

"Our culture," Emerson wrote, "is the predominance of an idea which draws after it this train of cities and institutions."[56] By the 1860s it was evident to an observer that ambitious middle-class persons were seeking a professional basis for an institutional order, a basis in universal and predictable rules to provide a formal context for the competitive spirit of individual egos. The practice of regional self-interest and community good works had led to superficiality, poor judgment, incompetence, and undue praise of the versatile amateur. The word "amateur," which earlier in the eighteenth century had simply referred to a person who pursued an activity for the love of it, increasingly acquired negative and pejorative references as the nineteenth century developed. *Amateurish,* a new midcentury word, connoted faulty and deficient work, perhaps defective, unskillful, superficial, desultory, less than a serious commitment, the pursuit of an activity for amusement and distraction. The middle-class person required a more reliable institutional world in which to liberate individual energy than amateurs

55 "Emancipation in the British West Indies," *Emerson Works,* 11, *Miscellanies,* 125–26. The effect of the war on Emerson is described by George M. Fredrickson, *The Inner Civil War: Northern Intellectuals and the Crisis of the Union* (New York: Harper & Row, Publishers, 1965), pp. 176–80 *passim.*

56 "Circles," *Emerson Works,* 2, *Essays: First Series,* 302, 310.

had previously known. Lawyers, medical doctors, teachers, managers, civil servants all now required working definitions of such elaborate concepts as "contract," "disease," "curriculum," "system," and "bureacracy," which average and prudent men throughout the nation could accept.

In the "rich thicket" of American reality, the middle class required the partitioning of space and the scheduling of time beyond what *ad hoc* methods and impetuous minds could accomplish. The organization of the North for the Civil War itself gave a substantial boost to institutional trends that were under way: in such areas as financing and banking, the gathering of vital statistics about the population, and social science applied to education, public health, and philanthropy.[57] "The two dominant words of our time are *law* and *average,* both pointing to the uniformity of the order of being in which we live," Oliver Wendell Holmes, Sr., said in 1860: "Statistics have tabulated everything— population, growth, wealth, crime, disease. We have shaded maps showing the geographical distribution of larceny and suicide. Analysis and classification have been at work upon all tangible and visible objects."[58] By the third-quarter of the century, a practical empiricism that waited upon successful local usage and informal public pressure was disastrous in a nation industrializing with the haste of America. Abstract principles were necessary—science, a formal conceptual framework in which calculating individuals could determine the natural course and limits of expectations.

Holmes, for instance, criticized the active medical pro-

[57] See for instance Robert H. Bremner, "The Impact of the Civil War on Philanthropy and Social Welfare," *Civil War History* 12 (December 1966): 293–303.

[58] Oliver Wendell Holmes, "Currents and Counter-Currents in Medical Science," in *Medical Essays: 1842–1882* (Boston and New York: Houghton Mifflin Company, 1895), p. 180. For one impulse behind this movement, see Richmond Laurin Hawkins, *Positivism in the United States (1853–1861)* (Cambridge, Mass.: Harvard University Press, 1938); W. M. Simon, *European Positivism in the Nineteenth Century: An Essay in Intellectual History* (Ithaca, N.Y.: Cornell University Press, 1963).

fession for dangerously overdosing the community with "noxious agents" because the average doctor thought he "earned his money" only when the patient received a "recipe." Semieducated practitioners remained ignorant of the natural course or special science of particular diseases, especially environmentally contagious ones that demanded an awareness of circumstances rather than the dispensing of powerful drugs—drugs which themselves might produce new and baffling symptoms, only to be treated with additional poisonous medication. Because more doctors might be prescribing for medically induced symptoms than for actual diseases, Holmes "firmly believe[d] that if the whole materia medica, *as now used,* could be sunk to the bottom of the sea, it would be all the better for mankind,—and all the worse for the fishes."[59]

After the Civil War, American spokesmen publicly endorsed middle-class ambitions within the context of a growing number of institutions that both employed and satisfied the needs of the middle class. Among those institutions, for instance, was the American university, including its professional schools. In his inaugural address at the new University of Minnesota in 1869, William Watts Folwell commented that "so long as there is open to young men the prospect of a name and a home, of a high social position to be won with clean hands and unsoiled garments by headwork, and without capital, the learned professions, so called, will continue to absorb the best blood of the country."[60] In a nation without an effective apprenticeship system and without a significant gentry, the school diploma more and more served as the license with which an individual sought entry into the respectability and rewards of a profession. By 1870, there were more institutions in America awarding bachelor's degrees, more medical schools, and more law schools than in all of Europe. Chairs in some proprietary medical schools sold like seats on the stock exchange. And why? Because, as

59 Holmes, *Medical Essays*, p. 203.

60 William Watts Folwell, "Inaugural Address," in *University Addresses* (Minneapolis: The H. W. Wilson Company, 1909), pp. 10–11.

the visiting James Bryce observed: "In a country where there is no titled class, no landed class, no military class, the chief distinction which popular sentiment can lay hold of as raising one set of persons above another is the character of their occupation, the degree of culture it implies, the extent to which it gives them an honourable prominence."[61] For the middle class in America, degree-granting education was an instrument of ambition and a vehicle to status in the occupational world.

In 1860, the sentiment was heard that "Americans all wanted to be clerks, professionals or bosses, or to drive something."[62] Success in the middle class increasingly depended upon providing a service based on a skill, elevating the status of one's occupation by referring to it as a profession. Funeral directors, for instance, seized the word—*profes-sional*—when they decided not to follow in "the wake of broom makers, box and basket-makers." As legal agents certified by county boards of health, they proposed that the members of the National Funeral Directors' Association be educated, examined, and licensed as professionals. In 1884, the first Code of Ethics concluded with the statement: "There is, perhaps, no profession, after that of the sacred ministry, in which a high-toned morality is more imperatively necessary than that of a funeral director's." A man of the world, the undertaker knew better from experience, that the claim for respectability was itself an initial step to "get the public to *receive us as professional men*," as one president of the Association phrased it.[63] In 1891, a plumber praised the dignity of his work before the American Public Health Association in words that were becoming familiar:

[61] William G. Rothstein, *American Physicians in the Nineteenth Century: From Sects to Science* (Baltimore and London: The Johns Hopkins University Press, 1972), pp. 292–93; James Bryce, *The American Commonwealth*, 2 vols., 3d ed. rev. (New York: Macmillan and Co., 1895), 2:626.

[62] Montgomery, *Beyond Equality*, p. 32.

[63] Habenstein, Lamers, *History of American Funeral Directing*, pp. 476, 472–73.

Plumbing is no longer merely a trade. Its importance and value in relation to health, and its requirements regarding scientific knowledge, have elevated it to a profession. It is clothed with the responsibility of the learned professions and the dignity of the sciences. The high qualities of mechanical skills are combined with the best of the sciences of the most practical utility. It unites skilled labor and high educational qualifications in one. This being the nature of plumbing today, it becomes the duty of the plumber to maintain in every way the dignity of his calling. It should be his special care to have the profession as free as possible from the deleterious effects of the incompetent and unscrupulous.[64]

The Sanitary News, a trade weekly from Chicago which first appeared in 1882, exhorted the community to pay the price of high-grade professional skills in plumbing for the sake of the public's safety. "As a matter of fact," the editor concluded, "an ignorant or incompetent man can do more damage to health and life with plumbing materials than he can with a wad of prescription paper or a store full of drugs."[65]

By the 1890s, one historian has recently speculated, "perhaps one-third of the American population was distinctly middle class."[66] While the shrinking size of the family and falling birth rates—especially among the American born—indicated a greater concern with both the education of and the expectations for individual lives, the middle class was expanding throughout the nineteenth century. In the later eighteenth century six children were commonly found in a single family. The birth rate began declining after 1820, and by 1900 three children was the more familiar number.[67]

---

[64] Cited in Barbara Gutmann Rosenkrantz, "Cart Before Horse: Theory, Practice and Professional Image in American Public Health, 1870–1920," *Journal of the History of Medicine and Allied Sciences* 29 (January 1974): 60.

[65] *The Sanitary News* 13 (December 1, 1888): 49.

[66] C. K. Yearly, "The 'Provincial Party' and the Megalopolises: London, Paris, and New York, 1850–1910," *Comparative Studies in Society and History* 15 (January 1973): 54.

[67] In 1810, a thousand white women had 1,358 children under five years old; in 1860 a thousand white women had 905 children; and in

After 1870, occupational statistics from the federal census pointed to the rising importance of the types of work in which middle-class attitudes were rewarding. Clerical occupations, for instance, rose most dramatically in relative importance to the entire labor force: from .6 percent in 1870 to 2.5 percent in 1900 to 4.6 percent in 1910. According to the census summary, the professional class "increased markedly in relative importance," from 2.6 percent in 1870 to 4.1 percent in 1900.[68] Clerical, semiprofessional, and professional persons shared certain characteristics. Rather than producing a material product, they provided the public a service; the quality of that service depended upon the accurate knowledge, the efficient methods, the good judgment, the

1900, 666. The largest decline occurred between 1840 and 1850. *Historical Statistics of the United States: Colonial Times to 1957: A Statistical Abstract Supplement* (Washington, D.C.: U.S. Department of Commerce, Bureau of the Census, 1960), Series B 37, p. 24. Concerning family planning, the female role, and such issues as abortion in the nineteenth-century American middle class, see David M. Kennedy, "The Nineteenth-Century Heritage: The Family, Feminism, and Sex," in *Birth Control in America: The Career of Margaret Sanger* (New Haven, Conn., and London: Yale University Press, 1970), pp. 36–71; Carroll Smith-Rosenberg and Charles Rosenberg, "The Female Animal: Medical and Biological Views of Woman and Her Role in Nineteenth-Century America," *Journal of American History* 60 (September 1973): 332–56. The Rosenbergs note that "it is significant that discussions of birth control in the United States always emphasized the role and motivations of middle-class women and men; in England, following the canon of the traditional Malthusian debate, the working class and its needs played a far more prominent role. Not until late in the century did American birth-control advocates tend to concern themselves with the needs and welfare of the working population" (345n).

68 Alba M. Edwards, *Population: Comparative Occupation Statistics for the United States, 1870 to 1940; Sixteenth Census of the United States, 1940* (Washington, D.C.: U.S. Government Printing Office, 1943), pp. 101–2. After 1870 the trend was "plainly away from production of physical goods and toward distribution and service, toward pursuits in transportation, communication, and trade; service pursuits; and clerical pursuits." In 1870, 75.4 percent of the labor force was engaged in the production of physical goods; in 1900, the figure had dropped to 65.4 percent. The erosion was relatively steady, especially after 1880. In 1910 the figure stood at 62.7 percent and in 1930 at 52.9 percent. See also P. K. Whelpton, "Occupational Groups in the United States, 1820–1920," *Journal of the American Statistical Association* 21 (1926): 335–43.

positive outlook, and the persuasive style of the total person himself. People were judged by their entire performance rather than by any isolated skill. Moreover, by means of both personal defensiveness and an inflated estimation of their status, persons in these occupations protected themselves in competitive situations against criticism and failure, which aimed at demeaning the very character of an individual.

More than considerations of profits and capitalism entered into middle-class attitudes toward work. Prestige did, especially the prestige of white-collar employment that took pride in its competent service and its basis in science. For instance, the clerical secretary in the school office and the semiprofessional technician assisting the medical doctor admired, emulated, and envied the professionals for whom they worked. They shared his prestige, identified with his status, boasted about his knowledge, repeated his technical language, guarded his secrets, and measured their own respectability in terms of both his and their own symbolic titles, positions, and advancement. The middle-class person constantly needed to exaggerate the importance of his activity. To think only in the linear dimension of salary or wages demoted any work to a mechanical job, befitting the lowly manual laborer.

Though the number of white-collar workers was small at first, the trend was evident. The number of stenographers and typists grew from 154 in 1870 to 112,364 in 1900; the number of bookkeepers, cashiers, and accountants from 38,776 to 254,880.[69] National statistics for the number of managerial personnel, industry by industry, are difficult to obtain for the years before 1900. However, the census did suggest that such tasks multiplied. In the transportation and communications industries, the number of managers, proprietors, officials, and inspectors increased more than five fold in the period 1870 to 1900, from 12,501 to 67,706. In the mineral industry, the number of chemists, assayers, and metallurgists increased more than eleven fold, from 774 to

[69] Edwards, *Population: Comparative Occupation Statistics*, p. 112.

8,847; and the number of foremen, overseers, and coal-mine operatives rose from 186,036 to 676,997.[70]

The inflation of titles accompanied the proliferation of tasks in service-oriented occupations that advertised their superior skills. Most often, Americans adopted a generic title—president, dean, editor, engineer, general, doctor— and multiplied the possible number of variations and hyphenates. A modest American business might employ three vice-presidents. Assistant deans, associate deans, and just plain deans for this and that function appeared everywhere in American colleges. The varieties of engineers reached into the thousands with elegant names adorning such special work as picking up garbage (sanitation engineer) and poisoning rats (exterminating engineer). In the twentieth century, "surgeons" began operating on trees, and "beauty doctors" practiced in parlors.

Historically, the middle class in America prospered because it did not depose any identifiable social group or compete for a fixed and scarce amount of wealth. Americans were consumer oriented, sensitive to the expanding possibilities of popular demand, and they expressed less fear about overcrowded professions and restricted white-collar occupations than did the English. The middle class in America grew, metaphorically speaking, by piling layer upon layer. An individual or group sought to cultivate a new clientele, to develop a new service or function, to apply a skill in a new kind of way, and enlarge the social need for an occupation. After 1870, for instance, lawyers excluded from the successful corporate elite did not necessarily leave the profession; they reached out for new types of practices in real estate, insurance, personal injury, divorce, government, and of course criminal law and politics. Moreover, few lawyers could afford to be so specialized and inflexible that they neglected the opportunities for new work available in a general practice.[71]

---

[70] *Ibid.,* pp. 109, 104, 111.
[71] Lawrence M. Friedman, *A History of American Law* (New York: Simon and Schuster, 1973), pp. 549–61.

Middle-class persons in America appeared to perform a proliferating number of specialized services and novel tasks which a progressive civilization defined as essential and which the middle-class person himself viewed as previously nonexistent opportunities.[72] Between 1870 and 1900, for instance, the number of trained nurses increased eleven times; veterinarians, eight times; and technical engineers, six times. The number of architects increased five times; dentists, four times; and editors and journalists, three times.[73] Educational standards for proficiency and certification rose throughout the later nineteenth century; and such fields of female employment as librarianship and nursing attempted to acquire the schooling, the status, and the independence (without the income) of a profession. By 1900, forty-one states by statute licensed pharmacists, thirty-five states licensed dentists, and thirty-four states licensed physicians. In other occupations the record was much less impressive in 1900, but legislators dramatically reversed the situation by 1915. Of a list of thirty-eight occupations, twenty-five were now licensed in more than a third of the states, and thirteen in all forty-eight states.[74]

By continually heightening the level of the client's and the consumer's expectations, the middle-class person in America believed that he continually elicited a constructive need for more and more scientific knowledge. Even the pursuit of such commonplace activities as playing baseball, planning meals, vacation traveling, and courtship now required special information about reality which, according to the middle class, only aggressive, curious, and competitive people sought out and applied. In America's expanding social universe, middle-class culture was designed to be as complete as life itself.

[72] Joseph Schumpeter discusses this phenomenon as a way for understanding the meaning of the middle class in *Social Classes; Imperialism* (Cleveland and New York: Meridian Books, The World Publishing Company, 1955), pp. 132–34, 137, 157, 166.

[73] Edwards, *Population: Comparative Occupation Statistics*, p. 111.

[74] *Occupational Licensing Legislations in the States* (Chicago: The Council of State Governments, 1952), pp. 22–23, 78–80.

THE FORTUNATE MIDDLE CLASS

Toward the end of the century, a conscious awareness of the everyday behavior of the middle class was reaching down into popular culture, and writers began routinely to describe both the social prescriptions and the mores of this group. George Ade, a Chicago journalist, for instance, wrote a newspaper piece entitled "The Advantage of Being 'Middle Class.'" Why is it, he asked, that the "fortunate" middle class "has a monopoly of the real enjoyment in Chicago?" Theoretically no classes existed in that big city. "But the 'middle class' means all those persons who are respectably in the background, who work either with hand or brain, who are neither poverty-stricken nor offensively rich, and who are not held down by the arbitrary laws governing that mysterious part of the community known as society."[75]

The middle-class person lived in the middle, sharing both the ambition of the competitive individual and the reputability of the gentleman, avoiding both the excessive emotionalism of the menial laboring class and the excessive probity of polite society. In part, Ade emphasized the freedom of the middle-class person, his right to be a fool or a victim if he wished. More generally, Ade succeeded in capturing the complexity of real people who thought that they both had liberated their lives from arbitrary restraints and had bound their lives with a rational social morality. "The middle class people wouldn't scourge a man simply because he wore a morning coat in the afternoon. Again, if his private life were redolent of scandals they would not tolerate him as a companion, no matter how often he changed his clothes." The middle-class person cultivated a social condition in which prudish decorum did not imprison an individual and demonic urges did not obsess him. He moved freely between the levels of the exclusive rich and the

[75] George Ade, "The Advantage of Being 'Middle Class,'" collected in Franklin J. Meine, *Chicago Stories* (Chicago: The Henry Regnery Company, 1963), p. 75.

vulgar poor. "It is quite a privilege to belong to the middle class," Ade described vividly,

especially during the warm weather in June. A middle-class family may sit on the front stoop all evening and watch the society people go to the weddings in their closed carriages. Father doesn't have to wear a tight dress coat all evening and have a collar choking him. He may take off coat or vest, or both, and smoke either pipe or cigar without scandalizing any one. If he and mother wish to get some ice-cream they go around the corner to get it, or else they may send one of the children with a pitcher. If they were above the middle class, of course, it would never do for them to be seen in a common ice-cream place, and the idea of sending a pitcher would be shocking.

At once, the middle-class person both retained his symbols of respectability and security and released his desires for advancement and success.[76]

By means of slang, phrases, and the original use of words, the middle class created its own language, which expressed its special thoughts. Active verbs dominated the evolving forms of speech. Middle-class Americans, for instance, spoke approvingly about the intensity of a man's energy. A successful person was "on the go," "all set," "spoiling for a fight," "getting his spunk up," "spreading it on thick," "snapping up" an opportunity, and "going one better." A desirable human trait was nearly always set off by its countertrait. The failing man who exhausted and dissipated his energy might be "petered out," "skunked," "run into the ground," "gone under," "struck out," "hitting the booze," or "on the bum."

Phrases that represented intelligence, knowledge, skill, and good judgment proliferated in American speech. It was important for an individual to know a "good thing," to "acquire" or "get the hang of it," to be able to "run"—manage, control, guide—any organization, including a church. The "fool," by contrast, demonstrated bad judgment; he

[76] *Ibid.*, pp. 75–76.

"lost the run of" a thing or lost touch, he made "snap judgments" that were usually uninformed and wrong, he lived
by a "hit-or-miss" pattern. "Easy-going" men were not eager
to learn and they might be "cleaned out," "roped in," or
swindled through their own ignorance.

The middle-class person believed in perseverance, independence, commitment, and self-glory. It was important for
this individual to "make himself solid," to be "self-poised,"
to show a "strong suit," to "handle" life well by mastering
it. He must avoid the damaging reputation of being a "bad
egg," "small potatoes," or a "flunky." The confident person
would "stick up for" and "set a great deal by" his convictions, "strike for" his goal, "hang to the ropes," "run his
luck," "stick it out," and persist until he "hit the mark."
The pressures upon an individual intensified as competitive
society "turned the screws," and in order not to be "screwed"
himself or "hung up" the anxious middle-class person was
advised to "take it easy."

Culturally, the middle class was finding its literary voices,
refining its private thoughts, and formalizing its institutions
and organizations. Like Ade, Mark Twain instinctively
understood the range of middle culture in which he felt
comfortable. "Indeed I have been misjudged, from the very
first," Twain complained. "I have never tried in even one
single instance, to help cultivate the cultivated classes. I was
not equipped for it, either by native gifts or training. And
I never had any ambition in that direction, but always
hunted for bigger game—the masses."[77]

In his own words, Twain catered to the Belly and the
Members as well as to the Head. Old-fashioned Reason,
with its harmonies and laws, was antiquated in the gamy
world where men played upon each other's "confidence."
Middle-class life was a game in which individuals were
played for the fool, were "played out," "played it alone,"
"played even," and played tricks.

For Twain, the common entertainer rather than the

[77] Albert Bigelow Paine, ed., *Mark Twain's Letters,* 2 vols. (New
York: Harper & Brothers, Publishers, 1917) 2: 527.

precious artist would redefine reason, in the parlance of everyday amusement. "Honestly, I never cared what became of the cultured classes," Twain wrote, "they could go to the theatre and the opera. They had no use for me and the melodeon." Twain's emotional medium was ordinary melodrama, not high tragedy; and he observed that the middle class, including himself, was in the process of defining the standards by which work and people could be judged. "My audience is dumb, it has no voice in print, and so I cannot know whether I have won its approbation or only got its censure." A minimal measure, at least, was the "sanctity which comes with cash."[78]

As a cultural symbol, money played a profound role in the career of such Americans as Twain. On the one hand, middle-class persons pursued wealth as a source of pleasure, wholeness, and instinctual fulfillment. They dreamt about spending the dollar, fantasied about its power, equated it with an elemental solution to all problems, and measured their self-worth and status—indeed their manhood—in terms of its acquisition. On the other hand, middle-class persons renounced the solitary pursuit of wealth as unworthy of a human life. An exclusive concern with the accumulation of riches compromised ideals of sacrifice, corrupted creative urges, and reduced the insatiable seeker to a state of helplessness, hate, and anger. By portraying heroes whose professional code of behavior transcended a concern with payment for their services, middle-class culture prevented people from believing that they were working for mere money. In episode after episode, Twain reinforced that culture by writing about the obscenity of the dollar in American life.

Mark Twain styled himself the literary spokesman for the middle class in the Gilded Age. And by means of hyperbole, humor, cynicism, and sarcasm, he emphasized both his attraction to and his revulsion for American values. In the

[78] *Ibid.*, p. 528. Twain cited in Justin Kaplan, *Mr. Clemens and Mark Twain: A Biography* (New York: Pocket Books, 1968), p. 82.

preface to the London edition of *The Gilded Age,* he expressed this ambivalence:

In America nearly every man has his dream, his pet scheme, whereby he is to advance himself socially or pecuniarily. It is this all-pervading speculativeness which we have tried to illustrate in "The Gilded Age." It is a characteristic which is both bad and good, for both the individual and the nation. Good, because it allows neither to stand still, but drives both for ever on, toward some point or other which is ahead, not behind nor at one side. Bad, because the chosen point is often badly chosen, and then the individual is wrecked; the aggregation of such cases affects the nation, and so is bad for the nation. Still, it is a trait which it is of course better for a people to have and sometimes suffer from than to be without.[79]

Twain satirized, mocked and gibed at the fantasies, gullibility, and corruptibility of the American middle class. He described its aggressiveness; he characterized its frustration and remorse. But Twain never questioned the significance of his membership in that class. Culturally, it satisfied his basic needs for selfish, imaginative, and outlandish projects on the one hand, and for gentility, refinement and altruistic sacrifice on the other.

As a spokesman for persons who sought esteem, visibility, and comfort, the theatric Mark Twain had no trouble in distinguishing between and enjoying the pleasures of both the smoking room and the drawing room, the barroom and the parlor, the poolroom and the study, the bedroom and the nursery. Each was established in its exclusive space; each preempted a scheduled segment of a person's time; each had its appropriate language. Each made possible both the release of individual energy and the persistence of civilized conventions. And within each, middle-class persons played their competitive games and participated in their symbolic ceremonies. For the American aspiring to middle-class status, the generation between the Civil War and the turn

[79] Charles Neider has published separately Mark Twain's share of *The Gilded Age,* now entitled *The Adventures of Colonel Sellers* (Garden City, New York: Doubleday & Company, 1965), p. xvii.

of the century was a "guilded age," with new associations and social rules, in addition to being a "gilded age." An expanding American audience was taking for granted the advantages of the fortunate middle class.[80]

[80] On this final point, see for instance the suggestive case study by Daniel J. Walkowitz, "Working Class Women in the Gilded Age: Factory, Community and Family Life Among Cohoes, New York, Cotton Workers," *Journal of Social History* 5 (Summer 1972): 464–90. Walkowitz found that the values of the working-class people he studied did not differ greatly from the values of the middle–class people described by Richard Sennett in *Families Against the City: Middle Class Homes of Industrial Chicago, 1872–1890* (Cambridge, Mass.: Harvard University Press, 1970).

2

Space and Words

"THE COUNTRY IS A FOOL"

Life no doubt was changing in later nineteenth-century America. Industrial development hurt—12 to 14 percent unemployed in 1876, 18 percent unemployed in 1894—but there was industrial growth. The Gross National Product expanded from $147 per capita in the 1869–78 period to $234 in the 1894–1903 period. Between 1870 and 1900 the number of banks multiplied six fold and their principal assets and liabilities rose comparatively. The miles of main railroad track increased from 46,800 in 1869 to 190,000 in 1899. Proportionally, the urban population grew from 26 to 40 percent between 1870 and 1900, and the number of cities with over 100,000 inhabitants rose from fourteen to thirty-eight. In Massachusetts, life expectancy for a male at birth increased from 41.74 years in 1878–82 to 44.09 years in 1893–97, for a female from 43.50 years to 46.61. The amount of life insurance in force increased from two million dollars in 1870 to seven and a half million in 1900, while the assets of insurance companies rose from $269.5 million to $1,742 million.[1]

[1] The statistics were drawn from the following sources: Robert Higgs, *The Transformation of the American Economy, 1865–1914: An Essay*

It was the era of the "communications revolution."[2] The number of telephones, for instance, increased from three thousand in 1876 to 1.3 million in 1900. Daily newspaper circulation multiplied by seven times between 1870 and 1900, the number of post offices by nearly three times, the sale of ordinary postage stamps by eight times, the miles of telegraph wire by nine times, and the volume of telegraph messages by seven times. For many Americans the printing office and the patent office heralded the arrival of modern times. Between 1880 and 1900, the number of new books and editions increased three fold; between 1870 and 1900

in Interpretation (New York: John Wiley & Sons, Inc., 1971): unemployment, Table 5.4, p. 124; Gross National Product, Table 2.1, p. 19; railroad track, Table 2.4, p. 34; urban population, Table 3.1, p. 59. *Historical Statistics of the United States: Colonial Times to 1957: A Statistical Abstract Supplement* (Washington, D.C.: U.S. Department of Commerce, Bureau of the Census, 1960): banks and their assets, Series X 20–21, p. 624; life expectancy, Series B 84–85, p. 24; life insurance, Series X 436, 459, pp. 672, 675–76. See also for an extensive account of the economy Edward C. Kirkland, *Industry Comes of Age: Business, Labor, and Public Policy, 1860–1897* (New York: Holt, Rinehart and Winston, 1961). David T. Gilchrist and W. David Lewis, eds., *Economic Change in the Civil War Era* (Greenville, Del.: Eleutherian Mills-Hagley Foundation, 1965); Carter Goodrich, *Government Promotion of American Canals and Railroads, 1800–1890* (New York: Columbia University Press, 1960).

2 Robert G. Albion first used the phrase to separate the Industrial Revolution in factories from developments in transportation and such forms of media communication as telegraph, telephone, and radio: "The 'Communications Revolution,'" *American Historical Review* 37 (July 1932): 718–20. His suggestion was compelling. Nevertheless, historians of nineteenth-century America have examined with any degree of thoroughness only aspects of transportation such as canals and railroads. Arthur Meier Schlesinger in *The Rise of the City, 1878–1898* (New York: The Macmillan Company, 1933) did describe at length the cultural influences of myriad forms of communication. Perhaps because of his encyclopedic method, Schlesinger stimulated only peripheral interest in further research. A synthetic account of the same period, such as Samuel P. Hays, *The Response to Industrialism, 1885–1914* (Chicago: The University of Chicago Press, 1957), typically neglected the theme of the "communications revolution." In the illuminating introduction to *The Land of Contrasts, 1880–1901* (New York: George Braziller, 1970), pp. 1–28, Neil Harris has recently rekindled interest. Harris has also used the phrase "guilded" age to characterize the era.

the number of copyright registrations increased eight fold, and the number of patents applied for and issued for inventions two fold.[3]

Witnesses testified that the psychological tensions were nearly unbearable. In 1881, an American medical doctor named George Beard popularized the term "neurasthenia" to describe the symptoms of his harassed urban patients.[4] James Bryce, the most famous English visitor in the later nineteenth century, observed that life in America "is that of the squirrel in his revolving cage, never still even when it does not seem to change. . . . [I]t is unusually hard for any one to withdraw his mind from the endless variety of external impressions and interests which daily life presents, and which impinge upon the mind." Daniel Coit Gilman, president of Johns Hopkins University, described the ambivalence of his colleagues toward college government: "We have broken away from the restricted notions of the past; we have not yet learned how to adjust ourselves to the broader domains in which we are now walking." Frederick Engels observed that "in a country as untouched as America, which has developed in a purely bourgeois fashion without any feudal past . . . the people must become conscious of

3 *Historical Statistics of the United States:* telephones, Series R 1, pp. 480–81; newspaper circulation, Series R 176, p. 500; post offices and postage stamps, Series R 139, 142, pp. 496–97; telegraph wire and messages, Series R 44, 45, pp. 483–84; new books and editions, Series R 165, p. 499; copyrights, Series W 69, pp. 607–8. For a more detailed account of one phase of these developments, see Frank Luther Mott on the newspapers, "The Rise of the Independent Press, 1872–1892," in *American Journalism: A History, 1860–1960,* 3d ed. (New York: The Macmillan Company, 1962), pp. 411–516.

4 George M. Beard, *American Nervousness: Its Causes and Consequences: A Supplement to Nervous Exhaustion (Neurasthenia)* (New York: G. P. Putnam's Sons, 1881). See also Nathan G. Hale, Jr., *Freud and the Americans: The Beginnings of Psychoanalysis in the United States, 1876–1917* (New York: Oxford University Press, 1971), pp. 24–68; Donald Meyer, *The Positive Thinkers: A Study of the American Quest for Health, Wealth and Personal Power from Mary Baker Eddy to Norman Vincent Peale* (Garden City, N.Y.: Doubleday & Company, Inc., 1965), pp. 21–31; David M. Kennedy, *Birth Control in America: The Career of Margaret Sanger* (New Haven, Conn., and London: Yale University Press, 1970), pp. 54–56.

their own *social* interests by making blunder after blunter."[5]

On the surface, contradictions appeared to tear away at American society. Mark Twain, for instance, could embrace both the preindustrial past and the technological future. America's first big-money professional author and humorist, he celebrated his boyhood on the Mississippi and his young manhood in the West. Twain also numbered among the first to submit a typewritten manuscript to a publisher, to be a connoisseur of fountain pens, and to dictate part of a book into a phonograph. The potential of machines for accelerated communications and profits fascinated the man. His speculative investment in the Paige typesetter, an excessively complex mechanism which Twain tended to endow with human characteristics, drove him into bankruptcy.[6] He satis-

[5] James Bryce, *The American Commonwealth*, 2 vols., 3d ed., rev. (New York: Macmillan and Co., 1895), 2: 771; Fabian Franklin, *The Life of Daniel Coit Gilman* (New York: Dodd, Mead & Company, 1910), p. 330; Karl Marx and Frederick Engels, *Letters to Americans, 1848–1895: A Selection* (New York: International Publishers, 1953), p. 161.

Certainly differences divided the decades between the Civil War and the turn of the century, though historians have preferred to overlook similarities and focus upon the apparent gap that separated The Gilded Age from the Progressive Era. For recent studies on the transition from the seventies to the eighties, see Geoffrey Blodgett, "Reform Thought and the Genteel Tradition," in H. Wayne Morgan, ed., *The Gilded Age*, 2d ed., rev. (Syracuse, N.Y.: Syracuse University Press, 1970), pp. 55–76; Alan Trachtenberg, Introduction, *Democratic Vistas, 1860–1880* (New York: George Braziller, 1970), pp. 1–32. For an excellent examination of comparative values in the seventies and the nineties, see John G. Cawelti, "America on Display: The World's Fairs of 1876, 1893, 1933," in Frederic Cople Jaher, ed., *The Age of Industrialism in America: Essays in Social Structure and Cultural Values* (New York: Free Press, 1968), pp. 317–46. On the nineties, see John Higham, "The Reorientation of American Culture in the 1890's," in John Weiss, ed., *The Origins of Modern Consciousness* (Detroit: The Wayne State University Press, 1965), pp. 25–48; Larzer Ziff, *The American 1890s: The Life and Times of a Lost Generation* (New York: The Viking Press, 1966); Frank Luther Mott, "The Magazine Revolution and Popular Ideas in the Nineties," *Proceedings of the American Antiquarian Society* 64 (1954), 195–214. For impressionistic descriptions see Thomas Beer, *The Mauve Decade: American Life at the End of the Nineteenth Century* (New York: Alfred A. Knopf, 1926).

[6] "But it's a cunning devil, is that machine!" Twain wrote, "—and knows more than any man that ever lived. You shall see. . . . It is a

fied the mania for gambling and "booming," for the pushing
and rushing and the pliable morals: "The country is a fool,
I think," he had one of his characters proclaim.[7] But Twain
knew he spoke about himself as well. "Ah, well, I am a great
and sublime fool," he wrote to William Dean Howells in
1877. "But then, I am God's fool, and all His works must be
contemplated with respect."[8]

In the era Mark Twain and Charles Dudley Warner called
"The Gilded Age," Americans played the game of fortune seriously. Twain's sympathetic character, Eschol Sellers—
Mr., Captain, Major, General, or just plain *Old Sellers,*
depending upon the state of his credit—proposed to strike it
rich with his Infallible Imperial Oriental Optic Liniment
and Salvation for Sore Eyes, the Medical Wonder of the
Age. John Oakhurst, the cool and impassive gambler in Bret

magnificent creature of steel, all of Pratt & Whitney's superbest work-
manship, and as nicely adjusted and as accurate as a watch. In construction it is as elaborate and complex as that machine which it ranks
next to, by every right—Man—and in performance it is as simple and
sure." Albert Bigelow Paine, ed., *Mark Twain's Letters,* 2 vols. (New
York: Harper & Brothers, Publishers, 1917), 2: 507, 516. See Tom Bur-
nam, "Mark Twain and the Paige Typesetter: A Background for Despair," *Western Humanities Review* 6 (Winter 1951–52), 29–36; Samuel
Charles Webster, ed., *Mark Twain, Business Man* (Boston: Little,
Brown and Company, 1946), pp. 171–73, 307–8, 310–11, 330–31, 396–97.

7 The voice belonged to Washington Hawkins in Twain and Warner's
novel *The Gilded Age.* Mark Twain, *The Adventures of Colonel
Sellers,* ed. Charles Neider (Garden City, N.Y.: Doubleday & Company,
1965), p. 195. See also Justin Kaplan, *Mr. Clemens and Mark Twain: A
Biography* (New York: Pocket Books, 1968), p. 189. Kaplan excels at
presenting biographic detail on Twain and information on the popular
culture of the era. On the latter, see Henry Nash Smith, ed., *Popular
Culture and Industrialism, 1865–1890* (Garden City, N.Y.: Anchor
Books, 1967), pp. vii–xx; Robert R. Roberts, "Popular Culture and
Public Taste," in Morgan, ed., *The Gilded Age,* pp. 275–88; R. Rich-
ard Wohl, "The 'Country Boy' Myth and Its Place in American Urban
Culture: The Nineteenth Century Contribution," ed. Moses Rischin,
Perspectives in American History, 3 (1968), pp. 77–158; Richard Weiss,
"Horatio Alger, Jr., and the Response to Industrialism," in Jaher, ed.,
The Age of Industrialism in America, pp. 304–16.

8 Henry Nash Smith and William M. Gibson, eds., *Mark Twain–
Howells Letters: The Correspondence of Samuel L. Clemens and William D. Howells, 1872–1910,* 2 vols. (Cambridge, Mass.: Harvard University Press, 1960), 1: 215.

Harte's "The Outcasts of Poker Flat," accepted the fact that "with him life was at best an uncertain game, and he recognized the usual percentage in favor of the dealer." Luck was a mighty queer thing: "All you know about it for certain is that it's bound to change. And it's finding out when it's going to change that makes you."[9] The wreckage of human ambition was strewn across the fictional scene of the Gilded Age. "What is the use of struggling, and toiling and worrying any more?" Laura Hawkins, a Twain heroine, lamented. "Let us give it all up."[10] Many Americans seemed to capitulate to what the next generation judged to be an ideological veil for self-indulgence: the gospel of wealth.[11] "Nothing lost save honor," the rascal Jim Fisk pronounced in defiance of the conventional notion of "virtue."

Disguises, masquerades, and confidence men appeared in the actual world, beyond the imaginary confines of the new regional fiction. The malodorous reality of profits in steel, for instance, belied the heroic image of Andrew Carnegie's triumphant individualism. Even the visiting Herbert Spencer reacted to Carnegie's Pittsburgh, polluted and reeking, as "repulsive." "Six months' residence here would justify sui-

[9] Twain, *Adventures of Colonel Sellers,* pp. 58–59. Bret Harte, *The Luck of Roaring Camp and Other Tales* (Boston and New York: Houghton Mifflin Company, 1906), pp. 15, 22.

[10] Twain, *Adventures of Colonel Sellers,* p. 231. "This is a desperate game I am playing," Laura reflected, "a wearing, sordid, heartless game. If I lose, I lose everything—even myself. And if I win the game, will it be worth its cost after all? I do not know. Sometimes I doubt. Sometimes I half wish I had not begun. But no matter; I *have* begun, and I will never turn back; never while I live" (p. 159).

[11] A description of that ideology is found in Ralph Henry Gabriel, *The Course of American Democratic Thought,* 2d ed. (New York: The Ronald Press Company, 1956), pp. 151–69; Robert Green McCloskey, *American Conservatism in the Age of Enterprise, 1865–1910: A Study of William Graham Sumner, Stephen J. Field and Andrew Carnegie* (Cambridge, Mass.: Harvard University Press, 1951); Joseph Frazier Wall, *Andrew Carnegie* (New York: Oxford University Press, 1970), pp. 805–15. See also Edward Chase Kirkland, *Dream and Thought in the Business Community, 1860–1900* (Ithaca, N.Y.: Cornell University Press, 1956); Gail Kennedy, ed., *Democracy and the Gospel of Wealth* (Boston: D. C. Heath and Company, 1949).

cide," the English apostle of industrialism and Social Darwinism proclaimed, to the dismay of his host.[12]

Self-deception went deep. As a self-appointed *"custojeen
iv money,"* John D. Rockefeller was called by Mr. Dooley,
"a kind iv a society f'r th' previntion of croolty to money."[13]
Henry Ward Beecher gained fame as the most eloquent and
qualified clergyman in his day; yet none of his respectable
middle-class congregation in Brooklyn, New York, seemed
to object when "The Great Preacher" received one thousand
dollars to endorse a truss, or when the following advertisement for a commercial brand of soap ran in popular American magazines:

> If cleanliness is next to Godliness, soap must be considered as a
> means of Grace, and a clergyman who recommends moral things
> should be willing to recommend soap. I am told that my com-
> mendation of Pears' Soap has opened for it a large sale in the
> United States. I am willing to stand by every word in favor of it
> that I ever uttered. A man must be fastidious indeed who is not
> satisfied with it.
>
>   Henry Ward Beecher

Little scandal was heard when Beecher received fifteen
thousand dollars' worth of stock from Jay Cooke for the
expressed purpose of influencing the public mind by writing
favorable editorials on the Northern Pacific Railroad in the
Christian Union.[14]

In a literal sense, Beecher was not acting dishonestly. He

12 Herbert Spencer, *An Autobiography*, 2 vols. (New York: D. Appleton and Company, 1904), 2: 468; Wall, *Carnegie*, p. 386.

13 "Rockefeller," in Louis Filler, ed., *The World of Mr. Dooley* (New
York: Collier Books, 1962), p. 157.

14 Frank Luther Mott, *A History of American Magazines: 1885–1905*
(Cambridge, Mass.: Harvard University Press, 1957), p. 32; Paxton Hib-
ben, *Henry Ward Beecher: An American Portrait* (New York: George
H. Doran Company, 1927), pp. 229, 263, 223; Kaplan, *Mr. Clemens and
Mark Twain*, p. 178. For Beecher as a spokesman for middle-class
values, see William G. McLoughlin, *The Meaning of Henry Ward
Beecher: An Essay on the Shifting Values of Mid-Victorian America,
1840–1870* (New York: Alfred A. Knopf, 1970); Clifford E. Clark, Jr.,
"The Changing Nature of Protestantism in Mid-nineteenth Century
America: Henry Ward Beecher's *Seven Lectures to Young Men*," *Jour-
nal of American History* 57 (March 1971): 832–46.

was the kind of religious individual who both anticipated enormous profits from his book on the life of Christ and was convinced that such a work could uplift public morality. As a moralist and realist, Mark Twain was less the mountebank than Beecher. After a tour through New York City's worst slums, Twain declared: "I wish to become rich, so that I can instruct the people and glorify honest poverty a little, like those good, kind-hearted, fat benevolent people do."[15]

SPACE AND THE GUILDED AGE

The era was a fool, indeed, but serious things were happening historically to overshadow the peccadillos and peculations of unsavory characters. Mid-Victorian America was maturing, and social life in America was being transformed.

The emergence and consolidation of the culture of the middle class was a nineteenth-century phenomenon. And between 1840 and 1915 that culture dominated American social thought and institutional developments. The Reform or Romantic era before the Civil War and the Progressive era at the turn of the century have been subjected to extensive historical investigation. Historians have not, however, established the all-important continuity between these two epochs in the American past. They have ignored or neglected "the missing link," the transitional Mid-Victorian era. Three generations made up a continuous—an "organic" —whole, to borrow a popular metaphor from the period. Generally speaking, the Reformers were born in the first decade of the nineteenth century and intellectually matured in the years 1835–60, the Mid-Victorians were born in the decade of the 1830s and matured in the years 1865–90, and the Progressives were born in the decade of the 1860s and matured in the years 1890–1915.

The lives of individuals from different generations frequently crisscrossed, and subsequent research must examine

15 Kaplan, *Mr. Clemens and Mark Twain*, p. 29.

the middle class in generational and even half-generational periods. Though there was a basic continuity of attitudes one identifies as middle class, there was no lack of serious conflict between Americans. Indeed, persons who agree upon basics often threaten and repel each other, more so than those with little in common. The former accentuate their differences, intensify their mutually felt hatreds, and consume each other with envy and jealousy. Violence in American history has been related to, and accelerated by, shared expectations and shared frustrations, especially between generations and half-generations of men.

In the nineteenth century, Americans who shared middle-class pretensions wanted respectability, orderliness, control, and discipline. But they also celebrated their own energy, their capacity for booming, boosterism, and the lust for power. Passion, passion was everywhere in America, and as Herman Melville noted, it no longer demanded a palatial stage. Average persons were now psychologically "tormented with an everlasting itch for things remote," with the desire to light out for the territories, with the need at least to taste those "invisible spheres formed in fright."[16] Ambition, health, surplus, waste, and competition often ran contrary to control and concentration. But what source of social discipline could opportunistic persons voluntarily share in a liberal society, what source of social discipline neither superimposed nor aristocratic, nor privileged, nor physically coerced, nor artificially contrived?

The answer was ingenious. Every person was bound by his "nature" in the everyday world. By uncovering and defining one's particular nature, every person became conscious not only of his ability but of his limitations. By freeing one's nature, by releasing one's inborn capacities, by being one's real self, a person became aware of the boundaries that

16 The concept of plenitude is examined by F. O. Matthiessen, *American Renaissance: Art and Expression in the Age of Emerson and Whitman* (New York: Oxford University Press, 1941), p. 380; Arthur O. Lovejoy, *The Great Chain of Being: A Study of the History of an Idea* (Cambridge, Mass.: Harvard University Press, 1936), pp. 288–314.

circumscribed common abilities and talents. In the inner-most self, in one's natural gifts and inheritance, a person recognized the restrictions of an individual life. For ex-ample, by defining her true nature and its potential for fulfillment, the American woman also defined such "nat-ural" restraints confining her activities as the physiology of sex, the inner space of the home, and the time schedule of children.[17] One of the deepest dualities of middle-class America was its simultaneous potential for determinism and acquiescence, self-control and self-knowledge within liberty; the potential for fate within freedom.

The processes of nature at once both liberated the energy of the individual and confined it. With intense interest Mid-Victorians in the latter half of the nineteenth century sought to describe in meticulous detail the everyday physical world surrounding them. Every subject was made into a natural "science," from calisthenics to the architecture of the home to religious worship.[18] What strikes the historian is the totality of the Mid-Victorian impulse to contain the life ex-periences of the individual from birth to death by isolating them as science. Describing the outer structure of the visible universe, Mid-Victorians believed that they also described the inner structure of the invisible one. Control of the physi-cal movements of a person in his course of life meant control of the confines of his spiritual attitudes. Though this cul-tural response was not peculiarly American, its frequency and intensity did set American life apart.

[17] See Catharine E. Beecher, *A Treatise on Domestic Economy, for the Use of Young Ladies at Home, and at School* (Boston: Marsh, Capen, Lyon, and Webb, 1841); Anne L. Kuhn, *The Mother's Role in Childhood Education: New England Concepts, 1830–1860* (New Haven, Conn.: Yale University Press, 1947); Kathryn Kish Sklar, *Catharine Beecher, a Study in American Domesticity* (New Haven, Conn., and London: Yale University Press, 1973).

[18] See for instance Catharine Beecher's efforts in *Physiology and Calisthenics: For Schools and Families* (New York: Harper & Brothers, Publishers, 1856) and *Calisthenic Exercises, For Schools, Families, and Health Establishments* (New York: Harper & Brothers, Publishers, 1856).

Space and time were the most elementary categories in everyday experience, and in a simple mental step individuals could recognize that space and time effectively delimited human behavior. Indeed, an individual located in a particular space was identifiable, given a name by his acquaintances. Space in particular commended itself to Americans, whose heritage endowed them with an abundance of space and a limited amount of time. Mid-Victorians turned their interest toward identifying every category of person who naturally belonged in a specific ground-space: the woman in the residential home, the child in the school, the man in his place of work, the dying person in a hospital, and the body in the funeral parlor; the immigrant in the ghetto, the criminal in the prison, the insane in the asylum, the Indian on the reservation, the Negro in his segregated area, the Irishman in the saloon, the prostitute and the pimp in the red-light district. Within broad spheres, of course, the specialization of space and the increasingly complex human roles within it went on endlessly.

The Gilded Age was also a guilded age, developed around the novel uses of space and protective boundaries to regulate the social experience of the individual. Mid-Victorians in America, for example, formally distinguished between public spaces and private spaces, an all-important division. Earlier Americans had separated public and private only informally and vaguely. In the 1829 edition of Webster's dictionary, *public* referred to "publican, general, the people; open for the comon use by everyone without restriction." *Private,* on the other hand, meant "separate, unconnected with others, secret, secluded, isolated, closed," and by implication "opposed to the people, subversive." *Private* was a negative notion that appeared only as the contradiction of *public*. In the ideological world of the eighteenth-century republican, all desirable things were public. "Every man in a republic," stated Benjamin Rush, "is public property. His time and talents—his youth—his manhood—his old age— nay more, life, all, belong to his country." Broadly conceived, the space of a township or county or community belonged to everyone and was a general responsibility.[19]

Not only did Mid-Victorians regard the notion of "private," especially in terms of property, as positive and desirable; they created public spaces which were truly public, theoretically excluding private uses. In the newly founded national parks—Yellowstone in 1872, Sequoia and Yosemite in 1890—spatial boundaries now protected wild nature itself. Moreover, the maintenance of specialized space required the development of a culture with specialized training, uncommon knowledge, administrative ability, and a professional code of ethics and dedication that lent itself to a distinct way of life, in this case the forestry service and the conservationist movement. Zoological gardens, confining wild animals behind barriers in carefully restricted spaces, opened their gates to the public in this period: Lincoln Park in Chicago in 1873; Philadelphia in 1874, followed by Cincinnati; and the National Zoological Park in Washington, D.C., established by Congress in 1890. Institutionalized public space attended by professional keepers could control and safely exhibit the most savage specimens in nature's kingdom. Symbolically, what was designed for animals could extend to the animal in humans.[20]

[19] Dagobert D. Runes, ed., *The Selected Writings of Benjamin Rush* (New York: Philosophical Library, 1947), p. 31. See Michael Zuckerman, *Peaceable Kingdoms: New England Towns in the Eighteenth Century* (New York: Vintage Books, 1972); David H. Flaherty, *Privacy in Colonial New England* (Charlottesville, Va.: University Press of Virginia, 1972): I do not believe Flaherty's evidence supports the thesis. According to John S. Whitehead, the distinction in America between public and private colleges did not emerge until the later part of the century, most explicitly with Charles William Eliot at Harvard, *The Separation of College and State: Columbia, Dartmouth, Harvard, and Yale, 1776–1876* (New Haven, Conn., and London: Yale University Press, 1973), pp. 191–240.

[20] See Roderick Nash, "The American Invention of National Parks," *American Quarterly* 22 (Fall 1970); Nash, *Wilderness and the American Mind* (New Haven, Conn.: Yale University Press, 1967); Thomas G. Manning, *Government in Science: The U.S. Geological Survey, 1867–1894* (Lexington, Ky.: University of Kentucky Press, 1967), pp. 151–67; Henry Clepper, *Professional Forestry in the United States* (Baltimore:

The specialized structuring of public space appeared everywhere. The civic building and the public high school, often with an impressive tower housing a magnificent public clock, were the most formidable and enduring buildings erected in most later nineteenth-century American communities. In 1879 arc lighting first illuminated the public squares of Cleveland, distinctly setting off the outdoor public areas and making them accessible for evening recreation. Architects like Frederick Law Olmsted and Daniel Burnham designed elaborate city park systems, especially in New York and Chicago.[21] Bellevue was built into a modern hospital in the 1850s; Cook County opened its doors as a general hospital for the poor in 1865; and the Presbyterian Hospital in upper Manhattan, later to become part of the Columbia-Presbyterian Medical Center, was considered to be the most advanced hospital structure in its time when its two main buildings, each four stories high were completed in 1872.[22]

The Johns Hopkins Press, 1971). On the conservationist movement see Samuel P. Hays, *Conservation and the Gospel of Efficiency: The Progressive Conservation Movement, 1890–1920* (Cambridge, Mass.: Harvard University Press, 1959); Martin Nelson McGeary, *Gifford Pinchot: Forester-Politician* (Princeton, N.J.: Princeton University Press, 1960). See also, for its cultural interpretation, Peter J. Schmitt, *Back to Nature: The Arcadian Myth in Urban America* (New York: Oxford University Press, 1969). Founded in 1859, the Philadelphia zoo was the first in America, but it did not open its gates to the public until 1874.

[21] See Albert Fein, *Frederick Law Olmsted and the American Environmental Tradition* (New York: George Braziller, 1972); Laura Wood Roper, *FLO: A Biography of Frederick Law Olmsted* (Baltimore and London: The Johns Hopkins University Press, 1974); Thomas S. Hines, *Burnham of Chicago: Architect and Citizen* (New York: Oxford University Press, 1974).

[22] See Robert J. Carlisle, *An Account of Bellevue Hospitals, with a Catalogue of the Medical and the Surgical Staff from 1763 to 1894* (New York: The Society of the Alumni of Bellevue Hospital, 1893). For the history of the American hospital, see Leonard K. Eaton, *New England Hospitals, 1790–1833* (Ann Arbor, Mich.: The University of Michigan Press, 1957); Albert R. Lamb, *The Presbyterian Hospital and the Columbia-Presbyterian Medical Center, 1868–1943* (New York: Columbia University Press, 1955); Mary Risley, *House of Healing: The Story of the Hospital* (Garden City, N.Y.: Doubleday & Company, Inc., 1961), pp. 215–32. The "pavilion" plan in which the building was designed with corridors alongside the wards thus separating the traffic from the patients characterized the construction of the new American

Civic groups sponsored the founding of symphony orchestras —New York (1878), Boston (1881), Chicago (1891)—and grand opera houses and auditoriums were inevitably built: New York's Metropolitan Opera House (1883), the Chicago Opera House (1884–85), the Auditorium Building in Chicago (1887–89).[23] Consolidated from scattered collections, the great public libraries with their imposing structures appeared in the 1890s in New York, Boston, and Chicago.[24]

Appearing for the first time in America, department stores comprehensively structured commercial public space. In Philadelphia, John Wanamaker inaugurated his "new kind of store" in 1877, a collection of specialized shops gathered and organized in one large building. In New York, Alexander T. Stewart built a structure in the 1860s that covered two acres, the largest retail store in the world, employing two thousand persons. And in Chicago, Marshall Field and Levi Leiter built three stores between 1868 and 1878. After the partnership dissolved, Leiter moved his business to the south end of the Loop and erected the building which is currently the downtown retail store of Sears, Roebuck, and Company, founded in 1886.[25] Several streets north on State,

hospitals after 1850. See also George Rosen, "The Hospital: Historical Sociology of a Community Institution," in Eliot Friedson, ed., *The Hospital in Modern Society* (Glencoe, Ill.: The Free Press, 1963), pp. 1–36.

[23] See Mark Antony De Wolfe Howe, *The Boston Symphony Orchestra, 1881–1931* (Boston and New York: Houghton Mifflin Company, 1931); Ellis Allen Johnson, "The Chicago Symphony Orchestra, 1891–1942: A Study in American Cultural History" (Ph.D. diss., Dept. of History, University of Chicago, 1955).

[24] See Phyllis Dain, *The New York Public Library: A History of Its Founding and Early Years* (New York: New York Public Library, 1972); Walter Muir Whitehill, *Boston Public Library; a Centennial History* (Cambridge, Mass.: Harvard University Press, 1956); Gwladys Spencer, *The Chicago Public Library: Origins and Backgrounds* (Chicago: University of Chicago Press, 1943). See also S. R. Warren and S. N. Clark, eds., *Public Libraries in the United States of America: Their History, Condition and Management*, Special Report, Department of the Interior, Bureau of Education (Washington: Government Printing Office, 1876).

[25] See *Golden Book of the Wanamaker Stores: Jubilee Year, 1861–1911* (n.p., 1911); *Sears, Roebuck and Co.: Our March to Victory and*

the Palmer House was built on a square city block. Large and sumptuous hotels such as the Palmer House, the Grand Union in New York, and Baldwin's in San Francisco became famous in the 1880s.

The most dramatic quasi-public use of defined space in the later nineteenth century occurred in professional athletics and recreational sports. Rising interest in such activities was unmistakable. In 1866, wealthy sportsmen acquired 230 acres in Westchester County and built a park for horse racing which accommodated eight thousand people in the grandstand. In 1885, an unprecedented forty thousand people paid admission to see the four games of the second World Series between the Chicago and New York teams.[26]

Games require playgrounds which are almost always uniquely shaped and measured: baseball's diamond, football's field, horse racing's track, golf's course, basketball's court, boxing's ring, cycling's path, swimming's pool. In this era, architects laid out arenas, fields, stadiums, and parks for spectators. Not only did the new structures consume large amounts of space; more often than not the use of the space was restricted to one sport and one season. The closed space was permanent and functionally inflexible. In the form of exclusive country clubs, well-to-do communities from Palm Beach to Puget Sound enclosed large tracts of land for golf courses, the first apparently being Brookline near Boston in

Grand Removal Notice (Chicago: n.p., 1895). Wm. Cooke Daniels defined the department store as "an institution which, so far as local conditions permit, aims to supply all the material wants of all its possible customers." *The Department Store System* (Denver: n.p., 1900). See William Amelius Corbion, *The Principles of Salesmanship, Deportment and System: a Text-book for Department Store Service* (Philadelphia: George W. Jacobs & Company, 1907); John William Ferry; *A History of the Department Store* (New York: The Macmillan Company, 1960).

26 Allan Nevins, *The Emergence of Modern America, 1865–1878* (New York: The Macmillan Company, 1927), p. 219; Schlesinger, *The Rise of the City*, p. 312. On the early years of baseball, see Harold Peterson, *The Man who Invented Baseball* (New York: Charles Scribner's Sons, 1973); David Quentin Voigt, *American Baseball: From Gentleman's Sport to the Commissioner System* (Norman: University of Oklahoma Press, 1966); Harold Seymour, *Baseball* (New York: Oxford University Press, 1966); John M. Rosenburg, *The Story of Baseball* (New York: Random House, 1972).

1882. Yacht clubs purchased beach and harbor facilities. Colleges built gymnasiums. In the 1870s, the popular YMCA and YWCA movements began drawing average people into structured indoor recreational space.[27]

In the period, the enclosure and definition of private space received even more attention than public. The appearance of Yale locks, burglary and fire-alarm systems, lighted streets, and anti-tramp legislation indicated the extent to which Americans were becoming concerned with protecting their private spaces. Mid-Victorians turned inward and described a natural and special function for every particular space, especially as the number of spaces multiplied and grew more complex. For instance, the common floor-plan of a Mid-Victorian home showed a breakfast nook or room, a dining room, kitchen, and large pantry; a master bedroom, separate children's bedrooms, a maid's room off the kitchen, often a nursery and a den, and at least two bathrooms; a large living room, a sun porch, and an ample foyer. Each room was separate and distinct, permanently set off by walls, doors, halls (dominated by a center hall), small passageways, closets, nooks, wood molding, and high ceilings.

Mid-Victorians associated each space with a function or activity that assumed cultural, indeed ceremonial, meaning. The breakfast meal, for example, had its own nook or room, its own types of food, its own nutritional mystique described in a literature, its own time of day, and its own morning newspaper. With the introduction of "grits," Quaker Oats, Wheatena, and other packaged cereals, Americans ceased eating pie, steaks, fried potatoes, baked beans, and heavy

[27] See Caspar W. Whitney, "Evolution of the Country Club," *Harper's New Monthly Magazine* 90 (December 1894), 16–33. The appearance of college gymnasiums is discussed in Chapter 7. At a YMCA convention in 1867, it was stated that the effect of owning a building added "immeasurably to the influences of our societies. . . . It is more than the mere power of property. The ideal of permanency or real power flows from the fact." C. Howard Hopkins, *History of the Y.M.C.A. in North America* (New York: Association Press, 1951), pp. 159, 246–70. The "physical work" of the YMCA is also discussed in Fred E. Leonard, *Pioneers of Modern Physical Training*, 2d. ed., rev. (New York: Association Press, 1919), pp. 119–25.

meat meals on a weekday morning. Meals were regularized
and differentiated. Even bread, now commercially baked,
took on a distinct form at breakfast; hot out of the toaster,
it was spread with the new synthetic oleomargarine. At more
psychological levels of consumption, Mid-Victorians identified breakfast with clean faces and neat clothes, a cheerful
greeting, a measured haste, and suppression of those hateful
feelings in family members that might erupt, blighting a
new day and perhaps a new fortune.[28]

Although trivial and ordinary, the example of women's
magazines vividly symbolizes the meaning Mid-Victorians
could attach to a defined space. For the uninformed, such
journals as [Women's] Home Companion (1873), Women's
Home Journal (1878), Ladies Home Journal (1883), and
Good Housekeeping (1885) advised the concerned matron

[28] The changing diet at breakfast disturbed George Augustus Sala, a
public lecturer and writer. He described the ideal meal in a volume
entitled, *Breakfast in Bed; or Philosophy Between the Sheets: A Series
of Indigestible Discourses* (New York: John Bradburn, 1863): "A
mutton-chop, or a rump-steak, or a good plateful from a cold joint, or
a couple of eggs broiled on bacon, or a haddock, or a mackerel, or
some pickled salmon, or some cold veal-and-ham pie, or half a wild
duck, or a devilled partridge, with plenty of bread-and-butter, or toast,
or muffins, and perhaps some anchovy sauce, or potted char, or preserved beef; the whole washed down by a couple of cups of tea or
coffee." The justification for the morning feast then followed: "I have
scarcely any need to point out that variety in what you have for
breakfast is the prime essential to enable you to eat any breakfast at
all. Man was not meant to live on bread—nay, nor on toasted bacon,
nor homoeopathic cocoa—alone. If you don't vary his diet, if you don't
give him something by way of a change, he will pine away, or refuse
his victuals, and grow morose and refractory as a wild animal." pp. 187,
189–90. Sala acknowledged that his cause was a losing one.
After the turn of the century, the government sponsored serious,
scientific studies of the nutritional and economic value of breakfast
foods. See Charles D. Woods and Harry Snyder, *Cereal Breakfast Foods*,
U.S. Department of Agriculture, Farmer's Bulletin no. 249 (Washington, D.C.: U.S. Government Printing Office, 1906); William Frear,
Breakfast Foods, Commonwealth of Pennsylvania, Department of Agriculture, Dairy and Food Division, Bulletin no. 162 (Harrisburg, Pa.:
Harrisburg Publishing Co., State Printer, 1908). See also Richard William Schwarz, "John Harvey Kellogg: American Health Reformer"
(Ph.D. diss., Dept. of History, University of Michigan, 1964), pp. 414–
41.

on the proper management of her increasingly elaborate household, including her own deportment. The first issue of *Good Housekeeping*, for instance, ran articles on "Home Decoration: Vestibule, Hall, and Staircase in Detail," what to do with "leftovers" and scraps at meals, and how the application of cheap varnish both kills bedbugs and improves the appearance of furniture. The new magazine devoted an entire column to the proper use of the three billion toothpicks made annually for "people who turn their mouths into pulp mills by reducing wooden toothpicks into fibrous splinters, damaging to the gums and throat, to say nothing of the disgusting offensiveness when mixed with saliva, in the process of expectoration." Not an "article of diet," toothpicks should never be placed on the meal table, but kept near at hand in another room where they could be used "as quietly and privately as possible" and then *"religiously thrown away."*[29]

Natural functions accompanied every structured space; the more spaces an individual inhabited, the more power and knowledge the person needed to command, the more complex and successful an American he or she might become. In the seventies, San Francisco's Nob Hill, Chicago's Prairie Avenue, and New York's Fifth Avenue came into their own. Spatially removed from common life, the mansions of the wealthy assumed an unprecedented elegance, with conservatories, music rooms, billiard rooms, balconies, and even theaters. In 1875, Mark Twain built a house in Connecticut that was three stories high, with nineteen large rooms and five bathrooms with indoor plumbing.

It was in the eighties that aspiring Americans began patronizing luxurious restaurants like Delmonico's in New York City, and the middle class began traveling in the com-

---

[29] *Good Housekeeping: a Family Journal; Conducted in the Interests of the Higher Life of the Household,* 1 (May 2, 1885): 14. Everything had a proper place in the household, including pets; however "pet children and pet animals, when given undue place and prominence, turn the milk of human kindness sour in many a heart, and draw dark clouds about many an otherwise peaceful home." *Ibid.,* 1 (May 30, 1885): 9.

fortably appointed Pullman railroad car, a new dimension
in mobile living space. The elegant car Pullman built for
himself at a cost of $38,000 in 1876 was appropriately called
a "mansion on wheels," and was lent on occasion to every
president from Grant to McKinley, as well as to visiting
foreign dignitaries. From its own personal experience, the
middle class knew that the Pullman car made travel "comfortable, inexpensive, safe," clean, and according to the
promoting agent, educational. Pullman understood his clientele as well as he understood himself. Striving Americans
respected and emulated few status symbols more than the
ability to own one's own Pullman car, a very rich man's
mobile home.[30]

Well-heeled Americans cultivated more and more space
for their private uses. The affluent began supplementing
their winter residences with vacation homes in Newport, Bar
Harbor, Long Branch, Saratoga Springs, Lenox, and Tuxedo.
Over time, the fashions of the well to do had a way of becoming the necessities of the middle class. Summer vacations
fell within the means of middle-class families, and white-
collar workers frequented resorts in the White Mountains
of New Hampshire, or at Denver and Colorado Springs in
the Rockies.

The Mid-Victorian taught that everyone naturally belonged in a specific space, especially the poor. In the 1860s,
environmental reformers began designing tenement houses
for immigrants. Ideally the apartment in a tenement was
meant to preserve the privacy and cohesion of the single
family, as if the family resided in the space of the suburban
middle class's detached home. With its room to store coal
and wood, which now would not have to be purchased daily;
with its own privy making it unnecessary for the individual
to frequent the saloon in order to relieve himself in the
public facility; with its icebox to store perishables like milk
so that the woman did not have to shop outside for every

[30] See Stanley Buder, *Pullman: An Experiment in Industrial Order
and Community Planning, 1880–1930* (New York: Oxford University
Press, 1967), pp. 29, 22.

meal or serve her children nonperishable beer—the ideal
tenement would turn the face of the immigrant away from
the outward street culture with its numerous dangers and
temptations. It would face him inward toward self-sufficiency
and independence now symbolized by the new resources
found in the privacy of his own home. The tenement apartment was a spatial way-station for the immigrant on his way
to self-reliance, respectability, and responsible citizenship.
As a working wage-earner, he would prove himself to be
dependable, reliable, and disciplined, a model of patriotism
and probity to his children, whose wholesome domesticity
would make joining street gangs or loitering in saloons unnecessary. The structured space of the tenement house
would both liberate and confine the urban poor.[31]

WORDS AND THE COMMUNICATIONS REVOLUTION

Mid-Victorians not only isolated and structured space; they
filled that space with words. Words rather than face-to-face
or direct human contact became the favorite medium of
social exchange. Confined in its space, every serious activity
found a literary expression, including a distinct vocabulary
that sympathetic persons could share.

The bicyclist, for example, could subscribe to the *Veloci-
pedist* (1869), or the "Velocepede Notes" in *Scientific
American, American Bicycling Journal* (1877–79), *Bicycling*

31 See Jacob August Riis, *How the Other Half Lives: Studies Among
the Tenements of New York* (New York: Charles Scribner's Sons, 1890);
Marcus T. Reynolds, *The Housing of the Poor in American Cities*,
Publications of the American Economic Association, vol. 8, nos. 2, 3
(Baltimore: 1893); Alfred Tredway White, *Improved Dwellings for the
Working Classes, 1877, 1879; Better Homes for Workingmen, 1885;
Riverside Buildings, 1890* (Brooklyn, N.Y., 1891); Lawrence Veiller,
Housing Conditions and Tenement Laws in Leading American Cities
(New York: The Evening Post Job Printing House, 1900); J. W. Sulli-
van, *Tenement Tales of New York* (New York: Henry Holt and Com-
pany, 1895); Roy Lubove, *The Progressives and the Slums: Tenement
House Reform in New York City, 1890–1917* (Pittsburgh: University of
Pittsburgh Press, 1962).

World (1879–1915, under various titles), *The Wheelman* (1882–83), *The Wheel* (1880–1900), *The Wheelman's Gazette* (1883–1908). Even the casual rider could follow and participate in the professional developments of the sport. *Velocinasiums* or schools were established for instruction. "The art of walking is becoming obsolete," *Scientific American* noted in 1869. At one school in New York City,

On any week-day evening may be seen upward of a hundred and fifty gentlemen—doctors, bankers, merchants, and representatives from almost every profession—engaged in this training school preparatory to making their appearance upon the public streets and fashionable promenades. . . . Here are two well-known stock brokers, jaded by the excitement of Wall street, with their coats off, and faces burning with zeal, gyrating around the room in the most eccentric manner. Some of the time they were upright in the saddle, but more frequently they were engaged in mounting and dismounting their refractory steeds: they looked fatigued, they gave forth the sigh of discouragement; but after an expert had mounted and raced gracefully around the room, they began to rally for another effort, and seemed to be satisfied that the fault was not in the machine after all.[32]

Cycling was more than a pastime. It was a subculture with its own slang and verbal gestures; its ceremonies, competitive races, and prizes; its special knowledge, habits of thought, discipline, and pride; its spatial interest in good roads and in safe paths through parks and public squares; its concern with reform in dress and properly lit vehicles. One expert rider typically bragged that "a horse costs more, and will eat, kick, and die; and you cannot stable him under your bed." Tribune Bicycle advertised that "when *Mile-a-Minute* Murphy accomplished his wonderful feat of riding a Tribune a full mile in less than 60 seconds behind a special train, he established a wheeling record which is likely to remain the record for years." Selling for forty to sixty dollars, the Tribune combined "strength and speed in such a way that full confidence is placed in the wheel." The Wright brothers were bicycle mechanics from Canton,

Ohio, who expanded their skills into gliders and aircraft, as others expanded their skills into motorcycles and automobiles.[33]

Sports, the circus, gardening, physical health, mental hygiene, cooking, clothing, fashions, spiritualism, courtship and marriage, art, reform, secret societies, trades, unions, professions—few activities in America lacked some form of enduring literary expression. Through their writings, devotees often attempted to raise interest in an activity to the level of a mental science, even a profession. High schools and universities, for instance, introduced courses of study in home economics which were intended to dignify in the name of domestic science what earlier had been a chore called housekeeping. Educated women with professional standards would distinguish a science with its distinct literature from folklore.[34]

[33] Leonard De Vries and Ilonka Van Amstel, *The Wonderful World of American Advertisements, 1865–1900* (Chicago: Follett Publishing Company, 1972), p. 73. See Richard Harmond, "Progress and Flight: An Interpretation of the American Cycle Craze of the 1890s," *Journal of Social History* 5 (Winter 1971–72): 235–57; Gary Allan Tobin, "The Bicycle Boom of the 1890's: The Development of Private Transportation and the Birth of the Modern Tourist," *Journal of Popular Culture* 7 (Spring 1974): 838–49.

[34] Courses in cooking and sewing, with lectures on the chemistry of food and nutrition, were found in land-grant colleges in Iowa, Kansas, and Illinois in the 1870s. By 1905, there were thirty-six land-grant institutions with departments of home economics. This development also found expression in secondary schools, and in the establishment of cooking schools throughout the nation. The government entered the field of scientific research in nutrition in 1894. See Helen Campbell, *Household Economics: A Course of Lectures in the School of Economics of the University of Wisconsin* (New York and London: G. P. Putnam's Sons, 1896). See also Isabel Bevier, *Home Economics in Education* (Philadelphia, London, Chicago: J. B. Lippincott Company, 1924); Paul V. Betters, *The Bureau of Home Economics: Its History, Activities and Organization,* Institute for Government Research Service Monograph no. 62 (Washington, D.C.: The Brookings Institution, 1930), pp. 1–43; Beulah I. Coon, *Home Economics in Colleges and Universities of the United States,* Federal Security Agency, Office of Education, Home Economics Education Series, no. 26 (Washington, D.C.: U.S. Government Printing Office, n.d.), pp. 1–4; Emma Seifrit Weigley, "It Might Have Been Euthenics: The Lake Placid Conferences and the Home Economics Movement," *American Quarterly* 26 (March 1974), 79–96.

Mid-Victorians would not leave life to chance, miscellania, floating categories, or fleeting impressions. They filled structured space with structured thoughts and words that preoccupied any individual concerned with self-fulfillment and the improvement of natural talent. Visitors in the early part of the century, for instance, remarked that children in America acted like premature adults, not like children. Nature did visibly identify children, and Mid-Victorians relentlessly pioneered in confining children to their appropriate spaces, in defining delinquency, and cultivating a children's literature together with a science of pedagogy. Parents, teachers, and librarians were determined to make children choose childhood.[35] By 1885, *Youth's Companion* had achieved the largest magazine circulation of the period. In the 1870s, sixty or more different juvenile periodicals were published each year, apart from the expanding market in children's books. Mark Twain, for one, expressed hopes of catering to that lucrative market, especially with *The Prince and the Pauper* (1882).[36] The kindergarten and primary-school movement established three professional journals in the 1870s alone.[37] The expanding field of childhood opened

[35] See Kuhn, *The Mother's Role in Childhood Education:* Bernard Wishy, *The Child and the Republic: The Dawn of Modern Child Nurture* (Philadelphia: University of Pennsylvania Press, 1968); Joseph M. Hawes, *Children in Urban Society: Juvenile Delinquency in Nineteenth-Century America* (New York: Oxford University Press, 1971); Dorothy Ross, *G. Stanley Hall: The Psychologist as Prophet* (Chicago and London: University of Chicago Press, 1972), pp. 279–308; Robert H. Bremner, John Barnard, Tamara K. Hareven, Robert M. Mennel, eds., *Children and Youth in America: A Documentary History,* 3 vols. (Cambridge, Mass.: Harvard University Press, 1970–74); Richard L. Rapson, "The American Child as Seen by British Travelers, 1845–1935," *American Quarterly* 17 (Fall 1965): 520–34; Joseph F. Kett, "Adolescence and Youth in Nineteenth-Century America," *Journal of Interdisciplinary History* 2 (Autumn 1971): 283–98.

[36] Frank Luther Mott, *A History of American Magazines, 1865–1885* (Cambridge, Mass.: Harvard University Press, 1957), pp. 174–80; Kaplan, *Mr. Clemens and Mark Twain,* pp. 277–79. See also R. Gordon Kelley, "Publishing: the Institutional Matrix," *Mother was a Lady: Self and Society in Selected American Children's Periodicals, 1865–1890* (Westport, Conn., and London: Greenwood Press, 1974), pp. 3–31.

[37] On the early literature, see W. N. Hailman, *Kindergarten Culture in the Family and Kindergarten* (New York, Cincinnati, Chicago: Amer-

up significant opportunities for adults with literary and professional ambitions.

Mid-Victorians were seldom reluctant to capitalize personally on the expression of their reform ideas. Writing and lecturing in specialized areas "paid." Indeed, the line between conventional greed and the excitement of intellectual and scientific discovery usually blurred upon close examination, as a contemporary portrait of leading American physicians revealed in 1876:

We have in our cities, great and small, a . . . class of physicians whose principal object is to obtain money, or rather the social position, pleasures, and power, which money only can bestow. They are clear-headed, shrewd, practical men, well educated, because "it pays," and for the same reason they take good care to be supplied with the best instruments, and the latest literature. Many of them take up specialities because the work is easier, and the hours of labour are more under their control than in general practice. They strive to become connected with hospitals and medical schools, not for the love of mental exertion, or of science for its own sake, but as a respectable means of advertising, and of obtaining consultations. They write and lecture to keep their names before the public, and they must do both well, or fall behind in the race. They have the greater part of the valuable prac-

ican Book Company, 1873); Henry Barnard, *Papers on Froebel's Kindergarten with Suggestions in Principles and Methods of Child Culture in Different Countries* (Hartford, Conn.: American Journal of Education, 1881); Harvey Carpenter, *The Mother's and Kindergartner's Friend* (Boston: Cupples, Uppham and Company, 1884); [Anne L. Page, Angeline Brooks, Alice H. Putnam, Mary H. Peabody], *The Kindergarten and the School, By Four Active Workers* (Springfield, Mass.: Milton Bradley Co., 1886); Elizabeth Palmer Peabody, *Lectures in the Training Schools for Kindergartners* (Boston: D. C. Heath and Company, 1888). Susan E. Blow, *Kindergarten Education,* vol. 2 in *Monographs on Education in the United States,* ed. Nicholas Murray Butler (Division of Exhibits, Department of Education, Universal Exposition, St. Louis, 1904).

On the history, see Nina C. Vandewalker, *The Kindergarten in American Education* (New York: The Macmillan Company, 1908); Evelyn Weber, *The Kindergarten: Its Encounter with Educational Thought in America* (New York: Teacher's College Press, Columbia University, 1969); Marvin Lazerson, "Urban Reform and the Schools: Kindergartens in Massachusetts, 1870–1915," *History of Education Quarterly* 11 (Summer 1971): 115–42.

tice, and their writings, which constitute the greater part of our medical literature, are respectable in quality, and eminently useful.[38]

Merely publicizing one's social importance could not, however, cover up the basic ambiguity of Mid-Victorian motives. Gratification of venal desires, at first delayed and then intensified by the requisite professional education, jarred against equally strong desires to benefit society and to make permanent contributions to civilization. Nowhere was that ambiguity better demonstrated than in the manipulation of words.

Like no other class in history before them, Mid-Victorians dealt in words. Words were their primary social currency, and this relatively unexplored medium of cultural exchange began profoundly to affect everyday human relationships. In the world of mass advertisement that opened up in the 1860s and 1870s, for example, words served as surrogates for products. National companies began buying space units in magazines and newspapers. Proctor and Gamble's Ivory Soap, "99 and 44/100 percent pure . . . it floats"; Eastman Kodak's "You press the button; we do the rest"; Schlitz's, "The Beer that Made Milwaukee Famous": such slogans, repeated incessantly, became familiar advertising leaders in the 1880s and 1890s. The facility with language rather than the quality of the commodity sold manufactured goods.[39] The slogan, "Cheapest Supply House on Earth," appeared on every page of Sears, Roebuck, and Company's mail-order catalog, another innovation in the era. Within the enormously successful catalogs, verbal superlatives competed with one another to raise every ordinary item to the

[38] J. S. Billings, "Literature and Institutions," in [Edward H. Clarke, Henry J. Bigelow, Samuel D. Gross, T. Gaillard Thomas, J. S. Billings], *A Century of American Medicine, 1776–1876* (Philadelphia: Lea, 1876), pp. 363–64.

[39] For delightful examples of the advertisements of the period, see the reproductions in De Vries and Van Amstel, *American Advertisements;* Edgar R. Jones, *Those Were the Good Old Days: A Happy Look at American Advertising, 1880–1930* (New York: Simon and Schuster, 1959), pp. 9–106. Mott concentrates on a narrative, *American Magazines, 1885–1905,* pp. 22–34.

level of the extraordinary and the special. Typically, a
product was advertised in America as the "best," "first,"
"largest," "greatest," "remarkable," and "cheapest." Scott's
Emulsion, for instance, a cod-liver-oil substance, was promoted as "human nature's kindest friend." One Scott's ad
bannered, "Truth Stranger Than Fiction." In the illustration, a distraught mother asked at the bedside of the failing
child: "Oh, doctor, must my darling die?"—"There's very
little hope, but try *Scott's Emulsion*."

Advertisers in America employed words to portray substance, purity, and health, which associated a product in the
mind of a consumer with self-esteem, control, place, power,
energy, and new life. Pabst advertised its malt extract as
"spring medicine," and Anheuser-Busch called its ale "food
drink." Vigoral, the trade name for Armour's concentrated
beef, claimed to "make weak people strong." Heinz boasted
of forty-seven varieties of pickles, presumably for persons
with sturdy stomachs. As portrayed, the use of an advertised
product represented a way of life, a set of solid values, a
genuine activity set in its special space. Pear's soap belonged
in the modern bathroom, because the mistress of the house
took pride in keeping that space odorless and antiseptic, and
because Pear's "is the best, the most elegant, and the most
economical of all soaps for general toilet purposes. It is not
only the most attractive, but the purest and the cleanest."
As symbols of permanence, such famous trademarks as
Quaker Oats' double-chinned Quaker holding a package of
food in one hand and a scroll marked "Pure" in the other,
Prudential's Rock of Gibraltar, and King C. Gillette's face
imprinted themselves on American life. By 1878, J. Walter
Thompson had acquired his own advertising firm, which
he headed for thirty years. Successfully promoted products
left a familiar impression on the American's awareness.
Bromo-Seltzer "will cure that headache" for those who kept
"late hours"; Chase and Sanborn was "justly called the
aristocratic coffee of America"; and Hires' "improved root
beer" was the "most delicious and wholesome Temperance
drink in the world."

Technological developments in the era made unprecedented communication of the written word possible. In the seventies, Remington's new typewriter model was capable of printing both lowercase and capital letters. ("Nothing succeeds like success," Simplex Typewriter Company advertised; "A typewritten letter has a successful look about it and makes business.") In the eighties, Waterman manufactured the first successful fountain pen. In 1885, Ottmar Mergenthaler perfected the linotype machine which in the hands of a skilled operator cast whole lines of lead type ready for print. Henry Holt, Charles Scribner, and E. P. Dutton established aggressive publishing houses in the seventies. The economics of publishing and distribution began significantly reducing the price of the printed word, including illustrations and photographs, to the consumer.[40]

"Writing for the magazines has become a profession, employing a considerable number of trained experts," the *National Republic* wrote in 1877.[41] A reliable audience, for instance, now financially supported John Burroughs and his nature studies; a generation earlier, Henry David Thoreau, far the superior naturalist and writer, had only a scant audience and received no income from his writings. It was only after 1870 that Ralph Waldo Emerson began making money from his books, as did a native American literary class, including Twain and Howells from the Midwest, Harte from the West, and Cable from the South. In 1871, *Atlantic Monthly* made Bret Harte an unprecedented offer of $10,000 for the exclusive rights to at least twelve poems or sketches for one year. The offer was based on the strength

[40] Developments in the publishing world are discussed by Raymond Howard Shove, *Cheap Book Production in the United States, 1870 to 1891* (Urbana, Ill.: University of Illinois Library, 1937); John Tebbel, *A History of Book Publishing in the United States,* 2 vols. (New York and London: R. R. Bowker, 1972–) vol. 2, *The Expansion of an Industry, 1856–1919* (1975); Madeleine B. Stern, *Imprints on History: Book Publishers and American Frontiers* (Bloomington: Indiana University Press, 1956).

[41] Cited in Mott, *American Magazines, 1865–1885,* pp. 17–18.

of Hart's collection of stories *The Luck of Roaring Camp,* one of the best-sellers in the decade, and his poem "The Heathen Chinee," which achieved faddish popularity. In three years, Mark Twain's combined royalties from the book and the play versions of *The Gilded Age* earned him $100,000.[42]

Here was a real meaning for the communications revolution. A man was his "word" or the words others used about him. Nature excluded few persons from the acquisition of American words. Universally and freely shared, available to all, words could provide a measure for categorizing people in a democratic society. Mid-Victorians were competitive, and the serious contests of the future would be verbal. Americans would probe, joust, and examine each other in a war of words that occurred in the classroom, the courtroom, the salesroom, and the living room. The confidence man knew that not only could facility with language sell commodities, it could also sell persons. Those armed with words would get ahead in the new society; the inarticulate, barely literate, and foreign speaking would not. The fictional immigrant Jew David Levinsky typically associated mastery of the American language with assimilation and eventual material success in American life. Learning new words transformed the itinerant Jew into a first-class citizen, one who was comfortable in a variety of spaces, a "greenhorn no longer," an active participant in the American dream.[43] For the success-

[42] Margaret Duckett, *Mark Twain and Bret Harte* (Norman: University of Oklahoma Press, 1964), pp. 32, 51, 94–95, 119; Kaplan, *Mr. Clemens and Mark Twain,* pp. 145–46, 191; Webster, ed., *Mark Twain, Business Man,* pp. 188–90.

[43] See Abraham Cahan, *The Rise of David Levinsky* (New York: Harper & Row, Publishers, 1917; reprinted 1960), pp. 83–144; Hutchins Hapgood, *The Spirit of the Ghetto: Studies of the Jewish Quarter of New York* (New York: Schocken Books, 1967), pp. 27–32, originally published in 1902. On the importance of English literacy in immigrant life, see Timothy L. Smith, "Immigrant Social Aspirations and American Education, 1880–1930," *American Quarterly* 21 (Fall 1969): 523–43; Robert Higgs, "Race, Skills, and Earnings: American Immigrants in 1909," *The Journal of Economic History* 31 (June 1971): 420–28.

ful writer, journalist, and orator such as Mark Twain, Ben
Franklin's adage required amendment: *time* was no longer
money—*words* were, each and every one of them.

Twain used the vernacular to return words to their vivid,
material, sensuous basis in nature. A Mid-Victorian understood that words were more than an external medium of
social exchange, more than outward appearances or window
dressing, more than a conveyance of intercommunication.
Words liberated reality itself, as they revealed the deepest
emotional life of a person in his or her expressions. Words
uncovered and exposed the nature of a self, the wants,
desires, expectations, corruptions, and compromises of a
certain group of people. By means of vivid and descriptive
journalism, Helen Hunt Jackson portrayed in 1881 a "century of dishonor," the rape of the American Indian. In the
same year, Henry Demarest Lloyd told the story of the
feudalistic oil trust.[44]

By making words clear, plain, direct, and tangible, Mid-
Victorians believed that they were incarnating reality,
plumbing its depths, raising its potential, and immortaliz-
ing its true nature. After George Pullman built his planned
town in which every movement was calculated to impress
Americans with spatial order, cause and effect, efficiency,
and a superintelligence, he sought out the distinguished
Andrew Dickson White, president of Cornell University, to
publicize the middle-class utopia in *Harper's,* the country's
best-known magazine. The simplicity of words from the pen
of a disciplined writer was essential to the success of Pullman's special creation. Not coincidentally did Americans
publish more utopian novels in the eighties and nineties
than in any other period in American history.[45] Populists,

[44] Helen Hunt Jackson, *A Century of Dishonor: The Early Crusade
for Indian Reform* (New York: Harper & Brothers, 1881); H. D. Lloyd,
"Story of a Great Monopoly," *Atlantic Monthly* 47 (1881): 317–34.

[45] White recommended as a substitute Richard T. Ely, who wrote the
article, "Pullman: a Social Study," *Harper's New Monthly Magazine*
70 (February 1885): 452–66. See Buder, *Pullman,* pp. 100–1; Vernon
Louis Parrington, *American Dreams: A Study of American Utopias*
(Providence, R.I.: Brown University Press, 1948), pp. 232–41.

for instance, identified with Edward Bellamy's *Looking Backward* (1888), and few thought that they were escaping through literature. Instead they were clarifying and transforming social reality. Indeed, perhaps the ultimate embodiment of reality in America occurred in 1893, when Frederick Jackson Turner wrote about the elemental nature of America's "frontier." Through a poetic essay, Turner defined a unique field of endeavor, confined in its own space, described in its own words, a culture unto itself: American history.[46]

Mid-Victorians taught that words liberated the nature of a self by bringing it to consciousness, the "American Character" in Turner's case. But Mid-Victorians also taught that words, more than any other medium of communication, confined and restricted the nature of a self. Indeed, this second dimension of the value of words stimulated as much interest as the first, especially since words were a common denominator among all persons in American life. The printed word was an ideal form of expression for business contracts, professional recommendations, and abstract public relationships between Americans.

A Mid-Victorian used the written word as if he were defending it in a public courtroom. To place an opinion in writing was to make it final, commit the writer to its veracity, document a position and submit that position to the impartial reading of a third party and even subject it to legal action. Written words, by their very nature, made people hesitate and seriously consider their thoughts and possible actions. The printed page was intimidating, restraining, even emotionally forbidding and paralyzing. A document filed away for permanent reference could be recovered at any future date and be used to damage irreparably a person's reputation. In this atmosphere, every word

[46] On the populists, I am drawing upon dissertation research by Christine McHugh, department of History, University of Illinois, Chicago Circle. Frederick J. Turner, "The Significance of the Frontier in American History," *Annual Report of the American Historical Association for the Year 1893* (Washington, D.C.: U.S. Government Printing Office, 1894), pp. 197–227.

was potentially damning, every word suspect. A fear of words inhibited people from committing themselves to a position, impressed upon people their helplessness, and inevitably had the effect of moderating public behavior.

As a form of social exchange, words were eminently impersonal, and vulnerable to regulation and alteration. Words created distances between people, distances a Mid-Victorian welcomed. At its best, the printed page exemplified detachment, calm consideration, order, permanence, and responsibility for judgment, all Mid-Victorian virtues. With the written word, for instance, an author could censor, correct, revise, and edit his thoughts. He controlled them. The audience was removed, the excitement of a listener's emotional approval or disapproval absent, as the author worked in the office, study, or library. In a cerebral and detached environment, a writer could carefully structure the word, and plan the result. At its worst, therefore, the printed page filled with forbidden ideas might endanger civilization itself, and this threat increasingly became a source of impenetrable Mid-Victorian earnestness.

When Anthony Comstock and the Watch and Ward Society successfully lobbied for a tighter postal obscenity law in 1873, the growing influence of the written word in America had become evident. If public space could be regulated, why could not the public words and morals within that space? For the next generation, vice societies in America preached the cleansed printed page as civilization's salvation and the tainted page as barbarism's chief advocate. "[B]ad books," declared one spokesman, "are worse, far worse, than bad companions." Obscene books produced lust, according to Comstock, and lust was *"the boon companion of all other crimes."*[47] Forged by criminals, the written word provoked

[47] Cited in Paul S. Boyer, *Purity in Print: The Vice-Society Movement and Book Censorship in America* (New York: Charles Scribner's Sons, 1968), pp. 20, 21. Comstock himself wrote two books, *Frauds Exposed; or, How the People are Deceived and Robbed, and Youth Corrupted. Being a Full Exposure of Various Schemes Operated through the Mails, and Unearthed by the Author in a Seven Years' Service as a*

all other violations of society. Social hygienists drew the link between eroticism in dirty books and the brothel in the city streets. Public trustees charged professional librarians, keepers of childhood purity, with scrutinizing the classics of literature for pornographic filth. Such educators as President Charles William Eliot of Harvard, President Alice Freeman Palmer of Wellesley, and President G. Stanley Hall of Clark exhorted the audiences of the annual meetings of Boston's Watch and Ward Society. Mid-Victorians prominently displayed the expurgated edition and the forbidden list, both sanctioned by the most distinguished cultural authorities in America.

The Mid-Victorian's obsession with disseminating the printed page was no crank's reaction. Words influenced human relationships in a new way. To be isolated with a book was to be isolated as never before. Mid-Victorians recognized that such isolation could restrain people, confine them within their spatial boundaries, their literary images, and their vicarious experiences. The entire experience of reading was internal and contemplative. Detached from any face-to-face confrontation, apart from any mass audience, oblivious to any restriction of time, the individual alone could read and reread the written word in the privacy of any room. A reader could review a single sentence continuously; he could read backward or forward, slowly or quickly. He could direct the imagination to be sanguine rather than morbid, to soar rather than to sink, to love proper thoughts and to hate perverse ones. But the imagination did not necessarily cooperate upon conscious demand. Isolated, the reader required no intermediary as interpreter, no set stage, no responsive listener. He could proscrastinate reading a book or magazine, start and lose himself in reverie, stop at

Special Agent of the Post Office Department and Secretary and Chief Agent of the New York Society for the Suppression of Vice (New York: J. Howard Brown, 1880), and *Traps for the Young* (New York: Funk & Wagnalls, 1883). On censorship, see also Tebbel, *Book Publishing in the United States*, 2:609–34.

any point, and resume the activity at a later time. In contrast, the actor or the musician interpreted the theatrical drama or the musical symphony within an established social setting, and the theme of the performance developed within an established period of time.

Intensified by the abundance of reading matter that Mid-Victorian America began publishing, the effect of the printed page was to fragment the attention of people, to encourage confusion and frustration that gave way to self-doubt and mistrust. Overpowered by their own insecurity, Americans found themselves turning toward such professional spokespersons as Eliot, Palmer, and Hall, who would distinguish the true words from the false ones, the wholesome from the degenerate, and the safe from the subversive. Noah Porter's *Books and Reading: Or, What Books Shall I Read and How Shall I Read Them?* (1870), for instance, was a publishing success that guided Godfearing, middle-class audiences through lists of books about history, fiction, poetry, and science. Public spokesmen and educators were increasingly expected to assist respectable Americans to discriminate in their reading matter. Charles William Eliot's "Five-Foot Book-Shelf," or The Harvard Classics, fifty volumes of selected readings, grew out of the movement to further the self-education of "working people." Eliot claimed in his Introduction, "I proposed to make such a selection as any intellectually ambitious American family might use to advantage, even if their early opportunities of education had been scanty."[48] If read for only fifteen minutes a day over a number of years, the selections would provide a good substitute for a liberal education. The reception, success, and status attached to the books exceeded both Eliot's expectations and the publisher's.

A riot of words and a crisis of confidence alarmed a society which began placing its faith in professional persons. In Mid-Victorian America, the citizen became a client whose

---

[48] Henry James, *Charles W. Eliot: President of Harvard University, 1869–1909*, 2 vols. (Boston and New York: Houghton Mifflin Company, 1930), 2:196.

obligation was to trust the professional. Legitimate authority now resided in special spaces, like the courtroom, the classroom, and the hospital; and it resided in special words shared only by experts.

3

The Culture of Professionalism

A RADICAL IDEA

The structuring of space and words belonged to a larger process: the professionalization of American lives. The pattern manifested itself everywhere, in popular culture, the academy, and spectator sports, indeed in the ordinary habits of a middle-class life as an individual learned the hygienic way to bathe, eat, work, relax, and even have sexual intercourse. The middle class in America matured as the Mid-Victorians perfected their cultural control over the release of personal and social energies. And the professions as we know them today were the original achievement of Mid-Victorians who sought the highest form in which the middle class could pursue its primary goals of earning a good living, elevating both the moral and intellectual tone of society, and emulating the status of those above one on the social ladder. Americans after 1870, but beginning after 1840, committed themselves to a culture of professionalism which over the years has established the thoughts, habits, and responses most modern Americans have taken for granted, a culture which has admirably served individuals who aspire to think very well of themselves.

In the 1870s and 1880s, examples of professional trends were already numerous. At the level of popular culture, the mass distribution of books by subscription both rationalized marketing procedures and created a vast new audience. Grant's *Personal Memoirs* (1885), for instance, was a publishing bonanza, earning the family a fortune in royalties.[1] In 1868, James Redpath began eliminating the confusion, duplication, and waste in the lecture rooms of the American lyceum by organizing a national lecturing bureau —Redpath Lyceum Bureau—which now became responsive to particular and local needs. Founded in 1874, the Chautauqua movement began drawing renowned scholars inside its brown canvas tents, first with its national program in adult education and then with its university extension.[2]

Spectator sports quickly displayed tendencies toward professionalization. The first Kentucky Derby was run at Churchill Downs in 1875.[3] Baseball became the country's most popular late-nineteenth-century pastime, and Cincinnati organized the first professional club in 1869, the Red

[1] In a little more than six months after publication, the publisher sent Mrs. Grant a royalty check for $200,000, the largest amount ever sent an author in one sum. Within a year, the book had earned the publisher $600,000. John Tebbel, *A History of Book Publishing in the United States*, vol. 2, *The Expansion of an Industry, 1856–1919* (New York and London: R. R. Bowker, 1975): 524–26.

[2] See Carl Bode, *The American Lyceum: Town Meeting of the Mind* (Carbondale and Edwardsville, Ill.: Southern Illinois University Press, 1956), pp. 200, 249; Justin Kaplan, *Mr. Clemens and Mark Twain: A Biography* (New York: Pocket Books, 1968), pp. 88–94; Joseph E. Gould, *The Chautauqua Movement: An Episode in the Continuing American Revolution* (New York: State University of New York, 1961); Theodore Morrison, *Chautauqua: A Center for Education, Religion, and the Arts in America* (Chicago and London: University of Chicago Press, 1974).

[3] On the early history of the Derby, see Lamont Buchanan, *The Kentucky Derby Story* (New York: E. P. Dutton and Company, 1953), pp. 11–31; Brownie Leach, *The Kentucky Derby Diamond Jubilee, 1875–1949* (New York: Dial Press, 1949), pp. 16–17; Frank G. Menke, *The Story of Churchill Downs and the Kentucky Derby* (n.p., 1940), pp. 11–15.

Stockings. Professional recognition required distinctive forms of dress with which the public was familiar, and the Red Stockings became the first team to wear the traditional baseball uniform, designed by a local dressmaker. In 1868, Henry Chadwick, editor of the weekly *The Ballplayer's Chronicle,* wrote a book entitled *The [American] Game of Baseball: How to Learn It, How to Play It, and How to Teach It.* At the outset, he distinguished between amateur interest in the game for the sake of recreation, and the more serious interest of the "professional player" or "professional expert" who

> not only requires an attentive study of the rules of the game, and of those special applications of them known as "points," together with perfect familiarity with each and every rule; but also a regular course of training, to fully develope the physical powers, in order to ensure the highest degree of skill in each and all of the several departments of the game. . . . To play the game up to its highest point of excellence requires as great a degree of mental ability, and the possession of as many manly physical attributes as any known game of ball.[4]

The National League was formed in 1876, the American Association in 1882, and the first "World" Series was played in 1884.

The rules of collegiate football developed following the first Harvard-Yale contest in 1875 and the first Princeton-Yale contest in 1885. The fears widely expressed by college

4 Henry Chadwick, *The [American] Game of Baseball: How to Learn It, How to Play It, and How to Teach It* (New York: George Munro & Co., Publishers, 1868), pp. 13, 14. Chadwick's weekly, *The Ballplayer's Chronicle,* first appeared on June 6, 1867. In 1886, he published two books, *The Art of Pitching and Fielding* and *The Art of Batting and Base Running.* Both were published by A. G. Spalding & Bros. (based in New York and Chicago), who advertised themselves in Chadwick's books as "the largest sporting goods house in America. . . . Manufacturers, Importers, and Dealers in General Sporting Goods, Guns and Gun Accoutrements, Fishing Tackle, Base Ball Supplies, Lawn Tennis, Cricket, Croquet, Ice and Roller Skates, Foot Balls, Lacrosse, Polo, Cutlery, Gymnasium, Theatrical, and General Sporting Goods. Send for illustrated catalogue." See also Harold Seymour, "The Coming of the Professionals," in *Baseball* (New York: Oxford University Press, 1966), pp. 59–72.

faculty only fed the contagious obsession of the public, alumni, and students with winning the annual rivalries and participating in the increasingly elaborate ceremony. Given the intensity of the gridiron competition and the disgrace of losing, the direction of events was predictable. To little avail, the editor of the *Nation* complained in 1882 that "the college base-ball, boating, and foot-ball which make so much talk in the newspapers are shared in really by about two or three dozen young men in each college, whose expenses are paid by their fellows. All the 'athletic sport' that the great majority of the students get consists in the payment of money to the 'college eight,' or 'college nine,' as the case may be."[5] In 1889, Walter Camp named the first All American team, and in 1893 Harvard appointed its first salaried athletic coordinator.[6] Football meant fame and prestige even to the best colleges and universities, and administrators soon knew better than to handle amateurishly the munificence that derived from athletic honors.[7]

In more traditional fields of specialization, the outline of

[5] *Nation* 35 (November 30, 1882): 458. For a detailed summary of reactions to the big success of college football in the later part of the century, see Henry D. Sheldon, *Student Life and Customs* (New York: D. Appleton and Company, 1901), pp. 230–55.

[6] Scientific treatises on the subject quickly followed. See A. Alonzo Stagg and Henry L. Williams, *A Scientific and Practical Treatise on American Football for Schools and Colleges* (Hartford, Conn.: The Case, Lockwood & Brainard Company, 1893); Walter Camp, *Football Facts and Figures: A Symposium of Expert Opinions on the Game's Place in American Athletics* (New York: Harper and Brothers, 1894); Walter Camp and Lorin F. Deland, *Football* (Boston and New York: Houghton Mifflin Company, 1896).

[7] On the early history of collegiate sport, see Guy Lewis, "The Beginning of Organized Collegiate Sport," *American Quarterly* 22 (Summer 1970): 221–29; Ronald A. Smith, "Athletics in the Wisconsin State University System: 1867–1913," *Wisconsin Magazine of History* 55 (Autumn 1971): 2–23; W. Carson Ryan, Jr., *The Literature of American School and College Athletics*, Bulletin no. 24 (New York: The Carnegie Foundation for the Advancement of Teaching, 1929), Frederick Rudolph, *The American College and University: A History* (New York: Alfred A. Knopf, 1962), pp. 373–93; Robin Lester, "The Rise, Decline and Fall of Intercollegiate Football at the University of Chicago, 1890–1940" (Ph.D. diss., Dept. of History, University of Chicago, 1974), pp. 1–99.

professional structures emerged boldly. The law established its first national professional association in 1878, librarianship in 1876, and social work in 1874. Dentistry founded its first university school (in contrast to a training school) in 1867, architecture and pharmacy in 1868, schoolteaching and veterinary medicine in 1879, and accounting in 1881. The Wharton School of Finance and Economy was founded in 1881, a prelude to the declaration that business was a profession. The first state license law for dentistry appeared in 1868, for pharmacy in 1874, for veterinary medicine in 1886, for accounting in 1896, and for architecture in 1897. By 1894, twenty-one states had established an examination system for medical doctors, and fourteen others permitted only graduates from accredited medical schools to practice.[8]

The number of professional schools and students, and the standards for graduation, rose quickly in the last quarter of the century. A study of professional education in the United States published in 1899 showed the following increase in the number of schools over the century:

	1801–25	1826–50	1851–75	1876–1900
THEOLOGY	18	25	72	47
LAW	3	7	24	50
MEDICINE	12	22	33	86
DENTISTRY	0	2	7	47
PHARMACY	2	4	8	38
VETERINARY	0	0	2	15
TOTAL	35	60	146	283

Theology, with the largest number of schools, grew the most slowly. However, in ratio to the population, all professional fields were increasing. And higher standards for graduation were being adopted everywhere. By 1899, the majority of law schools taught a three-year course of studies; by contrast only one school had in 1875. By 1899, nearly all the medical-

[8] Harold L. Wilensky, "The Professionalization of Everyone," *American Journal of Sociology* 70 (September 1964): 143; *Occupational Licensing Legislations in the States* (Chicago: The Council of State Governments, 1952), pp. 22, 28–30.

school programs were four years in length, whereas most had been two years in 1875, and none had been four.[9]

By 1880, medical specialization so dominated the profession, especially in urban areas, that one physician warned, "there is now danger lest, all being specialists, none shall be general practitioners."[10] It was generally acknowledged that the specialist's work was easier, his hours more manageable, his prestige greater, and his fees higher than the general practitioner's. Specialists were determining the direction of American medicine, and they identified their professional interests with the exclusive national speciality medical societies, the following of which were founded between 1864 and 1888:

1864	American Ophthalmological Society
1868	American Otological Society
1875	American Neurological Association
1876	American Dermatological Association
1876	American Gynecological Society
1879	American Laryngological Association
1880	American Surgical Association
1886	American Association of Genito-Urinary Surgeons
1887	American Orthopedic Association
1888	American Pediatric Society

"In the brief period of less than fifty years," N. S. Davis, president of the American Medical Association, told his colleagues in 1883, "we have specialities for almost every part or region of the human body."[11] But Davis also implied more. Specialists were consolidating their considerable status as they moved to monopolize the presidency of the AMA,

9 James Russell Parsons, Jr., *Professional Education*, vol. 10 in *Monographs on Education in the United States*, ed. Nicholas Murray Butler (Division of Exhibits, Department of Education, Universal Exposition, St. Louis, 1904), pp. 2, 6–7, 11.

10 Cited in William G. Rothstein, *American Physicians in the Nineteenth Century: From Sects to Science* (Baltimore and London: The Johns Hopkins University Press, 1972), p. 210.

11 N. S. Davis, "Address on the Present Status and Future Tendencies of the Medical Profession in the United States," *Journal of the American Medical Association* 1 (July 21, 1883): 37.

control the faculties of medical colleges, pressure for the creation of speciality hospitals, dominate the staffs of general hospitals and dispensaries, and establish a clientele among persons with means and power.

Mid-Victorians appreciated the value to a career of membership in professional associations with "distinguished" titles. In the 1870s and 1880s, at least two hundred learned societies were formed, in addition to teachers' groups. Scientists, for instance, began establishing specialized associations beyond the American Association for the Advancement of Science, a prestigious organization which itself had been founded as a specialized group in 1848. With relative haste, it spawned:

1876	American Chemical Society
1880	American Society of Chemical Engineers
1882	American Forestry Association
1883	American Ornithologists' Union
1883	American Society of Naturalists
1884	American Climatological Society
1885	American Institute of Electrical Engineers
1888	Geological Society of America
1888	National Statistical Association
1888	American Mathematical Society
1889	American Physical Society

Also in the 1880s, historians (1884), church historians (1888), economists (1885), political scientists (1889), modern-language scholars and teachers (1883), and folklorists (1888) all established their associations, which stepped beyond the American Social Science Association, originally founded in 1865. Nearly every group included "American" in its title, a symbol that served to emphasize the scope of both its membership and its professional interest.

What was the meaning of this professional interest? As commonly understood, a profession was a full-time occupation in which a person earned the principal source of an income. During a fairly difficult and time-consuming process, a person mastered an esoteric but useful body of systematic knowledge, completed theoretical training before entering a practice or apprenticeship, and received a degree or license from a recognized institution. A professional person in the role of a practitioner insisted upon technical competence, superior skill, and a high quality of performance. Moreover, a professional embraced an ethic of service which taught that dedication to a client's interest took precedence over personal profit, when the two happened to come into conflict.[12]

Yet, in the mind of the Mid-Victorian, professionalism meant more than all this. Professionalism was also a culture which embodied a more radical idea of democracy than even the Jacksonian had dared to dream. The culture of professionalism emancipated the active ego of a sovereign person as he performed organized activities within comprehensive spaces. The culture of professionalism incarnated the radical idea of the independent democrat, a liberated person seeking to free the power of nature within every worldly sphere, a self-governing individual exercising his trained judgment in an open society. The Mid-Victorian as professional person strove to achieve a level of autonomous

[12] For definitions of the concept of profession see Wilbert E. Moore, *The Professions: Roles and Rules* (New York: Russell Sage Foundation, 1970); Howard M. Vollmer and Donald L. Mills, eds., *Professionalization* (Englewood Cliffs, N. J.: Prentice-Hall, 1966); A. M. Carr-Saunders, *Professions: Their Organization and Place in Society* (Oxford: At The Clarendon Press, 1928); Everett C. Hughes, *Men and Their Work* (Glencoe, Ill.: The Free Press, 1958); Philip Elliott, *The Sociology of the Professions* (New York: The Macmillan Company, 1972); Talcott Parsons, "The Professions and Social Structure," in *Essays in Sociological Theory*, rev. (New York: The Free Press, 1964), pp. 34–49; Parsons, "Professions," *International Encyclopedia of the Social Sciences*, 17 vols., ed. David L. Sills (New York: The Macmillan Company and The Free Press, 1968), 12: 536–47; Everett C. Hughes, "Professions," in Kenneth S. Lynn, ed., *The Professions in America* (Boston: Beacon Press, 1967), pp. 1–14; Ernest Greenwood, "Attributes of a Profession," *Social Work* 2 (July 1957): 45–55; William J. Goode, "The Theoretical Limits of Professionalization," in Amitai Etzioni, ed., *The Semi-Professions and their Organization: Teachers, Nurses, Social Workers* (New York: The Free Press, 1969), pp. 266–313; Goode, "Community Within a Community: The Professions," *American Sociological Review* 22 (April 1957): 192–200.

individualism, a position of unchallenged authority hereto-
fore unknown in American life.

In contrast to the tradesman and the craftsman, the
professional person defined the unique quality of a subject,
its special basis in an exclusive and independent circle of
natural experiences. The craftsman traditionally handled a
series of individual objects, according to the custom of his
work, varying his own specific practices by trial and error.
The professional excavated nature for its principles, its
theoretical rules, thus transcending mechanical procedures,
individual cases, miscellaneous facts, technical information,
and instrumental applications. Frederick Jackson Turner,
for instance, isolated the unique nature of American history,
and Oliver Wendell Holmes, Jr., the unique nature of the
law in America; G. Stanley Hall isolated the distinctive
characteristics of "adolescence," and Jane Addams the professional woman social worker's special, natural sensitivity
to injustice.[13] The intellectual pretensions of these persons
were specific in aim and definite in purpose. As professionals, they attempted to define a total coherent system of
necessary knowledge within a precise territory, to control
the intrinsic relationships of their subject by making it a
scholarly as well as an applied science, to root social existence in the inner needs and possibilities of documentable
worldly processes.

In contrast to the empiricists, the professional person
grasped the concept behind a functional activity, allowing
him both to perceive and to predict those inconspicuous or
unseen variables which determined an entire system of

[13] For comments on the differences between craft and professional
activities, see Alfred North Whitehead, *Adventures of Ideas* (New York:
Mentor Books, The New American Library, 1955), pp. 64–65. See Jill
Conway, "Jane Addams: An American Heroine," in Robert Jay Lifton,
ed., *The Woman in America* (Boston: Beacon Press, 1967), pp. 247–66;
Conway, "Women Reformers and American Culture, 1870–1930,"
Journal of Social History 5 (Winter 1971–72): 164–77; Dorothy Ross,
G. Stanley Hall: The Psychologist as Prophet (Chicago and London:
University of Chicago Press, 1972), pp. 279–340; Burton J. Bledstein,
"Frederick Jackson Turner: A Note on the Intellectual and the Pro-
fessional," *Wisconsin Magazine of History* 54 (Autumn 1970): 50–55.

developments. The professional penetrated beyond the rich confusion of ordinary experience, as he isolated and controlled the factors, hidden to the untrained eye, which made an elaborate system workable or impracticable, successful or unattainable: for instance, a deep-level mining operation for low-grade ore, a suspension bridge or a skyscraper with its network of internal stresses, a commercial farm in the West, with its delicate ecological balance, producing cereals for export.[14] Before submitting a report, to take the first instance, the mining engineer surveyed the ground, studied the geology, assayed a representative sample of ore, estimated its tonnage, determined the cost of extraction and marketing, and evaluated the dangers of production both to financial investment and to human life within the context of the rugged circumstances. Normally the risks were high in writing these reports, but in addition the educated ability of the consultant to sample accurately and estimate tonnage could never be taken for granted, and miscalculation ruined many reputations. The experienced engineer with a solid record of professional achievement was literally worth his weight in precious metal.

Utilizing his trained capacity, the professional person interpreted the special lines along which such complex phenomena as a physical disease, a point of law, a stage of human psychological growth, or the identity of an historical society developed in time and space. The professional did not vend a commodity, or exclusively pursue a self-interest. He did not sell a service by a contract which called for

14 For historical examples of these processes of professionalization, see Clark C. Spence, *Mining Engineers and the American West: The Lace-Boot Brigade, 1849–1933* (New Haven, Conn. and London: Yale University Press, 1970); Carl W. Condit, *American Building Art: The Nineteenth Century* (New York: Oxford University Press, 1960), pp. 103–96; Condit, "Sullivan's Skyscrapers as the Expression of Nineteenth-Century Technology," *Technology and Culture* 1 (Winter 1959): 78–93; Condit, *The Rise of the Skyscraper* (Chicago: University of Chicago Press, 1952); Alan Trachtenberg, *Brooklyn Bridge: Fact and Symbol* (New York: Oxford University Press, 1965), pp. 66–67; Clarence H. Danhof, *Change in Agriculture: The Northern United States, 1820–1870* (Cambridge, Mass.: Harvard University Press, 1969).

specific results in a specific time or restitution for errors. Rather, through a special understanding of a segment of the universe, the professional person released nature's potential and rearranged reality on grounds which were neither artificial, arbitrary, faddish, convenient, nor at the mercy of popular whim. Such was the august basis for the authority of the professional.

The jurisdictional claim of that authority derived from a special power over worldly experience, a command over the profundities of a discipline. Such masterful command was designed to establish confidence in the mind of the helpless client. The professional person possessed esoteric knowledge about the universe which if withheld from society could cause positive harm. In the cases of the doctor, the lawyer, the engineer, and the chemist, the consequences could be lethal. No less, however, did society require the minister to recite knowingly at the grave, the teacher to instruct intelligently in the classroom, the national historian to discover a meaning that related the present to the past. Laymen were neither prepared to comprehend the mystery of the tasks which professionals performed, nor—more ominously—were they equipped to pass judgment upon special skills and technical competence. Hence, the culture of professionalism required amateurs to "trust" in the integrity of trained persons, to respect the moral authority of those whose claim to power lay in the sphere of the sacred and the charismatic. Professionals controlled the magic circle of scientific knowledge which only the few, specialized by training and indoctrination, were privileged to enter, but which all in the name of nature's universality were obligated to appreciate.

For middle-class Americans, the culture of professionalism provided an orderly explanation of basic natural processes that democratic societies, with their historical need to reject traditional authority, required. Science as a source for professional authority transcended the favoritism of politics, the corruption of personality, and the exclusiveness of partisanship. And science as an attitude for professional discipline required inner control and an individual respect for rules, proven experience, and a system of hygienic laws concerned with such personal habits as diet, bathing, sex, dress, work, and recreation. Typically, middle-class Americans with professional pretensions translated the moral cause of temperance into a scientific truth for successful living.[15] In the same way they transformed masturbation into a legitimate medical "disease," an abnormality of nature with its set of related signs and symptoms. Medical doctors made it possible for the deviant afflicted by masturbation to control his or her unnatural excitement by prescribing such radical treatments as vasectomy, clitoridectomy, castration, electrodes inserted into the bladder and rectum, and the cauterization of the prostatic urethra.[16]

The person who mastered professional discipline and

[15] In a copious literature, see George M. Beard, *Stimulants and Narcotics: Medically, Philosophically, and Morally Considered* (New York: G. P. Putnam & Sons, 1871); *The Cyclopaedia of Temperance and Prohibition: A Reference Book of Facts, Statistics, and General Information on all Phases of the Drink Question, the Temperance Movement and the Prohibition Agitation* (New York: Funk & Wagnalls, 1891); Martha M. Allen, *Alcohol: A Dangerous and Unnecessary Medicine, How and Why, What Medical Writers Say* (Marcellus, N.Y.: Department of Medical Temperance of the National Women's Christian Temperance Union, 1900). See also Joseph S. Gusfield, *Symbolic Crusade: Status Politics and the American Temperance Movement* (Urbana: University of Illinois Press, 1963); and, exceptionally well done, Brian Harrison, *Drink and the Victorians: The Temperance Question in England 1815-1872* (London: Faber and Faber, 1971).

[16] See J. H. Kellogg, *Plain Facts for Old and Young: Embracing the Natural History and Hygiene of Organic Life* (Burlington, Iowa: I. F. Segner, 1886), pp. 169-327; Joseph W. Howe, *Excessive Venery, Masturbation, and Continence: The Etiology, Pathology and Treatment of the Diseases Resulting from Venereal Excesses, Masturbation and Continence* (New York: E. B. Treat & Co., 1887); Bernarr A. MacFadden, *The Virile Powers of Superb Manhood: How Developed, How Lost: How Regained* (New York: Physical Culture Publishing Company, 1900). See also Tristram Engelhardt, Jr., "The Disease of Masturbation: Values and the Concept of Disease," *Bulletin of the History of Medicine* 68 (Summer 1974): 234-48; R. P. Neuman, "Masturbation, Madness, and the Modern Concepts of Childhood and Adolescence," *Journal of Social History* 8 (Spring 1975): 1-27; Arthur N. Gilbert, "Doctor, Patient, and Onanist Diseases in the Nineteenth Century," *Journal of the History of Medicine and Allied Sciences* 30 (July 1975): 217-34.

control emerged as an emulated example of leadership in American society. He was self-reliant, independent, ambitious, and mentally organized. He structured a life and a career around noble aims and purposes, including the ideal of moral obligation. But most importantly, the professional person absolutely protected his precious autonomy against all assailants, not in the name of an irrational egotism but in the name of a special grasp of the universe and a special place in it. In the service of mankind—the highest ideal— the professional resisted all corporate encroachments and regulations upon his independence, whether from government bureaucrats, university trustees, business administrators, public laymen, or even his own professional associations. The culture of professionalism released the creative energies of the free person who was usually accountable only to himself and his personal interpretation of the ethical standards of his profession.

THE CONSERVATIVE CONSEQUENCES

An unusual advantage inhered in the Mid-Victorian position: the radical idea of the democrat as autonomous professional had only socially conservative consequences. The culture of professionalism liberated the nature of persons and activities, but it also restricted them to that nature. By professionalizing a sphere of American life such as poverty, criminality, or disease, Mid-Victorians planned both to isolate and control the phenomenon, with dispassion and disinterest.[17] Every sphere of American life now came

[17] On the professionalization of poverty, see Nathan Irvin Huggins, *Protestants Against Poverty: Boston Charities, 1870–1900* (Westport, Conn.: Greenwood Publishing Corporation, 1971); Roy Lubove, *The Professional Altruist: The Emergence of Social Work as a Career, 1880– 1930* (Cambridge, Mass.: Harvard University Press, 1965). The claim for poverty as a reformer's science appears in Robert A. Woods *et al., The Poor in Great Cities: Their Problems and What is Doing to Solve Them* (New York: Charles Scribner's Sons, 1895); Robert Hunter, *Pov-*

within the power of the Mid-Victorian professional to set apart, regulate, and contain.

Indeed, American medicine was a good example of how conservative values came to prevail in the culture of professionalism. In the 1890s, for instance, physicians invoked their authority both to rationalize the containment of the poor in the ghettos and to justify the freedom of movement of the middle class. The organized medical profession, serving its middle-class patients who would tolerate neither the inconvenience nor the indignity of a quarantine, refused to cooperate with public boards of health which required the reporting of tuberculosis cases. Respectable physicians argued that disease thrived in the dirty living conditions of the tenements, conditions which of course were not found in the private residences of their fortunate patients. Only the poor should be isolated by quarantine. The medical notion that the middle class might be infecting the poor by means of communicable, air-borne tubercle bacilli seemed radical.[18]

The conservative consequences of professional behavior were many and commonplace, especially after an individual completed years of training followed by lifetime membership affiliation. By means of ceremonies and rituals, for instance, the professions cultivated the inner aristocratic or elitist social instincts often found in the democrat. The autonomy of a professional person derived from a claim

erty (New York, London: The Macmillan Company, 1904); Jane Addams *et al., Philanthropy and Social Progress: Seven Essays* (New York: Thomas Y. Crowell and Company, Publishers, 1893).

18 See Hermann M. Biggs, "Sanitary Science, the Medical Profession, and the Public," *Medical News* 72 (January 8, 1898): 48–49; Lawrence F. Flick, *The Crusade Against Tuberculosis: Consumption a Curable and Preventable Disease: What a Layman Should Know About It* (Philadelphia: David McKay, Publisher, 1903); John Duffy, *A History of Public Health in New York City, 1866–1966* (New York: Russell Sage Foundation, 1974), pp. 241–42, 539–40, 545–46; Barbara Gutmann Rosenkrantz, *Public Health and the State: Changing Views in Massachusetts, 1842–1936* (Cambridge, Mass.: Harvard University Press, 1972), pp. 111–12; George Rosen, *A History of Public Health* (New York: MD Publications, Inc., 1958), pp. 387–89; Rothstein, *American Physicians,* pp. 271–72.

upon powers existing beyond the reach or understanding of ordinary humans. Special rituals, including many of the activities formalized in a graduate school, reinforced the mysteriousness of those powers and enhanced the jurisdictional claim. Specifically, comprehensive examinations for higher degrees, such as the Bar examination or medical boards, tested the larger resources of a candidate, not only the individual's superior intellectual accomplishments but superior emotional control under duress. Moreover, the Ph.D. dissertation was an exercise not only in scholarly method, but in the human endurance and delayed gratification necessary to make an "original contribution to knowledge." Internships, professional oaths, ordination, association meetings, scholarly papers, awards, prizes, recognition of a priesthood of elders: all served ceremonial functions that both indoctrinated the select participants and transmitted general information to the client public. Mid-Victorians favored formidable, enduring, massive displays of their legitimacy and influence. Professional structures provided an excellent forum.

The more elaborate the rituals of a profession, the more esoteric its theoretical knowledge, the more imposing its symbols of authority, the more respectable its demeanor, the more vivid its service to society—the more prestige and status the public was willing to bestow upon its representatives. Common sense, ordinary understanding, and personal negotiations no longer were the effective means of human communication in society, as the old-fashioned egalitarian had once thought they should be. Now clients found themselves compelled to believe on simple faith that a higher rationality called scientific knowledge decided one's fate. The professional appeared in the role of a magician casting a spell over the client and requiring complete confidence; and the client listened to words that often sounded metaphysical and even mystical. "Once the priests were physicians," a speaker told the American Public Health Association in 1874, "now the physicians are becoming, in their way, priests, and giving laws not only to their own patients, but to society. . . . The Pope himself takes modern medicine, and has a modern cook, and seeks health as the doctors advise."[19]

Charismatic figures presided over the rituals and ceremonies that Americans began playing out in the later nineteenth century: in the medical doctor's office, the home, the school, the seminar room, the athletic arena, the fraternity house, the settlement house, and the charity ward. Within carefully established spaces, rituals and ceremonies began to dominate human relationships and to consolidate the emerging culture of professionalism. Often those rituals and ceremonies centered upon the conspicuous display of new tools and equipment which not only struck the client with awe but impressed the professional practitioner himself with his power. For instance, with the new use of anesthetics, the ophthalmoscope, the laryngoscope, the microscope, the cardiograph, the thermometer, and soon the X ray, the number of professional procedures and tests to which a patient might be subjected significantly multiplied.[20] With the increasing number of those procedures the patient's mixed feelings of fear and respect inevitably grew, the same feelings perhaps experienced by the spectator in a religious rite. New technology did improve the quality of practice and service, but in the hands of professional entrepreneurs that same technology could also be employed to take advantage of the emotional insecurity of the client.

Mid-Victorians magnified and multiplied the symbols which emphasized professional authority in American society. Degrees, diplomas, and honorary awards, for instance, appeared on the office walls of a certified practitioner, whose code of ethics might prevent the commercial advertisement

---

[19] Samuel Osgood, "Health and the Higher Culture," *Public Health*, Reports and Papers, Presented at the Meeting of the Public Health Association 2 (1874–75): 207.

[20] See Rothstein, *American Physicians*, pp. 207–9; W. J. Reader, *Professional Men: The Rise of the Professional Classes in Nineteenth-Century England* (London: Weidenfield and Nicolson, 1966), p. 166.

of his credentials.[21] The lawyer now displayed before his client his "casebooks" and legal library; the professor his collection of original documents, artifacts, specimens, notes, published articles, and books.

Idealism and monopolistic self-interest often played an indistinguishable role in the new images professionals cultivated about their expertise. For instance, numerous professional associations worked for more stringent preparation and higher standards in licensing in order to protect the public from incompetence and quackery.[22] However, this reform also worked to restrict the number of practitioners, thereby raising their incomes.[23] Social workers, public-health officials, and academics sponsored new governmental agencies which transcended private interest and served the public directly. This reform also served to enhance the status, opportunities, public recognition, and

[21] See Donald E. Konold, *A History of American Medical Ethics, 1847–1912* (Madison: The State Historical Society of Wisconsin, 1962), pp. 22, 35, 43–55; James Willard Hurst, *The Growth of American Law: The Law Makers* (Boston: Little, Brown and Company, 1950), pp. 329–30.

[22] In medicine see Austin Flint, "Medical Ethics and Etiquette: Commentaries on the National Code of Ethics," *The New York Medical Journal* 37 (1883): 285–87, 312–15, 340–45, 369–76, 395–400, 429–32, 453–56; "Announcement of The Johns Hopkins Medical School, 1893," in Gert H. Brieger, ed., *Medical America in the Nineteenth Century: Readings from the Literature* (Baltimore and London: The Johns Hopkins Press, 1972), pp. 313–30; Abraham Flexner, *Medical Education in the United States and Canada: A Report to the Carnegie Foundation for the Advancement of Teaching*, Bulletin no. 4 (New York: The Carnegie Foundation for the Advancement of Teaching, 1910); Richard Harrison Shryock, *Medical Licensing in America, 1650–1965* (Baltimore: The Johns Hopkins Press, 1967), pp. 43–76.

[23] "The country needs fewer and better doctors," Flexner wrote, and "the way to get them better is to produce fewer." *Medical Education,* p. 17. On the increasing elitism of the turn-of-the-century medical profession, see Gerald E. Markowitz and David Karl Rosner, "Doctors in Crisis: A Study of the Use of Medical Education Reform to Establish Modern Professional Elitism in Medicine," *American Quarterly* 25 (March 1973): 83–107. On the concern with income, see George Rosen, *Fees and Fee Bills: Some Economic Aspects of Medical Practice in Nineteenth Century America* (Baltimore: The Johns Hopkins Press, 1946).

interests of special occupations by means of creating permanent civil-service positions.[24] To prevent well-known abuses in the marketplace, physicians campaigned for the sole privilege both to authorize admissions into hospitals and to write prescriptions for drugs. But the physician now made himself and his fees central to the administration of all legitimate medical services, including the most pedestrian and routine.[25]

The uncertainty and anxiety of a client heightened his receptivity to the commanding voice of professional authority. With such power over others, and with his judgment usually beyond both public and professional criticism, the ambitious practitioner often could not resist the opportunities for financial corruption. In the 1890s, for instance, a number of middle-class physicians—concerned with the personal doctor-client relationship and its accompanying fees for private office visits, home calls, and medication—

[24] Steven J. Novak has told this story in "Professionalism and Bureaucracy: English Doctors and the Victorian Public Health Administration," *Journal of Social History* 6 (Summer 1973): 440–62. On the emergence of public administration as an applied field of political science, see Woodrow Wilson, "The Study of Administration," *Political Science Quarterly* 2 (June 1887): 197–222; Frank J. Goodnow, *Comparative Administrative Law: An Analysis of the Administrative Systems National and Local, of the United States, England, France and Germany* (New York and London: G. P. Putnam's Sons, 1893); Goodnow, *Municipal Problems* (New York: Published for the Columbia University Press, The Macmillan Company, 1897); Goodnow, *Politics and Administration: A Study in Government* (New York, London: The Macmillan Company, 1900); R. Gordon Hoxie *et al.*, *A History of the Faculty of Political Science, Columbia University* (New York: Columbia University Press, 1955), pp. 68–75; Mary O. Furner, *Advocacy and Objectivity: A Crisis in the Professionalization of American Social Science, 1865–1905* (Lexington, Ky.: The University Press of Kentucky, 1975), pp. 283–87.

[25] I say legitimate medical services because James Harvey Young demonstrates the persistence of quackery following the passage of the Pure Food and Drug Act in 1906: *The Medical Messiahs: a Social History of Health Quakery in Twentieth-Century America* (Princeton, N.J.: Princeton University Press, 1967). Young traces the nineteenth-century story in *The Toadstool Millionaires: A Social History of Patent Medicines in America before Federal Regulation* (Princeton, N.J.: Princeton University Press, 1961).

opposed the manufacture and the free distribution of the diphtheria antitoxin by the state. Professional arguments were mustered. Claiming that private enterprise's antitoxin was more pure and effective than the state's, the physicians purchased the serum from commercial companies at from two to five dollars a bottle and sold it to their patients. One state public-health doctor wryly pointed out that all anti-toxin was produced "inside the horse."[26] But how was the ordinary patient to know which antitoxin was better, and for the price of a routine office or home visit what concerned middle-class parent would take the risk of his child catching diphtheria?

Symbols of professional authority emphasized the com-plexity of a subject, its forbidding nature to the layman, the uninitiated, and even the inexperienced practitioner. By the later nineteenth century, for instance, judges were not builders of the Bench but its protectors who constructed legalisms, jargon, and formalities in a humorless defense of the legitimacy of the law. There was a nearly uncontroll-able growth in the publication of casebooks, and the style of legal opinions now tended toward the heavy, labored, and unimaginative.[27] In the Bar, technical expositions on such specialized subjects as the laws of electric wire on streets and highways now appeared; and both pragmatic treatises and local manuals, inbred and ignoring any social

[26] Cited in Barbara Gutmann Rosenkrantz, "Cart Before Horse: Theory, Practice, and Professional Image in American Public Health, 1870–1920," *Journal of the History of Medicine and Allied Sciences,* 29 (January 1974): 71; Rosenkrantz, *Public Health and the State,* pp. 124–26. In New York City, where physicians had a financial interest in the private laboratories, one spokesman for the county medical society ar-gued that the state should not enter into competition with its citizens. A spokesman for the health department pointed out that the depart-ment's laboratory had reduced the cost of the antitoxin from $12 to $1 a vial. Duffy, *Public Health in New York City,* pp. 241–42.

[27] Lawrence M. Friedman, *A History of American Law* (New York: Simon and Schuster, 1973), pp. 538–43. In the first teaching casebook, C. C. Langdell at Harvard simply collected particular cases on con-tracts. Apart from Langdell's brief introduction, the massive volume lacked any editorial elucidation or commentary: *Selection of Cases on the Law of Contracts: With References and Citations* (Boston: Little, Brown and Company, 1871).

commentary, proliferated.[28] As symbols of authority, these arid statements had the effect of both intimidating the bold, young lawyer from attempting to summarize or restate the whole of the law and preventing the client from any thought of participating in his own case. Paradoxically, the obscure and technical formalisms of an occupation, even its minutiae and tedium, now opened to the ambitious middle-class American the avenue of opportunity, adventure, prestige, and success.

Symbols of professional authority—including the number of technical aids in an office, the number of articles and books on a vita, the income and life style of a successful practitioner—reinforced the public's consciousness of its dependence. Indeed, the pattern of dependence was the most striking conservative consequence of the culture of professionalism. Practitioners succeeded by playing on the weaknesses of the client, his vulnerability, helplessness, and general anxiety. The client's imagination easily did the rest.

Professionals tended to confide the worst, often evoking images of disaster and even a horrible death. The physician might hint at the possibility of an undetected cancer, leaving the patient to his own thoughts. The lawyer might threaten the client with high bail, a long trial, and visions of being locked up and sexually abused in jail. The professor might intimidate the student with failure in his studies, which might permanently obstruct the pursuit of a promising career. The policeman might menace the average citizen with pictures of meaningless, catastrophic, and racial violence in the streets, especially at the hands of a mugger or a psychopath. The minister might vividly portray for the juvenile the hideous ruin of the inebriated and the oversexed. The insurance man might warn the client of sudden destitution and moral irresponsibility toward one's family. The accountant might confront his client with the discovery of fraud and financial disgrace.

28 See Edward Quinton Keasbey, *The Law of Electric Wires in Streets and Highways*, 2d ed. Rev. (Chicago: Callaghan and Company, 1900); Friedman, *History of American Law*, pp. 542–43.

By pointing to and even describing a potential disaster, the professional often reduced the client to a state of desperation in which the victim would pay generously, cooperate fully and express undying loyalty to the knowledgeable patron who might save him from a threatening universe. The culture of professionalism tended to cultivate an atmosphere of constant crisis—emergency—in which practitioners both created work for themselves and reinforced their authority by intimidating clients.

In the 1870s, a wonderful example appeared in the extensive publicity Allan Pinkerton gave to the professional private detective, a new kind of man who practiced violence in order to protect helpless citizens. Through fictional stories, true-life accounts of the cases handled by his nationally known agency, and autobiographic narratives, Pinkerton described the comprehensive achievements of professional criminals. "Their modes of working and plans of operation have reached a degree of scientific perfection never before attained."[29] Criminal activity was as prosperous and sophisticated as the expanding services in American society, and no individual was safe, perhaps even against his own close friends. Highly intelligent, often educated, careful in his planning, concealing his operations in mystery, knowledgeable about technology, personally aggressive, self-reliant, and resourceful, the successful criminal frequently appeared "as the well-dressed, polished, and educated gentleman, as the distinguished foreigner and as the profound scientist."[30] His presence was ubiquitous. Pinkerton

[29] Allan Pinkerton, *Thirty Years a Detective: A Thorough and Comprehensive Exposé of Criminal Practises of all Grades and Classes, Covering a Period of Thirty Years' Active Detective Life* (New York: G. W. Dillingham, 1887), pp. 15–16. Pinkerton authored books entitled *The Expressman and the Detectives, The Detective and the Somnambulist, The Model Town and the Detectives, Spiritualists and Detectives, Claude Melnotte as a Detective, The Spy of the Rebellion, Criminal Reminiscences and Detective Sketches.* On the detective story in the nineteenth century, see Edmund Pearson, *Dime Novels: Or, Following an Old Trail in Popular Literature* (Boston: Little, Brown and Company, 1929), pp. 138–97.

[30] Allan Pinkerton, *Professional Thieves and the Detective: Containing Numerous Detective Sketches Collected from Private Records* (New York: G. W. Carleton & Co., Publishers, 1880), p. vi.

extended his list of subversives who victimized the community to include the Molly Maguires, labor-union men, strikers, communists, and tramps. Indeed, what honest American could know when and where the malignancy of professional crime might strike? In the year following the civil turmoil of 1877, Pinkerton wrote:

The spectacle of so vast a country as ours being even for a short time palsied, its local authorities paralyzed, its State governments powerless, and its general government almost defied, was so sudden, so universal, and so appalling, that the best judgment of our best minds were found unequal to cope with so startling and extreme an emergency.[31]

Only the professional detective in plain clothes, infiltrating the "entire school of crime" by means of his own "quick conceptions and ready subterfuges," his own "superior intelligence" and "high moral character," could protect the constantly threatened client. "His calling," Pinkerton said of the detective, "has become a profession. . . . Few professions excel it."[32]

To turn to another example, professional reporters and editors who practiced the new journalism drew the public's attention to themselves by exaggerating the importance of the daily news, especially its apocalyptic and menacing overtones. The public was simultaneously fascinated and frightened. In the popular press of the 1890s, for instance, Joseph Pulitzer of the *World* and William Randolph Hearst of the *Journal* calculated to prepare the nation for war with Spain by means of their own well-organized army of reporters, boats, and communication facilities. The press boldly publicized Spanish atrocities such as the slaughter of innocent victims, the execution of patriots, and the persecution of American citizens. Even the United States government depended upon the information provided by the press. Americans read in the newspaper that gross violations

[31] Allan Pinkerton, *Strikers, Communists, Tramps and Detectives* (New York: G. W. Carleton & Co., Publishers, 1878), p. 13.

[32] Allan Pinkerton, "The Character and Duties of a Detective Police Force," *Transactions of the Third National Prison Reform Congress* 3 (1874): 242; Pinkerton, *Thirty Years*, pp. 16, 17, 18.

of the basic laws of civilized humanity were occurring, and that Spanish barbarism threatened any self-respecting freedom-fighter who both cherished his decency and considered himself an effective human being. The anticipated response of the outraged American public was forthcoming.[33]

Professionals not only lived in an irrational world, they cultivated that irrationality by uncovering abnormality and perversity everywhere: in diseased bodies, criminal minds, political conspiracies, threats to the national security. An irrational world, an amoral one in a state of constant crisis, made the professional person who possessed his special knowledge indispensable to the victimized client, who was reduced to a condition of desperate trust. The culture of professionalism exploited the weaknesses of Americans— their fears of violent, sudden, catastrophic, and meaningless forces that erupted unpredictably in both individual and mass behavior. Indeed, the ascending culture took advantage of the instinctive mistrust an apprehensive client might feel toward the universe around him. That universe itself intensified human suspicion of an all-pervasive cosmic irrationality, when the frightened client failed to come up with an adequate response to such an elemental personal question as, "What have I done to deserve this grisly fate?—Why me?"

Perhaps no Calvinist system of thought ever made use of the insecurities of people more effectively than did the culture of professionalism. The professional person extended the gift of his special powers to the client who was by definition unworthy of such attention. And in return the professional expected at the very least to receive the psychic reward of the client's unqualified gratitude; when appropriate he expected to receive an ample tangible reward from

[33] See Charles H. Brown, *The Correspondents' War: Journalists in the Spanish-American War* (New York: Charles Scribner's Sons, 1967); George Juergens, *Joseph Pulitzer and the New York World* (Princeton, N.J.: Princeton University Press, 1966), pp. 217–18; Gerald F. Linderman, *The Mirror of War: American Society and the Spanish-American War* (Ann Arbor, Mich.: The University of Michigan Press, 1974), pp. 148–73.

the client's pocketbook. The client would make payment in the magnanimous spirit of a thankful subject who offered an appreciative token in return for the original gift—a gift which could never adequately be returned or repaid. In the professional order of values, no client merited a crueler fate, no client was quite so undeserving and detestable, as the one who betrayed his patron by appearing to be ungrateful.

The state of a client's dependence could become psychologically unbearable. In the emerging academic profession, for instance, the tenured faculty could easily exploit the complete insecurity and fragile confidence of the untenured instructors, who competed to be retained. At Harvard in the 1880s, nervous breakdowns occurred frequently. Promising young men wore themselves down through worry and overwork as they exhausted themselves in the classroom, anxiously curried the favor of their mentors and patrons, neglected their health, postponed marriages, moonlighted and borrowed money to make ends meet.[34] The victims of such a system, their emotions paralyzed, proceeded cautiously and conservatively in all their movements. In 1888, for example, Josiah Royce discovered himself growing dull and indecisive, and he too now "joined the too great army of scholarly blunderers who break down when they ought to be at their best." After taking a leave of absence and embarking on a long voyage, he described his disintegration and collapse to a sympathetic William James, who both personally and professionally knew the experience only too well:

There was indeed a long period of depression—not exactly the sort of discontent that was to be feared, i.e. not exactly a *longing* for anything good or evil, but simply the dullness that Tolstoi describes in his Confession, or the "grief without a pang, voiceless and drear," that Coleridge so well portrays. It was a diabolically interesting nervous state, although while it lasted I never

[34] Robert A. McCaughey, "The Transformation of American Academic Life: Harvard University 1821–1892," *Perspectives in American History* 8 (1974): 302–5.

could make out precisely why I ate my meals, or kept aboard at all. To call the thing misery would be a mistake. It was an absolute negation of all active predicates of the emotional sort save a certain (not exactly "fearful") looking-for of judgment and fiery indignation.

It was an entire year before Royce shook off his "head-weariness" and recovered his wits.[35]

In its very idealism, the culture of professionalism bred public attitudes of submission and passivity. For instance, reformers in the later nineteenth century proposed to make American politics more professional and less partisan, more attentive to the will of the individual citizen rather than to the desire of the venal boss. But a significant consequence of that democratic reform was to discourage the public's participation in its own political affairs. The direct primary, the direct election of senators, woman's suffrage: these progressive ideas had the conservative effect of emphasizing the individual citizen's isolation, ignorance, and relative helplessness, the voter's need to subordinate himself to the expertise of the political manager or the newspaper endorsement, or to decline to take part in the political process.[36]

In another instance, similar patterns of dependency and submission began occurring among the rank and file of the labor-union movement. As professional leadership assumed command, the worker became a client whose main responsibility was to trust the careerist. Jealous of his authority, Samuel Gompers unilaterally demanded a free and unopposed hand in collective bargaining. Union leaders were acutely sensitive to encroachments upon their power, espe-

[35] *The Letters of Josiah Royce,* ed. John Clendenning (Chicago and London: The University of Chicago Press, 1970), pp. 211, 215, 214.

[36] See Walter Dean Burnham, *Critical Elections and the Mainsprings of American Politics* (New York: W. W. Norton & Company, 1970), pp. 72–90. On professionalizing tendencies in nineteenth-century American government, see David J. Rothman, *Politics and Power: The United States Senate 1869–1901* (Cambridge, Mass.: Harvard University Press, 1966).

cially by socialists calling for direct public intervention in the internal affairs of labor.[37]

The professions obligated the trained person to detect and treat potential dangers to the public, at the same time that the professions encouraged the ordinary citizen to go about the absorbing business of making a living. It was within the power of the professional person to define issues and crises—threats to life and security—perhaps real and perhaps unreal. And it was within the power of the professional to justify his actions, including the use of socially sanctioned violence, by appealing to a special knowledge called scientific fact. No metaphysical authority more effectively humbled the average person.

THE VERTICAL VISION

Mid-Victorians would structure life, its space, its words, its time, and its activities. And professionalism with its cultural rituals, ceremonies, and symbols satisfied this need. Mid-Victorians cultivated a new vision, a vertical vision that compelled persons to look upward, forever reaching toward their potential and their becoming, the fulfillment of their true nature. This new vision liberated Americans skyward, in space, time, and rhetoric. Mid-Victorians rejected those persons as misfits who either called for a horizontal social unity of their fellowmen based on income and a common plight in the marketplace, or who uncondescendingly merged their identity with the unworthy poor below.

In the later nineteenth century, for instance, an instructor in a college might earn less income than a policeman, but the wide difference in the status of their occupations pre-

[37] See David Brody, "Career Leadership and American Trade Unionism," in Frederic Cople Jaher, ed., *The Age of Industrialism in America: Essays in Social Structure and Cultural Values* (New York: Free Press, 1968) pp. 288–303.

cluded any common or class sympathy. Whatever their means, the professor and the policeman socially lived worlds apart, and their mistrust of each other in the everyday world—the horizontal one—was mutual. That mistrust, moreover, went deeper than ethnic hostilities and would outlive them. Indeed, the young doctor, lawyer, college instructor, and eventually the young policeman, were oriented in a vertical direction, toward emulating the successful professionals in their own fields, though in fact those elders above well might exploit young practitioners both in terms of income and work-load, as the example of Josiah Royce at Harvard indicated.

In a vision restricted to uplifting, to enthusiasm, confidence, and trust, middle-class Americans with professional ambitions began comparing themselves to those of higher status, looking up to the next rung of the social ladder. However, not only the human failures who had lost the ability to climb looked downward. Everyone did. The fear of falling knawed away at every climber, and this fear—ubiquitous in the middle class—was often the source of a general anxiety within individuals which no amount of monetary security, public honors, or personal confidence seemed to eliminate.[38] In competition with society, the professional ego was constantly sensitive to its achievement, and it toiled mightily even as it attempted to relax.

The vertical vision obstructed any horizontal recognition as middle-class Americans refused to relate to each other as equals. For instance, with ambiguous feelings of nostalgia and contempt, the middle-class American might gaze at his previous station in life in the old neighborhood and with the old folk.[39] But even as he condemned the old-

[38] Advice literature on the fragile nature of success proliferated in America after 1840, and the fear of failure was evident throughout, as it was in much of the popular fiction of the century. For two examples, nearly a half century apart, see "Success in Life," *Harper's New Monthly Magazine* 7 (1853): 238–40; Theodore Roosevelt, "Character and Success," *The Outlook* 64 (1900): 725–27.

[39] The ambivalence expressed by Abraham Cahan about his historical past as an orthodox Jew in the nineteenth century is a case in

fashioned ways of the past, mocked its quaintness, and asserted the superiority and progress of the present, the American needed to commemorate and perhaps even participate in the restoration of his historical origins. An individual's first concern was with his present position and future prospects in the vertically oriented society, and the edited past served to boost a struggling ego in continual need of both succor and stimulation.[40]

Looking vertically, middle-class Americans lacked a corporate sense of community, and nowhere was this more evident than in the emerging professions, which were instrumental in institutionalizing the ground rules for individual ambition. Professional associations in the nineteenth century such as the American Medical Association regularly mistitled practical codes of etiquette by referring to them in the lofty name of "codes of ethics." The latter prescribed the moral responsibility of a professional to the public, while the former described the conventional forms

point. See, *The Rise of David Levinsky* (New York: Harper & Row Publishers, 1917; reprinted 1960); Sanford E. Marovitz, "The Lonely New Americans of Abraham Cahan," *American Quarterly* 20 (Summer 1968): 196–210. These feelings also emerged as Theodore Dreiser reflected in his short story on "The Old Neighborhood" (1918) in *Chains: Lesser Novels and Stories* (New York: Boni & Liveright, 1927), pp. 219–47.

[40] The popularization of American history through textbooks and colorful narrative accounts is already evident in mid-nineteenth-century lower education. See Ruth Miller Elson, *Guardians of Tradition: American Schoolbooks of the Nineteenth Century* (Lincoln: University of Nebraska Press, 1964), pp. 186–218; George H. Callcott, *History in the United States, 1800–1860* (Baltimore and London: The Johns Hopkins Press, 1970). By the later part of the century, American magazines were filled with literary-historical pieces. Between 1884 and 1888, for instance, *The Century Magazine* ran a successful series, "Battles and Leaders of the Civil War" (vols. 29–35). Meanwhile, *Century* serialized J. J. Nicolay and John Hay, "Abraham Lincoln: A History," which ran between 1886 and 1890 (vols. 33–39). On the industry of popular historical fiction in America, see Ernest Leisy, *The American Historical Novel* (Norman: University of Oklahoma Press, 1950); Robert A. Lively, *Fiction Fights the Civil War: An Unfinished Chapter in the Literary History of the American People* (Chapel Hill: University of North Carolina Press, 1957); A. T. Dickinson, Jr., *American Historical Fiction*, 2d ed. (New York: The Scarecrow Press, Inc., 1963).

of intercourse by which practitioners related to each other.[41] Lawyers protected their individual ways and private dreams of success by failing to adopt any national code until 1908. But the more exclusive medical profession found it necessary to protect its tangible interests with a national code as early as 1847.

In the nineteenth century, the medical code of etiquette became the means by which practitioners attempted to outlaw consultants unacceptable to an association, to restrict competitive practices within the select group of regular physicians, to secure and maximize fee schedules, and to protect themselves against the public airing of a controversy, including a colleague's testimony in a malpractice suit. In the case of the latter, etiquette served to defeat ethics and the public's right to know and be safeguarded against incompetence. For publicly expressing a difference of opinion that diminished the client's confidence in a professional's authority, an individual might be charged with unprofessional conduct and deprived of his position or his right to practice. The actual sin of the accused was to damage the credibility of his fellow professionals in the marketplace, perhaps contributing to the already difficult task of collecting bills. Only the worst abuses in a profession tended to surface, such as the charging of outlandish fees by surgeons for performing unnecessary operations. The general policy of the organized medical profession in the nineteenth century was to charge as much as the public would pay, and physicians actually banded together to crusade for less charity work and less public medicine because they feared that Americans with means would take advantage by viewing medicine as a free commodity available in public dispensaries and clinics to every person.[42]

---

41 Flint, "Medical Ethics and Etiquette," 286.

42 Konold, *A History of American Medical Ethics,* pp. 54–63. On the resistance of the medical profession to public medicine, see also Charles E. Rosenberg, "Social Class and Medical Care in Nineteenth-Century America: The Rise and Fall of the Dispensary," *Journal of the History of Medicine and Allied Sciences* 29 (January, 1974): 51–53; Duffy, *Public Health in New York City,* p. 490.

In the 1890s, an active movement lobbied for and published several books about the teaching and establishment of formal business procedures in medicine.[43]

Vertically oriented professionals who lacked a corporate sense of community could easily adapt a personal perspective to an intellectual one. The scientific response of the trained physician was to seek a specific medical etiology in an individual case for a specific problem. Thereby he isolated a subject by minimizing the significance of its social context and ignoring the root causes, which might require social and ideological reform. For instance, psychiatrists, neurologists, and gynecologists who treated such a "fashionable disease" of middle-class women as hysteria in the later nineteenth century were convinced that they were diagnosing a medical problem with a specific etiology, a predictable course of development, and an origin in an organic malfunction of the uterus.[44] The disease stemmed not from society but from an individual's sexual organs. "It is

[43] Among the early titles see Charles Ralph Mabee, *The Physician's Business and Financial Adviser* 4th ed. (Cleveland, Ohio: Continental Publishing Company, 1900); Joseph McDowell Mathews, *How to Succeed in the Practice of Medicine* (Louisville, Ky.: J. P. Morton & Company, 1902). See also, in the twentieth century, Thomas Francis Reilly, *Building a Profitable Practice; Being a Text-Book on Medical Economics* (Philadelphia & London: J. B. Lippincott Company, 1912); Charles Elton Blanchard, *Medical Dollars and Sense: The Story of the Building of a Large Office Practice* (Youngstown, Ohio: Medical Success Publishing Company, 1912); Verlin C. Thomas, *The Successful Physician* (Philadelphia and London: W. B. Saunders Company, 1923); George David Wolf, *The Physicians Business; Practical & Economic Aspects of Medicine* (Philadelphia and London: J. B. Lippincott Company, 1938); Theodore Wiprud, *The Business Side of Medical Practice* (Philadelphia and London: W. B. Saunders Company, 1939).

[44] See Carroll Smith-Rosenberg, "The Hysterical Woman: Sex Roles and Role Conflict in 19th-Century America," *Social Research* 39 (Winter 1972): 652–78; Ann Douglas Wood, "'The Fashionable Diseases': Women's Complaints and their Treatment in Nineteenth-Century America," *Journal of Interdisciplinary History* 4 (Summer 1973): 25–52; Carroll Smith-Rosenberg and Charles Rosenberg, "The Female Animal: Medical and Biological Views of Woman and Her Role in Nineteenth-Century America," *Journal of American History* 60 (September 1973): 332–56; John S. Haller, Jr., and Robin M. Haller, *The Physician and Sexuality in Victorian America* (Urbana, Chicago, London: The University of Illinois Press, 1974), pp. 5–43.

almost a pity that a woman has a womb," one professor of gynecology in 1864 concurred with a remark he had read.[45] Moreover, physicians described the cultural and social needs of women in the most restrictive ways. In 1875, another gynecologist reported, on the basis of scientific evidence, that women were physiologically and mentally unfit for the professions and skilled labor.

We have been studying woman . . . as a sexual being; and . . . we must arrive at the conclusion that marriage is not an optional matter with her. On the contrary, it is a prime necessity to her normal, physical, and intellectual life. . . . The end and aim of woman's sexual life is perfected by maternity. . . . Physically, children are necessary to the married woman. The sterile wife is constantly exposed to diseases that the fecund wife is comparatively exempt from. The sterile wife is not a normal woman, and sooner or later this physical abnormality finds expression in intellectual peculiarities.[46]

In another instance of the individual focus of a professional's "science," spokesmen for the New Public Health after the turn of the century hoped to avoid both the political controversy and the medical profession's opposition to proposals for environmental reform by strictly confining the movement to scientific preventive techniques and individual cases. The effect was to lessen criticism and pacify the public-health movement, which increasingly fragmented

[45] William H. Byford, *A Treatise on the Chronic Inflammation and Displacements of the Unimpregnated Uterus* (Philadelphia: Lindsay & Blakiston, 1864), p. 41. Concerning the physical health of woman, one contemporary wrote: "In this country . . . it is scarcely an exaggeration to say that every man grows to maturity surrounded by a circle of invalid relatives, that he later finds himself the husband of an invalid wife and the parent of invalid daughters, and that he comes at last to regard invalidism . . . the normal condition of that sex—as if Almighty God did not know how to create a woman." Cited in Howard D. Kramer, "The Beginnings of the Public Health Movement in the United States," *Bulletin of the History of Medicine* 21 (1947): 366–67.

[46] Ely Van De Warker, "The Relations of Women to the Professions and Skilled Labor," *Popular Science Monthly* 6 (1875): 465, 467. See also Carl N. Degler, "What Ought To Be and What Was: Women's Sexuality in the Nineteenth Century," *American Historical Review* 74 (December 1974), 1467–90.

into such areas as public hygiene, mental hygiene, and dental hygiene. As public-health doctors grew conscious of their field as a specialty in scientific medicine, they perceived that the unprofessional enthusiasm of the aggressive reformer was decidedly a liability to a professional image of authority and attitude of deference and respect in the mind of the dependent client.[47]

However, it was at the level of the individual life which aspired to schedule its development in ascending stages that the vertical vision had its most real consequences. Nothing less than a conceptual revolution began to structure the perceptions of ambitious Americans who were shaping and trimming their attitudes according to the upright sights of the middle class. Not one idea but a whole system of interrelated ones—career, character, child nurture, formal education, vocational crisis and decision, personal management—directed the attention of the individual person upward toward the future. And those ideas were meant to take hold of a person practically from the moment he was conceived. An American who proved himself to be calculating, decisive, and personally resourceful when constantly confronted by risk and uncertainty merited the best life the society had to offer. And American society did not offer its best comfort, luxury, and prestige to "pikers."

The loftiness of the vertical vision translated into the aloofness of the Mid-Victorian predisposition. In the new idea of "career," for example, the Mid-Victorian graded his occupational advancement upward through the measured course of a lifetime. Career meant scheduled mobility, from the distinct and ascending levels of schooling, to the distinct and ascending levels of occupational responsibility and prestige. What formed a career was not disconnected ends, not conditioned habits, not *ad hoc* actions, not practical good works, not an infinite series of jobs, but the entire

[47] Rosenkrantz, *Public Health and the State*, pp. 131 ff.; Duffy, *Public Health in New York City*, pp. 265–69, 495–97.

coherence of an intellectually defined and goal-oriented life. That coherence was manifested at every stage of a career.[48]

For the careerist by definition committed himself totally, not merely to private concerns, personal results, particular accomplishments, and the welfare of neighbors. He committed himself to a continuous performance in the service of universal ends. Horizontally the careerist "boomed," fought, energetically competed, wasted the obstacles in the way, and overcame all impediments, especially his own inertia. Vertically he escalated, mounting the successive platforms of achievement. The dispassionate ability to analyze, the "promise" of a professional life, a confident "style": these qualities made the difference in a Mid-Victorian's struggle to triumph over inability and inefficiency, to conquer partisanship and subjectivity.

The careerist was a person in flight, striving to realize the total resources of an inner nature, and moving aloft supported by that profound representation of natural power called character.[49] The upward-looking Mid-Victorian revered no spiritual possession more. Character was the internal and psychological symbol of continuity that corresponded to the sociological course a person ran in a career. Character and career were the two faces of a single phenomenon.

In part, the success of the culture of professionalism could be attributed to the fact that American Mid-Victorians constructed a secular theodicy. Despite its flux, madness, and seeming irrationality, the world was a rational place, and every person could discover his "real me" within the natural confines of space and time. Such firm notions as career and character, for instance, organized a human life totally, from beginning to end. In the normal schedule of development, Mid-Victorians came to anticipate such events as an individual's vocational crisis, and to a lesser degree his religious crisis. To know that every occurrence had a

48 The new idea of career is discussed more fully in Chapter 5.
49 See the discussion in Chapter 4.

reason, a justification, both emboldened and inspired a Mid-Victorian. The scientific assurance that the most despised weakness—human failure—was rooted within the nature of the fallen victim resolved the thorny question of responsibility. Success was a personal triumph for the middle-class individual, as failure was a personal disaster.

The locus of evil is focal to any cultural vision. Evil in the Mid-Victorian theodicy stemmed from the inability to realize one's potential, the inability to commit oneself to place and time, to subjugate carnal desires and their distractions, to approach a life professionally. The flaw was internal. Society blamed the ineffectual individual for his own failure. No one else was at fault. The conservative consequences of a radical idea again became evident. Sustained by an unfinished career and a vertical vision, the consummate Mid-Victorian individual—the professional—never lost faith in the promise of his "becoming," despite adversity. He never gave up on "making it." He stuck by his training and discipline, was patient and trusting, contained his anger, never committed himself to extreme judgments or actions that might jeopardize a career, and refused to blame the social system for the momentary irrationality of a life. All irrationality vanished within a higher rationality, even for the individual who committed himself to the very system that was "turning the screws" on him. Mid-Victorians believed that worldly reversals were tests of will, commitment, and endurance. A fall now and then would eventually prove to have been "fortunate," when one looked back from the heights after the long race upward.

Mid-Victorians were increasingly isolated in their private spaces, confined to the self-realization of their special natures, and admonished by the need to act professionally and responsibly. Not surprisingly, they viewed the motives of their fellowmen with cynicism and suspicion, as the darker side of the culture of professionalism came into view. Mark Twain, the American master of sarcasm, for instance, described the scandal-ridden American politics as a "Kakistocracy," meaning a government "for the benefit of knaves at the cost of fools." There was no tempering Twain's misanthropy. He reflected that since the California Gold Rush every American had posted his price, including Mark Twain, and it was always within reach of being dishonestly satisfied. Twain was an envious man: jealous of the success of others; anxious that he was missing out on a symbol of public recognition such as money; and terrified that he was prostituting his talents, exhausting them, for ephemeral gain. Competition consumed Twain, who in his thrill with life as a contest could not distinguish his ego from his profession; indeed, he could neither sustain periods of undiminished concentration nor shake off periods of enervating hatred and accusation.[50]

As a function of their vertical vision, Mid-Victorians such as Twain expected people to behave perversely toward each other. By joining law-and-order leagues, purity crusades, or temperance societies, many Mid-Victorians refused to be disappointed, either in the satanic actions of others or in their own saintliness.[51] Twain well knew that the two were inseparable.

Beneath public proclamations of trust in American society and its competence, personal expressions of self-doubt by Americans were everywhere. The distrust of self was more than a passing phase of a rapidly industrializing society; it was intrinsic to the culture of professionalism with its vertical angle of vision. Personal self-doubt and insecurity caused an individual to slump into inertia, confusion, indecision, and submission. Mistrust checked all passion, riddled all plans with doubt, and blasted any hope of undivided attention. The weakness of the Mid-Victorian's own character was revealed in his anxiety about failing to prove himself tough-minded and vigilant—a man—and in

50 This interpretation of Twain draws substantially from Kaplan, *Mr. Clemens and Mark Twain.*

51 For a discussion of these movements in the later nineteenth century, see David J. Pivar, *Purity Crusade: Sexual Morality and Social Control, 1868–1900* (Westport, Conn., and London: Greenwood Press, 1973).

his fear of losing out to the competition and being compromised. A Mid-Victorian was capable of behaving as assertively as a self-righteous bully or as passively as an indifferent coward.

The Mid-Victorian depended upon the false mental confidence that his case was the true one and the opposing case was false. But that fragile confidence easily shattered, often sending the victim into a state of depression. *"American nervousness is the product of American civilization,"* psychiatrist George Beard emphasized in 1881.[52] The mind of the Mid-Victorian was overwhelmingly involved in all events impinging upon the life of an individual, especially emotional disorders. "We live in an age of intense mental activity and ever-increasing cerebral strain," wrote E. L. Youmans, founder and editor of the *Popular Science Monthly,* in an article entitled "Observations on the Scientific Study of Human Nature":

The fierce competitions of business, fashion, study, and political ambition, are at work to sap the vigour and rack the integrity of the mental fabric, and there can be no doubt that there is, in consequence, an immense amount of latent brain disease, productive of much secret suffering and slight aberrations of conduct, and which is liable, in any sudden stress of circumstances, to break out into permanent mental derangement. The price we pay for our high-pressure civilization is a fearful increase of cerebral exhaustion and disorder, and an augmenting ratio to shattered intellects. We are startled when some conspicuous mind strained beyond endurance . . . crashes into insanity and suicide, yet these are but symptoms of the prevailing tendencies of modern life.[53]

[52] George M. Beard, *American Nervousness: Its Causes and Consequences: A Supplement to Nervous Exhaustion* (New York: G. P. Putnam's Sons, 1881), p. 176. cf. Chapter 2, n. 4.

[53] E. L. Youmans, ed., *The Culture Demanded By Modern Life: A Series of Addresses and Arguments on the Claims of Scientific Education* (New York: D. Appleton and Company, 1867, 1897), pp. 402–3. The fascination with mind sciences in the era also took the direction of spiritualism, a subject that captivated the professional interest of the psychologist William James. For recent literature on this theme, see Howard Kerr, *Mediums, and Spirit-Rappers, and Roaring Radicals:*

Invalidism, failing eyesight, mysterious organic malfunctions, sick headaches, and even paralysis occurred all too frequently in the medical histories of educated middle-class Americans, and the symptoms could vanish as suddenly as they had appeared.

Within the Mid-Victorian theodicy, evil and failure—either one's own or others'—never wanted for an explanation. In Wisconsin, for instance, successful middle-class farmers blamed the local populists themselves. Ignorance of scientific agriculture and professional farming caused the poor farmer's plight, the prosperous farmer concluded. Neither the railroads, the banks, nor the monetary system had essentially persecuted the populist. Rather, the lack of educated sophistication, the poor farmer's own internal inadequacies, had determined his condition, hence depriving his threatening cause of credibility.[54] Mid-Victorians threw responsibility pitilessly inward. They saw the populist as undisciplined, ignorant, and hysterical, projecting his own personal failure upon the social system and calling for artificial remedies. Had the populist been rational, he would have first examined his own inefficiency as a farmer, and then realized that he plagued himself.

The single tax, greenbacks, free silver, the abolition of the wage system: all these contrivances displayed the same amateurish thinking, from the Mid-Victorian's point of view. Old-fashioned egalitarians naively crusaded for panaceas in order to reverse their own economic disaster. They responded broadly and emotionally, couching their appeals in sentimental descriptions of human need. Too trustful of their fellowmen and too mistrustful of experts, these demo-

Spiritualism in American Literature, 1850–1900 (Urbana, Ill. University of Illinois Press, 1972); R. Laurence Moore, "Spiritualism and Science: Reflections on the First Decade of the Spirit Rappings," *American Quarterly* 24 (October 1972): 474–500; Moore, "The Spiritualist Medium: a Study of Female Professionalism in Victorian America," *American Quarterly* 27 (May 1975): 200–21.

54 The Wisconsin example is described by Gerald Prescott, "Gentlemen Farmers in the Gilded Age," *Wisconsin Magazine of History* 55 (Spring 1972): 197–212.

crats should first have critically questioned their own professional competence to deal with their own specific problems.

To borrow a metaphor from football, a sport increasingly popular in the day, Mid-Victorians executed a successful end run around the older egalitarians with their indiscriminate Jeffersonianism. Individuals on the new team knew their positions, planned strategy, made a scientific study of the game, and studied the rulebook, which they were in the process of writing. The old group of players was unstructured, uncoordinated, and ignorant of the possibilities of the game. In 1893, A. Alonzo Stagg and Henry Williams wrote a book about football as a "science" in which the object was to defeat the opposition, and win competitive matches rather than simply play for pleasure or amateur sport. Several years later, Walter Camp and Lorin Deland elucidated with a "deeper insight" the reasons for the "great popularity" of the sport:

It calls out not merely the qualities which make the soldier,—bravery, endurance, obedience, self-control,—but equally that mental acumen which makes the successful man in any of the affairs of life—perception, discrimination, and judgment. . . . The great lesson of the game may be put into a single line: *it teaches that brains will always win over muscle!*[55]

Committed to a new, more intense, and more discriminating democracy, Mid-Victorians intellectually proposed to discover the true nature of every subject, to locate its position in space and time, to establish its duties and coin its words. After the uncritical social promiscuity of the earlier egalitarianism, no American could reasonably complain against such a natural, structured society.

In the later nineteenth century, America's celebrated equality of opportunity began pointing in a true vertical direction. If the "character" of the poor, the ethnic, and the criminal was flawed, Mid-Victorians expressed confidence that no aristocratic caste had conspired to weaken

[55] Camp, Deland, *Football*, pp. iii–iv; cf. n. 6 of this chapter.

these people or cause their defects. The professional responsibility to restrain the "dangerous classes," to perfect such institutions as asylums and schools, stemmed from a growing body of expert knowledge that described the universe as it actually functioned. The culture of professionalism was for the Mid-Victorian a modern metaphysics. Written documents, facts, and authorities supported every disinterested decision. If the nature of women confined this class to domesticity, for instance, it was not because Mid-Victorian men proposed to enslave their wives. It was because informed Mid-Victorian women, students of their own nature, voluntarily chose to develop their given inner potential, their special gifts and sensitivities. And within the spheres of the home and the charitable organization, these liberated women cultivated the symbols of their own professional authority. It was a positive sign of power, independence, and respectability in Mid-Victorian life that women no longer worked alongside their husbands, that they were mistresses of a special space and a class called children, and that they participated in their own cultural rituals and ceremonies.[56]

Not coincidentally did Vassar College open its doors in the sixties, Smith and Wellesley in the seventies, Bryn Mawr and Barnard in the eighties, and Mount Holyoke (converted from a seminary to a college) and Radcliffe in the nineties.[57] Special people founded specialized institu-

[56] See the images of womanhood projected in the study by Michael Gordon and M. Charles Bernstein, "Mate Choice and Domestic Life in the Nineteenth-Century Marriage Manual," *Journal of Marriage and the Family* 32 (November 1970): 665–74. The professionalization of woman's functions, especially motherhood, is a central idea in the writings of Charlotte Perkins Gilman, perhaps the most penetrating voice on woman's position in society at the end of the nineteenth century. See her *Women and Economics: A Study of the Economic Relation Between Men and Women as a Factor in Social Evolution* (Boston: Small, Maynard & Company, 1898), and *The Home: Its Work and Influence* (Urbana, Chicago, London: University of Illinois Press, 1972), originally published in 1903.

[57] For a survey of the new institutions, see M. Carey Thomas, *Education of Women*, vol. 7 in *Monographs on Education in the United States*, ed. Nicholas Murray Butler (Division of Exhibits, Department

tions, though nearly all state universities and western colleges had been coeducational since the sixties. The faculty administrator in the new elite women's college hastened to discuss the distinct mission of "the refined, the trained, the growing woman"—the professional woman. "The smallest village, the plainest home, give ample space for the resources of the trained college woman," wrote Alice Freeman Palmer, president of Wellesley and the most eminent woman college president of her generation:

Little children under five years die in needless thousands because of the dull, unimaginative women on whom they depend. Such women have been satisfied with just getting along, instead of packing everything they do with brains, instead of studying the best way of doing everything small or large; for there is always a best way, whether of setting a table, of trimming a hat, or teaching a child to read. And this taste for perfection can be cultivated.[58]

With their college degrees, Mid-Victorian women cultivated domestic virtues in nursing, librarianship, the teaching of music, increasingly in social work, and especially in schoolteaching.[59] According to the census, the number of

of Education, Universal Exposition, St. Louis, 1899, 1904), pp. 18–33. See also Annie Nathan Meyer, *Barnard Beginnings* (Boston and New York: Houghton Mifflin Company, 1935); L. Clark Seelye, *The Early History of Smith College, 1871–1910* (Boston and New York: Houghton Mifflin Company, 1923); Arthur C. Cole, *A Hundred Years of Mount Holyoke College: the Evolution of an Educational Ideal* (New Haven, Conn.: Yale University Press, 1940), pp. 180–203; Marion Talbot and Lois Kimball Mathews Rosenberry, *The History of the American Association of University Women, 1881–1931* (Boston and New York: Houghton Mifflin Company, 1931).

[58] Alice Freeman Palmer, "Why Go To College," in George Herbert Palmer and Alice Freeman Palmer, *The Teacher: Essays and Addresses on Education* (Boston and New York: Houghton Mifflin Company, 1908), p. 385. See also Palmer's article "Three types of Women's Colleges," *Ibid.*, pp. 324–27; *An Academic Courtship: Letters of Alice Freeman and George Herbert Palmer, 1886–1887* (Cambridge, Mass.: Harvard University Press, 1940), pp. 178–79; and the ideological exposition in John P. Rousmaniere, "Cultural Hybrid in the Slums: The College Woman and the Settlement House, 1889–1894," *American Quarterly* 22 (Spring 1970): 45–66.

[59] See Dee Garrison, "The Tender Technicians: The Feminization of Public Librarianship, 1867–1905," *Journal of Social History* 6 (Winter

female educators increased from 84,500 in 1870 to 325,500 in 1900. By 1900, male educators numbered a third as many as females, and the male percentage of the profession had dropped from 34 percent in 1870 to 26.5 percent.[60] "Never before," Palmer concluded, "has a nation intrusted all the school training of the vast majority of its future population, men as well as women, to women alone."[61]

Mid-Victorians advocated that natural specialization and not artificial discrimination characterized the new American society. "To discover and cultivate the special aptitudes of women, as distinguished from those of men," said Charles William Eliot at the first commencement of Smith College in 1879, "should be the incessant effort of the managers of colleges for women."[62] The pattern for females gainfully employed in professional services was self-evident. In contrast to the educators, the number of women employed in other professional services was minimal. In 1900, 84 female technical engineers were counted compared to 43,200 males; 100 female architects compared to 10,500 males; 1,000 female lawyers compared to 113,500 males; 7,400 female doctors compared to 124,600 males. The appearance of 11,000 female trained nurses compared to 760 males left no doubt that Americans distinguished between female professional services and male.[63]

1972–73): 131–59; Ann Douglas Wood, "The War Within a War: Women Nurses in the Union Army," *Civil War History* 18 (September 1972): 197–212; Richard L. Simpson and Ida Harper Simpson, "Women and Bureaucracy in the Semi-Professions," in Etzioni, ed., *Semi-Professions and their Organization*, pp. 196–275.

[60] Alba M. Edwards, *Population: Comparative Occupation Statistics for the United States, 1870 to 1940* (Washington, D.C.: U.S. Government Printing Office, 1943), pp. 128, 120. By 1930, males made up only 19 percent of the teaching profession.

[61] Alice Freeman Palmer, "Women's Education in the Nineteenth Century," in Palmer and Palmer, *The Teacher*, p. 350.

[62] From excerpts of Eliot's address in Seelye, *Early History of Smith College*, p. 49.

[63] Edwards, *Population: Comparative Occupation Statistics*, pp. 128, 120.

A SEMINAL INSTITUTION

In nineteenth-century America, higher education emerged as the seminal institution within the culture of professionalism. No institution would continue to be more important, more primary for the success of Mid-Victorian social values. The theme cannot be stated too emphatically. By building up its higher schools and drawing upon the graduates for positions of leadership, the middle class hoped to dominate all the institutional services Americans were increasingly requiring. By the end of the century, for instance, nearly half the graduates from American colleges were entering such fields as teaching, administration, and business.[64]

Historically, the bourgeoisie had fought to eliminate such gentry-controlled institutions as state government, which restricted the free play of individual energy and ambition. In his own mind the bourgeois placed the direct connection between effort and reward, work and income, capital and power, talent and merit above all else; and the patronage and sinecures of undeserving noblemen in unearned legislative and administrative positions broke that all-important connection. In mid-century England, for instance, a bourgeois spokesman like Herbert Spencer vehemently disapproved of free public education, in addition to inveighing against such free public services as vaccinations against smallpox and the construction of sanitation facilities in order to combat cholera epidemics.[65] "Nature demands that every being shall be self-sufficing," Herbert Spencer reasoned in his popular *Social Statics:*

[64] Bailey B. Burritt, *Professional Distribution of College and University Graduates,* United States Bureau of Education Bulletin no. 19, whole number 491 (Washington, D.C.: U.S. Government Printing Office, 1912), pp. 74–78.

[65] Herbert Spencer, *Social Statics: Or, The Conditions Essential to Human Happiness Specified, and the First of Them Developed* (New York: D. Appleton and Company, 1865, 1870), pp. 360–90, 406–32; J. D. Y. Peel, *Herbert Spencer: the Evolution of a Sociologist* (New York: Basic Books, 1971), pp. 96–97.

All that are not so, nature is perpetually withdrawing by death. . . . Mark how the diseased are dealt with. Consumptive patients, with lungs incompetent to perform the duties of lungs, people with assimilative organs that will not take up enough nutriment, people with defective hearts that break down under excitement of the circulation, people with any constitutional flaw preventing the due fulfillment of the conditions of life, are continually dying out, and leaving behind those fit for the climate, food, and habits to which they are born. Even the less-imperfectly organized, who, under ordinary circumstances, can manage to live with comfort, are still the first to be carried off by epidemics; and only such as are robust enough to resist these—that is, only such as are tolerably well adapted to both the usual and incidental necessities of existence, remain. And thus is the race kept free from vitiation. Of course this statement is in substance a truism; for no other arrangement of things is conceivable.[66]

Americans, however, were seeing things differently by the later part of the century. In the eighties, James Bryce observed that middle-class Americans were neither dogmatically committed to a relentless policy of laissez-faire nor fixated on some vicious version of Spencerian Darwinism.[67] More accurately, the middle class opposed institutions it could not control and favored those it could. For example, government began losing its invidious image when educated professional types began to view themselves as experts in the science of government rather than gentlemen public servants in the art of government. The professional transformed public administration into an instrument of opportunity for the middle class and an instrument of regulation for the society.[68] Indeed, an increasing number

[66] Spencer, *Social Statics,* p. 414. The Social Darwinian influence upon the Americans is examined by Richard Hofstadter, *Social Darwinism in American Thought,* rev. ed. (Boston: The Beacon Press, 1955).

[67] James Bryce, *The American Commonwealth,* 2 vols., 3d ed., rev. (New York: Macmillan and Co., 1895), 2:539–40. See Robert C. Bannister, " 'The Survival of the Fittest is our Doctrine,' History or Histrionics?" *Journal of the History of Ideas* 33 (April–June 1972): 265–80.

[68] See Peter Woll, *American Bureaucracy* (New York: W. W. Norton & Company, 1963), pp. 29–49. The Interior department of the federal

of college graduates in the later nineteenth century were taking advantage of the employment opportunities developing in the service sector of the society. And those graduates were establishing minimum standards for entry and advancement into occupations as they proceeded to exclude both the unqualified and the undesirable. Behind all these developments was the burgeoning American university. When Henry Adams dared to ask his enthusiastic students at Harvard in the 1870s, "what they thought they could do with education when they got it," he was surprised to hear an answer, " 'The degree of Harvard College is worth money to me in Chicago.' " Adams's own earlier experience had been that the degree of Harvard College was "rather a drawback" in the real world.[69]

The institution of higher education did not simply level American society; it leveled the society upward—vertically. Higher education satisfied two essential but conflicting needs of the emerging middle class in America. On the one hand, the middle-class individual identified with the public's interest and established his credentials as a democrat committed to opportunity for the hard working, the ambitious, and the meritorious. On the other hand, the middle-class individual asserted his position of leadership and reacted unkindly to criticism and assaults upon his authority from those he considered to be his inferiors. Far more than other types of societies, democratic ones required persuasive symbols of the credibility of authority, symbols the majority of people could reliably believe just and warranted. It became the function of the schools in America

government was created in 1849, Justice in 1870, the Post Office in 1872, Agriculture in 1889 (originally in 1862 with a commissioner), Commerce and Labor in 1913. See Robert E. Cushman, *The Independent Regulatory Commissions* (New York: Oxford University Press, 1941): The Interstate Commerce Commission was established in 1887; the Federal Reserve Board in 1913, and the Federal Trade Commission in 1914. See Warren Frederick Ilchman, *Professional Diplomacy in the United States, 1779–1939: A Study in Administrative History* (Chicago: The University of Chicago Press, 1961), pp. 41–131.

69 *The Education of Henry Adams: An Autobiography* (Boston and New York: Houghton Mifflin Company, 1918), pp. 305–6.

to legitimize the authority of the middle class by appealing to the universality and objectivity of "science." The fact that most Americans learned to associate the scientific way with democratic openness and fairness made the relationship convincing.[70]

By screening students upon entrance, formalizing courses of study, publishing textbooks, standardizing examinations, and awarding degrees, higher educators convinced the public that objective principles rather than subjective partisanship determined competence in American life. Intelligence prevailed over family inheritance as a requisite for accomplishment in society. Educators successfully advocated that the proliferation of schools in America prevented any privileged social class, any closed guild, or any preferential apprenticeship system from monopolizing the services of an occupation or from angling the truth according to the private perceptions of a few men. As early as 1847, for instance, one noted physician justified the existence of twenty-eight medical schools in America, more than in all of Europe, in terms of the genuine requirements of the American public. "Cheapness of education, and a corresponding adaptation of time," he wrote, "are found indispensable to the general condition of society. . . . We have not the means, we have not the leisure, to follow the standard of European wealth." Any attempt to compare America to Europe was seen as "fictitious."[71]

An expansive system of schools served as a common denominator in America, as an instrument of a democratic society. That society constantly needed to balance itself between the countervailing forces of ambition and authority, both basic cultural requirements of the middle class. Even though American schools might cultivate fewer geniuses and train fewer exquisite minds than the more refined and restricted systems of Europe, the larger numbers

[70] This theme is developed in Chapter 8.
[71] M. Paine, "Medical Education in the United States," *Boston Medical and Surgical Journal* 29 (November 29, 1843): 332.

of school-trained Americans were broadly competent, and they would benefit from the simplified norms, rules, and procedures established to maintain a respectable level of standards in any occupation. The average American practitioner was neither creative nor imaginative, but he was not a quack. What the middle class in America sacrificed in high quality, fine craftsmanship, originality, and durability in the work of its producers, it gained in the public's strenuous support of middle-class authority and the credibility of that authority over time. The public came to accept the middle-class article of faith that the regularly trained professional, however dubious his reputation and shoddy his record, however crude his technique and rude his behavior, however rigid his attitudes and inadequate his knowledge, was superior to the merely experienced operator. The difference was the role played by the school.

The cultural demands upon higher education in America, especially the university, compelled it to be far more flexible and diversified than European systems. Any occupation and any subculture of American life achieved recognition and status when it became deserving of study as a professional and academic science with its distinct theory and intellectual requirements. "The true pursuit of mankind is intellectual," an American educator proclaimed in the 1880s. And Mid-Victorians began formulating the intellectual pursuit for vocation-minded Americans, in colleges of education and departments of physical education, in schools of social work, business and finance, and nursing. In the 1960s, for instance, both the expansion of such programs as Latin American Studies and American Civilization and the institutionalization of such areas as Black Studies, Jewish Studies, urban sciences, and criminal justice only extended a trend that had begun in the later nineteenth century. When Mid-Victorians boldly defined such new subjects as sociology and American history, they only peeked at the possibilities of pluralism. The notion that a student in the twentieth century could earn a bachelor's degree in radio announcing within a department of speech would have horrified them. Yet, the Mid-Victorians had prepared the logic.

Mid-Victorians did not conceptualize the struggle confronting American higher education in terms of the "elitist" humanities versus the "democratic" natural sciences, Oxford versus the University of London, nobility versus working class. Rather, Mid-Victorians preferred to see their struggle in terms of professional studies versus practical ones, academic studies in any field versus on-the-job technical training, persons who discipline their minds versus persons who do not, qualified practitioners versus quacks. Often, the real struggle was fought *within* occupations and subcultures as younger, brighter, and better trained practitioners rebelled against the mediocrity of the elders above them and the incompetence of the entrepreneurial technicians below them. Within the context of democratic opportunity, Mid-Victorians worked in the culture of professionalism to structure American life vertically, so that every person should know and accept his rightful place in society. In the academic profession which developed within the American university, for example, such formally defined categories emerged as undergraduate student, graduate student, teaching assistant, instructor, assistant professor, associate professor, and full professor. Moreover, none doubted, though many might complain about, the upward direction in which power, privilege, prestige, and money flowed.

Higher education in America certified recognized spheres of cultural authority and autonomy, and Mid-Victorians designed that certification to transcend any public dispute. Any subject worthy of intellectual study at an authorized institution was worthy of independence, respect, and power. The authority and autonomy of professional persons in America was unprecedented in the century, perhaps in all of American history, and more than a few were prepared to take practical advantage of their extraordinary power.

There were few checks. By invoking the highest ideals—talent, merit, achievement—the educational system sanctioned the privileges, indeed, the affluence, of an accredited individual in American society. Theoretically, neither birth nor prejudice nor favoritism restricted those privileges.

Reflected within the structure and function of American higher education, the culture of professionalism was a frame of mind that trained Americans would take for granted. In contrast to the upper-class English elite with the artificiality of its nonacademic education, Americans compulsively felt the need for the objective measure of professional certification in order to identify people. Higher education in America was neither a luxury nor a way of life nor a source of alienation. It was a social necessity and a source of public acceptance. In contrast to Eastern and Central Europe, a professional class in America did not confine itself to a few large cities, was not chronically unemployed and frustrated, did not produce an estranged intelligentsia, and was not inclined to subversive activities and political revolution.[72]

The professional class in America lacked the cohesion, camaraderie, and consciousness of a traditional class. It lacked a corporate sensibility. Professionals in America poured out into the many spaces of society, providing leadership and organization for proliferating and often prospering middle-class subcultures—ethnic, racial, sexual, regional, and religious in nature. The educated Brahmin retained his private identity, as the educated Jew, Catholic, and southerner tended to retain their private identities.

By means of the calculated development of higher education, Mid-Victorians began bringing all of American life within the vertical vision of the culture of professionalism. The nineteenth-century individuals who became the first generation of university presidents in America faithfully

[72] For a comparison between professional classes in America and Europe, see Joseph Ben-David, "Professions in the Class System of Present-Day Societies," *Current Sociology* 12 (1963–64): 256–77.

represented this movement. We now turn to this group of men whose lives and opinions, mirror-like, magnified historical themes far more memorable than the men themselves.

4

Character

FROM CREDIT TO CREDENTIALS

Charles William Eliot at Harvard (1869–1909), Noah Porter at Yale (1871–86), Daniel Coit Gilman at The Johns Hopkins (1876–1902), Andrew Dickson White at Cornell (1868–85), Frederick A. P. Barnard at Columbia (1864–89), James McCosh at Princeton (1868–88), James Burrill Angell at Michigan (1871–1909), William Watts Folwell at Minnesota (1869–84), John Bascom at Wisconsin (1874–87)—what manner of men were these?[1]

They were nineteenth-century university presidents in America, instrumental both in forming such new institutions as Cornell, Johns Hopkins, and Minnesota, and in renovating such old institutions as Harvard and Columbia. They were Mid-Victorians, ideological spokesmen for a growing middle class in the post–Civil War decades, a class increasingly aware of the active relationship between higher education and the legitimacy of social power in America. They guided American colleges into the age of the uni-

[1] See the appendix for biographical sketches of the nine men. For the most comprehensive general history of the American university, see Laurence R. Veysey, *The Emergence of the American University* (Chicago and London: The University of Chicago Press, 1965).

versity, and they played an important role in institutionalizing the culture of professionalism.

Angell at Michigan, for example, created the first professorship in education and the first instruction in forestry;
he organized graduate studies in its own school, established
permanent admission requirements for medical school, required comprehensive examinations for the Bachelor of
Arts degree, and set the precedent for university certification of high schools in the state.[2] Barnard, at Columbia,
opened the School of Mines and was a moving force behind
equal education for women and the formation of Barnard
College.[3] Folwell at Minnesota conceived and worked toward establishing a comprehensive educational system in
the state, with the university at the pinnacle, and including
in the program junior colleges, state aid to high schools for
university-bound students, and a shortened winter course for
farmers.[4]

Eliot at Harvard concentrated all undergraduate studies
in the College, building around it semi-autonomous professional schools and research facilities, which subsequently
drew upon the talent graduated from the College. In 1872
graduate degrees (M.A., Ph.D.) were established, followed
in 1890 by the Graduate School of Arts and Sciences. In the
schools of Divinity, Law, and Medicine he formalized entrance requirements, courses of study, and written examinations. Instruction in private classes for women led to the
founding of Radcliffe College in 1894. Eliot raised faculty
salaries and introduced sabbatical leaves, retirement pensions, and exchange professorships in France and Germany.
In the College, Eliot's innovation, the "elective" system,

[2] See Howard H. Peckham, *The Making of the University of Michigan, 1817–1967* (Ann Arbor, Mich.: The University of Michigan Press,
1967), pp. 69–113.

[3] See *A History of Columbia University, 1754–1904* (New York: The
Columbia University Press, The Macmillan Company, 1904), pp. 140–
51; Marian Churchill White, *A History of Barnard College* (New York:
Columbia University Press, 1954), pp. 3–47.

[4] See James Gray, *The University of Minnesota, 1851–1951* (Minneapolis: The University of Minnesota Press, 1951), pp. 39–75.

presumed that students were qualified to enter, and he naturally interested himself in admission requirements and secondary-school preparation. He became active in such groups as the National Education Association and chaired the report of the Committee of Ten (1892), which recommended college preparatory programs in high school and encouraged the creation of the Board of College Entrance Examinations (1901).[5]

In his own realm, the new university president performed well. He appeared somewhat dramatically in the sixties and the seventies, and by the eighties was receiving professional recognition. In 1881, for instance, J. Franklin Jameson, a graduate student in historical studies at Johns Hopkins, noted in his diary that "college presidents all over the country are getting more absolute, as well as more specially fitted for their work."[6] In the mid-eighties, James Bryce was "struck by the prominence of the president in an American university or college. . . . The position of president is often one of honour and influence: no university dignitaries in Great Britain are so well known to the public, or have their opinions quoted with so much respect, as the heads of the seven or eight leading universities in the United States."[7] In 1893, after three decades of "reorganization" and "crisis" in American higher education, Hamilton W. Mabie, the editor and critic, sketched a composite portrait of the "new" university and college president:

There is no class in the community more influential to-day. . . . No class of men is rendering more important service to the Na-

5 See Hugh Hawkins, *Between Harvard and America: The Educational Leadership of Charles W. Eliot* (New York: Oxford University Press, 1972); Samuel Eliot Morison, *Three Centuries of Harvard, 1636–1936* (Cambridge, Mass.: Harvard University Press, 1936), pp. 323–99. Eliot's role on the Committee of Ten is described in Theodore R. Sizer, *Secondary Schools at the Turn of the Century* (New Haven, Conn.: Yale University Press, 1964).

6 Cited in Hugh Hawkins, *Pioneer: A History of The Johns Hopkins University, 1874–1889* (Ithaca, N.Y.: Cornell University Press, 1960), p. 98.

7 James Bryce, *The American Commonwealth*, 2 vols., 3d ed., rev. (New York: Macmillan and Co., 1895), 2:670–71, 672–73.

tion, none commands greater respect. . . . They are heard with respect on public questions no less than on academic and educational questions; they are credited with large intelligence, with disinterestedness, and with high aims. They are in a position to render notable public service by dealing with public questions with a breadth, courage, and freedom from party bias which are conceded to them on account of the position they occupy.[8]

In 1906, James Ford Rhodes, the historian of nineteenth-century America, commented that "for twelve years past no public addresses, save those of the Presidents of the United States themselves, have been so widely read throughout the country as have those of President Eliot."[9] In 1910, Woodrow Wilson also praised Eliot to a Princeton audience: "I suppose that no man has more fully earned the reputation of being the most useful citizen of the country than he."[10]

Rooted in the first half of the nineteenth century, the presidents were men whose personal lives began to reflect the new themes of the middle class and whose occupational lives were devoted to institutionalizing procedures and clarifying attitudes intrinsic to the development of professionalism. They were in the vanguard of the professional. Largely forgotten by history, however, the presidents were by no means heroic actors, memorable either for their extraordinary accomplishments or for their unusual personalities. To the contrary, it was their conventionality that commended them to the age. They were influential figures, representative men of the middle class who both enjoyed respectability and worked hard to reap its harvest of recognition. They all believed, as Eliot put it, that "serviceable

[8] Hamilton W. Mabie, "The American College President," *Outlook* 48 (1893): 341, 338.

[9] James Ford Rhodes, *History of the United States from the Compromise of 1850*, 7 vols. (New York: The Macmillan Company, 1893–1906), 6:385.

[10] Ray Stannard Baker, *Woodrow Wilson, Life and Letters: Princeton 1890–1910* (Garden City, N.Y.: Doubleday, Page and Company, 1927), p. 337.

institutions last," and here they found a worthy object for their considerable energies.[11]

The presidents were white Anglo-Saxon Protestant Americans. Their remarkably uniform origins revealed a common background in generally comfortable and educated surroundings. Of the eight American born, five came from New England and three from upstate New York. (Bascom was only one generation removed, and White two, from New England.) All were English in descent, and six of them traced their lineage to seventeenth-century New England. The only "foreigner," Scottish-born McCosh, called Scotch-Presbyterians like himself the first cousin to the Yankee.

Six of the men came from prosperous or distinguished families and enjoyed the privileges of study and travel. Among the remaining three none appears to have suffered poverty. Though Folwell's origins were both common and modest, he considered himself neither deprived nor exploited by the social structure. He took pride in his independent status, and he believed that his share in the opportunities of the age was commensurate with his talent. The presidents were traditional Anglo-Saxon types in nineteenth-century America. One can find no evidence that any of them felt personally misplaced, left behind, or victimized by a decline in status. In an increasingly aggressive, pushy, and impersonal society, the presidents joined in the pushing.

The presidents belonged to different generations. McCosh, Porter, and Barnard, born between 1800 and 1811, averaged 57.3 years of age when they assumed office, and they merited their posts on the basis of successful careers. McCosh and Porter were exceptional teachers and established scholars of moral philosophy. Barnard was an educator, writer, advocate of the new sciences, and university president at Mississippi. Bascom, Folwell, Eliot, Gilman,

[11] Cited in Henry James, *Charles W. Eliot: President of Harvard University, 1869–1909*, 2 vols. (Boston and New York: Houghton Mifflin Company, 1930), 2:303.

White, and Angell, born between 1827 and 1834, averaged 38.7 years of age when they assumed office, and they achieved fame during and through their presidencies. The younger men tailored themselves in more ecumenical and more secular garb than their elders, and certainly there were clashes of opinion. Nevertheless, changing fashions did not always indicate changing convictions.

One fundamental conviction all the presidents could agree upon was the importance of "character" in nineteenth-century American lives. As James Burrill Angell described the idea, "A society is always just what its members make it by their character; nothing more, nothing less."[12] The man of strong character stood for power, permanence, and fortitude—all virtues Mid-Victorians wished to display. The person of strong character transcended fickle public opinion and fleeting public repute. Mid-Victorians called character a democratic idea limited neither by social class nor by political partisanship. Character established special credentials, which the entire society could accept as lasting and unchanging. Webster's Dictionary, edited by Noah Porter, defined *character* as "the distinctive mark, the sum of qualities which distinguished one person or thing from another." The word derived from the classical languages, "to make sharp, to cut into furrows, to engrave." No idea was more formidable in the nineteenth-century American world, more a symbol of substance and durability.

The representation of character as "enduring credentials" took on heightened significance in light of the fact that an eighteenth-century spokesman such as Ben Franklin had used the word very differently. Franklin had spoken of "my credit and character as a tradesman"; and he defined *character* in terms of the amount of "credit" a community would extend to a person, based on an estimate of his "good repute," his "affluence," and his "felicity." In Franklin's description, character was an external acquisition, lacking any intrinsic or fixed meaning. Although community was

[12] Cited in Shirley W. Smith, *James Burrill Angell: An American Influence* (Ann Arbor, Mich.: University of Michigan Press, 1954), p. 30.

predisposed to judge the person who cultivated the virtuous habits of industry, frugality, and humility as one of good character, Franklin knew that habits not cultivated as ends in themselves but calculated to secure desirable results were appearances—moreover, appearances vulnerable to manipulation. To Franklin, a person's character was an exploitable object. "In order to secure my Credit and Character as a Tradesman," Franklin revealed in the full passage,

I took care not only to be in *Reality* Industrious and frugal, but to avoid all *Appearances* of the Contrary. I drest plainly; I was seen at no Places of idle Diversion; I never went out a-fishing or shooting; a Book, indeed, sometimes debauch'd me from my Work; but that was seldom, snug, and gave no Scandal: and to show that I was not above my Business, I sometimes brought home the Paper I purchas'd at the Stores, thro' the Streets on a Wheelbarrow.[13]

For Franklin, *credit* was a finite property, renegotiated in every contract; and *character* was an ephemeral possession, reconsidered in every case.

For the presidents, however, an individual's character was not his dress but his incarnation, the totality of his powers and control. A subtle shift occurred: from character as formed only by the habits of industry and frugality to character as formed also by aggressive mental initiative, self-reliance, and usefulness. By means of the independence of his confident intellect, the person with an admirable character now overcame circumstances and reached beyond the mutability of the environment. He calculated his course beyond specific cases, particular events, and *ad hoc* decisions. Knowledge acquired by the intellect was lasting authority, which was constantly meant to remind a client, a constituency, and an employer of the continuity and strength of a commanding individual's character. Within a structured

---

[13] *The Autobiography of Benjamin Franklin,* ed. Leonard W. Labaree, Ralph L. Ketcham, Helen C. Boatfield, Helena H. Fineman (New Haven, Conn.: Yale University Press, 1964), p. 125.

institution, Mid-Victorians favored formal educational training which would both establish the worldly credentials of an individual and develop his character.

It was the intention of the presidents that their credentials portray men of uncommon mental stability and foresight in a place James Bryce described as "more unrestful than any country we know of has yet been."[14] In their own sights, they were men of character. They held office for an average of twenty-three years, with no term being less than thirteen years. They all left ample autobiographical records of their activities, and they compiled extensive bibliographies of their addresses and writings. The presidents survived to an average age of eighty-four years. All were eventually selected to appear in the *Dictionary of American Biography,* and seven of the nine appeared in the *Encyclopaedia Britannica*'s eleventh edition, known as the scholar's edition. Gilman wrote the article for *Britannica* on the university in America.

THE BEST TYPE OF AMERICAN CHARACTER

The presidents chose to be symbols of permanence in their own era, and by their own measures they succeeded. They demonstrated a striking awareness of their cultural position within nineteenth-century American history. John Bascom's *Sociology,* for instance, became one of the pioneering documents in the growth of the social gospel movement. "Wisconsin was fortunate indeed," wrote Merle Curti and Vernon Carstensen, "to have such a mind during so critical a period of her intellectual history." Herbert W. Schneider called Noah Porter "in many ways the greatest and most erudite of the professors of philosophy" in the century. And Ralph Henry Gabriel added that Porter "forecast the think-

14 Bryce, *American Commonwealth,* 2:770.

ing of the social gospel, an aspect of Protestantism to achieve importance at the turn of the twentieth century."[15] Re-issued some thirty times, Porter's massive textbook *The Human Intellect* (1868) became a classic in its own day; and Porter's influence on the structure of the liberal-arts curriculum in American higher education was significant. A century later, James McCosh's works *The Scottish Philosophy* and *Christianity and Positivism* remain familiar statements of the type of moral philosophy that was pervasive in nineteenth-century American thought. Andrew Dickson White's *History of the Warfare of Science with Theology in Christendom* and his *Autobiography* made him a well-known man of letters in the day. Folwell's four-volume history of Minnesota remains a basic document in the social history of the region.[16] In the ongoing concern with the history of higher education in America, students continue to read the collected statements on educational philosophy by Eliot, Gilman, Angell, and Folwell, and the uncollected statements by Porter, McCosh, White, Bascom, and Barnard.[17]

15 John Bascom, *Sociology* (New York and London: G. P. Putnam's Sons, 1887); Merle Curti and Vernon Carstensen, *The University of Wisconsin: A History*, 2 vols. (Madison: University of Wisconsin Press, 1949), 1:295; on Bascom's thought see also Robert A. Jones, "John Bascom 1827–1911: Anti-positivism and Intuitionism in American Sociology," *American Quarterly* 24 (October 1972): 501–22; Herbert W. Schneider, *A History of American Philosophy* (New York: Columbia University Press, 1946), p. 245; Ralph Henry Gabriel, *Religion and Learning at Yale: The Church of Christ in the College and University, 1757–1957* (New Haven, Conn.: Yale University Press, 1948), p. 182.

16 Noah Porter, *The Human Intellect with an Introduction Upon Psychology and the Soul* (New York: Scribner Armstrong & Company, 1868); James McCosh, *The Scottish Philosophy: Biographical, Expository, Critical, From Hutcheson to Hamilton* (New York: Robert Carter and Brothers, 1875); McCosh, *Christianity and Positivism: a Series of Lectures to the Times on Natural Theology and Apologetics* (New York: Robert Carter and Brothers, 1871); Andrew Dickson White, *A History of the Warfare of Science with Theology in Christendom*, 2 vols. (New York: The Century Company, 1905); William Watts Folwell, *History of Minnesota*, 4 vols. (Saint Paul: The Minnesota Historical Society, 1921–30).

17 Charles William Eliot, *Educational Reform: Essays and Addresses* (New York: The Century Company, 1898); Charles William Eliot,

Responsibility to intellectual causes in America carried the presidents beyond the confines of the university. Andrew Dickson White twice served as president of the American Social Science Association, as well as the first president of the American Historical Association. James Burrill Angell was also a president of the American Historical Association, and a regent of the Smithsonian Institution. F. A. P. Barnard served as a president of the American Association for the Advancement of Science and was a member of the United States Coast Survey. Beginning with the 1864 edition, and including revised editions in 1879 and 1884, Porter was co-editor of Noah Webster's *American Dictionary of the English Language*. In 1890, he edited the first edition of the monumental *Webster's International Dictionary of the English Language*. Both James McCosh and John Bascom were active participants in the Concord School of Philosophy and published numerous books relating to social ethics. Daniel Coit Gilman was a president of the American Social Science Association, an influential voice in the many academic journals born at Johns Hopkins in its early years, and the first president of the Carnegie Institute. His many other activities included the Russell Sage Foundation, the John F. Slater Fund, the Peabody Educational Fund, and the National Civil Service Reform League. All the presidents frequently wrote on educational, scientific, professional, and current political issues for the growing number of journals and popular magazines in the later nineteenth century.[18] All

American Contributions to Civilization and Other Essays (New York: The Century Company, 1897); Daniel Coit Gilmann, *University Problems in the United States* (New York: The Century Company, 1898); Daniel Coit Gilman, *The Launching of a University and Other Papers, A Sheaf of Remembrances* (New York: Dodd, Mead & Company, 1906); James Burrill Angell, *Selected Addresses* (New York: Longmans, Green, and Company, 1912); William Watts Folwell, *University Addresses* (Minneapolis: The H. W. Wilson Company, 1909).

18 The growth of popular literary magazines and a public to support them was indispensable to these spokesmen. See John Tomsich, *A Genteel Endeavor: American Culture and Politics in the Gilded Age* (Stanford, Calif.: Stanford University Press, 1971), pp. 16–18.

of them took a personal interest in the reform of secondary education in America. "My life has had two sides; one employed in thinking, and the other in action," McCosh told a farewell audience in 1888. "I have not found the two inconsistent."

As institutional leaders, as transformers of the American college from boy's work to man's work, the presidents varied in their degrees of success. For example, after "twenty years of Princeton College," James McCosh told one of the modest but impressive accounts of university development in his farewell address. "These were the days of our prosperity," he said, summarizing his theme. Both as an efficient administrator and as an effective teacher, McCosh reversed the fortunes of the declining institution, which suffered from the loss of southern students during and after the Civil War. The faculty and the student body more than doubled in numbers during McCosh's tenure. The curriculum was liberalized, with half of the upperclassman's course of study now electives. The gymnasium, Dickinson Hall, Reunion Hall, a library building, University Hall, Witherspoon Hall, the president's residence, the observatory housed with a telescope, the College Chapel, the Biological Museum, the Art Museum, new dormitories—all were constructed in this period. The endowment for fellowships increased considerably. McCosh called the School of Science, founded in 1873, "the most important addition which has been made to the college in my day"; every summer an expedition of students supervised by Professor Arnold Guyot journeyed West to accumulate Princeton's biological and geological collections. In his "Library Meeting" for professors and upperclassmen, McCosh introduced a form of the graduate seminar. In 1877 graduate studies were permitted on a permanent basis, in 1887 Princeton began conferring degrees on the German pattern, and in 1888 McCosh boasted of seventy-eight advanced students. Already McCosh was aware that the educated public was tending to rate the status of a higher educational institution by the quality of its graduate program. "These graduate classes," McCosh concluded, "will force us on to become a university."[19]

Princeton's conversion into a university under McCosh was no fortuitous afterthought. In his inaugural address in 1868, McCosh had announced that he would steer a university-bound course during his presidency. He would not rest "satisfied till we have institutions to rival the grand old universities of Europe, such as Oxford and Cambridge, and Berlin and Edinburgh." Though his early hopes proved to be premature, they had not been misconceived. His successor secured official recognition of the new status, wrote Princeton's historian, but McCosh "worked the transformation."[20]

Among themselves, the presidents shared their sense of professional accomplishment. "You were our godfather," Gilman wrote to Eliot; and Eliot returned, "Words of praise from a man who, like you, knows what he is talking about, are always welcome." Both Angell and White influenced Gilman's election at Johns Hopkins, Angell calling his role "one of the few acts of my life which I have never regretted"; Andrew White wrote to Mrs. Gilman, "The success of Dr. Gilman as President of John Hopkins I have always regarded as the most remarkable of its kind achieved during my time." Years earlier, Folwell had written White: "Will you permit a friend and admirer to say that perhaps the practical working out of your idea [at Cornell] is of more account every way than any political service you can render the country." All responded to noteworthy public statements by their colleagues. Both Eliot and Porter, for instance, applauded Folwell's "Minnesota Plan" for organizing public education, and Folwell commended Mc-

[19] James McCosh, *Twenty Years of Princeton College: Being a Farewell Address* (New York: Charles Scribner's Sons, 1888), pp. 65, 11, 31.
[20] James McCosh, "Inaugural Address: Theme—Academic Teaching in Europe," *Inauguration of Rev. Jas. McCosh as President of Princeton College, 1868* (Princeton, N.J.: Standard Office, 1868), p. 30; McCosh, *Twenty Years,* pp. 34, 35; Thomas Jefferson Wertenbaker, *Princeton: 1746–1896* (Princeton, N.J.: Princeton University Press, 1946), pp. 303, 342.

Cosh's and Porter's stand against religious sectarianism in education. White described Angell's inaugural address as "masterly—the best presentation of the right doctrine I have ever seen." The presidents congratulated themselves that their audience spread as widely as the educated public, far beyond the confines of trustee meetings or commencement exercises.[21]

The presidents conducted themselves diplomatically, not only on the domestic scene but abroad. James Burrill Angell made time during his presidency at the University of Michigan to be Minister to China under Garfield, Minister to Turkey under McKinley, and a member of several important commissions at Cleveland's request. Daniel Coit Gilman served on the commission that investigated the Venezuela–British Guiana boundary dispute in the nineties. Andrew White, engaged in government missions while president of Cornell, was absent from campus for all but five months between 1876 and 1881. He was minister to Germany (1879–81), minister to Russia (1892–94), ambassador to Germany (1897–1903), and led the American delegation to the Hague Conference (1899). President Hayes offered the position of Minister of England to Noah Porter, and both Taft and Wilson offered the same position to Charles William Eliot.

The experience in diplomacy had ramifications for the American university. Angell, for instance, pioneered in the use of foreign archives in the writing of diplomatic history. And White, as a professor of modern European history, helped to develop the field pedagogically. He personally built up an impressive library of first editions, documents, sources, and historical artifacts, which he donated to the

21 Gilman and Eliot cited in Willis Rudy, "Eliot and Gilman: The History of an Academic Friendship," *Teachers College Record* 54 (March 1953): 309, 315; Angell cited in Smith, *Angell*, p. 163; White cited in Fabian Franklin, *The Life of Daniel Coit Gilman* (New York: Dodd, Mead & Company, 1910) p. 325; William Watts Folwell, *The Autobiography and Letters of a Pioneer of Culture*, ed. Solon J. Buck (Minneapolis: The University of Minnesota Press, 1933), p. 217; White cited in Smith, *Angell*, p. 100.

university. The new social sciences in particular benefited from the presidents' awareness of the world. These were not provincial men. Their own beliefs, based on ample observations abroad, committed them to perceiving a causal relationship between social knowledge and discipline in society. Their support for the sciences that had consequences for national development was usually forthcoming. White was the most outspoken, and he aggressively stated his position during a private audience with Leo Tolstoy. As the two walked and conversed, White recounted his advice to a Russian student of engineering at Cornell. The student should "bear in mind Buckle's idea" that building railways and telegraphs was the means to a better civilization and to the "enlightenment of the empire." Never, under any conditions, should the student divert his energies and "conspire against the government." Tolstoy and White stood face to face:

Tolstoi said the advice was good, but that he would also have advised the young man to speak out his ideas, whatever they might be. He said that only in this way could any advance ever be made; that one main obstacle in human progress is the suppression of the real thoughts of men. I answered that all this had a fine sound; that it might do for Count Tolstoi; but that a young, scholarly engineer following it would soon find himself in a place where he could not promulgate his ideas,—guarded by Cossacks in some remote Siberian mine.[22]

White was pointing the American university in an unmistakable direction.

Many Americans acknowledged the accomplishments of the presidents during their lengthy careers. The encomiastic testimonials revealed the prominent social and cultural circles in which the presidents were welcome. Referring to an address by Angell on internationalism, Secretary of State John Hay, a former pupil and friend, wrote: "I am sure I need not say what a comfort it is, in the confusion of tongues by which I am surrounded, to hear an occa-

[22] *Autobiography of Andrew Dickson White,* 2 vols. (New York: The Century Company, 1905), 2:93–94.

sional clear and authoritative voice like yours, which approves the work we are trying to do."[23] Theodore Roosevelt wrote Andrew Dickson White on his retirement from the German ambassadorship: "You have adhered to a lofty ideal and yet have been absolutely practical and therefore efficient, so that you are a perpetual example to young men how to avoid alike the Scylla of inefficiency and the Charybdis of efficiency for the wrong." Earlier Roosevelt had told White: "Do you know, I have come to the conclusion that I have mighty little originality of my own. What I do is to try to get ideas from men whom I regard as experts along certain lines, and then to try to work out those ideas."[24] Andrew Carnegie, seeking a director for his new institute, was supposed to have said to Daniel Coit Gilman, "You must be President."[25] And having offered the position of Minister to Great Britain to Noah Porter, Rutherford B. Hayes praised him to a Yale audience: "Knowing the desire of the American people that their representative to the nation to which we so largely trace our lineage should be a man reared up to the full stature of a mental and moral manhood, and wishing to select the best type of American character, in that emergency again I turned to Yale and found just the man."[26]

According to the testimonials, the presidents were impressive as men of character. Robert LaFollette, for instance, had never seen Ralph Waldo Emerson, but the Wisconsin progressive imagined that

John Bascom was a man of much his type, both in appearance and in character. He was the embodiment of moral force and moral enthusiasm; and he was in advance of his time in feeling the new social forces and in emphasizing the new social respon-

[23] Cited in Smith, *Angell,* p. 328.

[24] Elting E. Morison, ed., *The Letters of Theodore Roosevelt,* 8 vols. (Cambridge, Mass.: Harvard University Press, 1951–54), 3:309, 2:1118.

[25] Franklin, *Gilman,* p. 392; Joseph Frazier Wall, *Andrew Carnegie* (New York: Oxford University Press, 1970), pp. 858–61.

[26] George S. Merriam, ed., *Noah Porter: A Memorial By Friends* (New York: Charles Scribner's Sons, 1893), pp. 140–41.

sibilities. . . . It was his teaching, iterated and reiterated, of the obligation of both the university and the students to the mother state that may be said to have originated the Wisconsin idea in education.[27]

Both Washington Gladden and G. Stanley Hall praised Bascom as the instructor to whom they owed the most. F. A. P. Barnard "was among the most extraordinary men I ever knew," recalled the political scientist John W. Burgess: "He was a great theologian, a great scientist, and a great student of education." McCosh "made a powerful impression upon" Woodrow Wilson, wrote Ray Stannard Baker, an early Wilson biographer: McCosh "was the kind of man Wilson admired to the depth of his soul—the scholar, the wit, the leader—and he formed for him a kind of youthful adoration that he never lost."[28]

The success of the university as an institution paralleled the success of the university president as a public spokesman for the educational interests of the middle class. James Bryce, for instance, observed that the university was redressing the lack of competence upon the American scene. American universities were beginning to compare favorably with the "ancient universities of Europe." Bryce expressed surprise that "diligence is the tradition of the American colleges," and he called the era in America a renaissance. "There is an almost excessive anxiety among American scholars to master all that has been written," he observed, and he was struck by the passion with which the "young generation" pursued its studies—"even kinds of

27 *La Follette's Autobiography: a Personal Narrative of Political Experience* (Madison, Wis.: The Robert M. La Follette Company, 1919), p. 13.
28 Washington Gladden, *Recollections* (Boston and New York: Houghton Mifflin Company, 1909), p. 74; G. Stanley Hall, *Life and Confessions of a Psychologist* (New York: D. Appleton and Company, 1923), p. 157; John W. Burgess, *Reminiscences of an American Scholar: The Beginnings of Columbia University* (New York: Columbia University Press, 1932), p. 173; Ray Stannard Baker, *Woodrow Wilson, Life and Letters: Youth, 1856–1890* (Garden City, N.Y.: Doubleday, Page and Company, 1927), p. 84.

study which will never win the applause of the multi-tude."[29]

America's bright young men who in the past had been skeptical of an American education and gone off to Europe were now accepting the new American university. In 1882, after visiting the Continental universities, William James, for instance, became reconciled to his "home-lot," and was "readier to believe that it is one of the chosen places of the Earth." He intimated that the American mind, here-tofore athletic, could also be intellectual. The instruction and facilities at Harvard, James claimed, "are on the whole superior to anything I have seen." The American scholar lacked only the "abdominal depth of temperament and the power to sit for an hour over a single pot of beer without being able to tell at the end of it what we've been thinking about." Never at a loss for wit, James devised a solution for the American scholar's problem of "depth." Emerson might have been stunned by James's irreverence, but one suspects that in a perverse moment Concord's "seer" would have approved. "The first thing to do is to establish in Cambridge a genuine German plebeian Kneipe club, to which all instructors and picked students shall be admitted. If that succeeds, we shall be perfect, especially if we talk therein with deeper voices."[30]

By the nineties, middle-class Americans observed that higher education admirably served the nation. In 1893, Hamilton W. Mabie wrote in the *Outlook* that "the college belongs to the Nation, and the sooner the Nation recog-nizes the intimacy of the relation and the weight of the obligation, the better for the Nation." After twenty years, American higher education had achieved both the social recognition and the public support that assured its pros-perity. Even practical men and businessmen were affirming the importance of higher education to the structure of American society. "There is a dawning idea abroad,"

[29] Bryce, *American Commonwealth*, 2:694, 679, 778, 780.

[30] *The Letters of William James,* ed. Henry James, 2 vols. (Boston: The Atlantic Monthly Press, 1920), 1:216–17.

Mabie perceived, "that the colleges are not institutions for a fortunate few, who have leisure and means for prolonged study, but that they hold a very close relation to a sound national life, and are, indeed, the feeders of all that is noblest and safest in that life."[31] In 1895, a reviewer in the *Atlantic Monthly* described the phoenix-like American "zeal for learning." Also he was reminded "of the brilliant days of the Italian Renaissance." Grown men were devoting "to the abstract loyalties of the intellect the time, the strength, and the ambition which one would not expect to find."[32]

THE MAN OF CHARACTER

For the Mid-Victorians, a person's work was more than an unrelated series of jobs and projects, a utilitarian and functional response to need and limited desire. Work was the person: a statement to the world of his internal resources, confidence, and discipline; his active control over the intrinsic relationships of a life; his steadfast character. Indeed, the meaning of a Mid-Victorian life in America depended upon the tension and the confidence a man of character could sustain in a universe that did its best to neutralize tension, to demoralize confidence, and corrupt meaning. As an indwelling idea of self, as a core of continuous existence, one's character supported an ambitious individual as he exerted the supreme effort of attention to develop his real talents. Facile and witty, the wily old eighteenth-century Ben Franklin had played at being earnest. He had cultivated the character of the Odd Fellow. Solemn and judgmental, the nineteenth-century presidents *were* earnest. Each assumed the character of divinity. The smallest feature about a person's behavior now related to a higher meaning, to an ulterior purpose, to a potential basis

31 Mabie, "American College President," 340.
32 "The American College," *Atlantic Monthly* 75 (May 1895): 703.

for approval or condemnation of his innermost character. Mid-Victorians dismissed no utterance or act as a trifle, unrevealing about a person's character; and too often they eliminated those human tolerances that saved a life from misery.

The person with an ideal character was distinctive, intellectually and emotionally confident. He paced life properly, heard the true rhythm of the universe; and chose the real over the illusory, the natural over the artificial. He demonstrated such judiciousness, discretion, equanimity, and balance that right and wrong became clear to him, duty defined, and worldly matters set straight, perhaps for a lifetime. The person of character was in control, as Eliot's advice to his twenty-three-year-old son, "perplexed about the choice of a profession," illustrated:

> I hope you will not feel in haste to get through with your education, your "infancy," or period of training. There is no reason why you should, and I want you to enjoy a sense of ease and calm in that matter. . . . You need not feel that you ought to be earning your living, or doing something in the actual marketplace. That will come soon enough. There are fields of knowledge and philosophy which you have hardly set foot in. Take time to view them with a disengaged mind. The sense of being driven or hurried is very disagreeable to you; then arrange your life so that you cannot be driven or hurried.[33]

Beneath the warmth and the affection, Eliot was reminding his son about what was expected eventually from a Mid-Victorian life. Beyond confusion the person of character discovered meaning, beyond chaos he perceived a rational order, beyond doubt he settled upon hard facts, beyond youthful experimentation he pursued a career that suited his nature. The person of character was a source of faith sufficient unto himself. The person of character never wandered aimlessly in a bleak and dessicated world.

As self-appointed examples of the "man" of character, the presidents both pondered the irrationality of events

---

[33] James, *Eliot*, 2:36–37.

and survived, without any taint of cynicism, skepticism, and despair.[34] Was life worth living? "I have observed," Eliot commented, "in two instances this summer that laboring people find that question utterly absurd. They haven't a doubt on the subject." Neither did Eliot, though he was hardly a laboring person. Eliot wrote his son, suffering from indecision and instability: "You are unreasonable in expecting to know the sense of your existence. Nobody knows the meaning of any existence—of flower, beast, man, nation, or world. Live each day as usefully, innocently, and happily as you can, and leave the rest to God. It is time you were married. You are too solitary." The business of control, efficiency, and progress was cosmically serious with Eliot, who feared that a fault in the character of his son would correspond to a faltering career.[35]

As the presidents displayed their lives for public example, the man of character suppressed any sense of defeat, waste, or the dissipation of energy. He refused to consider the possibility that his efforts were futile or his performance inadequate. With typical conceit, Eliot recalled his attributes as a youth of fifteen: "He was reserved, industrious, independent and ambitious; he trod the giddy edge of precipices with a complete unconsciousness of danger." "Once born" described the presidents, and William James depicted the type: the "healthy-minded" for whom "happiness is congenital and irreclaimable," whose "consciousness . . . develop[s] straight and natural . . . with no element of morbid compunction or crisis." Eliot pompously wrote to his cousin, "It is a small virtue in me to speak plainly. . . . It is rather an Eliot quality—some people would say,

[34] In presentist terms, the presidents were male chauvinists who seldom clarified the usage of the word *man*, which meant both the generic mankind or humankind and the sexual male or masculine. A. D. White, for instance, both favored coeducation at Cornell and spoke out as a reformer and abolitionist for the rights of mankind. Nevertheless, White thought almost exclusively in male or masculine imagery.

[35] James, *Eliot*, 1:341–42, 2:39.

vice."[36] More than once James commented about Eliot's lack of tact, and his lack of human sympathy. Ralph Barton Perry wrote that Eliot "had something of that shallowness which seems to be the penalty of health." Eliot shared this trait with his colleagues. Perry perceived that

it is hard for a healthy man to plumb the depths of human suffering. It is hard for an effective man to recognize the limits of human capacity, and for a well-ordered man to appreciate the waywardness and inner conflict of genius. It is hard for a reasonable man to understand the tragic fatalities which encumber the wills of those who, though they be less virtuous, are sometimes more gifted.[37]

Healthy, effective, well-ordered, reasonable, somewhat shallow: these features typified the presidents.

Congenital Christians in a non-theological school, the presidents recorded their "once born" faith. "I feel very hopeful," Gilman wrote in 1867, "that the day of good things is at hand." Among Gilman's papers, this pledge from Schleiermacher's *Monologen* was found:

I will keep my spirits without flagging to the end of my days. The fresh courage of life shall never forsake me. What gladdens me now shall gladden me always. My will shall continue firm and my imagination vivid. Nothing shall snatch from me the magic key which opens to me those doors of the invisible world which are filled with mystery, and the fire of love in my heart shall never grow dim. I shall never experience the dreaded weakness of old age. I will treat with noble disdain every adversity which assails the aim of my existence, and I promise myself eternal youth.[38]

All the presidents shared Gilman's taste for the melodramatic. Reviewing his twenty years at Princeton, McCosh

---

[36] Eliot cited in Rudy, "Eliot and Gilman," 314, and in Ralph Barton Perry, "Charles William Eliot," in Allen Johnson and Dumas Malone, eds., *Dictionary of American Biography*, 11 vols. (New York: Charles Scribner's Sons, 1927–36), 6:77; William James, *The Varieties of Religious Experience: A Study in Human Nature* (New York: The Modern Library, 1929), pp. 78, 81.

[37] Ralph Barton Perry, "Charles William Eliot, His Personal Traits and Essential Creed," *New England Quarterly* 4 (January 1931): 27.

[38] Cited in Rudy, "Eliot and Gilman," 308; Franklin, *Gilman*, p. 434.

publicized the personal oath he had taken on acceptance of the office: "I devote myself and my remaining life, under God, to old Princeton, and the religious and literary interests with which it is identified, and, I fancy, will leave my bones in your graveyard beside the great and good men who are buried there, hoping that my spirit may mount to communion with them in heaven."[39] At the conclusion of his autobiography, White appeared to be no less earnest and no less self-certain:

I have sought to fight the good fight; I have sought to keep the faith,—faith in a Power in the universe good enough to make truth-seeking wise, and strong enough to make truth-telling effective,—faith in the rise of man rather than in the fall of man,—faith in the gradual evolution and ultimate prevalence of right reason among men. So much I hope to be pardoned for giving as an *apologia pro vita mea*.[40]

The flavor of these men was distinct. In their desire to succeed and conquer, they declined to reflect upon their own vanity, to admit to their own mistakes.

Speaking clear truths and advocating pure ideals, the man of character impressed society with the sincerity of his convictions. Andrew Dickson White, for example, repeatedly praised the "clear-headed, clear-voiced, earnest, and honest man." He recalled that Wendell Phillips, William Lloyd Garrison, and Stephen Douglas did not indulge in "rhetorical fustian and oratorical tall-talk. . . . [T]hey took strong hold upon me and gave me a higher idea of a man's best work in life."[41] Such educators as White were convinced of their own importance. "How real an influence an earnest teacher might . . . exercise upon his country," White proclaimed in the context of the slavery controversy. The man of character generated the power of positive persuasion. "You will be surprised," White wrote Folwell at Minnesota concerning legislatures and land grants, "to find how—

39 McCosh, *Twenty Years,* p. 5.
40 White, *Autobiography,* 2:509–10.
41 *Ibid.,* 1:16, 256.

despite the wretched tone upon such subjects in our legislature—an *earnest* man who understands *such a subject* is
listened to; and if he has tact he can set things right for a
century."[42] The man of character was an agent of destiny.

The earnestness of the presidents trod on naiveté, and
their exaggerated seriousness could assume comic propor-
tions. McCosh's exuberance caused him to speak more like
a Scottish Lord than a dignified higher educator: "I was
like the hound in the leash ready to start, and they [Prince-
tonians] encouraged me with their shouts as I sprang forth
into the hunt." Barnard's desire to be candid was perhaps
less studied: "I love young men," he exclaimed at his inaugural proceedings.[43] White was infatuated with mascu-
linity. He turned martial physical activity toward an intellectual end, when he justified the military training
program (ROTC) at Cornell:

Farmers' boys,—slouchy, careless, not accustomed to obey any
word of command; city boys, sometimes pampered, often way-
ward, have thus been in a short time transformed: they stand
erect; they look the world squarely in the face; the intensity of
their American individualism is happily modified; they can take
the word of command and they can give it. I doubt whether any
feature of instruction at Cornell University has produced more excellent results upon *character* than the training thus given.[44]

Muscular and nervous activity attracted White, who was
not an introspective man.

In White's effusive rhetoric, *earnest* and *manly* distinguished the character of an admirable individual. Indeed, White reiterated the word *manly* with the frequency
of an incantation. "In Heaven's name be men," he charged
the faculty, and called for faculty-student intercourse as a

42 Folwell, *Autobiography and Letters*, p. 198.

43 McCosh, *Twenty Years*, p. 7; *Proceedings at the Inauguration of
Frederick A. P. Barnard as President of Columbia College, 1864* (New
York: Hurd and Houghton, 1865), p. 40.

44 *The Inauguration of Cornell University: Reprinted from the Account of the Proceedings at Inauguration, October 7th 1868* (Ithaca,
N.Y.: Cornell University Press, 1921), p. 21; White, *Autobiography*,
1:388–89.

"relation simply of man to man." As a practical policy, White proposed that Cornell build no dormitories; students would room and board with local families in the town and benefit from the wholesome domestic influences that bred manly sentiments. White disdained the effete learned professionals who, in his view, were " 'tonguey' men taking positions of influence over substantial working men."[45]

The athletic view of life, which led White to stress the importance of physical and military education (ROTC), at times consumed him. "I fully believe that today in the United States physical education and development is a more pressing necessity even than mental development," he announced in his inaugural. And he proposed to introduce a work-study program in the Cornell curriculum. Earlier he had said that "as long as highly educated men are dyspeptics, so long will they be deprived of their supremacy in society by uneducated *eupeptics*—and so it ought to be."[46] The man of character exuded virility, a physical toughness that had moral consequences. White even extended the value of physical education into the problem of urban politics. He once stated:

There is perhaps nothing so wretched in our country to-day as the frequently servile acquiescence of many excellent men in the rule of "bosses." With a proper system of physical education, I believe the tyranny of unworthy leaders would be more and more difficult, and finally impossible. There is something in the possession of a sound physical frame in good training of great value to any man in resisting encroachments, whether physical or political.[47]

[45] *Inauguration of Cornell*, pp. 30, 25; Andrew D. White, *Address on Agricultural Education, Delivered Before the New York State Agricultural Society, 1869* (Albany, N.Y.: Chas. Van Benthuysen & Sons, 1869), p. 46.

[46] *Inauguration of Cornell*, p. 21; *Report of the Committee on Organization Presented to the Trustees of the Cornell University, 1866* (Albany, N.Y.: C. Van Benthuysen & Sons, Printers, 1867), p. 39.

[47] Andrew D. White, *Democracy and Education*, typescript, p. 28, Cornell University Archives, White MSS.

White had the good sense not to publish this feeble thought.

Cultivated attitudes caused university presidents to favor special programs on campus. In fact, White was in the vanguard of a later generation of presidents, including such men as Jacob Gould Schurman at Cornell, Arthur T. Hadley at Yale, and Woodrow Wilson at Princeton. They believed that military training, and in some cases organized athletics, hardened the moral character of students who were growing soft and lazy from the destructive effects of luxury and self-indulgence. For instance, Princeton's John Grier Hibben claimed that military "discipline is a tonic against all sloth and procrastination," and Cornell's Benjamin Ide Wheeler said that college football "tends to the production of manly, earnest character, to the throttling of pettishness and peevishness, and to the establishment of habits of punctuality, of a sense for discipline and authority, of a readiness for co-operation, and, last and chiefest, of the capacity for timely and unhesitating action."[48] The character traits of university administrators translated by means of specific policies into real actions in the educator's world.

Eliot's candor, McCosh's aggressiveness, White's virility surpassed personal idiosyncrasies. They shone as the visible, and often ugly, manifestations of a frame of mind consciously developed by the man of character. The presidents exhibited their personal asceticism as symbols of mental control and mental concentration for the average American to emulate. For instance, the first experience of the presidents and their rejection of such moderate vices as alcohol, tobacco, and coffee occurred in their early lives. Yet, the immoderate responses never ceased; responses which the

---

48 John Grier Hibben, "The Colleges and National Defense," *The Independent* 82 (June 28, 1915): 533; Benjamin Ide Wheeler, in Walter Camp, *Football Facts and Figures: A Symposium of Expert Opinions of the Game's Place in American Athletics* (New York: Harper and Brothers, 1894), p. 111.

presidents viewed as separating the civilized from the uncivilized, the superior from the inferior, the disciplined middle classes from the dissipated lower classes.

Temperance commanded the most attention as a symbol of reform. At least half the presidents professed teetotalism, and the remainder were silent. None even mentioned taking an occasional drink of wine at dinner. Folwell recalled that he drank his first and only liquor in combat during the Civil War; he "took enough to render him foggy and was quietly laid away to rest."[49] Bascom participated so actively in the temperance movement that he endangered his already weakened position at Wisconsin. Mid-Victorians perfected their own form of ego intoxication which was no less devastating than the overindulgence of liquid spirits. Barnard, a prominent member of the "Sons of Temperance," religiously preached both total abstinence and total dedication:

Whatever we may accomplish, we never can exterminate this vice, so long as there shall be a class of neutrals in the land. Neutrals! There can be no neutrals. Intemperance has no rampart of defence so nearly impregnable as that which is thrown up before it by the army of neutrals. If you would not fight for the perpetuation of drunkenness, you must fight against it! Think of this alternative from which there is no escape, and then—choose ye for yourselves.[50]

The crusade for civilization, as Barnard stated it, consumed Mid-Victorians, especially since they could distinguish only with difficulty among such "vices" as slavery, sex, poverty, and booze. In the total warlike effort to stimulate mental development and to structure American lives, there was no neutrality, and often there was little discretion. McCosh considered it important to tell the world in his farewell address that, " I cannot tell how happy I am to think that

49 Folwell, *Autobiography and Letters,* p. 129.

50 John Fulton, *Memoirs of Frederick A. P. Barnard* (New York: Published for the Columbia University Press by Macmillan and Co., 1896), pp. 107–8.

when I give up my office in the college, there is not a place for the sale of spiritous liquors in all Princeton."[51]

The use of tobacco concerned the presidents less, though they categorized it as a poison. The "disgusting" habit of sniffing, especially in "young women of good breeding," repulsed Angell. And Bascom described tobacco as a "habit . . . most unfortunate in the physical, social, aesthetical, and spiritual affiliations." Andrew Dickson White commented, "I expect next to hear of courses introducing young men to the beauties of absinthe, Turkish cigarettes, and stimulants unspeakable."[52] The presidents even condemned coffee as a stimulant, deleterious to moral and physical health, and a temptation to the weak will. Daniel Coit Gilman denounced the "vulgar and material" article, and also criticized graduate students who sipped tea while studying late at night. "I made a bad speech last night," Charles William Eliot was known to say, "I was garrulous and diffuse. In fact I was intoxicated—I had taken a cup of coffee." Eliot intimidated house guests at the breakfast table: "We can give you coffee. We also have Postum Cereal. It is excellent. Will you have Postum Cereal?"[53]

In Eliot's treatment of "character," one can discern a relationship between an extraordinary concern with control over the physical processes of a personal life and a professional interest in science. As early as 1820, according to a physician's magazine entitled *The Journal of Health,* "the middle classes" were distinguishable by their considerable attention to physical health.[54] Indeed, Mid-Victorians like Eliot seemed to spend a significant portion

[51] McCosh, *Twenty Years*, p. 51.

[52] James Burrill Angell, *Reminiscences* (New York: Longmans, Green, and Company, 1912), pp. 70–71; John Bascom, *Things Learned by Living* (New York: G. P. Putnam's Sons, 1913), p. 77; White, *Autobiography*, 1:385.

[53] Gilman, "The Johns Hopkins University," *Launching of a University*, p. 68; James, *Eliot*, 2:319–20.

[54] "The Middle Classes," *Journal of Health* 1 (Philadelphia, 1830): 357–58.

of their private time analyzing their ailments, urging the adoption of hygienic habits, traveling for the well-being of their nervous dispositions, and convalescing. Eliot's father, for instance, advised his son at college, "It is necessary to digestion that food be well masticated; and this cannot be, if swallowed greedily. Students, like men of business, are apt to be great deal too rapid in this process."[55] Charles William Eliot's personal letters were literally filled with lengthy descriptions of the physical condition of individual family members. Someone always seemed to be sick, infirm, or dying, or believed that he was. Concerning his own health, Eliot chose his words most revealingly. After amply describing an attack of dysentery, with the bloody discharge from the bowels and the extreme discomfort, he concluded: "It is queer how dysentery is my specialty. I shall die of it someday."[56] Eliot specialized not only in his occupation but in his disease.

A professional and even a legal approach to personal hygiene appealed to Eliot, especially as he became increasingly concerned toward the end of his life that alcoholism and venereal disease, "almost always" found closely associated, were destroying "us." "By 'us' I mean the white race, and particularly the American stock."[57] Eliot's ethnocentric fears of "race suicide" were alarming. Educated, white, Protestant Americans, the standard-bearers of civilization, were diminishing in absolute numbers. In 1902, Eliot noted that a selected group of Harvard graduates fell 28 percent below its original number, which meant "that the highly educated part of the American people does not increase the population at all, but on the contrary fails to reproduce itself."[58] The educated class could compen-

55 Letter from Samuel Eliot to C. W. Eliot, September 1, 1849, Harvard University Archives, C. W. Eliot MSS, Box 440.

56 Letter from C. W. Eliot to Mary Eliot, June 13, 1868, loc. cit.

57 Charles William Eliot, A Late Harvest (Boston: The Atlantic Monthly Press, 1924), p. 266.

58 Annual Reports of the President and the Treasurer of Harvard College, 1901–1902 (Cambridge, Mass.: Harvard University, January 31, 1903), pp. 31–32. For statements appearing contemporaneously with

sate for its shrinking size only by asserting the discipline of its superior character over the "undesirable races" in American society. Eliot became the first president of the American Social Hygiene Association, formed by middle-class professionals, to wipe out prostitution and promiscuity. Eliot proposed, for instance, to employ the public-health services to incarcerate prostitutes, and his justification was scientific:

Recent inquiries have demonstrated that more than half of the prostitutes in a modern city, or a rural community, are likely to be feeble-minded women. The effective confinement of feeble-minded women, at least till they are past childbearing, is, therefore, an indispensable part of the restriction of prostitution and the limitation of venereal disease.[59]

If character in America could not be preserved by education, it would be protected by legislation.

Character was the deepest self of the man that bound together the whole of the individual. It made possible the

Eliot's, see R. R. Kuczynski, "The Fecundity of the Native and Foreign Born Population in Massachusetts," *Quarterly Journal of Economics* 16 (November 1901): 1–36; (February 1902): 141–86. "It is probable that the native population cannot hold its own," Kuczynski concluded; "it seems to be dying out." Edward L. Thorndike, "The Decrease in the Size of American Families," *Popular Science Monthly* 63 (May 1903): 64–70. See also Kenneth M. Ludmeer, *Genetics and American Society: A Historical Appraisal* (Baltimore and London: The Johns Hopkins Press, 1972), pp. 7–43; Donald Pickens, *Eugenics and the Progressives* (Nashville: Vanderbilt University Press, 1968); Barbara Miller Solomon, *Ancestors and Immigrants: A Changing New England Tradition* (Cambridge, Mass.: Harvard University Press, 1956), pp. 152–75, 195–209. David M. Kennedy, *Birth Control in America: The Career of Margaret Sanger* (New Haven, Conn., and London: Yale University Press, 1970), pp. 42–44.

[59] Charles W. Eliot, "The Main Points of Attack in the Campaign for Public Health," *American Journal of Public Health* 5 (January 1915): 622; Eliot, *The Contemporary American Conception of Equality Among Men as a Social and Political Ideal*, Phi Beta Kappa Oration at the University of Missouri, June 2, 1909, pp. 19–22. On the movement for social hygiene, see also Egal Feldman, "Prostitution, the Alien Woman and the Progressive Imagination, 1910–1915," *American Quarterly* 29 (Summer 1967): 192–206; John C. Burnham, "The Progressive Era Revolution in American Attitudes Toward Sex," *Journal of American History* 59 (March 1973): 885–908.

self-reliant intellect that could both think irrespective of public approval and exert a supreme effort of human attention to overcome any personal obstacle. The impressiveness of a man's worldly credentials reflected the strength of his inner character, the permanence of his inner continuity, which corresponded to the outer continuity of a career. In the absence of other durable sources of social authority, Mid-Victorians began cultivating the idea of career as a source of confidence for middle-class Americans.

5

※

Careers

"What a tremendous question it is—what shall I be?" twenty-year-old Charles William Eliot wrote to a friend in 1854. The finality of the decision overawed the undecided Brahmin: "When a man answers that question he not only determines his sphere of usefulness in this world, he also decides in what *direction* his own mind shall be developed. The different professions are not different roads converging to the same end; they are different roads, which starting from the same point *diverge* forever, for all we know."[1]

Here lived no mean thought. The calculating Eliot would not take the future for granted. In the emerging industrial society, a decision about a profession would eclipse one's Brahmin origins. If the Brahmins expected to maintain their privileged position on the crest of society, they must necessarily reconsider the reaches of their thought. A decision about a profession involved one's identity, one's self-image, and indeed one's material prospects in the expanding social universe. When it came to his worldly fortunes, the young Eliot was discriminating, a trait he culti-

[1] Letter from C. W. Eliot to Theodore Tebbets, January 29, 1854, Harvard University Archives, C. W. Eliot MSS, Box 440.

vated through the years. "If I join the firm at 39 Milk St. tomorrow, I shall be an entirely different man 50 years hence from what I should have been had I gone into Cooke's [Harvard chemistry] laboratory, instead of the counting room." Eliot was considering the fate of the whole man, his life style and his future, for the next fifty years: "Now it seems to me that very few young men have the requisite data for an intelligent decision of the above question."[2]

At the age of nineteen, Eliot sensed that the social conditions for success in America were changing, and the gentleman merchant and Brahmin businessman types were slipping into the past. The current life of the Brahmin in the counting room was too complacent and comfortable. Did he have a future? Eliot traveled and observed, and he considered alternatives to commerce. Following an excursion in the summer of 1852, he wrote a friend:

One effect of my excursion has been to impress me with the mineral wealth of this country, and the vast resources which the future will unfold and employ; mining engineering will soon become one of the most respectable and useful professions which can engage the attention of American students, and the time is not far distant when we shall have a school of mining in this country to educate men for a profession which is daily becoming more needed and lucrative.[3]

In the long run, professional education could reward the student, both his pocketbook and his personality.

Eliot was making more than a decision about his profession. He was making a decision about his character, about his inner self that would be revealed in the struggles of a career. The crisis of a career decision—in its fullest stature a crisis of identity—deserves a hearing. Again and again the experience was repeated in professional lives in nineteenth-century America.[4] Some persons spoke out, such

---

2 *Ibid.*

3 Letter from C. W. Eliot to Theodore Tebbets, August 30, 1852, *loc. cit.*

4 See R. Jackson Wilson, *In Quest of Community: Social Philosophy in the United States, 1860–1920* (New York: John Wiley & Sons, 1968),

as Ralph Waldo Emerson; Henry James, Sr.; William James; Jane Addams; Charles Horton Cooley; G. Stanley Hall; and Lester Frank Ward. In varying degrees of intensity, most persons suffered in silence.

Young men such as Eliot, Gilman, Folwell, Angell, and White held college degrees, which numbered them among the privileged few in their day. These were no longer boys but often grown men in their twenties, and the practical world sought and would reward their talents. The college degree, the highest academic achievement in America, welcomed them directly into the learned professions or the managerial levels of the commercial world. Eliot's father, for instance, wrote a lengthy letter urging his son to become a merchant rather than a scientist. The former occupation did not wear the individual down through an excess of competition. To the contrary, it established the individual in an agreeable social position with influence, money, and the opportunity to know respectable people. The life of science was too reclusive and insecure, and its social status was dubious.[5]

The crisis of a young man's life, Erik Erikson has written, "may be reached exactly when he half-realizes that he is fatally overcommitted to what he is not."[6] Revealing

pp. 19–20; Bertram Wyatt-Brown, "New Leftists and Abolitionists: A Comparison of American Radical Styles," *Wisconsin Magazine of History* 53 (Summer 1970): 256–68; Silvan S. Tomkins, "The Psychology of Commitment: The Constructive Role of Violence and Suffering for the Individual and his Society," in Martin Duberman, ed., *The Antislavery Vanguard: New Essays on the Abolitionists* (Princeton, N.J.: Princeton University Press, 1965), pp. 270–98; Cushing Strout, "William James and the Twice-Born Sick-Soul," *Daedalus* 97 (1968): 1062–82.

[5] Letter from Samuel Eliot to C. W. Eliot, November 27, 1852, *loc. cit.*

[6] Erik H. Erikson, *Young Man Luther: A Study in Psychoanalysis and History* (New York: W. W. Norton & Company, 1962), p. 43. See also Erikson, *Identity: Youth and Crisis* (New York: W. W. Norton & Company, 1968), pp. 128–35; Kenneth Keniston, *Young Radicals: Notes on Committed Youth* (New York: Harcourt Brace Jovanovich, 1968); Keniston, "Youth: a 'New' Stage of Life," *American Scholar* 39 (Autumn 1970), 631–54; S. N. Eisenstadt, "Archetypical Patterns of Youth," in Erik H. Erikson, ed., *The Challenge of Youth* (Garden City, N.Y.: Anchor Books, Doubleday & Company, 1965), pp. 29–50.

their anxiety about occupational decisions in letters, Folwell, Eliot, and Gilman often confided in the dominant women of their early years. Following his education at Geneva College, Folwell, who returned home during the school year to help with the crops, anxiously wrote his mother concerning his inability to choose an occupation that would bring "success." "I am twenty-seven and most *great* men have achieved their *great deeds* before that age." That was in 1860. Again, the following year: "Dear Mother: Another of my now quite numerous birthdays has come and almost gone. According to the best of my knowledge I am *twenty eight* years old today. *Twenty eight!* And *nothing done.* My education unfinished—no immediate expectation of being 'settled in life'—rather a sorry picture."[7]

The family council, Folwell recalled, deprecated even a college education:

Here some practical business man would break in and say, "You were a foolish young fellow to be thinking so much about books and school and college. If you had had any brains and enterprise, you would have put your extra suit of clothes into a grip and started out to find a job. You might have made something of yourself." But for what seems a mere accident, I might have gone off on some such tangent, got into business, and perhaps made money, though that is doubtful.[8]

But Folwell also emphasized the positive as he asserted himself in letters to his mother. What appeared to be faulty grammar was a dialect which conveyed Folwell's strongest feelings: "Of the millions who have toiled in the world to acquire and perpetuate a name, how few have succeeded! And in most cases it would have been better for them could the world have forgotten them. So then, Mother, it don't pay a man to work for reputation, fame —and what the world calls success. They are not easy to get—and when got—are not worth the getting."[9]

[7] William Watts Folwell, *Autobiography and Letters of a Pioneer of Culture,* ed. Solon J. Buck (Minneapolis: The University of Minnesota Press, 1933), pp. 81, 120.

[8] *Ibid.,* p. 45.

[9] *Ibid.,* p. 81.

In the normal course of studies, Folwell's education might have brought a better-adjusted student to the legal profession. But that work in particular he felt compelled to discredit as "unmanly" and "unworthy":

I have, you know, talked of *law*. Well, I believe I could make myself a good lawyer and succeed in business. But I observe, on the other hand, that if a lawyer becomes refined, elevated, generally learned and *good* he must become so not by virtue of his profession, but in spite of it. The duties and employments of legal life are not of a nature to make a finished, manly and generous character. The objects of a lawyer are to get money and reputation, neither of which are worthy objects for a man who knows any better.[10]

Folwell claimed to know better; at stake in his worldly decision about a career was his character.

The Civil War saved Folwell some agonizing. After serving the Union as a civil engineer, he married and then worked for his father-in-law for several years, accepted a position at Kenyon College as professor of mathematics and civil engineering, and was elected to the presidency of the University of Minnesota in 1869. His decision against entering the law or commence vindicated, he wrote his mother in 1874: "I am sure your children are all better off than those of many of our neighbors. I am not worth any money, but I would not change places with many a millionare. I am very glad that my chief thought and care are not how to get more dollars together."[11]

Career patterns in the mid-nineteenth century were still uncertain as men jumped from profession to profession. Folwell was no exception. Angell practiced as a civil engineer, a journalist and editor, and a professor of modern languages, before becoming a university president. Lax entrance requirements facilitated occupational fluidity even in the established professions. In the Illinois Bar, for instance, Abraham Lincoln was a respected member of the

10 *Ibid.*, p. 82.
11 *Ibid.*, pp. 212–13.

Board of Examiners appointed by the state. Jonathan Birch from Bloomington applied for admission and arranged to be examined in Lincoln's hotel room. He related:

I knocked at the door of his room, and was admitted . . . but I was hardly prepared for the rather unusual sight that met my gaze. Instead of finding my examiner in the midst of books and papers, as I had anticipated, he was partly undressed, and, so far as the meager accommodations of the room permitted, leisurely taking a bath! I shall never forget the queer feeling that came over me as his lank, half-nude figure moved to and fro between me and the window on the opposite side of the room. Motioning me to be seated, he began his interrogatories at once, without looking at me a second time to be sure of the identity of his caller.

Lincoln inquired how long Birch had been studying, then asked him "in a desultory way" to define a contract and answer two or three basic questions:

Beyond these meager inquiries, as I now recall the incident, he asked nothing more. As he continued his toilet, he entertained me with recollections—many of them characteristically vivid and racy—of his early practice and the various incidents and adventures that attended his start in the profession. The whole proceeding was so unusual and queer, if not grotesque, that I was at a loss to determine whether I was really being examined at all or not.

Lincoln then addressed a few lines on paper to Judge Logan, another member of the committee, who gave the candidate the required certificate without any interrogation. Lincoln's note read:

My Dear Judge:—The bearer of this is a young man who thinks he can be a lawyer. Examine him, if you want to. I have done so, and am satisfied. He's a good deal smarter than he looks to be.[12]

12 Albert A. Woldman, *Lawyer Lincoln* (Boston and New York: Houghton Mifflin Company, 1936), pp. 153, 154; James Willard Hurst, *The Growth of American Law: The Law Makers* (Boston: Little Brown and Company, 1950), p. 282. For a description of the processes and controls of the frontier bar in this period, see William R. Johnson, "Education and Professional Life Styles: Law and Medicine in the

Such a system encouraged young men, however unprepossessing but alert, to try their hands at different trades.

Folwell's circumstances were modest compared to the affluent Gilman's and the Brahmin Eliot's, but the experience was similar. Young men of Eliot's Brahmin background and talents were advancing in both the textile mills and the import trade. Success, substance, and fame in the elitist Boston business community, the doors of which would easily open to Eliot, naturally attracted an ambitious, eager young man. Unemployed and with no definite prospect in the middle sixties, Eliot considered but rejected a lucrative offer to be a superintendent at Merrimack mills. The financial arguments "were all on one side," and his mother clearly wished that Eliot would accept the offer.[13] But Eliot was determined. Though unemployed, he would not turn to the business world until he was convinced that he could not make it as an educator. The key word in Eliot's thinking was "investment." In May 1865, Eliot wrote his mother: "I have invested nine years at home and two in Europe in the study of educational matters—I mean to try to get a chance to make my acquired knowledge useful."[14] In April 1865, Eliot had also objected that giving up teaching would "involve a sacrifice of years invested in this profession."

More than a decade earlier, Eliot had made his decision, and it had involved a considerable emotional investment in the future course of a professional life. In 1854 he had written his mother a lengthy letter, the tone of which suggested determination. *"Dear Mother,—*I have chosen the profession of a student and teacher of science, and it is you who should first know my choice, and understand the grounds of my decision. I shall try to write out here the pith of all the thought which I have given to the subject

Nineteenth Century," *History of Education Quarterly* 14 (Summer 1974): 187–92.

13 Letter from C. W. Eliot to Mary Eliot, April 21, 1865; letter from C. W. Eliot to Mr. Crowninshield, May 5, 1865, *loc. cit.*

14 Letter from C. W. Eliot to Mary Eliot, May 6, 1865, *loc. cit.*

for the last year and a half, and to show you the steps which led me to this conclusion."[15] Both the privations and the hazards of academic life were discouraging, a situation aggravated by the economic instability of the 1850s and 1860s. However, Eliot never thought that he was dedicating his life to poverty, or that he was retreating into scholarly solitude. He was calculating on the future importance of science and education, and he held out to his mother the real possibility of fame and success:

What a splendid opening what a magnificent field for young American science! New Colleges springing up everywhere, government expeditions by land and water, mines and factories, all requiring scientific aid, and very few scientific men to meet all this demand. The scientific men of America will make their mark on the page of history within the next fifty years, and the young man who starts now with a determination to be a good teacher and a thorough scholar stands a more than fair chance of becoming distinguished.

"My choice of a profession is made," Eliot declared.[16] But, of course, if science did not work out, there was always the business world; and his mother did not forget the alternative.

Gilman's elder sister "did more . . . at this period when he was seriously deliberating on his future course . . . than anything else to clarify his opinions and bring them to a just conclusion." The son of a wealthy New Haven merchant, Gilman renounced in the 1850s any ambition for wealth and the fame that accompanied it. "For some things I rejoice to find that my notions grow more and more definite," he wrote his sister: "For instance, in the desire to act upon the minds of men, to do my part, even though it may be but little, for the elevation and improvement of such society as my lot may be cast in. It seems to me I care less and less for money and for fame."[17]

[15] Letter from C. W. Eliot to Mary Eliot, March 16, 1854, *loc. cit.*
[16] *Ibid.*
[17] Fabian Franklin, *The Life of Daniel Coit Gilman* (New York: Dodd, Mead & Company, 1910), pp. 27, 30.

In the light of his comfortable background, Gilman might have been speaking gratuitously in his rejection of "money." However, he might also have been committing himself to a decision about a career that the family would not receive well. Writing home from St. Petersburg in 1854, young Gilman revealed what was on his mind: the future. "Every year makes me feel that I must draw nearer to a point. When I go home to America I must have some definite notions. Day and night I think of that time, and in all I see and do I am planning for being useful at home."[18]

Bright, educated, and privileged sons who clung to freedom in Europe gave an instance of the anxiety accompanying occupational decisions. Americans journeyed to the Continent as part of their larger American education. Europe could mean a spiritual limbo away from home when social expectations and obligations there pressured too greatly.

"We came out to Europe to learn what man can,—what is the uttermost which social man has yet done," Emerson wrote during his first visit in 1833, and disturbed by his own vocational crisis. Detached from the oppressive influence of home, he wished to gain a sense of proportion: "Perhaps the most satisfactory and most valuable impressions are those which come to each individual casually and in moments when he is not on the hunt for wonders."[19]

Porter and McCosh, like Emerson, traveled in the 1830s. White, Gilman, Eliot, Angell, and Folwell traveled in the 1850s and 1860s. All reflected more than they studied. Only Porter appeared to have dedicated himself to books.[20]

18 *Ibid.*, p. 28.

19 *The Journals of Ralph Waldo Emerson,* ed. William Waldo Emerson and Waldo Emerson Forbes, 10 vols. (Boston: Houghton Mifflin Company, 1903–4), 3:123. On Emerson's occupational crisis see Henry Nash Smith, "Emerson's Problem of Vocation—A Note on 'The American Scholar,'" *New England Quarterly* 12 (March–December 1939): 52–67; Ralph L. Rusk, *The Life of Ralph Waldo Emerson* (New York: Columbia University Press, 1949), pp. 151–67.

20 Noah Porter, "The American Student in Germany," *New Englander* 15 (November 1857): 574–602.

None acquired degrees, none pursued scholarship, none attached himself to a great man or mentor. The classroom bored Folwell, whose German was only "sufficient," and he later remembered the "indescribably bad air of the lecture rooms, where the attendance was large."[21] White's impression of Leopold Von Ranke was irreverent. On Tuesday, October 30, 1855, he jotted in his diary:

> To the usual lectures and at noon to Ranke's, more to see the "great gun" of the university than to understand or even hear him. Matter of lecture was no doubt good, but manner of delivery was comically atrocious. The great historian during most of his hour lay sprawled out in his chair looking upwards and talking to himself, now quickly, now slowly, now loud, now soft! Grinning and scrowling and not seeming to be aware of the presence of anybody.[22]

Angell, Eliot, and Gilman mentioned little about studies; like McCosh, they were more concerned with observing European school systems, talking, touring, and, when possible, reading.[23]

Andrew Dickson White perhaps best expressed the motive for going abroad: to extend those precious years of irresponsibility. As a robust adolescent, White had early been attracted to "hero worship," to admiring men who "do things." In his late teens, however, his "dream of becoming a locomotive-driver engineer faded, and while in college I speculated not a little as to what, after all, should be my profession." Neither the clergy nor medicine appealed, and politics repelled him "from an early period": "After my first sight of Washington in its shabby, sleazy, dirty, unkempt condition under the old slave oligarchy, political

---

21 Folwell, *Autobiography and Letters*, pp. 94–95.

22 *The Diaries of Andrew D. White*, ed. Robert Morris Ogden (Ithaca, N.Y.: Cornell University Press, 1959), p. 100.

23 James McCosh, "Notes on a Tour in Germany: Three Sketches, Present State of Philosophy, State of Theological Teaching, Lessons to be Gathered, 1859," in *Miscellaneous Publications* (Princeton University Library), 1:13–16.

life became absolutely repugnant to my tastes and desires."
The family urged White to enter its successful business.
He resisted and went off to Europe. "I shall study for no
degree," he wrote his mother, "[I] shall be perfectly free
and shall, in fact, only settle down and read a little and
study less, in times when extreme heat or cold render
travelling irksome to me. You must not think that I have
any intention of entering another fixed college course. I
have learned to love my liberty too well for that."[24]

It was in Europe that some of nineteenth-century America's most significant academic careers were decided. There
men often resolved finally that the expectations of their
fathers would not dominate their lives. The future president
of Clark University, G. Stanley Hall, for instance, would
not be a clergyman, the occupation his farm-bound parents
wished him to pursue. "Now Stanley," his mother wrote
him, "wherein is the great benefit of being a Ph.D. I think
a *preacher* should be a D.D. Just *what is* a Doctor of
Philosophy? and wherein would it give you *credit, influence,* or usefulness?"[25] After graduation from Williams
College, Hall went to Europe to avoid an occupation that
would have left him "out of place, a misfit, restless and
unhappy." So began "what might be called my long apprenticeship of fourteen years since graduation, during
much of which I had been very uncertain of my future."
After general studies in Germany, he returned home in
1871 and "passed through a period of acute discouragement for I was grievously in debt." For the next five years,
the bachelor Hall socialized with the educated elite, while
he moved through a number of temporary positions, both
tutorial and teaching. In 1876 he returned to Europe with
"a very definite purpose—to study experimental or physiological psychology with Wundt at Leipzig." He did not

24 *Autobiography of Andrew Dickson White,* 2 vols. (New York:
The Century Company, 1905) 1:253; *White Diaries,* p. 63.

25 Dorothy Ross, *G. Stanley Hall: The Psychologist as Prophet* (Chicago and London: University of Chicago Press, 1972), p. 41.

plan to take a degree, however, and he remained unsettled. Decisions were pending. "As my second stay abroad drew to a close and I had no prospects of a position I became, again, very anxious about my future, thought much of studying medicine and entering upon the practice of that profession, and finally decided that neither psychology nor philosophy would ever make bread and that the most promising line of work would be to study the applications of psychology to education."[26] The sobering alternative, "the dread one"—of going back to the farm—loomed before Hall. This irrational fear would continuously check his most rebellious and socialistic impulses.

As a source of individual discipline and isolation in a mobile society, the anxiety of returning (except in nostalgia) to the community of the past, one's home and origins, has been inestimable. "Safety first," became Hall's motto for future decisions concerning his career. He returned to America, "again in the depths because of debt and with no prospects, took a small flat on the edge of Somerville [Massachusetts] . . . and waited, hoped, and worked."[27]

In 1870, William Graham Sumner summarized the complaint of the aspiring professional academic: "There is no such thing yet at Yale as an academical *career*. There is no course marked out for a man who feels called to this work, and desires to pursue it." Speaking from personal experience, Sumner complained that the individual arrived at a professor's chair by taking an indirect route through the pulpit. Americans like Sumner were compelled

[to] go into the pulpit, engage in parish work, cultivate the homiletical faculties, and form the habits of clergymen, and then are elected professors, and have to form new habits, cultivate other faculties, and train themselves to other pursuits than those into which their lives have already hardened.

[26] G. Stanley Hall, *Life and Confessions of a Psychologist* (New York: D. Appleton and Company, 1923), pp. 183, 226, 196, 204, 215.
[27] *Ibid.*, p. 216.

Why such waste? Because, as Sumner said, "the pulpit is a career," and academic life had not yet graduated to the new idea.[28]

THE NEW COURSE

The word *career* derives from forms meaning "carry." The original definitions of *career* all referred to rapid and continuous action, movement, and procedure. For instance, an 1819 American edition of Samuel Johnson's eighteenth-century *Dictionary of the English Language* listed the following items: "1. The ground on which a race is run; the length of a course. 2. A course, a race. 3. Height of speed; swift motion. 4. Course of action; uninterrupted procedure." The most common usage of the word related to horse racing and falconry. As the nineteenth century progressed, however, the meaning of *career* took on a new dimension, cultural rather than physical, abstract rather than visual. The *Oxford English Dictionary* dated as 1803 the first example of the following usage: "A person's course or progress through life (or a distinct portion of life) so of a nation, party, etc. A profession affording opportunities of advancement." But it was not until midcentury that *Oxford* found an example of a person actively being told to "go and make a career for himself." The usage of the word was maturing. In American English by the late nineteenth century, to make the career meant to make a success, to become famous. The 1893 edition of the *Funk and Wagnalls* dictionary in America added the following definitions of *career* to the familiar ones: "1. A complete course or progress extending through the life or a portion of it, especially when abounding in remarkable actions or incidents, or when publicly conspicuous: said of persons, political

28 [William Graham Sumner], "The 'Ways and Means' For our Colleges," *Nation* 11 (September 8, 1870): 152.

parties, nations, etc. 2. A course of business activity, or enterprise: especially, a course of professional life or employment, that offers advancement or honor."

When speaking of occupational activities in the new usage of *career,* an individual no longer confined himself to the description of a random series of jobs, projects, or businesses which provided a livelihood. The individual could now speak of a larger and more absorbing experience —a career: a pre-established total pattern of organized professional activity, with upward movement through recognized preparatory stages, and advancement based on merit and bearing honor. By the late nineteenth century, *The Century Dictionary* and *Funk and Wagnalls* were acknowledging a new social concept, and they were citing examples of the new use of the word by such contemporary writers as Herbert Spencer and James Bryce.[29]

The new notion of career was striking for its totality and self-sufficiency. The new individual professional life had gained both an inward coherence and self-regulating standards that separated and defined it independently of the general community. The inner intensity of the new life oriented toward a career stood in contrast to that of the older learned professional life of the eighteenth and early nineteenth centuries. In the earlier period such external attributes of gentlemanly behavior as benevolence, duty, virtue, and manners circumscribed the professional experience. Competence, knowledge, and preparation were less important in evaluating the skills of the professional than were dedication to the community, sincerity, trust, permanence, honorable reputation, and righteous behavior. The qualifying credentials of the learned professional were honesty, decency, and civility. Hence, he did not think of a professional life in terms of ascending stages, each prepa-

29 The 1893 edition of *Funk and Wagnalls,* for instance, cited the following example from Bryce: " 'It is easier for women to find a *career* [in America], to obtain remunerative work of an intellectual as of a commercial or mechanical kind, than in any part of Europe,' *American Commonwealth* vol. II, Ch. 105, p. 585 [MACM.'88]".

ratory in training for the next, but as a series of good works or public projects, performed within a familiar and deferential society which heaped respectability on its first citizens.

In order to witness how the idea of community held the more specialized idea of career at bay, one need only turn to a well-known example of mobility in the eighteenth century, Ben Franklin. Despite his many occupations—printer, publicist, postmaster, scientist, diplomat, statesman—Franklin thought of his professional activities as a linear series of projects and good works. The end was the welfare of the public, which included Franklin's own "modest" return of Affluence, Reputation, and Felicity. In Franklin's mind, no structured or graduated career pattern, culminating in a senior professional stage associated with the height of accomplishment, knowledge, maturity, and recognition imposed itself on his life. Significantly, he began the *Autobiography* by writing his own epitaph, which revealed the man's self-identity. Who was Ben Franklin? For posterity he wished to project the image of his original vocation—printer. Here had lived the dutiful and common servant of the local community. Moreover, Franklin did not conclude the *Autobiography* by describing his acclaimed successes as a cosmopolitan scientist, diplomat, and statesman. He recounted the many and random community improvement projects in which he participated and took pride. The *Autobiography* was intended to advise youth, and Franklin's improvement projects testified to both a successful public life and a good character.[30]

A review of the ministry, the most admired and sought after of the learned professions, documents the changes that became noticeable within the first generation of the

[30] See John William Ward, " 'Who was Benjamin Franklin?'," *The American Scholar* 32 (Autumn 1963): 541–53. On Franklin as autobiographer see Robert F. Sayre, *The Examined Self: Benjamin Franklin, Henry Adams, Henry James* (Princeton, N.J.: Princeton University Press, 1964), pp. 3–43; Daniel B. Shea, Jr., *Spiritual Autobiography in Early America* (Princeton, N.J.: Princeton University Press, 1968), pp. 234–48.

nineteenth century. By the 1820s, the previous century's notion of "permanency" in the ministry had been seriously eroded in the expanding national society. The Lord's "calling" had committed His servant to perform his duties in a single congregation and community for a lifetime. But the meaning of an organic ministry, slowly maturing in intimate and familiar surroundings in which social order was paramount, was disappearing.[31] The profession of the ministry had entered a competitive society in which unrestrained individual self-determination undermined traditional life styles. No longer did Americans feel the restrictions imposed by a "calling" in which dependent man subordinated himself to the summons of an autonomous God who had determined the station in which every man could work most diligently for the public good and avoid idleness.[32]

Individual choice in a "calling" had never really been a choice at all. Few vocational alternatives presented themselves in a colonial society in which most people farmed.

[31] See Daniel H. Calhoun, *Professional Lives in America: Structure and Aspiration, 1750–1850* (Cambridge, Mass.: Harvard University Press, 1965), pp. 88–177.

[32] The classic source for the definition of "calling" was William Perkins, "A treatise of the Vocations or Callings of Men with the Sorts and Kinds of Them and the Right Use Thereof," *The Works of . . . Mr. William Perkins*, 3 vols. (London: John Legatt, 1626), 1:747–79. On the importance of the concept in America, see J. E. Crowley, *This Sheba, Self: The Conceptualization of Economic Life in Eighteenth-Century America* (Baltimore and London: The Johns Hopkins University Press), pp. 50–75; Stephen Foster, *Their Solitary Way: The Puritan Social Ethic in the First Century of Settlement in New England* (New Haven, Conn., and London: Yale University Press, 1971), pp. 99–103; Edmund S. Morgan, *The Puritan Family: Religion and Domestic Relations in Seventeenth-Century New England*, rev. (New York: Harper & Row, Publishers, 1966), pp. 66–79; James Axtell, *The School Upon a Hill: Education and Society in Colonial New England* (New Haven, Conn., and London: Yale University Press, 1974), pp. 100–101, T. H. Breen, *The Character of the Good Ruler: A Study of Puritan Political Ideas in New England, 1630–1730* (New York: W. W. Norton & Company, 1974), pp. 6–7. See also Michael Walzer, *The Revolution of the Saints: A Study in the Origins of Radical Politics* (New York: Atheneum, 1969), pp. 210–19.

The professional class committed its children at a young age to early apprenticeships or college education, which most people, including the youth concerned, presumed would make entrance into the occupation selected by the parent practically irreversible. However, the fluid environment of the nineteenth century made it possible for an ambitious young man with a will of his own to decline God's invitation in a calling, put his own feelings before social duty, and find easier access than ever before to a growing array of professions, including a number of new semi-public professions. A former minister himself, Emerson illustrated the case. With considerable wit and personal dismay, he described *"The New Professions:* The phrenologist; the railroad man; the landscape gardener; the lecturer; the sorcerer, rapper, mesmeriser, medium; the daguerreotypist. *Proposed:* The Naturalist, and the Social Undertaker."[33]

Confronted by both irreverence and competition, a traditional profession like the ministry came under intense pressures to approve of some internal changes. In part, the sociology of the profession played a role. Supported by scholarships and professional charity, a first generation of poor boys from the New England hills, displaced from family farms, began entering the ministry in the first quarter of the nineteenth century.[34] And these men began rejecting the social intimacy and family dominance of the older guild. There was an unprecedented element of individual effort and even drudgery in the new vision, which the older generation tended to deplore as corrupt, degen-

[33] *Emerson Journals,* 8:574.
[34] See David F. Allmendinger, Jr., *Paupers and Scholars: The Transformation of Student Life in Nineteenth-Century New England* (New York: St. Martin's Press, 1975), pp. 64–78; Lois Kimball Mathews, *The Expansion of New England: The Spread of New England Settlement and Institutions to the Mississippi River, 1620–1865* (Boston and New York: Houghton Mifflin Company, 1909), pp. 139ff. Refer to Chapter 1, n. 22, of the present text and the implications for crowding in New England in Kenneth Lockridge, "Land Population and the Evolution of New England Society," Chapter 1, n. 12 above.

erate, and materialistic. New expectations displayed themselves in a new style. In a social environment now offering vocational alternatives, young men could criticize, calculate, envision a ladder of advancement, and act with some measure of impunity toward their less flexible elders. Above all, young men could begin thinking in vertical rather than horizontal imagery. They meant, very literally, to move *up* and away.

The new minister thought more in terms of a career which he actively made than a "calling" into which he had been summoned. Lacking either a sense of permanency or commitment to a single congregation, the ambitious young minister now could express his concern with a rising salary. He could attend to the outward trappings of growing success, and the need to please laymen who were as ambitious, irritable, and status-conscious as himself. In the nineteenth-century world of movement, the social motives of the minister did not always differ greatly from the social motives of his congregation. Far from setting an elevated moral example of clerical detachment, the minister often appeared to be an entrepreneur, privately negotiating the contractual terms of a successful career as he moved upward from congregation to congregation. In the course of an individual's career, every congregation now became a conquest, a stepping-stone to the next challenge.

The new professional man often had nowhere to return, nothing to fall back upon except his own self-reliance and his own will. He balked at "inability," he deplored enervation and drift, he expected "commitment," and he accentuated "decision." He respected the trained capacity of his own mind to organize and control his surroundings. He believed in mental concentration and the spontaneous release of emotional energy.[35] He no longer heard William Perkins's classic definition of a calling, "a certain kind of life, ordained and imposed on man by God for the com-

[35] See Perry Miller, *The Life of the Mind in America: From the Revolution to the Civil War* (New York: Harcourt Brace & World, 1965), pp. 3–95.

mon good.''[36] Describing the events of the twenty years
following 1820, Emerson recalled that,

there was a new consciousness. . . . The young men were born
with knives in their brain, a tendency to introversion, self-
dissection, anatomizing of motives. . . . The key to the period
appeared to be that the mind had become aware of itself. . . . It
is the age of severance, of dissociation, of freedom, of analysis, of
detachment. Every man for himself. . . . People grow philosophical about native land and parents and relations. There is an universal resistance to ties and ligaments once supposed essential to
civil society.[37]

Perhaps close to thirty years old when he entered a profession, after having tasted life and rejected a series of pursuits; mature, competitive, and calculating about his prospects; believing in his expectations—the new type of professional man personally struggled to create his career, he
did not inherit it. He rejected the social forms and the
public conviviality associated with the shallow intellect of
the older learned professions.

A profession no longer circumscribed a man, confining
him to a preestablished station in life, including a calling
toward which sympathetic parents guided him. A man
now actively chose his profession, perhaps in defiance of
parents and friends. The world of movement and expectation focused on the spirited individual, his specialized
nature, his self-discipline, and the continuity of his rise
rather than his humility, his self-subordination to the social
order, and his dependence upon God's will. In the steps of
a career, an individual progressively discovered his potential, and his sense of worldly power rose accordingly. Professionals often made their livelihood from the misfortune
of people who in distress sought out the self-possessed man
—one who appeared to be a trustworthy character and in
whom confidence could be placed. To the layman, a pro-

---

[36] Perkins, *Works*, 1:750.
[37] "Life and Letters in New England," in *The Complete Works of Ralph Waldo Emerson*, 12 vols. (Boston: Houghton Mifflin Company, 1903–4), 10, *Lectures and Biographical Sketches*, 329, 326–27.

fessional character could be taken as a measure of competency in a career, as Charles William Eliot indicated when he wrote about his wife's ill health in 1867: "The problem is to find the most skillful man and the most trustworthy man at the same time. What you want is confidence in the physicians, and that is just what it is difficult for me to have."[38]

PROFESSIONAL CLAIMS ON ANTEBELLUM SOCIETY

Historians are only beginning to realize the extent to which our modern notions of career and profession were first becoming a recognizable experience in mid-nineteenth-century America. And that experience generally corresponded in time to the coming of age and the vocational decisions of such men as Eliot, White, Gilman, and Folwell—a generation of men born in the 1830s.

In 1849, Henry N. Day delivered an address specifically entitled *The Professions* at the medical school of Western Reserve College in Cleveland. Day left no doubt in the mind of a listener about the direction in which American life must head. "Civilized life," he reasoned, was founded on the "mutual dependence of men. Their social nature implies this dependence." And which social functions were "most important, most necessary. We find, in fact, that they are the professional tendencies." Everywhere incompetence threatened and endangered modern society, and Day argued that in order to be effective the public must view "professional life" as "in its very essence distinct" from the life of the "layman." The concept of the professional was perceived to be independent and autonomous. "Professional claims on society," according to Day, "differ in their essential nature from the claims" of everyone else, and he criticized the public for being too "slow to recognize its de-

[38] Letter from C. W. Eliot to Mary Eliot, July, 1867, *loc. cit.*

pendence" on professional services, and consequently for being "ungrateful."[39]

When Day spoke, professional claims were still in their infancy, but they were growing rapidly in the later 1840s and the 1850s. America's new social institutions were already revealing a pattern. The emergence of the school bureaucracy and the National Teachers' Association (renamed the National Educational Association in 1870) provided an instance of just how closely opportunity for the middle-class person seeking a career was to be tied to exercising social control over "undisciplined" lower-class persons. Elementary-school teachers enhanced their own professional positions at the same time that they cultivated in children the social restraint, patriotism, and respect for authority which families were failing to provide, especially lower-class rural and urban-immigrant families.[40]

In the new professions, social reform that, from the point of view of an ambitious middle class, liberated opportunities for the individual often accompanied social rehabilitation that, from the point of view of the lower class, confined people in close spaces, dictated private taste and morality, and regulated a person's time. In the 1840s, for instance, a professional consciousness began to appear

[39] Henry N. Day, *The Professions: An Address Delivered at the Commencement of the Medical Department of Western Reserve College* (Hudson, Ohio: The Observer Office, 1849), pp. 4, 5, 22.

[40] See Horace Mann, "Report for 1847: The Power of Common Schools to Redeem the State from Social Vices and Crimes," in *Annual Reports on Education* (Boston: Horace B. Fuller, 1868), pp. 559–639; Mann, *Lectures on Education* (Boston: Lemuel N. Ide, 1850), pp. 63–113, 117–62; Edward D. Mansfield, *American Education, Its Principles and Elements* (New York: A. S. Barnes & Co., 1851), pp. 48–49, 55–62; J. N. McJilton, "The National Importance of the Teacher's Profession," *Journal of the Proceedings of the Third Annual Meeting of the National Teachers' Association* (Georgetown: Waters and Hunt, Printers, 1861), 72. See also Michael B. Katz, *The Irony of Early School Reform: Educational Innovation in Mid-Nineteenth Century Massachusetts* (Cambridge, Mass.: Harvard University Press, 1968); Stanley K. Schultz, *The Culture Factory: Boston Public Schools, 1789–1860* (New York: Oxford University Press, 1973); and for the following generation, Marvin Lazerson, *Origins of the Urban School: Public Education in Massachusetts, 1870–1915* (Cambridge, Mass.: Harvard University Press, 1971).

among the administrators of America's asylums and prisons, institutions serving to incarcerate the increasing number of deviants in the American population.[41] Within this setting, professional psychiatry organized itself by founding in 1844 the Association of Medical Superintendents of American Institutions for the Insane, later to become the American Psychiatric Association.[42] In a significant body of literature, psychiatrists attempted to find natural explanations for mental illness, to justify its isolation and treatment, and write treatises on model institutions such as Thomas S. Kirkbride's, *On the Construction, Organization, and General Arrangements of Hospitals for the Insane* (1854). Insanity was a disease, Kirkbride wrote, "from which no age, sex, class, or profession in life can claim exemption, and . . . nowhere does it fail to make itself recognized as the great leveller of all the artificial distinctions of society."[43]

[41] On the rise of the asylum in America, see W. David Lewis, *From Newgate to Dannemora: The Rise of the Penitentiary in New York, 1796–1848* (Ithaca, N.Y.: Cornell University Press, 1965); David J. Rothman, *The Discovery of the Asylum: Social Order and Disorder in the New Republic* (Boston: Little, Brown and Company, 1971). See also Robert S. Pickett, *House of Refuge: Origins of Juvenile Reform in New York State, 1815–1857* (Syracuse, N.Y.: Syracuse University Press, 1969); James Leiby, *Charity and Corrections in New Jersey* (New Brunswick, N.J.: Rutgers University Press, 1967).

[42] The Association published the first volume of the *American Journal of Insanity* in July, 1844. In 1892, the Association reorganized itself into the American Medico-Psychological Association, which changed its name in 1921 to the American Psychiatric Association. The early consciousness of a profession was perhaps indicated by Isaac Ray's substantial book appearing in 1838 which set out legal definitions of insanity: *A Treatise on the Medical Jurisprudence of Insanity* (Boston: Charles C. Little and James Brown, 1838). For a discussion of this theme and its function in the professional consciousness of psychiatry, see Charles E. Rosenberg, *The Trial of Assassin Guiteau: Psychiatry and Law in the Gilded Age* (Chicago and London: The University of Chicago Press, 1968).

[43] Thomas S. Kirkbride, *On the Construction, Organization, and General Arrangements of Hospitals for the Insane; with Some Remarks on Insanity and its Treatment*, 2d ed., rev. (Philadelphia: J. B. Lippincott & Co., 1880), p. 22. In 1855, Edward Jarvis published his famous report commissioned by the Massachusetts legislature to help decide policy at the Worcester asylum: [Levi Lincoln, Edward Jarvis, Increase Sumner], *Report on Insanity and Idiocy in Massachusetts, by the Com-*

Universal problems in America's open society called forth professional responses. Indeed, as the asylums filled up with aliens, victims of impoverished and unstable lives, psychiatrists with their middle-class values confusedly employed medical descriptions of the etiology of lunacy to diagnose and detain "criminal" types with their lower-class values.[44]

By the later 1840s, the American interest in careers already reflected the interplay of two divergent themes: reform and rehabilitation. On the one hand, middle-class Americans expressed the reformer's desire to improve both the physical and spiritual quality of life for the average man, to break the historical trend toward the monopoly of knowledge and services by an exclusive and privileged class, and to establish public confidence in the republic by universalizing the standards for achievement in order to measure men in terms of merit. As one idealistic minister fervently stated his social faith in 1841:

In looking at our age I am struck immediately with one commanding characteristic, and that is, the tendency in all its movements to expansion, to diffusion, to universality. . . . This tendency is directly opposed to the spirit of exclusiveness, restriction, narrowness, monopoly, which has prevailed in past ages. Human action is now freer, more unconfined. All goods, advantages, helps, are more open to all. . . . That the world was made for all, and not for a few; that society is to care for all; that no human being

mission on Lunacy, Under Resolve of the Legislature of 1854 (Boston: William White, Printer to the State, 1855).

44 On the history of the psychiatric profession in nineteenth-century America, see Gerald N. Grob, *Mental Institutions in America* (New York: The Free Press, 1973); Grob, *The State and the Mentally Ill: A History of the Worcester State Hospital in Massachusetts, 1830–1920* (Chapel Hill: University of North Carolina Press, 1966); Ruth B. Caplan, *Psychiatry and the Community in Nineteenth-Century America: The Recurring Concern with the Environment in the Prevention and Treatment of Mental Illness* (New York: Basic Books, 1969); Norman Dain, *Concepts of Insanity in the United States, 1789–1865* (New Brunswick, N.J.: Rutgers University Press, 1964). See also George Rosen, *Madness in Society: Chapters in the Historical Sociology of Mental Illness* (Chicago and London: University of Chicago Press, 1968), pp. 172–225.

shall perish but through his own fault; that the great end of government is to spread a shield over the rights of all,—these propositions are growing into axioms.[45]

The new professions would be open. On the other hand, middle-class Americans were frightened by the excessive openness of American society, the intemperate habits of the immigrants, the casual display of erotic passions, the fierce competitiveness of men in the pursuit of material wealth, and the failure of moral restraint. Expansiveness had its perils. And many new professionals proposed to stabilize and control Americans by scientifically prescribing the rule of nature's law, by treating licentious behavior as abnormal and diseased, and rehabilitating virtue in men.

The interplay of both the reformer's idealism and the conservative's fear was displayed, for instance, in the early public-health movement, which received its initial professional impulse in the 1840s. Terrifying epidemics, conspicuously poor sanitation facilities, and sheer filth in the cities awakened people to a personal concern about disease and death.[46] In Boston late in 1839, the American Statistical Association was founded with the conscious purpose of collecting and interpreting vital statistics in a professional manner; "every rational reform must be founded on thorough knowledge," its constitution read.[47] In 1845, the first

[45] William E. Channing, "The Present Age," in *The Works of William E. Channing* (Boston: American Unitarian Association, 1885), pp. 159–60.

[46] See Charles E. Rosenberg, *The Cholera Years: The United States in 1832, 1849, 1866* (Chicago: University of Chicago Press, 1962), pp. 101–72; Howard D. Kramer, "The Beginnings of the Public Health Movement in the United States," *Bulletin of the History of Medicine* 21 (1947): 352–76; Barbara Gutmann Rosenkrantz, *Public Health and the State: Changing Views in Massachusetts, 1842–1936* (Cambridge, Mass.: Harvard University Press, 1972), pp. 8–36.

[47] Cited in Robert C. David, "Social Research in America Before the Civil War," *Journal of the History of the Behavioral Sciences* 8 (January 1972): 74. See the extensive statistics on towns, population, and taxation in Massachusetts in *Collections of the American Statistical Association*, vol. 1 (Boston: T. R. Marvin, 1847). See also Robert Gutman, "Birth and Death Registration in Massachusetts: The Inauguration of a Modern System, 1800–1849," *The Milbank Memorial Fund*

serious study of health problems in the city of New York was undertaken; and in 1849 the two-year-old American Medical Association investigated housing and health in New York, among other cities. The situation was serious.[48] In 1842, Massachusetts enacted a compulsory registration law, which, even despite imperfect enforcement, demonstrated that the rise in mortality rates was alarming. By midcentury, the rates in eastern American cities had begun to surpass the notorious London, and life expectancy in Boston and other American cities was lower than in London.[49]

In these years, public health began assuming the image of a profession. In 1846, Lemuel Shattuck reported to the Boston City Council that statistically "an increase in the number and density of population increases the liability to disease," and Shattuck concluded that the putrid conditions in which immigrants lived, stemming from their extravagant and

Quarterly 36 (October 1958): 373–402; John Koren, "The American Statistical Association, 1839–1914," in Koren, ed., *The History of Statistics: Their Development and Progress in Many Countries* (New York: Published for the American Statistical Association by The Macmillan Company, 1918), pp. 3–14.

[48] See John H. Griscom, *The Sanitary Condition of the Laboring Population of New York; with Suggestions for its Improvement* (New York: Harper and Brothers, 1845); Griscom, *The Uses and Abuses of Air: Showing its Influence in Sustaining Life, and Producing Disease; with Remarks on the Ventilation of Houses* (New York: J. S. Redfield, Clinton Hall, 1850). See also Carroll Smith-Rosenberg, *Religion and the Rise of the American City: The New York City Mission Movement, 1812–1870* (Ithaca, N.Y., and London: Cornell University Press, 1971), pp. 262–63. James H. Cassedy, "The Roots of American Sanitary Reform 1843–47: Seven Letters from John H. Griscom to Lemuel Shattuck," *Journal of the History of Medicine and Allied Sciences* 30 (April 1975): 136–47.

[49] Lemuel Shattuck, *Bills of Mortality, 1810–1849, City of Boston; with an Essay on the Vital Statistics of Boston from 1810 to 1841* (Boston: Printed for the Registry Department, 1893), pp. xi–xliii, 60–84. In 1850, life expectancy in Massachusetts at birth was 38.3 years for a male and 40.5 years for a female: *Historical Statistics of the United States: Colonial Times to 1957: A Statistical Abstract Supplement* (Washington, D.C.: U.S. Department of Commerce, Bureau of the Census, 1960), Series B 76–91, p. 24. See Rosenkrantz, *Public Health and the State*, pp. 8–36; Kramer, "Beginnings of the Public Health Movement," 358.

dirty habits, threatened the well-being of the entire community.[50] Physical health, as Shattuck defined it, was associated with clean living, self-control, and moral integrity. Rather than depend indiscriminately on voluntary help to perform the vital work of public health, Shattuck proposed that it be delegated to full-time, trained, and well-paid local "sanitarians." Moreover, he suggested that sanitary professorships be established in American colleges for the reason that "the science of preserving health and preventing disease should be taught as one of the most important sciences."[51]

In fact, the first really successful efforts at the professionalization of American life often waited until the later 1860s and the 1870s, in part because the events and the issues of the Civil War dominated the attention of men, absorbing their energies and wealth, in the decade of the 1850s. Nevertheless, in the antebellum years the idea of career and the possibilities of the culture of professionalism quietly influenced the vocational decisions of such college graduates as the presidents. What was evident to young men at the time was not the size but the novelty of the changes taking place in American society. Patience was required.

In the law, for instance, closed guilds lost their grip on the professional man as he began branching out into commercial and corporate practice. Banks, railroads, and industry increasingly hired lawyers away from the courtroom and the office. The growing number of partnerships, legal specializations, advertisements, and business retainers re-

[50] Lemuel Shattuck, *Report to the Committee of the City Council, Appointed to Obtain the Census of Boston for the year 1845, Embracing Collateral Facts and Statistical Researches, Illustrating the History and Condition of the Population, and their Means of Progress and Prosperity* (Boston: John H. Eastburn, City Printer, 1846), p. 176. Rosenkrantz, *Public Health and the State,* p. 19.

[51] [Lemuel Shattuck], *Report of a General Plan for the Promotion of Public and Personal Health, Devised, Prepared and Recommended by the Commissioners Appointed Under a Resolve of the Legislature of Massachusetts, Relating to a Sanitary Survey of the State* (Boston: Dutton & Wentworth, State Printers, 1850), p. 229.

flected the new realities, as did an emerging pattern of social recruitment in the profession. Until the 1830s, the
lawyer class in a state like Massachusetts and a city like
Philadelphia tended to be closely restricted and built on a
system of personal alliances including marriage, paternal
occupations, an extended apprenticeship, a college education, and economic means. An exclusive guild controlled
the local bar, and it easily prevented outsiders from qualifying for membership.[52]

Ironically, as the legal profession became more important
to the economy and politics of the nation in the second
quarter of the nineteenth century, it grew increasingly out
of touch with the sentiments of the society. Consequently,
in the 1830s the states, with the sanction of the public, began responding to the long-standing grievances against the
arrogance of the learned profession by removing the power
of certification from the local jurisdictions and investing
it in a representative of the state government itself.[53] By
1840 the states had ousted the guild-oriented bar from control of examinations in all of New England except Connecticut. The homogeneity of the older elite group dis-

[52] See Gerard W. Gawalt, "Sources of Anti-Lawyer Sentiment in
Massachusetts, 1740–1840," *The American Journal of Legal History* 14
(October 1970): 283–307; Gary Nash, "The Philadelphia Bench and
Bar, 1800–1861," *Comparative Studies in Society and History* 7 (Janu-
ary 1965): 203–20. Tocqueville observed that lawyers were more aristo-
cratic than any other group in America, *Democracy in America*, 2
vols. (New York: Alfred A. Knopf, 1963), 1:272–80; see also Capt.
Marryat, *A Diary in America, with Remarks on its Institutions*, 3 vols.
(London: Longman, Orme, Brown, Green, & Longmans, 1839), 3:192.
Descriptions of the legal profession in eighteenth-century America are
also found in John M. Murrin, "The Legal Transformation: The
Bench and Bar in Eighteenth-Century Massachusetts," in Stanley N.
Katz, ed., *Colonial America: Essays in Politics and Social Development*
(Boston: Little, Brown and Company, 1971), pp. 415–49; Milton M.
Klein, "The Rise of the New York Bar: The Legal Career of William
Livingston," *William and Mary Quarterly*, 3d ser., 15 (July 1958):
334–58.

[53] On public animosity toward the legal profession, see Charles Warren, *A History of the American Bar* (Boston: Little, Brown and Company, 1911), pp. 223–24. Perry Miller centers on the intellectual elitism
of the early profession: *Life of the Mind in America*, pp. 117–55.

solved as white, Protestant, middle-class sons from families of small businessmen, clerks, tradesmen, and artisans began entering the profession in significant numbers.[54]

Formal standards for admission to the bar were lowered in 1830–60. Under the new circumstances, the discipline of a deferential apprenticeship system was relaxed, relatively fewer lawyers held a liberal-arts college diploma, and several states began requiring from candidates only a good moral character and a fee.[55] Jealous of their disappearing prerogatives and the loss of a graded occupation, conservative members of a frightened establishment accused the barbarian invader of causing social anarchy, decay, and demoralization. Nevertheless, these compromised voices were unable to reverse the process. They served only to make the new and less restrictive bar more conscious of the importance of cultivating a new professional image in the generation before the Civil War.

In law magazines and public notices, lawyers began emphasizing that they were industrious and persevering craftsmen, persons of common origin whose systematic knowledge of the law as a rational science made both their special services and their independent judgment indispen-

[54] Portraits of both the new type and new style of lawyer in the nineteenth century are found in Howard Feigenbaum, "The Lawyer in Wisconsin, 1836–1860: A Profile," *Wisconsin Magazine of History* 55 (Winter 1971–72): 100–6; Calhoun, *Professional Lives in America*, pp. 59–87; Johnson, "Education and Professional Life Styles," 187–92; Nash, "Philadelphia Bench and Bar," 218–19.

[55] Roscoe Pound dramatized this as "The Era of Decadence," Chapter 8 in *The Lawyer from Antiquity to Modern Times with Particular Reference to the Development of Bar Associations in the United States* (St. Paul: West Publishing Company, 1953), pp. 223–42. See also W. Raymond Blackard, "The Demoralization of the Legal Profession in Nineteenth-Century America," *Tennessee Law Review* 16 (April 1940): 314–23; Anton-Hermann Chroust, *The Rise of the Legal Profession in America*, 2 vols. (Norman: University of Oklahoma Press, 1965), 2:155–59; Robert Stevens, "Two Cheers for 1870: The American Law School," *Perspectives in American History* 5 (1971): 416–18; Lawrence M. Friedman, *A History of American Law* (New York: Simon and Schuster, 1973), pp. 276–78.

sable to the administrative functions of an orderly society.[56]
Many frontier lawyers, for instance, were by no means
either uneducated or lacking in skills; and in the late
forties and fifties, many in the profession perceived that
the growing problems of social order, including the limits
of legal restraint, were more and more bringing the usefulness of legal services to the attention of Americans.[57] In
1849, the American Legal Association was founded

for the purpose of insuring safety and facility in the collection of
claims and the transaction of legal business throughout the
United States. Its design is to furnish professional and business
men with the name of at least one prompt, efficient and trustworthy Lawyer in every shire-town and in each of the principal
cities and villages in the Union, who will transact with dispatch
and for a reasonable compensation, such professional business as
may be entrusted to him.[58]

In 1850, John Livingston, secretary of the Association, published *The United States Lawyer's Directory and Official
Bulletin,* an authoritative listing of most of the practicing
lawyers and active judges in the various states. Listed in
the directory were 19,527 lawyers who were encouraged to

[56] See Maxwell Bloomfield, "Law vs. Politics: The Self-Image of
the American Bar (1830–1860)," *The American Journal of Legal History* 12 (1968): 306–23. Sidney H. Aronson notes that 83 percent of
the positions in Jackson's administration were held by lawyers, compared to 68 percent in Adams's administration and 62 percent in Jefferson's: *Status and Kinship in the Higher Civil Service: Standards of
Selection in the Administrations of John Adams, Thomas Jefferson, and
Andrew Jackson* (Cambridge, Mass.: Harvard University Press, 1964),
p. 85.

[57] For evidence of legal competence on the frontier, see Elizabeth
Gaspar Brown, "The Bar on a Frontier: Wayne County, 1796–1836,"
The American Journal of Legal History 14 (April 1970): 136–56;
Michael H. Harris, "The Frontier Lawyer's Library; Southern Indiana,
1800–1850, as a Test Case," *Ibid.* 16 (July 1972): 239–52.

[58] *Manual of the American Legal Association: Containing its Plan,
Constitution and Secretary's Report, Together with the Catalogue of
its Members, Embracing the Name and Address of at Least One Effi-
cient and Trustworthy Lawyer for Every Village and City in the Union*
(New York: Published by the Association, 1850), p. 11; Bloomfield,
"Law vs. Politics," 321.

take greater concern with the professional identity of their occupation and to broaden their professional "correspondence, acquaintance, and fellowship."[59]

In the period 1830–60, legal reformers with a nationalistic orientation called for scientific codification of an American law, universal codes based on the behavior and foresight of the prudent, average man. The movement was away from the artificial, burdensome, localistic, and particularistic common-law tradition that had supported the older guilds. Statutory principles would replace isolated precedents, bringing an intellectual element of standardization into both the practice and the teaching of the law.[60] Whig propaganda cried leveler, opportunist, and despot against the emerging realistic lawyer. Nevertheless, even the dean of the Whig legalists, Joseph Story, had to acknowledge the problem when he stated his wish "to avert the fearful calamity, which threatens us, of being buried alive, not in the catacombs, but in the labyrinths of the law."[61]

The legal reformers proposed to make systematic codes more effective in the negotiations of society. They tended to support the cause of labor and endorse such planks as the popular election of judges. The movement was irresistibly middle class—not leveling but egalitarian in terms

[59] John Livingston, *The United States Lawyer's Directory and Official Bulletin for 1850: Comprising the Name and Place of Residence of Every Practicing Lawyer in the Union—The Names and Places of Residence of the Commissioners of Deeds Appointed by the Governors of the Various States* . . . (New York: John Livingston, 1850), p. vi. Livingston bound both the *Manual* and the *Directory* together with the first volume of the *United States Law Magazine* (1850), which he edited. Expressing similar concerns in his book in 1854, George Sharswood published *An Essay on Professional Ethics,* 5th ed. (Philadelphia: T. & J. W. Johnson & Company, 1884), the first lengthy treatment on the subject in nineteenth-century America.

[60] See David Dudley Field, "Reform in the Legal Profession and the Laws: Address to the Graduating Class of the Albany Law School, March 23, 1855," in Perry Miller, ed., *The Legal Mind in America: From Independence to the Civil War* (Garden City, N.Y.: Doubleday & Company, 1962), pp. 285–95. See also Warren, *History of the American Bar,* pp. 508–39; Miller, *Life of the Mind in America,* pp. 239–65.

[61] *Ibid.,* p. 250.

of its legal advocacy of impartial opportunities. A scientific approach to the law knocked down privilege and unreasonable advantage, and it was directed toward the recognition and protection of individual rights, including those of women, criminals, and debtors. Rather than explicitly supporting capitalism, the reform movement called for protection of private property in order to preserve the independence of the private decision-maker against public or private monopoly. The intention was to disperse the power of decision and responsibility within the community. Americans now required in their law objective statements of liability and restraint, clear judicial protection against undue superiority, and accepted definitions of contracts. Mid-nineteenth-century American society, James Willard Hurst has written, "had a peculiar need to create and maintain a framework of reasonably well defined and assured expectations as to the likely official and nonofficial consequences of private venture and decision. Only within some minimum framework of reasonably predictable consequences were men likely to cultivate boldness and energy in action."[62]

Central to the establishment of the "minimum framework" for an open profession liberated from the local bar, the success of the law school with a national focus was tied to the state examination.[63] In the school, the student would begin to think like a lawyer who was familiar with the principles of his subject rather than like an apprenticed junior member of a prosperous family who was primarily concerned with the power relationships in his provincial region. By 1840, the law degree stood apart from the

[62] James Willard Hurst, *Law and the Conditions of Freedom in the Nineteenth-Century United States* (Madison: The University of Wisconsin Press, 1956), p. 22. See also Hurst, *Growth American Law: Law Makers*, p. 254; Warren, *History of the American Bar*, pp. 446–74; Miller, *Life of the Mind in America*, p. 251.

[63] See Gerard W. Gawalt, "Massachusetts Legal Education in Transition, 1766–1840," *The American Journal of Legal History* 17 (January 1973): 27–50; Warren, *History of the American Bar*, pp. 364–65; Friedman, *History of American Law*, pp. 525–56; Nash, "Philadelphia Bench and Bar," 207–8.

Bachelor of Arts, as indeed more and more students forsook the educational experience of the latter in favor of the career opportunities of the former. By 1845, a systematic course of legal instruction was insured at Harvard, and by 1854 Harvard advertised a professionally oriented law curriculum which served as the basic structure for many law schools through the turn of the century.[64]

The antebellum years did not witness impressive growth in the number either of law schools or of students.[65] Nevertheless, by 1860 a bright young man could easily predict the future and its meaning for his own career. Academic law was already demonstrating that it would be very successful in capturing legal education away from the practitioner and in locating it within the university. In 1860, though relatively few practicing lawyers had attended any law school, there were 1,200 students in twenty-two schools, more than half of them university schools. In 1890, there were 4,500 students in sixty-one schools, and most students expected to receive some formal instruction.[66] Significant developments occurred in the postbellum decades: the two and then the three-year curriculum became an established pattern for full-time students, teaching law was elevated from a pastime to a profession, annual examinations in school prepared students for written state bar examinations, formal training was required, and the number of schools doubled between 1870 and 1890. By 1860, the be-

[64] See Charles Warren, *History of the Harvard Law School; and of Early Legal Conditions in America,* 2 vols. (New York: Da Capo Press, Reprint edition, 1970), 2:84–94; Arthur E. Sutherland, *The Law at Harvard: A History of Ideas and Men, 1817–1967* (Cambridge, Mass.: Harvard University Press, 1967), p. 138; Gawalt, "Massachusetts Legal Education," 48–49; Stevens, "Two Cheers for 1870: American Law School," 432–33.

[65] See Sutherland, *Law at Harvard,* pp. 140–61; Stevens, "Two Cheers for 1870: American Law School," 418–19.

[66] *Ibid.,* 428, n. 171. See also James Russell Parsons, *Professional Education,* vol. 10 in *Monographs on Education in the United States,* ed. Nicholas Murray Butler (Division of Exhibits, Department of Education, Universal Exposition, St. Louis, 1904), p. 32; Jerold S. Auerbach, "Enmity and Amity: Law Teachers and Practitioners, 1900–1922," *Perspectives in American History* 5 (1971): 573.

ginning of a trend which would dominate American legal education for over a century was already manifested. If law was a science worthy of a professional career, and not a trade, then American higher education must dignify its instruction.

Similar developments were occurring in other fields. By 1850, medical degrees from schools had replaced the monopolistic licensing practices of privileged medical societies, and the source of controversy within medicine was not basically between professional physicians and empirical quacks but between two schools of professionals: the "regulars" and the "homeopaths."[67] A physician writing in *The Boston Medical and Surgical Journal* in 1843 blamed an oversensitive profession, straining for recognition, for producing "skepticism in the better portion of the community," thereby encouraging the public's subscription to quackery. Ironically, according to the writer, professional physicians defeated their own coveted authority when they told a patient "that each disease can be as accurately identified as can the various plants that grow in our gardens and fields, and that we have a specific medicine adapted to each particular disease." The professional motive of physicians pushed them to make exaggerated claims, "either to gain reputation over somebody else, or to give importance to professional character."[68]

At least a generation before the major innovations in medical science, doctors were beginning to seek the course of a career. By 1850, professionalism in medicine meant

[67] See Joseph F. Kett, *Formation of the American Medical Profession: The Role of Institutions, 1780–1860* (New Haven, Conn.: Yale University Press, 1968); Martin Kaufman, *Homeopathy in America: The Rise and Fall of a Medical Heresy* (Baltimore and London: The Johns Hopkins Press, 1971), pp. 1–75; William G. Rothstein, *American Physicians in the Nineteenth Century: From Sects to Science* (Baltimore and London: The Johns Hopkins University Press, 1972), pp. 152–74; Richard Harrison Shryock, *Medicine and Society in America, 1660–1860* (Ithaca, N.Y., and London: Cornell University Press, 1962), pp. 143–45.

[68] "Quackery," *The Boston Medical and Surgical Journal* 29 (December 26, 1843): 357.

something more than acquired knowledge and a trained skill, both of which were less than impressive in the eyes of the public. Professionalism meant a culture, a set of learned values which structured the attitudes and the responses of practitioners and their patients. Founded in 1847, the American Medical Association reflected those values in its first code of ethics.[69] For instance, concerning the obligation of the patient to the physician, the code said in Article II, Section 10:

A patient should, after his recovery, entertain a just and enduring sense of the value of the services rendered him by his physician; for these are of such a character that no mere pecuniary acknowledgment can repay or cancel them.[70]

However, in order to make professional services respected, the patient must sacrifice by paying, and the physician must perform his duty by charging. Concerning the financial obligation of the physician to his colleague, the code said in Article V, Section 9:

A wealthy physician should not give advice *gratis* to the affluent; because his doing so is an injury to his professional brethren. The office of a physician can never be supported as an exclusively beneficent one; and it is defrauding, in some degree, the common funds for its support, when fees are dispensed with which might justly be claimed.[71]

The days of the doctor as a learned gentleman, and an extension of the community, had passed. Indeed, concerning the public's right not to know about the quality of its care and the competency of its medical practitioners, the code said in Article VI, Section 2:

As peculiar reserve must be maintained by physicians toward the public in regard to professional matters, and as there exist nu-

[69] See the discussion in Morris Fishbein, *A History of the American Medical Association, 1847 to 1947* (Philadelphia and London: W. B. Saunders Company, 1947), pp. 35–40.

[70] Austin Flint, "Medical Ethics and Etiquette: Commentaries on the National Code of Ethics," *New York Medical Journal* 37 (1883): 343.

[71] *Ibid.*, 397.

merous points in medical ethics and etiquette through which the feelings of medical men may be painfully assailed in their intercourse with each other, and which can not be understood or appreciated by general society, neither the subject-matter of such differences nor the adjudication of the arbitrators should be made public, as publicity in a case of this nature may be personally injurious to the individual concerned, and can hardly fail to bring discredit on the faculty.[72]

By 1850, the status of the struggling medical profession, its ability to control its own members and be recognized as the only legitimate authority by the "lay" public, had become the paramount issue.

Signs of the professional claim on antebellum society were also observable in engineering and technology. "The task of surveying, planting, and building upon this immense tract requires an education and a sentiment commensurate thereto," Emerson wrote in 1844. "The arts of engineering and of architecture are studied; scientific agriculture is an object of growing attention; the mineral riches are explored; limestone, coal, slate, and iron; and the value of timber-lands is enhanced."[73] In 1852, the American Society of Civil Engineers was founded, though its effectiveness as an organization was more apparent after 1870. In the decade before the Civil War, engineers were already displaying a basic professional consciousness that made it possible for them both to distinguish between grades of engineers by task, title, and income, and to separate themselves from such marginal types of engineers as mechanics, architects, toolmakers, inventors, contractors, and scientists. Opportunities for mobility on such projects as canals and railroads made an early orientation toward career feasible among engineers, and they successfully preceded other groups in achieving professional status in the sphere of American technology.[74]

[72] *Ibid.,* 398.

[73] "The Young American," *Emerson Works,* 1, *Nature Addresses and Lectures,* 365.

[74] See Raymond H. Merritt, *Engineering in American Society, 1850–1875* (Lexington, Ky.: The University Press of Kentucky, 1969), pp. 1–26

Schools aided the process. In 1850, Benjamin Franklin Greene reorganized Rensselaer Polytechnic Institute. Founded in 1847 at Troy, New York, Rensselaer now turned from a school of science into a school of engineering, and Greene publicized the elaborate details of his new blueprint in *The True Idea of a Polytechnic Institute,* written in 1849 and issued in 1855:

A true idea of the Polytechnic Institute is . . . that of a *series of Special Schools* for the complete training of Architects, Civil Engineers, Mining Engineers, and other Scientific Technists,—all united under a common organization,—all alike aiming at the realization not only of exact and extended scientific culture, but of the utmost practical skill in the applications of science to the pursuits af active life.[75]

In Greene's mind it was imperative that Rensselaer protect its own special intellectual identity by not serving as an adjunct to any apprenticeship system of the crafts. *"What the Institute really is,"* he wrote, was "clearly apparent. . . . The idea of the Polytechnic Institution, fully worked out, embraces an array of appliances adapted to the most complete realization of true educational culture."[76] The Massachusetts Institute of Technology, similar in outlook, was founded in 1861, also with a strong curriculum in engineering. By 1870 more than seventy institutions in America offered students a curriculum in engineering, in-

passim; Daniel Hovey Calhoun, *The American Civil Engineer: Origins and Conflict* (Cambridge, Mass.: The Technology Press, Massachusetts Institute of Technology, distributed by Harvard University Press, 1960), pp. 190–91, 194, 54 ff.; Edwin Layton, "Science, Business, and the American Engineer," in Robert Perrucci and Joel E. Gerstl, eds., *The Engineers and the Social System* (New York, London, Sydney, Toronto: John Wiley & Sons, 1969), pp. 53, 55; D. L. Burn, "The Genesis of American Engineering Competition, 1850–1870," *Economic History* 2 (January 1931): 292–311; Mark Aldrich, "Earnings of American Civil Engineers, 1820–1859," *The Journal of Economic History,* 31 (June 1971): 407–19.

75 [Benjamin Franklin Greene], *The Rensselaer Polytechnic Institute: Its Reorganization in 1849–50; Its Condition at the Present Time; Its Plans and Hopes for the Future . . .* (Troy, N.Y.: D. H. Jones & Co., Printers, 1855), p. 38.

76 *Ibid.,* p. 56.

cluding courses in mathematics, geology, physics, chemistry, hydraulics, and mechanics.[77]

In the 1850s, American civil engineers began making their mark as innovators, managers, and specialists in the increasingly technical and rapidly developing railroad industry. "A very brief period, specifically from 1849 to 1855," according to historian Alfred D. Chandler, Jr., can "be identified as the time when modern business administration first appeared in the United States."[78] Trained engineers such as Benjamin H. Latrobe on the Baltimore and Ohio, J. Edgar Thompson on the Pennsylvania, and Daniel C. McCallum on the New York and Erie had worked up a career ladder, and they brought to the problems of corporate management on the railroad an analytic frame of mind similar to that of bridge-building, with its stresses and harmonies spanning very large spaces.

In the years before the Civil War, an aspiring middle class in America was beginning to build a professional foundation for an institutional order, a foundation in universal, scientific, and predictable principles. The attitudes that supported practical inquiry, trial and error, and local self-interest were leading to haste, incomplete results, and incompetence on the American scene. "Man is not for ever to be empiric," wrote Thomas Ewbank, director of the United States Patent Office, in 1855; "we know nothing, or next to nothing, of the principles by which . . . every object in nature is produced as it is. This knowledge is to be acquired."[79] Ewbank wished to think of the future American as a trained engineer with the world as his modern factory. The middle class was demanding both a reliable and a legitimate arena of laws, rules, and methods in which

77 Merritt, *Engineering in American Society*, p. 31.

78 Alfred D. Chandler, Jr., "The Railroads: Pioneers in Modern Corporate Management," *Business History Review* 39 (Spring 1965): 17. See also James A. Ward, *That Man Haupt: A Biography of Herman Haupt* (Baton Rouge: Louisiana State University Press, 1973).

79 Thomas Ewbank, *The World A Workshop; Or, the Physical Relationship of Man to the Earth* (New York: D. Appleton and Company, 1855), p. 111.

to operate. And the same young men who proposed to penetrate beyond observation to seek out principles and "science" would propose to do no less for their own individual lives by structuring their experience in the form of careers.

CHRISTIAN NURTURE

As young men, Eliot, Gilman, White, Folwell, Angell, and Bascom witnessed the failure of traditional expectations to provide their lives with meaning. Home, family, community, religion, college: none of these traditions, as the presidents experienced them before the Civil War, supplied a dependable basis, a "minimum framework," for the prediction and the control of an active life. The presidents were men in between, in the lurch, aware that the community of the past was proving itself inadequate. Yet, they were still groping for the new structure of career.

On the one hand, they reacted sympathetically to their formative experiences with home and community. In many ways these had been pleasant and educative influences. The preconscious years were the most influential ones, Barnard wrote. *"It's all in bringing up,"* Folwell commented to his mother. White traced his adult activities to boyhood interests. And from St. Petersburg, Gilman wrote to his elder sister, "If ever I make anything in this world or another I shall owe it to the blessed influences of *home.*" On his first trip to Europe as a young man, Eliot discovered "two horrible defects" in the French people: "They have no religion and no family life." And Bascom recalled that the town library of his youth planted the "germs" of his later life: it "was like fresh fruit to one long confined to sea fare." Angell wrote that his modest beginnings introduced him at an impressionable age to the variety of human nature:

I have always felt that the knowledge of men I gained by the observations and experiences of my boyhood in the country tavern has been of the greatest service. Human nature could be studied in every variety. . . . If, as I have sometimes been assured, I have any power of adaptation to the society of different classes of men, I owe it in no small degree to these varied associations of my boyhood.

Barnard credited "whatever of success may have attended me in life" to the "habits of concentration and perservering industry" instilled during his youthful apprenticeship on a newspaper.[80]

On the other hand, the presidents were understandably critical of a nurture that they increasingly perceived as both irrelevant and too undisciplined for American lives in the future. As adults recalled a bygone youth and gave thanks to parental concern, a perfunctory tone, somewhat wistful, crept in. Tradition had not been very useful to these men. Conventional religion, for instance, served to comfort their consciences, but it did little to guide them in the choice of careers.

According to traditional expectations, the college education of the younger presidents would have led them into the ministry, once they had rejected the practical world of business. Although several of the younger men started along this path, their experiences with religion were not decisive, but rather passive, dull, "anemic." Even ministers like Porter and McCosh, older men belonging to Emerson's generation, appeared more intellectual, secular, and moralistic than devout. Indeed, they always sounded more apologetic than evangelical, more concerned with being correct and clear than inspirational. In their day, bright young professionally ambitious men such as Porter and McCosh had entered the

---

[80] John Fulton, *Memoirs of Frederick A. P. Barnard* (New York: Published for the Columbia University Press by Macmillan and Co., 1896), pp. 9, 19; Folwell, *The Autobiography and Letters*, p. 64; Fabian Franklin, *The Life of Daniel Coit Gilman* (New York: Dodd, Mead & Company, 1910), p. 28; Henry James, *Charles W. Eliot: President of Harvard University, 1869–1909*, 2 vols. (Boston and New York: Houghton Mifflin Company, 1930), 1:126; John Bascom, "Books That Have Helped Me," *Forum* 3 (May 1886): 272; James Burrill Angell, *Reminiscences* (New York: Longmans, Green, and Company, 1912), p. 4.

learned profession of the ministry as a matter of accepted social course.[81]

However, professional patterns were changing. By 1835, for instance, the law rivaled the ministry as the professional choice of graduates at Yale, Bowdoin, Brown, and Dartmouth.[82] And the trend for the ministry was downward. At Williams, the ministry declined as a professional choice of graduates from 50 percent in 1826 to 20 percent in 1846 to 15 percent in 1866; at Yale, the ministry slipped from 33 percent in 1821 to 15 percent in 1861.[83] Nor was the curve at these two institutions atypical. The combined figures for thirty-seven representative colleges and universities showed that the ministry fell as a professional choice among graduates from 30 percent in 1820 to 25 percent in 1840 to 20 percent in 1860. In contrast, the law held its own throughout the period, at first ranking below the ministry and then surpassing it. By 1860, commercial pursuits had risen most dramatically as a professional choice of graduates, placing only slightly below the law and the ministry.[84]

In terms of religious experience, the presidents suffered no traumatic moment; they witnessed no dramatic vision, they were intoxicated by no pious ecstasy. Theirs was a religion of convenience. It posed no unanswerable problems or crises of conscience. Of course, a "sensible" man in the nineteenth century professed to be a Godfearing Christian, as he professed to be a patriot. But religion with its profuse rhetoric did not drive him to decision or motivate him to action. In 1854, Eliot, posing to his friend the tremendous

81 William Milligan Sloane, ed., *The Life of James McCosh: A Record Chiefly Autobiographical, with Portraits* (New York: Charles Scribner's Sons, 1896), pp. 21–23; George S. Merriam, ed., *Noah Porter: A Memorial by Friends* (New York: Charles Scribner's Sons, 1893), pp. 37–52.

82 Gawalt, "Massachusetts Legal Education," *American Journal of Legal History*, 38–40.

83 Bailey B. Burritt, *Professional Distribution of College and University Graduates*, United States Bureau of Education Bulletin no. 19, whole number 491 (Washington, D.C.: U.S. Government Printing Office, 1912), pp. 68, 107, 64, 85–86.

84 *Ibid.*, pp. 75, 143–44.

question of choosing a profession and remarking how few young men had the knowledge to make such a decision, felt obligated to conclude with the following perfunctory remark about the influence of his religious belief:

But I can't believe that any earnest inquirer was ever left without light on any question which concerned his eternal welfare. Hence the choice of a profession is a question which concerns us in this world, but not in the next; and one of two propositions must be true—either all human knowledge will be found to be equally worthless . . . or else all human knowledge is the birthright of every mortal, when he puts on immortality.[85]

Either way, religion was beside the point.

In mid–nineteenth-century America, religious commitments most often were peripheral to career decisions. The younger presidents, for instance, expressed only relief when their families deemed their religious attitudes adequate, and the issue was dropped. For one, William Watts Folwell was sensitive to his mother's wishes, and he patiently waited for a resolution of his spiritual status. The "light" did eventually arrive without the emotional storms of earlier ages. At the age of twenty-six, Folwell devoted one whole term to reading "nothing but theological matter." Aside from the possible but not probable "errors" in the *"doctrines* and *practice* of the church," Folwell became *"firmly* and *thoroughly* convinced" that the "true Church" in America was the Protestant Episcopal Church: "I don't see how any fair minded person who *knows the facts* can be of any other opinion."[86]

His mind systematically converted, his heart followed. Several years later in 1862, he sent his mother the "good news"; he had "accepted Baptism without hesitation, and now afterwards without regret." Other souls might anguish in torment and doubt; Folwell expressed only relief. He never became a "fully orthodox man." The quiet resolution

85 Letter from C. W. Eliot to Theodore Tebbets, January 29, 1854, *loc. cit.*

86 Folwell, *Autobiography and Letters,* pp. 79–80.

of religious conflict to "believe in God our Father . . . that he cares for us and will 'save' all who trust him" proved sufficient. Folwell trod the cerebral path to a resolution of the religious problem:

I feel glad to have closed up discussion on this great matter and to have declared myself upon what I must believe to be the right side. I have gone through no series of strange experiences, no ebullitions of passion, and have felt no pangs of disgrace. I have been entirely cool and have known what I have been about. I have now only to learn to live a Christian life.[87]

Excessive religious enthusiasm could be detrimental to an educator's career.

From their teens, the ministry attracted both John Bascom and James Burrill Angell. Bascom, the son of a Calvinist minister "whose library was a bristling phalanx of puritanic writers," attended Auburn Seminary after graduating from Williams College. But his distaste for theological creed made him uncomfortable in any church, except Nature. "Creation rather than grace," he explained, "is the watchword of the Kingdom of Heaven. . . . There is no position I would have more coveted than that of a professor in a theological seminary. But I came early to see that I could not keep step with any church, and must of necessity be a voice crying in the wilderness."[88]

Angell intended to pursue theological studies at Andover Seminary when a severe throat ailment "really changed the whole plan" of his life. The turn of events, however, did not seem to disturb him excessively. Though among Angell's family "none . . . were professors of religion," he became sufficiently devout after his college years to believe in personal immortality, oppose Sunday theater in Ann Arbor, and protest the abolition of scriptural readings at trustee meetings. His religion was comfortably noncontroversial in

---

[87] *Ibid.*, pp. 214, 144.

[88] John Bascom, *Things Learned by Living* (New York: G. P. Putnam's Sons, 1913), pp. 126–27.

the climate of the day. His piety expressed "a very practical faith in God, a present and living condition that He works in the world and that man exists for His service."[89]

The plain, earnest style of the charitable Christ set an example for the youthful Daniel Coit Gilman who looked "more and more" toward the ministry "as probably the place where I can do more good than anywhere else." In his own eyes, Gilman sought only a simple unalloyed satisfaction: "When any one believes in an inner life of faith and joy and is willing to talk about it in an earnest, every day style and tone, I do enjoy it most exceedingly." Gilman did not receive ordination, but he did acquire a license to preach. Religion for Gilman meant "the giving of kind thoughts and acts and words to those who are in need or trouble, in short, the giving of one's self."[90]

In Eliot it was apparent that anxiety, decision, and action did not accompany a concern with religion. Spiritual faith existed to give serenity, a fundamental condition in the gospel of worldly success. The personal struggle with fatalism, anguish, and despair evaporated in Eliot's piety. His was the springtime faith. His father knew scores of hymns, Eliot's son wrote, but "on the whole he did not care for hymn tunes that were melancholy or in a minor key."[91] Eliot's practical faith in a worldly order pervaded his sentiments. He wrote William James after reading *Varieties of Religious Experience:* "You seem to me to have not made allowance enough for the irresistible tendency of some imaginative human beings to 'spin yarns.'" "The subject," Eliot confided, was "an exciting or nervous one."[92] Excitement was never one of Eliot's religious qualities, and he did not wish it to be. Ralph Barton Perry summarized Eliot's prac-

89 Angell, *Reminiscences,* p. 77; Shirley W. Smith, *James Burrill Angell: An American Influence* (Ann Arbor, Mich.: University of Michigan Press, 1954), pp. 339, 157, 281, 33.

90 Franklin, *Gilman,* pp. 29, 38, 14, 36, 30, 29.

91 Cited in James, *Eliot,* 1:317.

92 Cited in Ralph Barton Perry, *The Thought and Character of William James,* 2 vols. (Boston: Little, Brown and Company, 1935), 2:336-37.

tical piety: "His was a religion without authority, mysticism, or other-worldliness, but it contributed effectually to his serenity and steadiness of purpose." Religion served to affirm Eliot's ego; it did not motivate him to pursue a career.[93]

[93] Ralph Barton Perry, "Charles William Eliot," in Allen Johnson and Dumas Malone, eds., *Dictionary of American Biography*, 11 vols. (New York: Charles Scribner's Sons, 1927–36), 6:77.

6

The Old-Time College

THE YOUNG AMERICAN

In what direction was an ambitious young man to turn in the antebellum years? The religious divine of the seventeenth century, the educated political statesman of the later eighteenth century, the learned professional of the new republic—none seemed to serve as a viable model for a life in mid–nineteenth-century America. The failure of these models was adequately mirrored in the inadequacy of the antebellum American college. At fault were not the curriculum, the repressive atmosphere of regulation, the efforts of the faculty, the lack of public financial support, and the proliferation of both mediocre and unstable institutions. These were obstacles to the success of the college, but not fatal ones. The old-time college was not an institution that catered to middle-class ambition and careers; this shortcoming doomed it. Its form of discipline and intellectual content were external to the novel needs of young men.[1]

1 The literature on the American college is voluminous. See Richard Hofstadter, *Academic Freedom in the Age of the College* (New York: Columbia University Press, 1961); Frederick Rudolph, *The American College and University: A History* (New York: Alfred A. Knopf, 1962); George P. Schmidt, *The Liberal Arts College: A Chapter in American*

By midcentury, middle-class Americans were actively beginning to impose their expectations on the higher educational system. But the system was unequal to the new
demands, in part because the traditional conception of
growing up and the obligation of the college to the student
were not relevant to the new realities. Among those better-
known realities was the movement of population in nineteenth-century America, especially after 1820. For instance,
the low proportion of people living in cities, between 4.5
and 5 percent, was nearly the same in 1820 as in 1730. But
after 1820 the percentage of the urban population began to
rise: to 8.5 percent in 1840, 16.1 in 1860, 22.6 in 1880,
32.9 in 1900.[2] Particularly in New England in the first part
of the century, fewer native sons could afford to remain on
the uneconomical farms of their fathers, and they either
sought out new western lands or migrated to the growing
cities and towns, where they became clerks, operatives,

Cultural History (New Brunswick, N.J.: Rutgers University Press, 1957);
Schmidt, *The Old Time College President* (New York: Columbia Uni-
versity Press, 1930); R. Freeman Butts, *The College Charts Its Course:
Historical Conceptions and Current Proposals* (New York: McGraw-Hill
Book Company, 1939); Charles F. Thwing, *American Colleges: Their
Students and Work*, 2d ed., rev. (New York: G. P. Putnam's Sons,
1883); Thwing, *The American College in American Life* (New York
and London: G. P. Putnam's Sons, 1897); Thwing, *The College Presi-
dent* (New York: The Macmillan Company, 1926); Russell Thomas,
The Search for a Common Learning: General Education, 1800–1960
(New York: McGraw-Hill Book Company, 1962); Thomas LeDuc, *Piety
and Intellect at Amherst College, 1865–1912* (New York: Columbia Uni-
versity Press, 1946); Frederick Rudolph, *Mark Hopkins and the Log:
Williams College, 1836–1872* (New Haven, Conn.: Yale University Press,
1956); John Barnard, *From Evangelicalism to Progressivism at Oberlin
College, 1866–1917* (Columbus: Ohio State University Press, 1969);
Richard Hofstadter, "The Revolution in Higher Learning," in Arthur
M. Schlesinger, Jr., and Morton White, eds., *Paths of American
Thought* (Boston: Houghton Mifflin Company, 1963), pp. 269–90.

2 [W. S. Rossiter], *A Century of Population Growth: From the First
Census of the United States to the Twelfth, 1790–1900*, Department of
Commerce and Labor, Bureau of the Census, S.N.D. North, Director
(Washington, D.C.: U.S. Government Printing Office, 1909), Table 4,
p. 15; *Historical Statistics of the United States: Colonial Times to 1957:
A Statistical Abstract Supplement* (Washington, D.C.: U.S. Department
of Commerce, Bureau of the Census, 1960), Series A 195–209, p. 14.

skilled workers, managers, teachers, doctors, ministers, and the like. Men without property, they sold their recently acquired skills as a service to society.

Another pertinent although lesser known reality influenced events in nineteenth-century America. A large group of youth and young adults in their late teens, twenties, and early thirties appeared in the population, a group which had not existed before either in such numbers or in relative size. By comparison with the nineteenth century, the population in colonial America had been very young, with half the people in 1790 estimated to be below the age of fifteen, a third below the age of ten, and more than two-thirds below the age of twenty-five.[3] The median age for a white male in 1790 was 15.9, and the ratio between dependent children under the age of sixteen and adults to support them over the age of twenty was 780 adults per 1,000 children. In 1790, there were nearly two children for every white female, and nearly 40 percent of the families contained between four and seven children.[4]

After 1830, however, the "young American" as young adult was more than a rhetorical phrase that nationalistic writers enjoyed invoking. During this decade, the ratio between adults over the age of twenty and children below sixteen drew even—.99 in 1840—and as the century progressed the ratio quickly turned in favor of the adults: 1.24 by 1870. John Todd did not exaggerate when in 1835 he wrote in *The Student's Manual:* "Our country is a youth, and nothing but what is elastic and youthful, is in fashion. Our legislators, our professional men, must all be young to be popular. The stars are to be looked at only while they are

---

[3] *A Century of Population Growth,* Table 25, p. 94; *Historical Statistics of the United States,* Series A 71–85, p. 10. See also J. Potter, "The Growth of Population in America, 1700–1860," in D. V. Glass and D. E. C. Eversley, *Population in History: Essays in Historical Demography* (Chicago: Aldine Publishing Company, 1965), pp. 653, 661–62.

[4] *Historical Statistics of the United States,* Series A 90, p. 11; *A Century of Population Growth,* Table 35, pp. 103–4; Table 37, p. 105; Table 28, p. 98.

rising. A man of fifty is considered almost superannuated, with us. Such is the fashion."[5] Todd called the country a youth, not a child or an infant, and population data tended to support his observation.

By 1840, the median age for white males had climbed to 17.9 and by 1860 to 19.7. On the one hand, both the percentage of children in the population and the average size of families were definitely declining in comparison to the colonial era. By 1850, there was only slightly more than a child and a half to every white woman; and between 1790 and 1860 the population per household had decreased from 5.79 to 5.28.[6] On the other hand, numerous older people were simply not to be found in a society in which only 8.3 percent of the white population was over the age of fifty in 1840, and 9.6 percent in 1860.[7]

Nineteenth-century America was a place for youth. Throughout the century, more than three-quarters of the population fell below the age of forty, and two-thirds below the age of thirty. The following averages illustrate the age distribution of the population after 1830: [8]

Age	Percentage of Population	
	1830–1860	1870–1900
0–14	42.4	36.9
15–29	29.0	28.4
30–49	19.6	22.6
50+	8.9	12.1

Nearly 30 percent of the entire population, including nearly 30 percent of the male population only, belonged to the broad category described as youth and young adulthood.

[5] *Ibid.*, Table 35, p. 103; John Todd, *The Student's Manual: Designed, By Specific Directions, to Aid in Forming and Strengthening the Intellectual and Moral Character and Habits of the Student* (Northampton, Mass.: J. H. Butler, 1835), p. 263.

[6] *Historical Statistics of the United States,* Series A 90, p. 11; Series A 257, p. 16; *A Century of Population Growth,* Table 38, p. 106.

[7] Tabulated from *Historical Statistics of the United States,* Series A 71–85, p. 10. See Potter, "Growth of Population," Table 9, p. 670.

[8] *Ibid.*

Moreover, as the century progressed, the percentage of the population in the fifteen-to-twenty-nine age group decreased only slightly, in contrast to the sharper declines in the younger ages and the increases in the older.[9]

Not even the casualties of the Civil War appeared to have diminished markedly the number of young men present in America after 1860. Throughout the century, additional millions of young Americans in their later teens and twenties began competing for jobs, distinction, and place in the society. Today the numbers are impressive.[10] To a young man at the time, as witnesses testified, the numbers could be both intimidating and frustrating, especially as the competition intensified. As the male population expanded, moreover, the median age continued to climb, from 20.2 in 1870 to 22.9 in 1900.

Increasingly it became the case in the nineteenth century

[9] With the drop in fertility rates in nineteenth-century America, children below the age of four declined from 18.0 percent of the white population to 15.3 in the years 1830–60, and from 14.0 percent to 11.9 in the years 1870–1900. In 1900, the population per household was 4.76. On the other hand, the white population over the age of fifty climbed from 8.3 percent in 1830, to 11.0 in 1870, to 13.6 in 1900. *Ibid.*

The shifting patterns of the entire century can be portrayed by employing the age categories used in 1800:

Ages	1800	1870	1900
1–9	34.7%	26.8%	23.8%
10–14	15.5	12.4	10.7
15–24	18.5	20.2	19.6
25–44	19.7	25.6	28.1
45+	11.7	14.9	17.8

[10] *Historical Statistics of the United States,* Series A 71–85, p. 10:

Male, Ages 15–29
[in millions]

Year	Total	15–19	20–24	[20–29]	25–29
1830	1.5	.57		.95	
1840	2.0	.76		*1.32*	
1850	3.4	1.23		*2.19*	
1860	4.6	1.65		*2.91*	
1870	5.3	1.99	1.83		1.51
1880	7.1	2.48	2.56		2.10
1890	9.0	3.25	3.10		2.70
1900	10.7	3.76	3.62		3.32

that college training and the college diploma were useful in order to identify individuals in the large crowd. But the old-time college was not intellectually prepared for the expansion of "youth" in American society, and it accommodated slowly to the vastness of this potential clientele. New provincial colleges were founded in the late eighteenth century and early nineteenth century—Williams (1795), Middlebury (1802), Bowdoin (1806), Amherst (1822)—especially to meet the needs of poor New England boys who wished to better themselves by entering the ministry.[11] But college officials responded reluctantly to the new kind of student, who was older, more mature and determined than the typical teenager in college. Students themselves were often cautious about changing the outmoded attitudes and practices by which they hoped to succeed. But inevitably, with the appearance in the nineteenth century of middle-class aspirations and career expectations, the idea of young manhood as a sphere all its own began taking on special meaning for Americans, and that idea eventually worked to transform the nature of American higher education.

In the eighteenth-century college, the stage of behavioral development called "young manhood" did not exist as a notable epoch, a distinct period or era in human time characterized by specific events, unique problems, and a distinct culture. College officials did not think of students as a special social group. Students were children, being prepared for a calling, who needed to be confined to a college or boarding school in order to survive the awful temptations of worldly vice during the "midpassage" to adulthood. In the self-contained college community, a student was housed under one roof with his instructors, and all proceeded together through the uniform daily routine of prayers, meals, recitations, and study. A constant regimen within a common group and a single curriculum would eradicate the deviant impulses of the willful child. Children required external

11 See David F. Allmendinger, Jr., *Paupers and Scholars: The Transformation of Student Life in New England* (New York: St. Martin's Press, 1975), pp. 1–42.

discipline, and the older the child, the more headstrong and stubborn his behavior was likely to be. Teachers responded to the largely petty offenses of their corruptible wards by corporal punishment, fines, and deprivation. The college served as a form of moral apprenticeship for the children of the gentry, who in their adulthood were expected to display a gloss of civilized manners, a parental concern for society, and exemplary Christian habits.[12]

Graduating a handful of gentlemen professionals to serve the society's relatively simple needs, the college existed at the periphery of colonial life. The number of college graduates in fact was very small. According to one count, the significant colonial colleges together graduated a total of 36.6 students per year between 1701 and 1750, and 123 students between 1751 and 1800. By the end of the eighteenth century, Harvard was averaging only 41.5 graduates per year (between 1787 and 1800), Columbia 14.9, Brown 18.1, Dartmouth 32.4, and Princeton 22.5.[13] The occupational preferences of the students were the ministry, the law, and medicine. However, the combined colonial colleges graduated only 2,505 ministers during the eighteenth century. In the second half of the century, the colleges averaged a total number of thirty-three graduates per year in the ministry, twenty-seven headed for the law, and thirteen for medi-

[12] See Henry D. Sheldon, *Student Life and Customs* (New York: D. Appleton and Company, 1901), pp. 81–94; Oscar Handlin and Mary F. Handlin, *The American College and American Culture: Socialization as a Function of Higher Education* (New York: McGraw-Hill Book Company, 1970), pp. 5–18; James Axtell, *The School Upon a Hill: Education and Society in Colonial New England* (New Haven, Conn., and London: Yale University Press, 1974), pp. 232–44, 112 ff. See also Edmund S. Morgan, *The Gentle Puritan: A Life of Ezra Stiles, 1727–1795* (New Haven, Conn., and London: Yale University Press, 1962), pp. 360–75; Richard Warch, *School of the Prophets: Yale College, 1701–1740* (New Haven, Conn., and London: Yale University Press, 1973), pp. 250–77; Samuel Eliot Morison, *Harvard College in the Seventeenth Century*, 2 vols. (Cambridge, Mass.: Harvard University Press, 1936), 1:74–138.

[13] Bailey B. Burritt, *Professional Distribution of College and University Graduates*, United States Bureau of Education Bulletin no. 19, whole number 491 (Washington, D.C.: U.S. Government Printing Office, 1912), pp. 143, 79, 90, 93, 95, 105.

cine.[14] At the very least, the college's social reason for existence was not greatly consequential to the concerns of the common man.

A society's perception of the "ages of man" influences the individual citizen's most fundamental attitudes toward life; indeed, it contributes to a society's decision to support one institution as culturally necessary rather than another. "All the world's a stage," Shakespeare wrote,

> And all the men and women merely players.
> They have their exits and their entrances,
> And one man in his time plays many parts,
> His acts being seven ages. At first the infant . . .

Infant, schoolboy, lover, soldier, justice, old man, and finally "second childishness and mere oblivion, / Sans teeth, sans eyes, sans taste, sans every thing": these seven ages, each seven years in duration, were as cosmic and continuous as the cycle of the seasons in their eternal return.[15] The Elizabethan world-view continued to impress eighteenth-century Americans, who believed that civilized man lived in rational harmony with the orderly principles of a lawful universe.

Colonial Americans conceived of growing up to adulthood in terms of a series of continuous or fluid periods in life, each normally appearing in its time or season with a minimum of stress and emotional turmoil. The child had little culture of his own, perhaps not even his own birthday to remember and celebrate. Until the age of seven, the child lived within the confines of the family and performed only modest household chores. Between the ages of seven and fifteen, he became the object of adult expectations which required that he curb idleness and mischievous passion, enter a calling or vocation usually that of his father, and master the habits of industry, frugality, and temperance. Patterns were informal and differed considerably from one person to

14 *Ibid.,* p. 143.

15 *As You Like It,* act 2, sc. 7, lines 139–166, *The Complete Plays and Poems of William Shakespeare,* eds. William Allan Neilson and Charles Jarvis Hill (Cambridge, Mass.: Houghton Mifflin Company, 1942), p. 225. Axtell, *School Upon a Hill,* p. 97.

another, from one community and region to another. There was no predetermined age at which a child would leave home, become apprenticed, or enter and leave school. A mature male frequently remained on the parental farm well into his twenties. Always facing toward manhood, the colonial child matured quickly, with little time for self-indulgence, few memorable ceremonies to distinguish his childhood, and the absence of an adolescent or pre-adult stage of life fraught with anxiety and emotional indecision. Growing up in eighteenth-century America was designed to be a rational, orderly, and somewhat impersonal public experience.[16]

In his dress, play, physical health, lessons, and skills, the colonial child was a small adult, incomplete and inadequate when measured against the adult norm. As John Demos observed, the shadow of the child gradually lengthened until it blended with the man's. From the ages of eight to twelve most boys began to work and learn some of the elementary skills—for instance, with tools and weapons—an adult would be expected to know. Boys began to receive some intermittent schooling and direct some attention to their religious life. Between the ages of twelve and twenty, boys most likely would be apprenticed at least for a short period

[16] See Monica Kiefer, *American Children Through Their Books, 1700–1835* (Philadelphia: University of Pennsylvania Press, 1948); John F. Walzer, "A Period of Ambivalence: Eighteenth-Century American Childhood," in Lloyd deMause, ed., *The History of Childhood* (New York: Harper Torchbooks, 1975), pp. 351–82; Oscar Handlin and Mary F. Handlin, *Facing Life: Youth and the Family in American History* (Boston, Toronto: Little, Brown and Company, 1971), pp. 26–66; Axtell, *School Upon a Hill*, pp. 97–99, 201–2; Jennie Holliman, *American Sports (1785–1835)* (Durham, N.C.: The Seeman Press, 1931), pp. 172–77; Michael Zuckerman, *Peaceable Kingdoms: New England Towns in the Eighteenth Century* (New York: Vintage Books, 1972), p. 73. John Demos, "The American Family in Past Time," *The American Scholar* 43 (Summer 1974): 422–46. "*Colonial society,*" Demos emphasized, "*barely recognized childhood as we know and understand it today.*" In response to Demos and others, see N. Ray Hiner, "Adolescence in Eighteenth-Century America," *History of Childhood Quarterly* 3 (Fall 1975): 253–80; Ross W. Beales, Jr., "In Search of the Historical Child: Miniature Adulthood and Youth in Colonial New England," *American Quarterly* 27 (October 1975): 379–98.

of time, try a number of jobs, or possibly intersperse some winter schooling with spring, summer, and fall farming. Whether a boy came from wealthy parents, a professional home, an artisan background, or a farm definitely influenced the course of his experience.

At the age of sixteen, the young man unceremoniously arrived at the age of discretion and often legal responsibility. Before him lay the roles and offices of adulthood, and the public reputation inherent in each. As Ben Franklin explained in his many articles of advice, the child learned to be an adult by dispassionately imitating the good character of a virtuous and successful grownup. Typically, Franklin signed his advice to a young tradesman, "written by an old one."[17] Age and practical experience tended to establish authority and discernment in colonial America, an attitude that would reverse itself in the rebellion of youth in the nineteenth century.

By the early part of the nineteenth century, young men were setting out on their own at an earlier age than ever before. And they were establishing their independence from apprenticeship, their fathers' occupations, and their state of dependence on the family farm into their twenties. When Tocqueville visited in the 1830s, he observed the discontinuity in the life of a young American, his early autonomy and his concern with individual freedom of choice. In America, the paternalistic and authoritarian family

does not exist. All that remains of it are a few vestiges in the first years of childhood, when the father exercises, without opposition, that absolute domestic authority which the feebleness of his children renders necessary and which their interest, as well as his own incontestable superiority, warrants. But as soon as the young American approaches manhood, the ties of filial obedience are relaxed day by day; master of his thoughts, he is soon master of his conduct. In America there is, strictly speaking, no adolescence:

17 *The Papers of Benjamin Franklin,* Leonard W. Labaree *et al.,* eds., 18 vols. (New Haven, Conn.: Yale University Press, 1959–), 3:306.

at the close of boyhood the man appears and begins to trace out his own path.[18]

Other foreign observers confirmed Tocqueville's impression. In 1839, Captain Frederick Marryat remarked that "any one who has been in the United States must have perceived that there is little or no parental control." The disciplinarian Marryat was profoundly offended: "At the age of six or seven you will hear both boys and girls contradicting their fathers and mothers, and advancing their own opinions with a firmness which is very striking. At fourteen or fifteen the boys will seldom remain longer at school. At college, it is the same thing; and they learn precisely what they please, and no more."[19]

The traditional social institutions Americans inherited from the eighteenth century were too informal and loose— too external in forms of discipline—to structure a young life in rapid motion.[20] Though an environmental discipline based on deference toward adults might survive within the family, the work situation, and the old-time college, that discipline was too limited by the particular setting to extend to the fluid circumstances of an adventurous youth's life. Social authority in America had become haphazard as the young American, concerned with his right to choice and perhaps a footloose existence, viewed earlier forms of discipline as excessive, arbitrary, and irrational. In the past, tired "old fogeys" concerned with maintaining local order had

[18] Alexis de Tocqueville, *Democracy in America*, 2 vols. (New York: Alfred A. Knopf, 1963), 2:192. See also Max Berger, *The British Traveller in America, 1836–1860* (New York: Columbia University Press, 1943), pp. 83–84.

[19] Capt. Marryat, *A Diary in America, with Remarks on Its Institutions*, 3 vols. (London: Longman, Orme, Brown, Green, & Longmans, 1839), 3:283, 286–87.

[20] See Joseph F. Kett, "Adolescence and Youth in Nineteenth-Century America," *Journal of Interdisciplinary History* 2 (Autumn 1971): 285–86; Kett, "Growing Up in Rural New England, 1800–1840," in Tamara K. Hareven, ed., *Anonymous Americans: Explorations in Nineteenth-Century Social History* (Englewood Cliffs, N.J.: Prentice-Hall, 1971), pp. 1–14.

found these forms of discipline appropriate, but in the present, energetic youth concerned with independence and opportunity found them stifling. "At fifteen or sixteen, if not at college, the boy assumes the man," Marryat observed; "he enters into business, as a clerk to some merchant, or in some store. His father's home is abandoned, except when it may suit his convenience, his salary being sufficient for most of his wants. He frequents the bar, calls for gin cocktails, chews tobacco, and talks politics." Where would this rebellious willfulness on the part of American youth end? asked the melancholic Marryat.[21]

Even at college the boy often assumed the man. In ever-increasing numbers, students abandoned supervised collegiate dormitories to room, board, and entertain themselves in town. They disappeared from the campus for extended periods of time to work, usually as schoolteachers. And they defiantly chose to burlesque and flaunt the paternalism of frequently vindictive college authorities whose police functions multiplied as their patience deteriorated.

THE NEW MORALITY

External discipline failed young America. In order to be effective, any new social morality would have to be internalized by the individual, built into his basic character, rooted in his instinctual habits, and carried universally into any situation. For the young American, character must transcend circumstance, the man must control his environ-

21 Marryat, *Diary in America*, 3:288. Useful theoretical considerations are discussed in Ruth Benedict, "Continuities and Discontinuities in Cultural Conditioning," *Psychiatry* 1 (1938): 161–67; S. N. Eisenstadt, *From Generation to Generation: Age Groups and Social Structure* (Glencoe, Ill.: The Free Press, 1956); Lewis S. Feuer, *The Conflict of Generations: The Character and Significance of Student Movements* (New York, London: Basic Books, 1969), pp. 318–84.

ment by mastering himself. In these terms, Ralph Waldo Emerson spoke to the "youth" of America in his address "The American Scholar" (1838):

Young men of the fairest promise, who begin life upon our shores, . . . are hindered from action by the disgust which the principles on which business is managed inspire, and turn drudges, or die of disgust, some of them suicides. What is the remedy? They did not yet see, and thousands of young men as hopeful now crowding to the barriers for the career do not yet see, that if the single man plant himself indomitably on his instincts, and there abide, the huge world will come round to him.[22]

The new social morality would assist rather than deny or attempt to suppress the individual's willpower, his unfulfilled desires and unrealized aspirations.

Tocqueville observed that as deferential and customary social arrangements loosened and even disappeared, allowing young Americans to assert their individual claims on society, natural ties based on familiarity and affection tightened. A youthful population, increasingly anxious and insecure about its future, voluntarily sought parental advice, and professional ministers hastened to cultivate this vast new audience. "So far as I know," John Todd wrote in his widely disseminated *The Young Man* (1844), "no one has occupied the ground which I have selected, nor said just the things which I am wishing to say."[23] An orphan whose poverty compelled him first to delay his education and then with inadequate preparation to struggle against illness and anxiety in order to get through Yale, Todd made good in the profession of the ministry. And he was brimming with advice for young men, based on his experience with his own self-determination, discipline, goals, struggle, and success. As he wrote about himself:

[22] "The American Scholar," in *The Complete Works of Ralph Waldo Emerson,* 12 vols. (Boston: Houghton Mifflin Company, 1903–4), 1, *Nature Addresses and Lectures,* 114–15.

[23] John Todd, *The Young Man: Hints Addressed to the Young Men of the United States,* 2d ed. (Northampton, Mass.: J. H. Butler, 1845), p. 15.

My father fell under a heavy blow of Providence; he fell in the morning of life. The same stroke crushed my mother, and I was born an ophan, shelterless, penniless. I was but six years old when I knelt over my father's grave, and vowed, even then, to rise above my circumstances. I soon determined to have a liberal education. My friends opposed, obstacles were thrown in my way, every thing opposed. I rose above all; I went to college, half-fitted; I was sick much of the time, owing to too severe application and anxiety; I pressed on, rose above all, and now stand where I can see my way clear.[24]

Todd's *The Young Man* was typical of a genre that began appearing in the 1830s and thereafter proliferated. Todd advised his audience on the importance of personal character in the triumph of a professional life; on the peculiar temptations of young men to throw away their "promise" in drink and flights of fancy; on the importance of the regular habits of rest, diet, industry, and economy; and on the worldly satisfactions drawn from self-improvement of the mind and self-government of the heart. The first edition of *The Young Man* sold out in one year, and Todd's earlier book, *The Student's Manual* (1835), sold in excess of one hundred fifty thousand copies.

Some individuals grew well-to-do by advising youth on the virtues of frugality. Lured on by success, both authors and publishers put together collections of lectures, sermons, and speeches. The results were impressive. Henry Ward Beecher's *Lectures to Young Men* (1844) sold more than fifty thousand copies before a revised edition appeared in the 1860s. Horace Mann's *A Few Thoughts for a Young Man* (1850) sold twenty thousand copies in its first edition and, according to Mann's wife, was the most "universally popular" treatise "the author ever wrote." Joel Hawes's early *Lectures to Young Men on the Formation of Character* (1828) had sold some ninety thousand copies before reissued in 1856.[25]

[24] John E. Todd, ed., *John Todd: The Story of His Life, Told Mainly by Himself* (New York: Harper and Brothers, Publishers, 1876), p. 118. See also Allmendinger, *Paupers and Scholars*, pp. 38–42.

[25] Perhaps mistakenly, I have taken the publishers at their word

The new genre also created a national demand for its authors as public speakers on college campuses, the lyceum circuit, and especially before the expanding number of urban young men's associations. By 1835, an American magazine observed that "in all the cities, and many of the larger and middling towns . . . there are . . . Young Men's Societies."[26] In 1839, Marryat complained that, by means of these youth associations, society in America "has been usurped by the young people, the married and old people have been, to a certain degree, excluded from it."[27] Marryat overreacted, but he did witness the emergence of a new and significant audience in nineteenth-century urban centers. In 1851, for instance, the first American branch of the Young Men's Christian Association was founded in Boston, with its goal to improve the "spiritual and mental condition of young men" by means of education, organized recreation, and the provision of decent living quarters. The movement met an overwhelmingly favorable response.[28]

The success of the advice literature can be attributed to its recognition of "youth" or young manhood as a distinct stage of life with its exceptional demands and dangers, a stage of life never fully acknowledged before. Through the books and pamphlets ran an undercurrent of anxiety and fear, conspicuously absent in the complacency of Ben Franklin's earlier remarks to the young. Now, at the very period of life when a young American was establishing his independence and making decisions that would determine the direction of his future, at the very moment when his pro-

about sales. Among the better known titles were William Dodd, *Discourses to Young Men* (1848); T. S. Arthur, *Advice to Young Men on their Duties and Conduct in Life* (1849); E. H. Chapin, *Duties of Young Men*, 9th ed. (1855); William G. Eliot, *Lectures to Young Men*, 4th ed. (1853). On the emergence of this literature, see John Demos and Virginia Demos, "Adolescence in Historical Perspective," *Journal of Marriage and the Family* 31 (November 1969): 632–34.

26 "Letters from New England—No. 4," *The Southern Literary Messenger* 1 (February 1835): 273.

27 Marryat, *Diary in America*, 3:290–91.

28 C. Howard Hopkins, *History of the Y.M.C.A. in North America* (New York: Association Press, 1951), pp. 16–36.

tected childhood was over and his professional character and morality were taking shape, he was emotionally vulnerable to "wild desires, restless cravings," and unpredictable fluctuations of mood. Personally the young man was unsure of himself, sexually he was unsteady, psychologically he was impatient, mentally he was distracted, and intellectually he was confused. Todd, for instance, warned the young man against building "castles in the air," the euphemism for masturbating. "I cannot speak on this subject as I would like to do," he suggested:

In no period of life are the appetites so strong and the relish so keen, as when we are young; and it is then too, that the imagination plays us all manner of tricks, and commences a system of domestic tyranny which is to last through life. . . .

In a few minutes we may so intoxicate the imagination that we fancy ourselves in positions which it would require years of effort to reach,—and which perhaps are for ever beyond our reach. The effects are, to waste, in dreaming, the time which might be profitably employed; to weaken the mind by committing it to the direction of fancy,—to indispose the soul to effort and labor, and to make the heart dissatisfied with the realities of life.[29]

Overstimulated worldly ambition drove young men to lose themselves in "reveries of imagination." At the very time of life when the young man should store up his energy and conserve it for the battle of life ahead, the temptations were greatest to waste it in daydreaming, dissipation, and frivolity.

Young manhood was a precarious age of life, made even more so by the precarious stage of American history. Characteristically, Beecher spoke in 1844 of the aimlessness of American life, the "unsettled times" which "foster dishon-

[29] Todd, *The Young Man,* pp. 141, 139, 142. See Ben Barker-Benfield, "The Spermatic Economy: a Nineteenth-Century View of Sexuality," in Michael Gordon, ed., *The American Family in Historical Perspective* (New York: St. Martin's Press, 1973), pp. 336–72; R. P. Neuman, "Masturbation, Madness, and the Modern Concepts of Childhood and Adolescence," *Journal of Social History* 8 (Spring 1975): 5–7.

esty," the "popular tumults" which have "swept over the land with desolation, and left their filthy slime in the highest places," and the "manifest decline" in both "family government" and "reverence for law."[30] Ministers tended to view the "convulsions" of the times as a national calamity, especially for vulnerable young men who had not yet learned to moderate their emotions by means of the internal flywheel of habit.

Most of the advice literature in the years between 1830 and 1860 read like an endless sermon on the importance of the bourgeois habits of industry, temperance, honesty, health, and especially moderation. For instance, Todd explained to college students that in rebellions "the faculties are always acting on right principles, and the students always on wrong." By pitting themselves against the "coolness of age and the wisdom of experience" of the faculty, Todd said, students made rebellion a "dishonorable business," which led only to "ruinous results" for their professional lives. As coercive institutional ties relaxed in democratic America, ministers recommended that moral control of the self stiffen. "The pursuits of ambition," Todd told the young man, "are successions of jealous disquietudes, of corroding fears, of high hopes, of restless desires, and of bitter disappointment. There is ever a void in the soul—a reaching forth towards the empty air."[31] Though Todd readily admitted to his own private ambition, he advised caution in young men when the bounds seemed to overreach familiar grounds.

Beyond the conventional wisdom, however, the responses of the ministers also struck a new theme. Young manhood was not a passing phase of life but a special one, characterized by aimlessness, vacillation, and indecision on the one hand; and overzealous commitments to principles and ideals on the other. The ministers could only express am-

[30] Henry Ward Beecher, *Lectures to Young Men, on Various Important Subjects,* 2d ed. (Boston: Ticknor and Fields, 1863), pp. 52–53.

[31] Todd, *Student's Manual,* pp. 248, 247–59, 372.

bivalence about the motives for reform of their new audience. "Youth" with its vigor and commitment implicitly indicted ministerial conservatism itself. Todd recalled that as a young man "every individual with whom I conversed endeavored to discourage me" from attending college, but he went anyway despite the predictions of failure.[32] Indeed, though the professional minister nurtured this new clientele of young men, he could not prevent it from rejecting his mature "wisdom of experience."

Within the reform movements of the 1830s and 1840s, a youth culture was emerging which strenuously identified itself by criticizing the lack of imagination, vitality, and internal discipline of the adult generation. The commitment to reform was more than a passing fancy of teenagers or an extension of teenage religious conversions. The commitment answered the need of young people in their twenties who were in college or had already trained for a vocation and were disillusioned with the compromises and corruptions of the successful elders they were told to imitate. One sample of 251 reformers found that the median age of entry into a reform career was 27.5, and another sample of 106 abolitionists revealed a median age of 29.[33] In temperance, feminism, dietary reform, education, and especially religion, young voices were speaking up which were disrespectful of mature ones, and though only a minority actively participated in reform, the sense of dissatisfaction among young Americans and the popularity of the new causes were contagious. In 1841, Emerson represented the mood of many when he said in a general way: "We are to revise the whole of our social structure, the State, the school, religion, marriage, trade, science, and explore their foundations in our

32 *Todd: Story of His Life,* p. 65.

33 An unpublished study by William G. Gilmore, cited in Lois W. Banner, "Religion and Reform in the Early Republic: The Role of Youth," *American Quarterly* 23 (December 1971): 679–80 n.5; David Donald, "Toward a Reconsideration of Abolitionists," in *Lincoln Reconsidered: Essays on the Civil War Era* (New York: Vintage Books, 1956), pp. 26–27.

own nature; we are to see that the world not only fitted the former men, but fits us, and to clear ourselves of every usage which has not its roots in our mind. What is man born for but to be a Reformer, a Re-maker of what man has made."[34] Young Americans did not have to approve of Emerson's strategy of reform in order to agree with the sources of his discontent.

A certain amount of discontent and rebellion among the young is to be expected. But the rebellion heard in America in the 1830s was more than temperamental. It was ideological and would become a permanent feature of the discontinuity in the experience of growing up. The youthful end of childhood no longer appeared as a diminished or preliminary stage during which parents and teachers watched for signs of adult stability and common sense. The youth no longer was seen as a miniature adult. To the contrary, as Henry David Thoreau now insisted, adulthood represented the loss or absense of the vitality of youth, the onset of inertia when human powers failed, and a stage of life when the individual began abdicating both his will to resist corruption and his inner freedom of choice. Adults minimized the possibilities of living: "The youth gets together his materials to build a bridge to the moon, or perchance a palace or temple on earth, and at length the middle-aged man concludes to build a wood-shed with them."[35] In contrast to the expansive youth, the diminished adult slowly lost his imagination, flexibility, and finally the principles which organized an active life; and he was reduced both to praying and well-wishing for his spiritual well-being:

When a man is young and his constitution and body have not acquired firmness, *i.e.*, before he has arrived at middle age, he is not an assured inhabitant of the earth, and his compensation is

---

[34] "Man The Reformer," *Emerson Works*, 1, *Nature Addresses and Lectures*, 248.

[35] *The Journal of Henry D. Thoreau*, eds. Bradford Torrey and Francis H. Allen, 14 vols. bound as 2 (New York: Dover Publications, 1962), 4 (July 14, 1852), 227.

that he is not quite earthy, there is something peculiarly tender and divine about him. . . . He really thinks and talks about a larger sphere of existence than this world. It takes him forty years to accommodate himself to the carapax of this world. This is the age of poetry. Afterward he may be the president of a bank, and go the way of all flesh. But a man of settled views, whose thoughts are few and hardened like his bones, is truly mortal, and his only resource is to say his prayers.[36]

Youth was a critical age, for it established the direction of the future. And the fear of entering adulthood and being prematurely overtaken by inertia, tedium, and dullness; the fear of failure in a competitive world pushed young men to extend their years of professional noncommitment, drift, and preparation. Their common anxieties made it natural for youth to fraternize in clubs, to relish its exuberance in athletics and active recreation, and to sentimentalize the excitement of "reforming" the world while a young man. Increasingly as the century wore on, autobiographies, memoirs, and personal accounts in magazines recounted the enthusiasm, promise, and virility of being a young man in America, the importance of struggle during those years, and how a sense of permanent self eventually arrived.

In order to contain the energies of this significant portion of the population, American higher education was uniquely placed. But it would have to redefine itself in the context of the emerging culture of young manhood, and it would have to cultivate more mature means of disciplining students than external constraint and parental regulation. Education was "root-and-branch" reform, Emerson wrote; causes such as abolitionism, pacifism, and temperance were "only medicating the symptoms."[37] Many middle-class Americans agreed with Emerson that higher education potentially came closer to meeting the internal needs of young manhood than either radical politics or repressive moral injunctions. But at mid-century the potential was largely unrealized.

36 *Ibid.*, 13 (December 18, 1859), 35.
37 "Culture," *Emerson Works*, 6, *The Conduct of Life*, 140–41.

BOYHOOD AT COLLEGE:
SELF-EDUCATION AND AMUSEMENT

In post–Civil War America, the university appeared less in response to the repressive nature, the authoritarianism, and the rigid piety of the old-time college than to its amorphousness. In a world of ambitious men, the goals of that college were unclear, its social authority weak, and its academic intentions obscure. The loose usage of the terms "college" and "university" in America symbolized the lack of form. In England, a university examined students, granted degrees, taught all the "arts and faculties," and housed the colleges in which students and instructors communally resided. Colleges did not award degrees. In America, however, the name "university" was used to describe nearly all institutions of higher learning, despite their functions, facilities, standards, and authority. The title served to inflate the importance of an institution in the eyes of its clientele. But not everyone was convinced. "It is a great mistake . . . to call any of our institutions by the name of Universities," Jared Sparks wrote at Harvard in 1829: "They are neither such, nor ever can be, without a radical change. They are mere schools. . . . I do not believe that a university can be engrafted on any of our old colleges."[38] Such statements continued to be heard in the 1880s.

Rather than face significant self-analysis, the traditional colleges tended to muddle along. The process of disintegration had begun in the second half of the eighteenth century, but it accelerated in the first half of the nineteenth, especially in the 1820s, an exceptionally violent and disorderly decade in many collegiate institutions. College faculties despaired over effective means of disciplining students, and what had originally been considered a solid classical curriculum had been worn to a thin veneer. By midcentury, in

[38] "Correspondence of George Bancroft and Jared Sparks, 1823–1832: Illustrating the Relation Between Editor and Reviewer in the Early Nineteenth Century," ed. John Spencer Bassett, *Smith College Studies in History* 2 (January 1917): 136.

some cases, only the ultimate threat of ruin compelled college administrators to listen to criticism and define a more precise function of a liberal arts institution in modern society.[39] Noah Porter and James McCosh, for instance, did not defend the old-time college against the criticism of formlessness and failure. They could hardly refute what they had long been saying as internal critics. Rather, they attempted to define the cultural function of the undergraduate college in the age of the university, that conglomerate of specialized schools.[40]

Historians have listened too closely to spokesmen like Eliot, White, and Gilman, who perhaps exaggerated the notion that the revolution in higher education occurred only after the Civil War. In fact, critical voices were raised within the colleges and led to some important changes at least a generation earlier. The American university that eventually emerged was, by and large, nurtured in that pre-war college. The personnel of the university, its original resources, and its formative experiences—all could first be found in the college. What came to distinguish the age of the postwar university from the prewar college was the consciousness of the effort to professionalize education, the comprehensiveness of the ideological justification, the effectiveness of the planning, and the resultant prospering of the institution, which grew rapidly in enrollment and faculty. But this "success story" had its beginnings in adversity, during the troubled days of the old-time college.

The American college in the first part of the nineteenth century was floundering. No serious-minded observer denied

[39] See Jurgen Herbst, "Liberal Education and the Graduate Schools: An Historical View of College Reform," *History of Education Quarterly* 2 (December 1962): 244–58; George E. Peterson, *The New England College in the Age of the University* (Amherst, Mass.: Amherst College Press, 1964).

[40] See Noah Porter, *The American Colleges and the American Public: With Afterthoughts on College and School Education*, 2d ed., rev. (New York: Charles Scribner's Sons, 1878). See also James Axtell, "The Death of the Liberal Arts College," *History of Education Quarterly* 11 (Winter 1971): 339–52.

it. Tocqueville's remark became a commonplace, repeated by many:

> It is not only the fortunes of men that are equal in America; even their acquirements partake in some degree of the same uniformity. I do not believe that there is a country in the world where, in proportion to the population, there are so few ignorant and at the same time so few learned individuals. Primary instruction is within the reach of everybody; superior instruction is scarcely to be obtained by any. . . . A middling standard is fixed in America for human knowledge.[41]

In the 1840s, Francis Wayland at Brown University, the most eloquent spokesman for new policies in American higher education, agreed. He emphasized that college reformers had responded to every significant complaint of the public. Science and modern-language courses were offered on a limited basis in the curriculum; students were allowed to select some portions of their program; more teachers were hired; and tuition was reduced below the actual cost of an education. Wayland urged that the college begin to satisfy the vocational interests of students. He introduced written examinations as a progressive method of evaluating merit; he abolished the mechanical recitation from textbooks; and he devised a system of marks "by which a parent could know the standing of his son at the close of every term."[42] Yet, because educators themselves showed little interest, the specific reforms languished.

Even when given the opportunity, most Americans did not value a college education. Emerson, for instance, sympathized with the "sturdy lad" from New England who did not consume valuable time by "studying a profession" in college, but "who in turn tries all the professions, who *teams it, farms it, peddles,* keeps a school, preaches, edits a

41 Tocqueville, *Democracy in America*, 1:51–52.

42 Francis Wayland, *Thoughts on the Present Collegiate System* (Boston: Gould, Kendall & Lincoln, 1842), pp. 1–17; Francis Wayland and H. L. Wayland, *A Memoir of the Life and Labors of Francis Wayland, Including Selections from his Personal Reminiscences and Correspondence,* 2 vols. (New York: Sheldon and Company, 1867), 1:205.

newspaper, goes to Congress, buys a township, and so forth, in successive years, and always like a cat falls on his feet."[43] The traditional college education offered little but a title, no hard knowledge about the natural world. Similarly, Henry George advised his son: "Going to college, you will make life friendships, but you will come out filled with much that will have to be unlearned. Going to newspaper work, you will come in touch with the practical world, will be getting a profession and learning to make yourself useful."[44] The desire of Americans to describe their work as professional was widespread. But when higher education was most needed to define new professions, especially other than the ministry, the college stood aloof from society. It had become overcommitted to a prescribed curriculum, limited goals, a ritualized way of life, and a defense of its failures. Newer institutions, usually poor and seeking respectability, tended to imitate the old.

Many colleges left their graduates incomplete, uncertain about the worth of the experience, negative about the ministry, indecisive about the future, unprepared for the world, critical of the intellectual philistinism of an American education, and envious of those peers who had launched themselves into secular occupations without delay. In part, the problem was due to the motivation of many parents who sent their boys to college, particularly the older and established institutions. "Parents without number," Wayland recounted, "when entering their sons in college, have come to me, and at great length have informed me of the peculiarities of their children, stating that their dispositions were excellent if they were only governed in some particular manner." Wayland learned what the parents were reluctant to admit, "that these *peculiar* young men were in fact, in almost every case, spoiled children, with whom I was likely to have more than the usual amount of trouble."[45]

43 "Self-Reliance," *Emerson Works*, 2, *Essays: First Series*, 76.
44 Charles Albro Barker, *Henry George* (New York: Oxford University Press, 1955), p. 339.
45 *Life and Labors of Wayland*, 2:262.

The original idea of the college sounded lofty—a place between home and society to prepare gentlemen for the manners, duties, and responsibilities of their station in life. But teachers were soon introduced to the sobering realities of supervising boys who had been sentenced to college by frustrated parents. Unfortunately, college officials were usually deceived by their own rhetoric, and the students easily resisted the legalistic collegiate restraints that were supposed to correct individual eccentricities and graduate a model of the well-rounded man. When Wayland became president at Brown in 1826, he proposed that "officers were to occupy apartments in college during the day and evening, and were to visit the rooms of students at least twice during the twenty-four hours."[46] In actual practice, discouraged instructors found themselves chained to drifting students, and even Wayland conceded defeat on the issue of discipline in the 1840s.

In part, the problem could be traced to the aristocratic pretensions of many who attended college, especially in the new colleges in western New England. Poor boys, the majority of whom were the sons of farmers and mechanics, sought a college degree—the first in the family—in order to secure their social status. They wished to acquire a title, remain in a declining New England, and identify with a provincial aristocracy, specifically the learned profession of the ministry. Their motive was reactionary, as Henry Ward Beecher depicted it:

The nearest approach to a line drawn between the common people and an aristocratic class in New England is that which education furnishes. And there is almost a superstitious reverence for a *"college education."* If a man has been to college, he has a title. He may be of slender abilities, he may not succeed in his business, but at least he has one claim to respect—he has been to college. It is like a title in a decayed family. It saves the pride and ministers pleasure to the vanity, long after it has in every other respect become utterly useless.[47]

46 *Ibid.,* 1:205.
47 Henry Ward Beecher, *Norwood: Or, Village Life in New England* (New York: Charles Scribner & Company, 1868), p. 181.

The intellectual pursuit of an education did not discipline these economically pressed students. Individually, they often boarded cheaply in the town away from the college, disappeared part of the year to work, ignored rules which inconvenienced their life style, and viewed school as a time to socialize with their college friends and indulge in the gregarious pleasures of an elite class. They viewed themselves as special.

In both the older colleges and the new, students showed their lack of restraint in a constant round of physical violence, often indiscriminate in its object and informally organized during the thrill of the moment. Fist-fighting and brawling were commonplace often taking the form of a "rush" in which, after prayers, a free-for-all broke out between groups of shoving, tramping, and clawing boys.[48] The hazing of freshmen could be a cold-blooded affair. As a prank, a blanket might be thrown over the head of a victim and tobacco smoke blown under it until he got sick or suffocated. In more extreme cases, the blindfolded and gagged victim could have his hair cut off, his body smeared with paint, his head held under a pump for a considerable period of time, his body floated in a barrel down a river or dumped in a locked cemetery. "Unmentionable indignities" of a sexual nature could be performed at night. "The preparations made and the deeds done," McCosh related,

are in all cases mean and dastardly, and in some horrid. I have seen the apparatus. There are masks for concealment, and gags to stop the mouth and ears; there is a razor and there are scissors, and there are ropes to bind, and in some cases whips or boards to inflict blows; there are commonly filthy applications ready, and in all cases unmanly insults more difficult to be borne by a youth of spirit than any beating.[49]

[48] See the description in Sheldon, *Student Life and Customs*, pp. 102–5. See also B. H. Hall, *A Collection of College Words and Customs,* rev. ed. (Cambridge, Mass.: John Bartlett, 1856), pp. 498–99; George R. Cutting, *Student Life at Amherst College: Its Organizations, Their Membership and History* (Amherst, Mass.: Hatch & Williams, 1871), p. 131.

[49] James McCosh, "Discipline in American Colleges," *The North American Review* 126 (1878): 439. See also Sheldon, *Student Life and*

Needless to say, people were hurt on the college scene, some fatally. "Crimes that were worthy of the penitentiary," recalled Andrew Peabody about Harvard, "were of frequent occurrence."[50]

The lack of student restraint was also directed at the college and its faculty. At Harvard, public rooms in inhabited buildings were blown up, and Yale students celebrated Christmas by smashing the windows of the college buildings and bolting the doors so that the professors had to smash them down with axes. Elsewhere, students called professors liars to their faces, and drunken revelers stoned faculty houses. Students formed clubs to steal chickens and borrow horses for nocturnal rides, to shave the manes and tails of favorite horses belonging to those whom they wished to punish, to serenade unpopular faculty members, and call strikes against the college by boycotting the commons with its pedestrian food. Yale, for instance, suppressed "bread and butter" rebellions in 1818 and 1828, and these ended only when the faculty expelled four students it thought to be the ringleaders and temporarily closed the college.[51] However, Yale came up with the permanent solution in 1842 when it closed the commons and students made their own eating arrangements for the next ninety years.

The food riots indicated the depth of the strains in college life. People quickly reveal themselves in their responses to food, its availability, preparation, taste, consistency, and surroundings. Food in the college at once became both the focus of division and discontent between rich and poor students and the source of camaraderie for all those, rich and poor, who gathered in the commons. Peabody represented both responses when he recounted that at Harvard in the early nineteenth century the quantity of the food was sufficient, "but it was so mean in quality, so poorly cooked,

50 Andrew P. Peabody, *Harvard Reminiscences* (Boston: Ticknor and Company, 1888), p. 32.

51 Related in Brooks Mather Kelley, *Yale: A History* (New Haven, Conn., and London: Yale University Press, 1974), pp. 215–16.

and so coarsely served, as to disgust those who had been accustomed to the decencies of the table, and to encourage a mutinous spirit, rude manners, and ungentlemanly habits; so that the dining-halls were seats of boisterous misrule, and nurseries of rebellion."[52] Students from better homes expected the "decencies of the table," and their social class sensibilities were offended when college kitchens accommodated the pocketbooks of poorer students. The evening meal at Harvard, for instance, consisted of tea and cold bread "of the consistency of wool." The Harvard kitchen, the largest in New England, fed about two hundred people, and a student could board for $1.75 per week, in contrast to upwards of $3.00 in a private home. Breakfast at Yale during this period was a dish called "slum," made from day-old boiled salt beef and potatoes and prepared in the form of fried hash. According to one Yale student, it was "enough to have produced any amount of dyspepsia. There are stomachs, it may be, which can put up with any sort of food, and any mode of cookery; but they are not those of students."[53] Of course, the pertinent question was, Which students?

In order to sustain enrollments, colleges carefully watched costs, and the austere space of a cheap dormitory room also irritated students whose families could afford better but in reality might not pay. At Harvard, the bare rooms were inadequately heated, carpetless, and furnished with a plain pine bed, table, desk, washstand, rocking-chair, and two to four simple chairs. Nothing else; a feather-bed was a luxury, mattresses were not in general use, coal and friction matches had not found their way into the college. Even "the evening-lamp could be lighted only by the awkward, and often baffling, process of 'striking fire' with flint, steel, and tinder-box." According to Peabody, a student's official life was both hard and monotonous, and like his room "remarkable

52 Peabody, *Harvard Reminiscences*, p. 29.

53 Hall, *College Words and Customs*, pp. 432–33; Sheldon, *Student Life and Customs*, p. 108; Allmendinger, *Paupers and Scholars*, pp. 82–86.

chiefly for what it did not have."[54] Under such circumstances, students responded normally by seeking excitement. Wealthier students, for instance, not only might take pleasure in resenting and demeaning the poorer students, they began abandoning the dormitories and commons for more interesting private accommodations in town, beyond the confines of the college and the control of its regulations.

Students rebelled in a variety of ways, even within the configurations of a geometry class. The most formidable student outburst at Yale, for instance, occurred in 1830 with the "Conic Section's Rebellion."[55] Students refused to accept a change in the method of teaching mathematics in which theorems would be explained from the "figure" on the blackboards instead of from the textbook. Students argued that most classes had recited from the book, while the faculty responded that demonstration from the figure was the method at Yale. The emotional involvement was irrational. At stake was the power of the college to enforce its will and the power of the students to resist that will, however petty the issue. Overreacting, the faculty repressed the revolt by expelling forty-three students, nearly half the class. Though the campus quieted down in the decade that followed, students began to carry weapons and vent their aggressions by fighting, burning, and looting in the town. Elsewhere, six insurrections shattered life at Princeton between 1800 and 1830.[56]

---

[54] Peabody, *Harvard Reminiscences,* pp. 196–97. See also Charles William Eliot, *Harvard Memories* (Cambridge, Mass.: Harvard University Press, 1923), pp. 115–16, 119–20. Eliot related that in the period 1849–59 the Yard lacked a sewage system as well as a water supply. Students carried water from outdoor pumps to their rooms in their own pails. "They had no hot water whatever, unless they heated a pot on their own fire, and very few did that. Consequently the amount of bathing done in the College was extremely limited." (P. 119.)

[55] Described in Kelley, *Yale,* pp. 168–69; Sheldon, *Student Life and Customs,* p. 110.

[56] John Maclean, *History of the College of New Jersey, From its Origin in 1746 to the Commencement of 1854,* 2 vols. (Philadelphia: J. B. Lippincott & Company, 1877), 2:40–41, 72–73, 86–93, 154–59, 167–

The apparently antiseptic, paternalistic, and isolated small-town environment of the college could nevertheless mask volcanic forces. In his *Autobiography*, Andrew Dickson White described the boredom and antics of college students, their rowdiness, profanity, and defiance of regulations. Nor did White recount "good old" collegiate nonsense, nineteenth-century versions of panty raids and "streaking." White told of murder, the infliction of physical disabilities that destroyed professional lives, the destruction of books and research,

the student brawl at the Harvard commons which cost the historian Prescott his sight, and the riot at the Harvard commencement which blocked the way of President Everett and the British minister . . . the fatal wounding of Tutor Dwight, the maiming of Tutor Goodrich, and the killing of two town rioters by students at Yale . . . the monstrous indignities to the president and faculty at Hobart of which I was myself witness, as well as the state of things at various other colleges in my own college days.[57]

The residents of small towns usually could not challenge the upper hand of the students. But where a fighting element emerged, as in the firemen and the sailors in New Haven, brutal and frequent conflicts ensued between the townsmen and the students.[58]

Students fulfilled adult expectations that they were unregenerate children. Peabody related that when he entered Harvard in the 1820s, "the entire Cambridge Common, then an unenclosed dust-plain, was completely covered, on Com-

72, 251–55, 267–70; " 'The Great Rebellion' at Princeton," *William and Mary Quarterly* 16 (July 1907): 119–21; "Glimpses of Old College Life," *Ibid.* 7 (July 1900): 19–20.

[57] *The Autobiography of Andrew Dickson White*, 2 vols. (New York: The Century Company, 1905), 1:353. See also G. Stanley Hall, "Student Customs," *Proceedings of the American Antiquarian Society*, n.s. 14 (October 1900): 107; David F. Allmendinger, Jr., "The Dangers of Ante-Bellum Student Life," *Journal of Social History* 7 (Fall 1973): 75–85.

[58] Kelley, *Yale*, pp. 216–20; [John Mitchell], *Reminiscences of Scenes and Characters in College: By a Graduate of Yale* (New Haven, Conn.: A. H. Maltby, 1847), pp. 215–16; Sheldon, *Student Life and Customs*, pp. 113–14.

mencement Day, and on the nights preceding and following it, with drinking-stands, dancing-booths, mountebank shows, and gambling-tables; and I have never since heard such a horrid din, tumult, and jargon, of oath, shout, scream, fiddle, quarreling, and drunkenness, as on those two nights."[59] George Ticknor learned that Harvard students were drinking brandy in the morning, and contracting venereal disease from women of ill repute. "The morals of great numbers of the young men who come to us," he gently concluded, "are corrupted."[60] In New Haven, Yale students could find pleasures to suit most any taste for perversion. At the most respected American colleges, students kept ale on tap with free access in the dormitories, shouted obscenities at tutors, burned textbooks in annual ceremonies, and persisted in the noisy and often disorderly burlesque of college life.

Student clubs that specialized in carousing and conspiring against the authorities proliferated. In the class of 1821 at Harvard, Emerson could choose between the gentlemanly Porcellian, better known as the "Pig Club," in part because of its dedication to gluttony; The Order of Knights of the Square Table, a festive group; or the Engine Club, a gang of delinquents who ran about town ostensibly to protect civic and college property.[61] Wayland told about a professor at the University of Virginia in the 1840s who "had incurred the ill will of some of the students" and was murdered by his own pupils.[62] In 1836 at Virginia a group of students who illegally constituted themselves a military company refused to surrender their guns to college officials. A riot followed with mob violence, random shooting, and attacks on the houses of professors. Armed soldiers finally

59 Peabody, *Harvard Reminiscences*, p. 26.

60 *Life, Letters, and Journals of George Ticknor*, 2 vols. (Boston and New York: Houghton Mifflin Company, 1909), 1:359; David B. Tyack, *George Ticknor and the Boston Brahmins* (Cambridge, Mass.: Harvard University Press, 1967), p. 96.

61 Ralph L. Rusk, *The Life of Ralph Waldo Emerson* (New York: Columbia University Press, 1957), p. 72. See also Sheldon, *Student Life and Customs*, pp. 116–22.

62 *Life and Labors of Wayland*, 2:93.

restored order, and the faculty dismissed charges against the students, who promised to behave.[63]

Nor did the religious revivals that periodically swept through the colleges in the first half of the nineteenth century run contrary to the pattern of emotional self-indulgence. Under the momentary influence of the penetrating evangelical spirit, students might wildly break down, weep, shout, and beg for forgiveness.[64] But the results were largely artificial. Invariably the faculty, which most students viewed as an adversary, planned and led the revivals in order to encourage moral reform and discipline. Significantly, the frequency of revivals at Yale corresponded to the intensity of student disorders. Yale underwent seven revivals in the particularly difficult 1820s, one every year and a half. And Yale's eleven revivals in the years 1821–40 surpassed the count of the previous eighty years.[65] Conversions, especially prevalent among teenage students, appeared to have had neither profound nor lasting effects, except perhaps in students inclined toward the ministry. During a prayer meeting at Williams, student friends led their fellow student G. Stan-

[63] Related in John S. Patton, *Jefferson, Cabell and the University of Virginia* (New York and Washington: The Neale Publishing Company, 1906), pp. 147–54; Handlin and Handlin, *American College and Culture*, pp. 40–41.

[64] Accounts of the revivals are found in *The American Quarterly Register*, the journal published by the American Education Society. See Henry Wood, "Historical Sketch of the Revivals of Religion in Dartmouth College, Hanover, N.H.," *Ibid.*, 9 (November 1836): 177–82; [C.] Goodrich, "Narrative of Revivals of Religion in Yale College," *Ibid.*, 10 (February 1838): 289–310; H. Humphrey, "Revivals of Religion in Amherst College," *Ibid.*, 11 (February 1839): 317–28; Joshua Bates, "Revivals of Religion in Middlebury College," *Ibid.*, 12 (February 1840): 305–23; Albert Hopkins, "Revivals of Religion in Williams College," *Ibid.*, 13 (February 1841): 341–51. See Allmendinger, *Paupers and Scholars*, pp. 119–21.

[65] Describing the revival of spring 1831, Goodrich commented: "The state of the college, for a long time after this revival, was peculiarly happy. For nearly or quite a year, there was not a single instance of punishment, so far as I can recollect, in the whole institution. The necessity of government seemed almost superseded, by the prevailing spirit of order, diligence and mutual affection." *American Quarterly Register* 10 (February 1838): 309. See also *Reminiscences . . . by a Graduate of Yale*, pp. 157–87.

ley Hall to believe "that I was suffering from conviction of sin, and accordingly, by various stages . . . that I had been converted." However, it made "no great change in my life," Hall recalled, and the emotional experiences were not "very deep."[66] Nevertheless, his parents were pleased .

Though religion did not impress Hall as a student, another experience, as a faculty member, did. He told of a chilling episode at Antioch in the early seventies when he was appointed chairman of a committee to break up a group of graduates "which supplied compositions to students in different colleges for a fee." One day on the street, Hall happened to come across the leader of the group, who drew a revolver and began loading it as he passed Hall:

Later, a bullet fired in my direction lodged in the post of the store a safe rod from where I was; another was fired through the window of my room a few nights later; while at a rhetorical evening exercise where I sat on the platform, a bottle of acid was thrown through the window, evidently directed at me but fell short and broke on the edge of the platform, spoiling my clothes and the dresses of some of the girls in the front row.[67]

More than some clothes were spoiled; so was the myth of the college as a refuge that sheltered gentlemanly types from the world. The sanctuary had collapsed.

The college failed to discipline its students in the first half of the nineteenth century, but not for any lack of written regulations, threats, and lectures on proper deportment. Indeed, the official atmosphere approached that of a military school. Upon entering Harvard in the 1830s, for instance, a student received a copy of the Orders and Regulations in which a system of merits and demerits was set out. Every proper act was rewarded with points and every transgression penalized, and the points accumulated over four

66 G. Stanley Hall, *Life and Confessions of a Psychologist* (New York: D. Appleton and Company, 1923), p. 163. Mark Hopkins described the ordinary revival as full of "noise or ostentation or vanity." *Early Letters of Mark Hopkins* (New York: The John Day Company, Incorporated, 1929), p. 127.

67 Hall, *Life and Confessions*, p. 202.

years, determining the student's rank in his class. Eight points were lost for being late at prayers (curiously, only two points for missing them entirely); sixteen points for lying on the grass, shouting from a window in the yard, or playing a musical instrument during study hours. Acting as investigator, prosecutor, and judge, a Parietal Committee that included nearly half the faculty supervised the detested system. On each side of the pulpit in the chapel, for instance, were sentry-boxes, manned during daily prayers by professors or tutors on the lookout for misconduct. Every activity by a student converted into a numerical value. A perfect recitation was worth eight points, a written assignment twenty-four, a declamation sixty. And the credits piled up, until a student graduated after four years with about twenty thousand points.

Students tended to express indifference if not hostility toward an indiscriminate system of ranking in which one unacceptable act of behavior could effectively cancel out the academic achievement of an entire year. These primitive efforts at grading students, and holding them accountable, were generally self-defeating. The excessive regulation and absolute standard of ranking only further goaded many students into flouting the arbitrary authority of the establishment and heaping ridicule on college procedures. "I think," Edward Everett Hale recalled, "the result was a very great indifference to college rank on the part of most of the students. But in the bosoms of our families there was a great respect for it."[68] However, the results were circular; families looked to the college for discipline, while the college looked back to the family.

[68] Edward Everett Hale, *A New England Boyhood* (Boston, Toronto: Little, Brown, and Company, 1893, 1964), p. 203. Descriptions of the parietal system at Harvard are found in Hall, *College Words and Customs*, pp. 343–44; Ernest Samuels, *The Young Henry Adams* (Cambridge, Mass.: Harvard University Press, 1948), pp. 12–13; Mary Lovett Smallwood, *An Historical Study of Examinations and Grading Systems in Early American Universities: A Critical Study of the Original Records of Harvard, William and Mary, Yale, Mount Holyoke, and Michigan from Their Founding to 1900* (Cambridge, Mass.: Harvard University Press, 1935), pp. 70–74.

The failure of discipline in the college was matched by the failure to challenge the student intellectually. "With a single exception, the instructors in my college life were little more than the driven stakes to which we were tethered," John Bascom remembered about Williams. The remark was commonplace. "On looking back, I think most of the old students will agree that too much value was attached to *memoriter* recitations," James Burrill Angell commented about Brown.[69] In the college classroom, students were first separated alphabetically into recitation groups. Then, young and inexperienced tutors, often only a few years older than the students, proceeded to mark the students on their ability to recite or memorize an assigned passage from a text. No discussion was permitted as the tutor perfunctorily called on each student who responded in turn by reciting mechanically. The average student displayed no interest in the text except to receive credit for the tedious daily drill. "Of course," Peabody recalled, "the endeavor—not always successful—was to determine what part of a lesson it was necessary for each individual student to prepare."[70] And once his turn had passed, the student naturally allowed his attention to wander, leaving plenty of time for daydreams.

The tutor played the role of a judge rather than a teacher, and his relationship to the students was normally imperious and unfriendly. The feelings of antagonism were mutual. A student seldom visited an instructor's room voluntarily, and then at night; and his peers accused a pupil of "bootlicking" and threatened him with reprisals if he went to a recitation early or remained after the exercise to ask a question. "Blue," "blue-light," and "blue-skin" were the humiliating nicknames for a student who was overconscientious in performing his duties and obeying the regulations. A student—a "toady"—who approached a teacher in friendly greeting, showed too much interest in his studies,

[69] John Bascom, *Things Learned by Living* (New York: G. P. Putnam's Sons, 1913), p. 47; James Burrill Angell, *Reminiscences* (New York: Longmans, Green and Company, 1912), p. 29.

[70] Peabody, *Harvard Reminiscences*, p. 201.

or wished to board in a faculty home was suspected of being a spy, as was the teacher who made an effort to relate to the students.[71] For his own part, the average tutor only abused the students in the same manner in which the faculty abused the tutors. Indolent professors exploited the lowly instructors by underpaying, overworking, and ignoring them. At Harvard, for instance, George Ticknor discovered that four tutors taught 2,364 exercises per year, while eleven professors taught only 824 exercises.[72] The tutors themselves were on trial, and they attended to their task by running a tidy classroom, knowing their place, and showing hostility toward students.

DULL PLACES AT BEST

"Colleges are dull places at the best," Theodore Parker wrote Noah Porter, "and the professors sometimes become as dead as any tooth in the brass wheels of the public clock, and like that only keep the college to *mean* time."[73] In a typical day at Harvard, students were required to attend chapel at six o'clock in the morning during the summer and six-thirty during the winter, since when daylight came later than six, according to Hale, "it had been proved, by sad experience, that the undergraduates took measures to put out the candles on which the chapel . . . depended for its light."[74] The chapel was bitter cold in winter. Following the ten-minute prayer service, a recitation session preceded breakfast, and then two and on rare occasion three recitation hours followed during the day, which officially closed at six in the evening again with prayers. The university re-

[71] Hall, *College Words and Customs*, pp. 30–31, 461–62; Cutting, *Student Life at Amherst*, p. 132; *Reminiscences . . . by a Graduate of Yale*, pp. 133–35; Peabody, *Harvard Reminiscences*, p. 200.

[72] Tyack, *Ticknor*, p. 95.

[73] Cited in George S. Merriam, ed., *Noah Porter: A Memorial by Friends* (New York: Charles Scribner's Sons, 1893), p. 122.

[74] Hale, *New England Boyhood*, pp. 179–80.

quired students to attend the two prayer services and recitations. Because any bright boy found it impossible to spend more than three hours a day preparing for the deadly class routine, a maximum of six hours a day was spent on academic work. In any average day, the boy was left nine or ten hours to educate and amuse himself, usually the latter. After the evening meal, Peabody recalled, "the dormitories rang with song and merriment." Expectedly, eager students became bored at college and apathetic ones troublesome. Hale spoke the sentiment of many when he concluded: "So we wrought through the four years, which for me were . . . tedious, as I had expected they would be."[75]

It was plainly observable after 1830 that the most respected American colleges were drifting, and the newer colleges founded in the nineteenth century did not correct the aimless movement. Noah Porter, Frederick A. P. Barnard, Daniel Coit Gilman, and Andrew Dickson White, for instance, attended Yale, and White commented upon the significance of Yale to Americans in the century:

Harvard undoubtedly had the greater influence on leading American thinkers throughout the nation, but much less direct influence on the people at large outside Massachusetts. The direct influence of Yale on affairs throughout the United States was far greater; it was felt in all parts of the country and in every sort of enterprise.[76]

The largest college in America in the first half of the nineteenth century, Yale became representative of the best collegiate education. Institutions such as Beloit and Western Reserve prided themselves on being known as the "Yale of the West," and according to one estimate, "at least sixteen

[75] Peabody, *Harvard Reminiscences*, p. 198; Hale, *New England Boyhood*, p. 201.

[76] White, *Autobiography*, 2:487. In the nineteenth century, the educated middle class widely accepted the impression that Harvard was more the "literary college" and Yale "more of a college fitting one for public life." In 1893 Charles Thwing wrote that "Yale seems to be more American than Harvard. Public life, politics, statesmanship represent a very important part of American life." "College Men First Among Successful Citizens," *Forum* 15 (June 1893): 500.

colleges were founded before the Civil War largely under the guiding hand of Yale College and its graduates."[77]

Nevertheless, the familiar failings of the college system marred the education of the presidents, even at Yale. The spirit of the classical, patriarchal, and rule-bound *Report* of 1828 endured. Barnard, for one, summarized the discontent: "Although I was apparently surrounded by many educational influences, and enjoying, or supposed to enjoy, the instruction of many eminent educators, it was to me a period of almost literal self-education."[78] Barnard felt most positively about his extracurricular writing and speaking in the literary society to which he belonged. And later he directly related the lack of student restraint in the American college with the lack of individual participation in the important decisions which effected a professional education.

In 1870, Barnard published a statistical study that confirmed what many educators thought they knew: that in the period 1850–70 New England colleges seemed to be serving a decreasing percentage of the general population.[79] In fact, whether the number of students was decreasing or increasing relative to the population was a debatable point, and irrelevant. None could reasonably dispute that the number of college graduates in the population was too small. For instance, between 1840 and 1860 an average of only 31 persons graduated each year from Columbia, located in a growing urban area. In the same period Yale averaged only 116 graduates in all departments and Harvard 146; Dartmouth averaged 78, Williams 43, Bowdoin 36, and Brown 32. In

[77] Donald G. Tewksbury, *The Founding of American Colleges and Universities Before the Civil War: With Particular Reference to the Religious Influences Bearing upon the College Movement* (New York: Teachers College, Columbia University, 1932), p. 14.

[78] John Fulton, *Memoirs of Frederick A. P. Barnard* (New York: Published for the Columbia University Press by Macmillan and Co., 1896), p. 33.

[79] F. A. P. Barnard, *Two Papers on Academic Degrees* (New York: McGowan & Slippers, Printers, 1880), pp. 10–12; Columbia College, *Annual Report of the President*, 1866, pp. 24–25. See also Arthur M. Comey, "The Growth of New England Colleges," *Educational Review* 1 (March 1891): 209–19.

1860, Yale was the largest college in the country with 521 students; Harvard had 457. Not until late in the century did the gross number of graduates in American institutions begin to rise substantially. In the decades of the nineteenth century, a combined list of thirty-seven leading colleges and universities averaged the following number of graduates per year:

1800s: 207
1810s: 295
1820s: 413
1830s: 528
1840s: 759
1850s: 908
1860s: 928
1870s: 1155
1880s: 1437
1890s: 2529

From decade to decade, the percentage of increase was erratic.[80]

Nor did a lack of colleges in the antebellum years deprive Americans of educational opportunities. Citing the American Almanac of 1842, Wayland counted 101 colleges, 39 theological seminaries, 10 law schools, and 31 medical schools.[81] According to Donald Tewksbury, 182 colleges were founded between the end of the colonial period and the Civil War, 133 of them between 1830 and 1871. Expansion in the student population occurred by means of the proliferation of new institutions rather than the dramatic growth of old ones. By 1870, more than 500 institutions in America awarded the bachelor's degree, more than in all of Europe. However, this manner of expansion created its own problems. Like shooting stars, colleges suddenly appeared and then vanished, witnessed only by those who attended or held a degree from an obscure place. Tewksbury estimated

---

[80] *Ibid.*, 211; Burritt, *Professional Distribution of College and University Graduates*, pp. 91, 85, 81, 96, 107, 113, 93, 143.

[81] Wayland, *Present Collegiate System*, p. 8.

that from the total number of 516 colleges founded in the sixteen states of the Union before the Civil War, 412 failed, a mortality rate of 81 percent.[82] Not only did such impermanence shake public confidence in the American college, it facilitated the appearance of the confidence man with the phony degree or the purchased one from an institution that may have never existed.

In America, the notions of college or university did not insure any organizing principles, uniform standards, patterns, or consistent definitions. Confusion and contradiction rendered higher education ineffective. Wayland observed that colleges had no relationships to each other, and "the educational system has no necessary connexions with any thing else. In no other country is the whole plan for the instruction of the young so entirely dissevered from connexion with the business of subsequent life."[83] Students established few ties to their institutions; any loyalty centered on the class. Even benefactors donated money to a college and then lost interest, acting "utterly indifferent as to the manner in which it is to be employed." Higher education "has almost got to be created," British historian and educator Goldwin Smith observed, arriving in America in 1868 to teach at the new Cornell University.[84]

Lack of direction in the course offerings typified American education. The curriculum looked like a crazy quilt, irritating even the traditionalists, as administrators tacked on random courses to fill the demand for such new areas of knowledge as the natural sciences. But when new courses were added, the number of hours required by the traditional subjects—Latin, Greek—was not reduced. The eager student faced an impossibility. When Emerson told an admirer that Harvard taught all the branches of learning, Thoreau retorted, "Yes, indeed, all the branches and none

82 Tewksbury, *Founding Colleges and Universities,* pp. 31, 28.

83 Wayland, *Present Collegiate System,* p. 41.

84 Cited in Ellis Paxson Oberholtzer, *A History of the United States Since the Civil War,* 5 vols. (New York: The Macmillan Company, 1917–37), 3:450.

of the roots."[85] Professors were called upon to teach subjects about which they knew nothing, hence the dependence upon arid textbooks. Lectures in modern subjects for juniors and seniors appeared to be superfluous within the context of the marking system and the prescribed curriculum. Despite official denials, the lectures often were extracurricular; the professor simply read his paper and dismissed the students, who had no reason either to take notes or remember a word.

Admissions policies also displayed discrepancies which usually damaged discipline in the college. Institutions competed for the limited pool of students, and most often admission and matriculation were a matter of form—one reason that college students extended in age from thirteen years to thirty-three. Hale, for instance, "was but thirteen years and five months old when I entered Harvard College." In 1819, the average age of the freshman class at Harvard was sixteen and a half, but the average reflected a relatively broad range. "Thirty-two or three is not an uncommon age for a candidate for the degree of Bachelor of Arts," observed Wayland at Brown.[86] The breadth of the scale was striking. Between 1830 and 1860, according to Allmendinger, nearly one-fourth of all graduates from New England colleges were over the age of twenty-five, including nearly one-third from such established new colleges as Amherst, Dartmouth, and Williams. Coming from more homogeneous and prosperous backgrounds, Harvard and Yale graduates tended to be younger, in their early twenties, while graduates from other New England colleges tended to be older. For instance, more than half the students were

[85] Cited in Henry Seidel Canby, *Thoreau* (Boston: Beacon Press, 1939), p. 40.

[86] Hale, *New England Boyhood*, p. 166; Wayland, *Present Collegiate System*, p. 31. Josiah Quincy, who attended Harvard between 1817 and 1821, remarked that the average age at entrance was fifteen, and some of the freshmen were twelve. Michigan had a fixed minimum age of fourteen. See W. Scott Thomas, "Changes in the Age of College Graduation," *Popular Science Monthly* 63 (1903): 159–71; Schmidt, *Old Time College President*, p. 78.

over the age of twenty-four in Mark Hopkins's class at
Williams in 1824.[87]

Wayland drew the obvious conclusion: "Here then are students of very dissimilar ages associated together, pursuing the
same studies and subjected to the same rules. It is obvious
that the rules suitable for one party, would be unsuitable
for the other."[88] Older students tended to come from
varied backgrounds and experiences. They had been out
in the world as "men," had worked at assorted jobs and
perhaps professions, delayed their college education, and
then independently returned to school, often without family assistance or a patron. However, upon returning to college, a mature student in his middle twenties also returned
to boyhood. From society's point of view, colleges were for
boys, and manhood did not arrive until after graduation.
Paradoxically, Americans recognized the sixteen-year-old
who left home and found a position as having already entered adulthood, an attitude which could only serve to
demean the self-image of older students and encourage
them to rebuff college authority.

The lack of consistent age-grading in the college meant
that natural leaders emerged from among the older and
more experienced students within a class to organize student
societies and rebellions. With capable heroes to emulate, a
teenage boy's sense of competition with others his own age,
and his need to accept an equal as a leader—an act he
might well resist—was minimized. Subjected to the social
pressures surrounding him, the boy fell under the influence
of the more mature individuals, who no doubt enjoyed and
cultivated the esteem. Moreover, because of the small student bodies and the demand for students, colleges hesitated
to discipline their pupils by expulsion, especially rowdy
boys who had earned the admiration of their class as student leaders. "The suspended student," Peabody related,
"was escorted in triumph on his departure and his return,
and was the hero of his class for the residue of his college

87 Allmendinger, *Paupers and Scholars*, pp. 9–10, 38, 129–38.
88 Wayland, *Present Collegiate System*, p. 31.

life."[89] When Harvard expelled forty-three of the seventy members of the class of 1823—after a history of secret partying, fighting in the commons, provoking the tutors, and defying the professors, all culminating with two days of rioting—administrators knew that few colleges, perhaps not even Harvard, could consistently afford to be so firm. In 1824 the Massachusetts General Court refused to renew Harvard's ten-thousand-dollar annual grant.[90]

Showdowns between faculties and students might harm all parties, and the notoriety of the "Great Rebellion" at Harvard did jolt the establishment into considering reforms. But student discipline remained a major problem, and college authorities fluctuated in their unimaginative responses between excessive harshness and excessive leniency. Students quickly learned to play on the insecurities of their college parents. After Yale's Bread and Butter Rebellion in 1828, the students who had been expelled were readmitted upon apologizing; and after the Conic Section's Rebellion in 1830, the forty-one expelled students, who were denied admission elsewhere, came to terms with an administration which had won the battle but was losing the larger war. The bloodiest events at Yale in New Haven were yet to come. The American college got by, avoiding issues as long as possible, and simultaneously attempting to be a boarding school, high school, reformatory, liberal arts university, professional school, church, monastery, and fraternal society.

Wayland emphasized that the American college failed as a system that could naturally control, remedy, hold itself accountable, and reform itself from within. Trustees, faculty, and students could neither monitor nor take responsibility for their own movements. The institution was *not* so arranged, as Wayland put it, that "it will go of itself."

[89] Peabody, *Harvard Reminiscences,* p. 32.

[90] See the account in Samuel Eliot Morison, "The Great Rebellion in Harvard College and the Resignation of President Kirkland," *Transactions,* Publications of the Colonial Society of Massachusetts 27 (April 1928): 54–112.

Internal self-discipline was lacking in everyone. Mistrust between faculty and students, for instance, prevented the appearance of officially sanctioned governing bodies among the students, who often found it difficult to resist the carnival atmosphere, the bohemianism, and the social pressures to join the fun. Exasperated students formed vigilante groups, which only heightened the atmosphere of lawlessness.

Reflecting their own lack of confidence in college teaching as a worthy career, faculty members were defensive on all fronts. "There is no step in the progress of colleges and universities," Andrew Dickson White was prompted to remark, "that has not been earnestly opposed on apparently cogent grounds by most worthy college officers."[91] The college consisted of self-serving groups. Neither trustees, administrators, faculty, nor students took pride in the educational activities indigenous to a college education. And lacking respect for their own function, members of the institution failed either to exercise any real understanding of the problems or to express any enduring loyalty to the corporate body. Except by coercive and authoritarian means, the college found it difficult to elicit discipline, run its affairs, and regulate its proceedings.

From the perspective of ambitious middle-class persons, the college had become an artificial institution, lacking a purposeful reason for existence in a society becoming increasingly conscious of national and universal standards. For instance, resources were both maldistributed and irrationally dispersed. One college proudly possessed a donated observatory without a telescope and another a telescope without an observatory. Moreover, political, local, religious, and personal influences played too large a role in the appointments both of trustees and faculty. Consequently, trustees viewed their positions as honorary, and generally concerned themselves little with their necessary duties. Faculty promotions were not based on merit and competitive accomplishment, and the effect was to drive many in-

[91] Andrew D. White, "College Fraternities," *Forum* 3 (1887): 253.

structors, especially the best, to devote their energy to outside interests where talent was better rewarded. Writing in 1839, the visiting Francis Grund was told that Harvard professors who did not inherit money looked to "marry rich women, who can afford paying for being entertained. They show their common sense in that. It's quite the fashion for our rich girls to *buy themselves a professor*, previous to taking a trip to Europe."[92] Was the professor not better off entertaining rich widows and prosperous daughters rather than students?

Many students suffered from both neglect and their own lack of confidence about spending time at college, and they let their disdain be known. Andrew Peabody's portrait of the clumsy Harvard professors making fools of themselves by chasing delinquent students symbolizes best the humiliating state of affairs at the country's most elite college:

The professors, as well as the parietal officers, performed police duty as occasion seemed to demand; and in case of a general disturbance, which was not infrequent, the entire Faculty were on the chase for offenders,—a chase seldom successful; while their unskilled manoeuvres in this uncongenial service were wont to elicit, not so much silent admiration, as shouts of laughter and applause, which they strove in vain to trace to their source.[93]

Widows and daughters were not so evasive. The faculty's hobnobbing in respectable society; pedestrian teaching based on shallow textbooks; an excessive reliance on the dependable structure of a four-year course in which serving time became more important than attaining proficiency in subjects; the social pressures to participate in mischief, and the constant examples of raw aggression—all told the truth that collegiate institutions were troubled.

---

[92] Francis J. Grund, *Aristocracy in America: From the Sketch-Book of a German Nobleman* (New York; Evanston, Ill.; London: Harper & Row, Publishers, 1959), p. 156.

[93] Peabody, *Harvard Reminiscences*, pp. 200–1.

7

An Emerging Culture

STUDENT CULTURE

Though college officials were moribund, students were not,
and outside the classroom they remade the college campus
into a distinct American phenomenon. With their emerging
consciousness of youth as a definite period of life between
childhood and adulthood, students began disciplining themselves by forming their own permanent institutions that
responded to their special needs. Amidst the rowdiness,
earnest searching was going on. In the generation before
the Civil War, the effective center of student life began
shifting away from the official college and its oppressive
routine. In the literary society, the fraternity, organized
athletics, and the student Young Men's Christian Association, a special American student culture slowly emerged
which reflected the attitudes and the ambitions of the new
middle class. The college of the future had a more important task than to cater to wild boys. It would serve the
broader requirements of American "youth." It is impossible
to say who played the greatest role in the changing culture
of the college: students, inspirational voices like Emerson's,
or academic critics. But the college was being transformed.

Young men needed time to prepare themselves to compete in a world of struggle, time to acquire the personal qualities of a steady nerve, courage, knowledge, self-reliance, and loyalty—qualities useful in any profession. The young man could not take his training, skill, and stratagems for granted; and he required customs and established roles that would make it possible for him to act out his young manhood: mixing in the coeducational social gathering, competing in the boat race and on the ball field, debating a public issue, committing himself to a "radical" reform, participating in student government and in religiously sponsored social-service projects.

Thomas Grattan, the British consul at Boston between 1839 and 1846, observed that the majority of American boys were a "melancholy picture" of premature aging and wasted energy. To the detriment of their careers, too many young men failed to choose to form their lives and expand their ambition in a period of life called youth:

It might be almost said that every man is born middle-aged. . . . The principal business of life seems to be to grow old as fast as possible. . . . The boys are sent to college at fourteen. They leave it, with their degrees at seventeen. They are then launched at once into life, either as merchants or attornies' clerks, medical students, or adventurers. . . . The interval between their leaving school and commencing their business career offers no occupation to give either gracefulness or strength to body or mind. Athletic games and the bolder field-sports being unknown . . . all that is left is chewing, smoking, drinking, driving hired horses in wretched gigs with a cruel velocity. . . . Young men made up of such materials as I describe are not young men at all. . . . They have no breadth, either of shoulders, information, or ambition. Their physical powers are subdued, and their mental capability cribbed into narrow limits.[1]

In the minds of its proponents, organized college athletics symbolized the cultural recognition of youth as a formative stage of human development which college life was in a unique position to support.

[1] Thomas Colley Grattan, *Civilized America*, 2 vols., 2d ed. (London: Bradbury and Evans, 1859), 2:318, 319, 320.

The new orientation was vertical. The student's focus of attention was removed from the college class with its *esprit de corps* and the dormitory, and turned inward toward the individual who was anxious about his personal destiny and identity. As the tension within individuals and the antagonisms between them grew more severe, students no longer tended to view the faculty as the natural enemy. If he was to be a serious contender in the struggle to succeed, the young man must concern himself with his own physical, moral, and intellectual education. And that concern could neither be relaxed nor reserved for the moments following pleasurable escapes. Indeed, dissipation itself turned into an organized social act when fraternities confined the activities of drinking, gambling, initiations, pranks, noisy singing, and conviviality with females to formal and customary settings.

Freedom to control one's social destiny meant that the private individual consciously and rigorously developed his nature along the lines of self-discipline and knowledge. The earnest young man regenerated himself during his college years; he purified his character and reformed his intelligence in order to fight out the battle of an American life on the terms of his own permanent choosing. Youthful exuberance and excitement helped to establish high ideals and permanent loyalties for the individual, who now learned to commit himself to goals beyond immediate self-interest and transient pleasure. Extracurricular student movements provided the context for individual growth in a structured group.

In the literary societies, for instance, the best students often received the most lasting features of their college education. They debated national public issues like slavery—issues which transcended the provincialism of the college and led a few committed students to form antislavery societies on campus.[2] They openly discussed religious doubts,

[2] See Thomas S. Harding, *College Literary Societies: Their Contribution to Higher Education in the United States, 1815–1876* (New York: Pageant Press International Corp., 1971), p. 309; George R. Cutting,

they wrote essays on current heresies like the foundation of divinity in "nature," and they invited public speakers like Emerson who might be unacceptable to college authorities and unwelcome on the campus itself. One society was actually known to recruit potential members from the preparatory schools. The societies absorbed the free time of students who pursued such extracurricular modern subjects as science, English, history, music, art, literature, and contemporary fiction. And with the college libraries hedged by restrictions and lack of funds, the societies maintained their own collections—ten thousand volumes each at Bowdoin and Williams—frequently the largest and most useful on campus.[3] As the interests of students expanded, and the student body itself grew more diversified in the generation before the Civil War, more specialized groups such as scientific clubs in the 1830s splintered away from the older debating societies.[4] Also appearing in the period, college magazines, periodicals, and poems drew away the attention of students.[5] And eventually the college itself in-

Student Life at Amherst College: Its Organizations, Their Membership and History (Amherst, Mass.: Hatch & Williams, 1871), p. 94; [John Mitchell], *Reminiscences of Scenes and Characters in College: By a Graduate of Yale* (New Haven, Conn.: A. H. Maltby, 1847), pp. 109–10; David F. Allmendinger, Jr., *Paupers and Scholars: The Transformation of Student Life in New England* (New York: St. Martin's Press, 1975), pp. 100–3.

3 See Harding, *College Literary Societies*, pp. 305–21; Henry D. Sheldon, *Student Life and Customs* (New York: D. Appleton and Company, 1901), pp. 125–42; Cutting, *Student Life at Amherst*, pp. 13–37; Edward Everett Hale, *New England Boyhood* (Boston, Toronto: Little, Brown and Company, 1893, 1964), pp. 181–83; Ralph L. Rusk, *The Life of Ralph Waldo Emerson* (New York: Columbia University Press, 1949), p. 73; *Reminiscences . . . by a Graduate of Yale*, pp. 105–22. A running account of the politics and activities of one society is found in William Gardiner Hammond, *Remembrance of Amherst: an Undergraduate's Diary, 1846–1848,* ed. George F. Whicher (New York: Columbia University Press, 1946).

4 See Cutting, *Student Life at Amherst*, pp. 56–59; Hale, *New England Boyhood*, pp. 187–89; Sheldon, *Student Life and Customs*, pp. 165–67.

5 An extensive listing is found in Cutting, *Student Life at Amherst*, pp. 66–78. See also Sheldon, *Student Life and Customs*, pp. 151–56; Frank Luther Mott, *A History of American Magazines, 1741–1850*

corporated in its curriculum the intellectual content that had initially generated interest in the societies.

Competition from the Greek-letter fraternities and secret societies such as Skull and Bones at Yale also drew off interest from the literary societies. Students formed the first fraternities in the later 1820s, and by 1870 the chapters had come to be a dominant and controversial feature of student social life. With their graduates to satisfy, their national reputations to protect, and expensive buildings and facilities to maintain, fraternities had ceased to be temporary clubs and spontaneous gatherings. Andrew Dickson White, for one, viewed their function as satisfying an important emotional need of students for both self-esteem and self-restraint. Fraternities filled a void in the life of many students on the college campus.[6]

By disciplining the aggression of its chosen members, and confining individual willfulness, fraternities served to mitigate "class" hostilities on campus, control hazing, channel dissipation, and set reasonable standards for deportment. The enduring importance of loyalty and corporate pride in a selective brotherhood were cultivated. Though unhappy with the cliquish and partisan nature of secret societies, Mark Hopkins conceded in 1846, "that I have reason to suppose that one object of some of the Societies here is the cultivation of manners, and so far they have im-

(New York, London: D. Appleton and Company, 1930), pp. 172, 488–89; Mott, *A History of American Magazines, 1865–1885* (Cambridge, Mass.: Harvard University Press, 1957), pp. 165–66. Both Daniel Coit Gilman and Andrew Dickson White were editors of college magazines.

[6] Andrew Dickson White, "College Fraternities," *Forum* 3 (1887): 243–47. The origins, manners, progress, and customs of the societies are described in William Raimond Baird, *American College Fraternities: A Descriptive Analysis of the Society System in the Colleges of the United States, with a Detailed Account of Each Fraternity* (Philadelphia: J. B. Lippincott & Company, 1879). See Cutting, *Student Life at Amherst*, pp. 159–90; Sheldon, *Student Life and Customs*, pp. 142–45, 167–78. See also Thomas LeDuc, *Piety and Intellect at Amherst College, 1865–1912* (New York: Columbia University Press, 1946), pp. 122–27.

proved."[7] But student manners improved at the cost of social exclusiveness and snobbery against scholarly pursuits. For instance, at the older eastern colleges especially, the financial expense of belonging to a secret society made its members conscious of a class other than that of the college—economic class. Ambitious students directed their energy to seeking entry into a privileged social caste. In the 1830s, one member of a fraternity at Williams suggested that the final qualification for selecting a new man should be the question, "Would you want your sister to marry him?"[8] Intellectually speaking, faculties enormously resented the political power of the secret society and its growing influence over the life of students, but practically speaking they feared their own lack of resolve in curbing this popular form of national association.[9]

After all, fraternities did permit college officials to scale down their involvement in the tedious business of lodging students and supervising dormitories—a move which in fact struck down the largely fictitious parental role of the American college. This trend had been occurring in American institutions for some time, and Yale and Harvard were among the last to abandon the compulsory commons. At poorer colleges, students had already formed clubs and devised alternative means for purchasing food more cheaply than that provided by the college kitchen.[10] Moreover, as members of the faculty moved into their own private residential housing, they no longer ate with the students, and to be compelled to do so was an unpleasant burden for many. When colleges again assumed the task of housing and feeding students in the later nineteenth century, the attitude was more practical than paternal, and by comparison the new regulations and supervision were modest.

[7] Cited in Frederick Rudolph, *Mark Hopkins and the Log: Williams College, 1836–1876* (New Haven, Conn.: Yale University Press, 1956), p. 115.

[8] *Ibid.*, p. 103.

[9] Sheldon, *Student Life and Customs*, pp. 178–92.

[10] Allmendinger, *Paupers and Scholars*, pp. 82–89.

After midcentury, fraternities increasingly made it possible for the individual to find both privacy in his lodging and intimacy in a small group—a second family—which both dormitory living and boarding in the town obstructed. Privacy and intimacy, White thought, were necessary for the formation of ambition in a modern young man. The individual living in a fraternity learned a "sense of proprietorship" for the property of his society and "a feeling of responsibility" for its permanent welfare. "Place twenty or thirty students in the ordinary college dormitory," White observed, "and there will be carelessness, uproar, and destruction; but place the same number of men belonging to any good fraternity in a chapter-house of their own, and the point of honor is changed; the house will be well cared for and quiet."[11] Self-discipline naturally developed within the fraternity brother as his possessive pride in associating with a group of socially promising young men grew.

With the organization of participants in college athletics, the ideological movement to regenerate the self, to purify the mind through the rational discipline of the body achieved its most explicit statement. In 1829, Princeton's *Biblical Repertory* supported the new gymnastics with the statement:

They not only minister present health, but look forward prospectively to firmness of constitution in subsequent life.

Most of the Gymnastic games, also, are of a social kind, and awaken an intense interest in the competitors; absorbing the attention, sharpening the perception, and communicating alertness to the motions of the mind as well as the body. Thus they become invaluable auxiliaries to the more direct methods of promoting intellectual culture.[12]

Americans began hearing a new refrain: the athletic youth was "manly" and his physical health was a "necessary con-

11 White, "College Fraternities," 246.

12 "Public Education," *Biblical Repertory* 5 (1829): 407; John R. Betts, "Mind and Body in Early American Thought," *Journal of American History* 54 (March 1968): 799. See also Edward Reynolds, "On the Necessity of Physical Culture to Literary Men, and Especially to Clergymen," *Biblical Repository* 2 (January 1832): 174–200.

dition of all permanent success." The notion that personal physical health was the basis of moral self-control and keenness of intellect became an obsession with many middle-class reformers, who crusaded against such flaws of character in their countrymen as the chewing of tobacco, spitting the juice everywhere, and drinking to excess. The sallow-faced, hollow-chested young man who sinned against his body demonstrated his bad manners, weak ambition, vulgar imagination, tired mind, and deteriorated virility. Moral advisers consistently warned young men that physical degeneration surpassed all other causes for the "terrible records of dyspepsia and paralysis" in professional careers.[13] To live in ignorance of the physical science of the body courted failure. As one writer put it, professional life was a battle which favored competitive persons with strong nerves, vigor, muscles, and a cool head:

A mind of great power, putting forth its full energy in some special effort, is like a warrior armed in heavy mail, going forth to battle. If the horse which carries him be small and puny, the warrior must needs fail. If, on the other hand, the horse be a powerful and generous animal, fully equal to the occasion, how much is the force of the rider himself increased thereby. So the mind gathers impulse and force from the body, whenever the latter is in high health and vigor.[14]

College athletics were equal to the task.

The old-time college had frowned upon games and sports as carnal and frivolous diversions, amusements both harmful to the mind of a gentleman and subversive of the duties

13 The concern with physical health was practically synonymous with educational reform. See, for instance, Charles Caldwell's widely distributed treatise *Thoughts on Physical Education: Being a Discourse Delivered to a Convention of Teachers* (Boston: Marsh, Capen & Lyon, 1834). Caldwell claimed to "show the essential connexion between mind and matter, and make it clearly appear, that, for its sound and vigorous operations, the former depends on the condition of the latter" (p. 4). See also Horace Mann, "Report for 1842: The Study of Physiology In The Schools—Dissertation Upon the Subject," *Annual Reports on Education* (Boston: Horace B. Fuller, 1868), pp. 129–229.

14 John S. Hart, *Mistakes of Educated Men,* 4th ed. (Philadelphia: J. C. Garrigues, Publisher, 1862), pp. 18–19.

of a Christian, not to speak of the damage inflicted on clothing and college property.[15] Colonial Americans measured physical effort by its useful industry, not its pleasure, and college officials advised the distracted student to take a long walk or plant a garden, if he must. Parents did not send their children to college to play ball. "In almost all our Colleges, young men suffer severely from intense physical indolence," Wayland observed in 1842; "They spend day after day in warm rooms, leaving them only at the hours of recitation, prayers and commons, and then only to cross a small court or pass from one building to another."[16] When students did gather informally as a group to play games which had no rules or system, carnage might ensue. For instance, during "Bloody Monday" at Harvard, the presence of a ball gave students the excuse to assault each other indiscriminately. "We had foot-ball in tumultuous throngs," Hale recalled, "we had base-ball, in utter ignorance that there were ever to be written rules for base-ball, or organized clubs for playing it."[17] No wonder students remained indoors rather than be bloodied in a free-for-all.

But the lack of disciplined athletic activity, and the absence of the virile qualities it embodied, was intolerable to many in the college by midcentury, especially students concerned with secular careers. Saints and ministerial students thought they could live without bodies, Thomas W. Higginson complained, and quite naturally they lacked physical stamina, died prematurely, and were deficient in the "vigorious manly life." Were saints celibate as a matter of choice and willful restraint? Men like Higginson thought that if the "pallid, puny, sedentary, lifeless, joyless, little" student continued to represent the professional class in America's future, the prognosis was for a degenerated

15 Jennie Holliman, *American Sports (1785–1835)* (Durham, N.C.: The Seeman Press, 1931), pp. 64–65.

16 Francis Wayland, *Thoughts on the Present Collegiate System* (Boston: Gould, Kendall & Lincoln, 1842), p. 118.

17 Hale, *New England Boyhood*, pp. 200–1.

and exhausted race.[18] No specter haunted ambitious middle-class individuals more than the image of their own human decay.

In the 1840s students began forming sports clubs both for their own pleasure and to challenge rivals at other schools; in the later 1850s colleges built indoor gymnasiums furnished with the apparatus necessary for an individual to develop his body according to physical laws; in 1860 Amherst created the first professorship of hygiene and physical education.[19] These were beginnings which prospered. Organized crew and boat-racing were introduced in the forties, baseball now with teams and rules captured the enthusiasm of students in the fifties, and football began assuming the outlines of a modern sport in the sixties. The science of gymnastics and calisthenics developed quickly, with trained instructors and manuals to assist the student.[20] Undeniably, the trend during the century was away from individual exercise to team sports, and away from intramural competition to intercollegiate contests, the fierceness of which forged school loyalty by directing aggression against the detested outsider.

However, the proponents of physical education never ceased to emphasize the disciplinary value of sports to the average individual, its usefulness in nurturing the mental and emotional control necessary for success in professional life. In the early 1880s, for instance, one advocate estimated that one-half of the Yale men exercised regularly, two-

[18] Thomas W. Higginson, "Saints, and their Bodies," *Atlantic Monthly*, 1 (March 1858): 584, 585–86, 590. See also Higginson, *Out-Door Papers* (Boston: Ticknor and Fields, 1863).

[19] See Nathan Allen, *Physical Culture in Amherst College* (Lowell, Mass.: Stone & Huse, 1869); Allen, *Physical Development: or the Laws Governing the Human System* (Boston: Lee and Shepard, Publishers, 1888), pp. 17–30; Cutting, *Student Life at Amherst*, pp. 111–17.

[20] See Sheldon, *Student Life and Customs*, pp. 192–95; Fred E. Leonard, *Pioneers of Modern Physical Training*, 2d. ed., rev. (New York: Association Press, 1919), pp. 63–94; Guy Lewis, "The Beginning of Organized Collegiate Sport," *American Quarterly*, 22 (Summer 1970): 221–29; Betts, "Mind and Body," 801–5. See also Foster Rhea Dulles, *America Learns to Play: A History of Popular Recreation, 1607–1940* (New York, London: D. Appleton-Century Company, 1940), pp. 136–47.

thirds of the Harvard men, and five-sixths of the Amherst men, who were required to work out four days a week in the gymnasium. "It is a commonplace to say that regular physical exercise is a condition of the best mental exertion," he wrote; "But as a matter of fact it is true that the best students are most conscientious regarding their exercise. It is not the working eight or ten hours a day which kills students, but it is the lack of exercise. . . ." By physically exerting himself daily, the student could be certain of keeping "his mind clear, and his rank near the head of his class."[21] He was an achiever.

Another outlet for achievers was the student Young Men's Christian Association movement. In 1858, organizations were first established at the universities of Michigan and Virginia, and the success of the movement on campuses in the second half of the century cannot be minimized. In contrast to the earlier prayer-meeting type of religion with its stress on the dramatic experience of conversion, the student YMCA nurtured the constant inner discipline of the individual who quietly chose to be an enthusiastic Christian in the totality of his daily routine. The new stress was educational. Increasingly the movement was supported by a superior institutional organization, permanent facilities, and professional planning. But its success was due to self-motivated students willing to dedicate themselves, who as young men found purpose in a Christian gospel of cultural self-improvement, a gospel that also included the improvement of society. The practical achievements were real. The movement not only held Bible classes and encouraged missionizing work; it also supported public lectures of general interest as well as secular educational programs. It oriented freshman to the campus and helped them find suitable lodging. It assisted students who were ill and counseled students in distress. It served as an employment bureau and extended loans. It organized social-service projects in the urban slums. Finally, it satisfied the

21 Charles F. Thwing, *American Colleges: Their Students and Work* (New York: G. P. Putnam's Sons, 1883), p. 90.

needs of young men who sought a carefully organized but ambitious student life in a sphere broader than the formal college.[22]

RE-FORM: LET EACH MIND DECLARE HIS OWN

Youth sought out its own spokesmen, and Ralph Waldo Emerson emerged as a favorite lecturer on college campuses and before young men's associations in the 1840s and 1850s. Emerson's engagements sent him across the nation, into small towns and large cities, as he cultivated the new audience of youth. "With his coming, adolescence ended and virility began," Charles Woodbury recalled, "he *belonged* to the young men."[23] Though Emerson did not talk specifically about gymnasiums or student societies, he confronted a young man with the crisis of his individual ambition and his need to make decisions. Emerson justified the dissatisfaction of youth with the "American system of education" and its incongruity with the occupational world. He articulated the subconscious fears of youth about its own lack of worth as he touched upon the emotional sources of human feelings of inadequacy. Emerson laid out an ideology that established young manhood as the critical period of genesis for the maturing mind, a period when the success or failure of a developing life hung in the balance. In sum, Emerson made young men think about themselves; as Woodbury phrased it, "he first taught us to think, and who can forget the opener of that door?"[24]

22 Sheldon, *Student Life and Customs*, pp. 271–75; C. Howard Hopkins, *History of the Y.M.C.A. in North America* (New York: Association Press, 1951), pp. 271–308.

23 Charles J. Woodbury, *Talks with Ralph Waldo Emerson* (New York: The Baker & Taylor Co., 1890), pp. 11, 12. For an extensive list of the groups of young men's associations before which Emerson appeared, see Ralph L. Rusk, ed., *The Letters of Ralph Waldo Emerson*, 6 vols, (New York and London: Columbia University Press, 1939), 6:632–33.

24 Woodbury, *Talks with Emerson*, p. 11.

Not many did forget. Andrew Dickson White recalled that Emerson's lectures on the college circuit "made the greatest impression upon me." And G. Stanley Hall wrote that when Emerson came to Williams College in the 1860s, "few of the faculty attended but the students heard him gladly, and in my set a veritable Emersonian craze ran rampant. . . . I felt that I had come into personal contact with the greatest living mind."[25] Upon popular demand, Emerson's one-day visit stretched into an entire week, and when college officials denied the use of the chapel, the students procured the largest hall in town and filled every seat. After hearing Emerson, James A. Garfield was unable to sleep that night, and recalled that "the beginning of his intellectual life was a lecture delivered by Emerson."[26] Emerson would have been pleased. Under the heading of *"Notes for Williamstown,"* he jotted in his *Journal:* "I gain my point, gain all points, whenever I can reach the young man with any statement which teaches him his own worth."[27] The competition of life in America relentlessly chipped away at the confidence of individuals, it degraded their intelligence and demoralized their self-esteem, and no one knew this better than young men.

As a cultural spokesman for the slumbering powers of nature within the individual, for self-sufficiency and struggle, Emerson boosted the ego of the student looking toward a career. The testimony of his influence was staggering. "I listened to him as an oracle," John Fiske exclaimed

[25] *The Autobiography of Andrew Dickson White,* 2 vols. (New York: The Century Company, 1905), 1:29; G. Stanley Hall, *Life and Confessions of a Psychologist* (New York: D. Appleton and Company, 1923), p. 163.

[26] Theodore Clarke Smith, *The Life and Letters of James Garfield,* 2 vols. (New Haven, Conn.: Yale University Press, 1925), 1:76. On Emerson's visit to Williams, see *The Journals of Ralph Waldo Emerson,* ed. William Waldo Emerson and Waldo Emerson Forbes, 10 vols. (Boston: Houghton Mifflin Company, 1903-4), 10:107, 116-18; *Emerson Letters,* 5:433-34; Rudolph, *Mark Hopkins and the Log,* pp. 162-63.

[27] *Emerson Journals,* 10:107. "It is a singular fact," wrote James Russell Lowell, "that Mr. Emerson is the most steadily attractive lecturer in America," *Lowell Works,* 4 vols. (Boston: Houghton, Mifflin Company, 1892), 1:349.

after visiting Emerson at Concord. "Yesterday I shall never forget," he wrote his mother; "Of all the men I ever saw, none can be compared with him for depth, for scholarship, and for attractiveness,—at least so I think. . . . I thought him the greatest man I ever saw."[28] Emerson was the favorite author of the young Chauncey Wright. And setting out as a lawyer, Oliver Wendell Holmes, Jr., wrote Emerson that "more than anyone else [you] first started the philosophical ferment in my mind."[29] William James, Franklin Sanborn, Moses Coit Tyler, Moorfield Storey, William Torrey Harris, Edwin Mead: these men and others concerned with professional decisions and careers responded to Emerson's words.[30] After initially expressing

28 John Spencer Clark, *The Life and Letters of John Fiske*, 2 vols. (Boston: Houghton Mifflin Company, 1917), 1:212–14; Milton Berman, *John Fiske: The Evolution of a Popularizer* (Cambridge, Mass.: Harvard University Press, 1961), p. 26.; H. Burnell Pannill, *The Religious Faith of John Fiske* (Durham, N.C.: Duke University Press, 1957), p. 45.

29 James Bradley Thayer, *Letters of Chauncey Wright; with some Account of his Life* (Cambridge, Mass.: John Wilson and Son, 1878), pp. 30, 87; Mark DeWolfe Howe, *Justice Oliver Wendell Holmes: The Shaping Years, 1841–1870* (Cambridge, Mass.: Harvard University Press, 1957), p. 203; Felix S. Cohen, ed., "The Holmes-Cohen Correspondence," *Journal of the History of Ideas* 10 (January 1948): 15; *Holmes-Pollock Letters: The Correspondence of Mr. Justice Holmes and Sir Frederick Pollock, 1874–1932*, ed. Mark De Wolfe Howe, 2 vols., 2d ed. (Cambridge, Mass.: Harvard University Press, 1961), 2:264.

30 See William James, "Address at the Emerson Centenary in Concord," in *Memory and Studies* (New York: Longmans, Green, and Company, 1912), pp. 17–34; William T. Stafford, "Emerson and the James Family," *American Literature* 24 (January 1953): 433–61; F. B. Sanborn, *Recollections of Seventy Years*, 2 vols. (Boston: Richard G. Badger: The Gorham Press, 1909), 2:261; *Moses Coit Tyler, 1835–1900: Selections from His Letters and Diaries*, ed. Jessica Tyler Austen, (Garden City, N.Y.: Doubleday, Page & Company, 1911), p. 18; Moorfield Storey, "Speech," in *The Centenary of the Birth of Ralph Waldo Emerson* (Boston: The Riverside Press, 1903), pp. 105–6; William Torrey Harris, "Ralph Waldo Emerson," *Atlantic Monthly* 150 (August 1882): 238–52; Harris, "The Dialectic Unity in Emerson's Prose," *The Journal of Speculative Philosophy* 18 (1884): 195–202; Harris, "Emerson's Philosophy of Nature," in *The Genius and Character of Emerson: Lectures at the Concord School of Philosophy*, ed. F. B. Sanborn, (Boston: James R. Osgood and Company, 1885), pp. 339–64; Edwin D. Mead, *The Influence of Emerson* (Boston: American Unitarian Association, 1903).

the traditional Unitarian's dislike of Emerson, Charles William Eliot became converted, and reportedly knew the Concord philosopher's essays "almost as well as he knew the Bible." [31]

Emerson said some hard things that young men, driven by parental expectations and their own confusion about the future, found relevant. For one, the problem of an American education surpassed the "deadness" of the curriculum that Emerson himself often criticized. After all, the classical curriculum had trained for centuries the best minds in Western civilization, including those of the Founding Fathers and Emerson himself. Moreover, intellectuals of the caliber of Thomas and Matthew Arnold and John Henry Newman were attempting to renovate and rejuvenate that very curriculum in English schools. But every educator knew that any curriculum taught badly was damned.

An American education, Emerson observed, was "open to graver criticism than the palsy" of its details. It was open to the gravest criticism: death within. "It is a system of despair." The inertia of the adult world with its mechanical, pedestrian routine stifled all inspiration. Dissatisfied young men, unhappy about their uncertain fates and their lack of direction, questioned the motivation of their instructors. They listened to Emerson and agreed with him in principle: "Men do not believe in a power of education." [32]

The educator himself, crucial to any system, did not seriously ask his right to be, his right to interact with students, his right to encourage students to build woodsheds

[31] Henry James, *Charles W. Eliot: President of Harvard University, 1869–1909*, 2 vols. (Boston and New York: Houghton Mifflin Company, 1930), 2:198n; Hazen C. Carpenter, "Emerson, Eliot, and the Elective System," *New England Quarterly* 24 (March 1951): 13. See also Charles William Eliot, "Emerson," in *Four American Leaders* (Boston: Beacon Press, 1906), pp. 75–126.

[32] "New England Reformers," in *The Complete Works of Ralph Waldo Emerson*, 12 vols. (Boston: Houghton Mifflin Company, 1903–4), 3, *Essays: Second Series*, 267, 268.

rather than temples on earth. Emerson indicted the teaching profession:

The cause of education is urged in this country with the utmost earnestness,—on what ground? Why on this, that the people have the power, and if they are not instructed to sympathize with the intelligent, reading, trading, and governing class; inspired with a taste for the same competitions and prizes, they will upset the fair pageant of Judicature, and perhaps lay a hand on the sacred muniments of wealth itself, and new distribute the land.

Fear prompted cautious public servants to urge their claims: " 'This country is filling up with thousands and millions of voters, and you must educate them to keep them from our throats.' " [33] Both a former teacher and minister himself, Emerson was sensitive to the argument that American society required greater discipline from its educational system, especially as the influence of the church declined. Indeed, the Law now touched "the business of Education with the point of its pen," and the system became "frozen stiff," a defense of the status-quo. Legalists and administrators managed the business of education, which Emerson viewed as a social system of detention.[34]

Missing in American higher education was the focus upon the individual student, and the demands of his young manhood. Without the individual placed at the center of the system, the enforcement of discipline was a farce, and despair became the dominant mood of the educator, who could not define the purpose of his effort except in repressive and supervisory terms. Student, instructor, administrator: everyone was dehumanized by an institution which condoned evasion. "Our skill is expended to procure alleviations, diversion, opiates," Emerson complained; "So have we cunningly hid the tragedy of limitation and inner death

[33] *Ibid.*, 268; "The Conservative," *Emerson Works*, 1, *Nature Addresses and Lectures*, 320.

[34] *Emerson Journals*, 5:250–51. See Virginia Wayman, "A Study of Emerson's Philosophy of Education," *Education* 56 (April 1936): 474–82; Howard Mumford Jones, "Introduction," in *Emerson on Education: Selections* (New York: Teachers College Press, Columbia University, 1966), pp. 1–23.

we cannot avert. Is it strange that society would be devoured by a secret melancholy which breaks through all its smiles and all its gayety and games?"[35] The American college suffered from depression, a social illness which paralyzed the will, softened the character, and weakened the identity.

It disheartened Emerson to see a young man after ten years of college education "come out, ready for his voyage of life,—and to see that the entire ship is made of rotten timber, of rotten, honeycombed, traditional timber without so much as an inch of new plank in the hull." Why did the young man graduate a "dunce?"[36] Because his college education remained external and peripheral to the student. It failed to cultivate his mind, nurture his talent, perfect his character, and help him decide upon a career. College concluded the years of boyhood, and when the graduate embarked into the world, already he had become old and rigid before his time. Emerson deplored the appearance of stunted humanity which gathered at the Harvard reunions, alumni attempting to reenact the antics of their frivolous boyhood at college. "I avoid the Stygian anniversaries at Cambridge, those hurrahs among the ghosts, those yellow, bald, toothless meetings in memory of red cheeks, black hair, and departed health. Most forcible Feeble made the oration that fits the occasion, that contains all the obituary eloquences."[37] Puerilism characterized American higher education.

Emerson's irreverence was at once shocking, stimulating, repulsive, and attractive. He would place individual development at the center of the student's life, the student at the center of the teacher's attention, the active intellect at the center of the curriculum, knowledge at the center of the classroom, the classroom at the center of the school's administration, and the school at the center of the community's interest. Common principles, definitions of role, and accountability would organize every concentric circle, from

[35] "New England Reformers," *Emerson Works*, 3, *Essays: Second Series*, 268–69.

[36] *Emerson Journals*, 5:254.

[37] *Ibid.*, 7:60.

the individual student outward. For instance, Emerson wrote following a student rebellion at Harvard in 1842: "Let the college provide the best teachers in each department, and for a stipulated price receive the pupil to its lecture-rooms and libraries; but in the matter of morals and manners, leave the student to his own conscience, and if he is a bad subject to the ordinary police."[38] The artificial *in loco parentis* supervision degraded the function of the college, so why not turn criminal offenders over to the public authorities? The transformed college would rely on its own natural methods of discipline, such as the competitive desire of the student to achieve excellent marks on examinations, earn high standing on merit rolls, and succeed among his peers. If the college's forms of discipline failed the young man, then he did not belong in school. Let him find his own way in life without artificial protection and unfair advantage. Independence, self-reliance, natural accountability, and self-determination applied to education as well as to every other sphere of social life. Let the teachers earn a living by satisfying the intelligence of their students, not their pleasure in defying authority.

At the level of human relationships, the entire system of education called for "re-form." "The teacher should be the complement of the pupil," Emerson insisted; "now, for the most part, they are Earth's diameters wide of each other." And Emerson proposed a novel test by which college professors should be appointed: "A college professor should be elected by setting all the candidates loose on a miscellaneous gang of young men taken at large from the street. He who could get the ear of these youths after a certain number of hours, or of the greatest number of these youths, should be the professor. Let him see if he could interest these rowdy boys in the meaning of a list of words."[39] Horrifying! Here was yet another example of Emersonian "infidelity" and heresy. However, ambitious young men who wished to be-

---

[38] [Ralph Waldo Emerson], *The Dial: A Magazine for Literature, Philosophy and Religion* 3 (July 1842): 134.

[39] *Emerson Journals*, 7:224.

lieve in themselves and the honesty of their rebellious impulses listened.

By insisting that knowledge was the foundation of a successful career, that knowledge was superior to physical power and wealth, Emerson sounded a note of integrity in American education. "Knowing is the measure of the man," he told college audiences; "By how much we know, so much we are."[40] A speaker who told young men to respect their own private minds and make the special bent of that mind the basis of an individual life captivated them. Moorfield Storey recalled that "during our college life many of us learned our most valuable lessons" from Emerson. It was he who expressed the vital thought: "Nature arms each man with some faculty which enables him to do easily some feat impossible to any other, and this makes him necessary to society." The corollary of that thought was "that each is bound to discover what his faculty is, to develop it, and to use it for the benefit of mankind."[41]

Each man had a social contribution to make, but it demanded the active involvement of the individual in his own personal development. Speaking from the confines of his own vertical vision, Emerson advised students about the constructive uses of their aggressive feelings. They must conquer their own laziness, arrest the desire to be self-indulgent, and resist effeminacy. They must persist in informing their minds, train their patience, harden their will-power, and calculate on the eventual triumph of their own cause. The ideal young man exhibited self-commitment, preparation, and endurance—all unified by a knowledgeable conception of his purpose.

Emerson proposed that higher education in America expand social opportunity in correspondence with the recently released energies and talents of middle-class individuals. The chance of success would be within the reach of everyone

40 "Natural History of Intellect," *Emerson Works*, 12, *Natural History of Intellect and Other Papers*, 10.
41 Storey, "Speech," in *Centenary Emerson*, p. 105.

who exerted himself, as long as he lived by an inner idea which remained constant throughout an ever-changing existence. As Storey summarized Emerson's lesson: "Every man, able or dull, superior or inferior, white, brown, or black, had his right to his chance of success, and it followed that no other man had a right to take that chance away or to insist that his fellow man should be remade according to his ideas."[42] Emerson had spoken to students more clearly than to his peers. Education was an original activity in America. "The secret of Education," Emerson said, "lies in respecting the pupil. . . . [L]et each mind his own, and declare his own."[43]

Persons who perfected their natural talent in a worldly profession prepared themselves for greatness. Genius was an act of concentration, the preparation of human ability for achievements in specialized endeavors. Every profession was honorable, every man a specialist: "One man is born to explain bones and animal architectures; and one, the expression of crooked and casual lines, spots on a turtle, or on the leaves of a plant; and one, machines, and the application of coil springs and steam and water-wheels to the weaving of cloth or paper; and one, morals; and one, a pot of brandy, and poisons."[44] In the romantic metaphor employed by Emerson, education as a *mirror* no longer reflected the general state of the community. More radical than politics, religion, and the law, education as a *lamp* threw light on the new opportunities of the student as a young man. Emerson imagined an American education to be active rather than merely reactive, constructive rather than merely reconstruc-

---

42 *Ibid.*, pp. 105–6.

43 "Education," *Emerson Works*, 10, *Lectures and Biographical Sketches*, 143. For a description of the curriculum and educational ideas to which Emerson was responding, see Edgeley Woodman Todd, "Philosophic Ideas at Harvard College, 1817–1837," *New England Quarterly* 16 (March 1943): 63–90; George P. Schmidt, "Intellectual Crosscurrents in American Colleges, 1825–1855," *American Historical Review* 42 (October 1936): 46–67.

44 *Emerson Journals*, 9:41.

tive. He conceived that a "college should have no mean ambition. . . . Here, if nowhere else in the world, genius should find its home." He referred to the college as "essentially the most radiating and public of agencies."[45]

After an absence of years, Emerson returned to Harvard Yard in the middle sixties, and the trustees elected him to the board of overseers. He was hopeful. "At present, the friends of Harvard are possessed in greater or less degree by the idea of making it a University for men, instead of a College for boys." Emerson, however, would not neglect the college: "These are giddy times, and, you say, the college will be deserted. No, never was it so much needed." Emerson believed that he was witnessing the birth of a new era: "The treatises that are written on university reform may be acute or not, but their chief value to the observer is the showing that a cleavage is occurring in the hitherto firm granite of the past, and a new era is nearly arrived."[46]

Indeed, Emerson's observations were not fanciful. He cherished his contacts with young men and had visited more colleges and spoken with more students than most educators. In the 1840s and 1850s, Emerson personally experienced the new importance being attributed to such phrases as "college life," the "college campus," "college training," the "college chum," and the "college president." His own invitations to speak testified to the changing interests within the college. Like the inner individual in Emerson's vertical angle of vision, the inner college was aiming high and specifically at a new kind of professional man—earnest, informed, combative, skillful, persistent, and self-contained. It was only a matter of time before eager students graduated and decided upon the academic profession as a career. Now came the real test of their ambition.

[45] "The Celebration of Intellect," *Emerson Works*, 12, *Natural History of Intellect and Other Papers*, 126, 115.

[46] *Emerson Journals*, 10:290–91; "The Celebration of Intellect," *Emerson Works*, 12, *Natural History of Intellect and Other Papers*, 116; *Emerson Journals*, 10:197.

ACADEMIC CULTURE

Above all, what had been missing in the old-time college was an academic culture. Professors did not take sufficient pride in their work to train specifically for it, decide early upon the course of a career, and commit themselves to the sacrifices necessary to make a contribution to knowledge. When William Graham Sumner said that no such thing as an academic career existed at Yale, he meant that young teachers tended to view their work as temporary until something better came along, that middle-aged men sought an interlude or an escape from the rigors of an active profession such as the ministry, and the elderly found a berth for retirement. Being a professor was a "poor business," wrote Henry Ward Beecher: "Who ever heard of a college professor that was not poor? They dry up in a pocket like springs after the wood is cut off from the hills. They are apt to get very dry in other ways, too. A man that teaches cannot afford to know too much. A teacher is like a needle. He should be small and sharp. If large, he cannot run easily through the garments to be made."[47] Americans slipped in and out of college teaching, and like Sumner, who had practiced as a minister, professors often took a college position because of dissatisfaction with their earlier professional decisions and lives.

After midcentury, educators began to show some signs of discontent with the quality of academic life. In the use of words, for instance, Americans began referring to an "academic" function as distinguished from a professional and a technical one. And they began disputing the difference between a college and a university, as when Noah Porter stimulated controversy by insisting upon defining Yale as a college. Controversy pointed to a rising level of consciousness among academics, and a concern with their status. Colleges themselves were becoming more specialized. In the 1850s, Americans began hearing about commercial colleges, and in

[47] Henry Ward Beecher, *Norwood: Or, Village Life in New England* (New York: Charles Scribner & Company, 1868), pp. 26–27.

the 1860s, about business colleges and state teachers' colleges. And college life began assuming a new level of social complexity, as the "college store" appeared, "college clothes," the "college catalogue," college newspapers and humor magazines, and the "college widow," a young woman who remained about a college year after year in order to associate with the male students. Though he did not record it until later, Henry Seidel Canby left a remarkable portrait of the most interesting woman on a later nineteenth-century campus, indeed perhaps one of the most shadowy, sympathetic, and neglected bearers of culture on the scene:

The college widow had a depth and richness of emotional experience never developed in American life . . . outside of the few metropolises, and seldom there. She began at sixteen or eighteen, as a ravishing beauty, the darling of freshmen; she passed on in the years of her first blooming from class to class of ardent youngsters, until, as her experience ripened, she acquired a taste, never to be satisfied by matrimony, for male admiration, abstracted from its consequences; and more subtly, for the heady stimulant of intimacy with men in their fresh and vigorous youth. By her thirties she had learned the art of eternal spring, and had become a connoisseur in the dangerous excitement of passion controlled at the breaking point, a mistress of every emotion, and an adept in the difficult task of sublimating love into friendship. The students lived out their brief college life and went on; she endured, and tradition with her, an enchantress in illusion and a specialist in the heart. Twenty, even thirty years might be her tether; when suddenly on a midnight, a shock of reality, or perhaps only boredom, ended it all, she was old—but still charming and infinitely wise. To smoke a cigarette with her when cigarettes were still taboo for women, and drink her coffee and liqueur, was a lesson in civilization.[48]

In the physical presence of the college widow, civilization and young manhood awakened together inside the suggestible student.

[48] Henry Seidel Canby, *Alma Mater: The Gothic Age of the American College* (New York: Farrar & Rinehart, 1936), pp. 14–15; Brooks Mather Kelley, *Yale: A History* (New Haven, Conn., and London: Yale University Press, 1974), pp. 230–31.

In the final third of the nineteenth century, the number of faculty members increased dramatically. It doubled between 1870 and 1880, and rose more than 300 percent between 1870 and 1900:[49]

	Number of Institutions	Number of Faculty
1870	563	5,553
1880	811	11,552
1890	998	15,809
1900	977	23,868

Interest in teaching at all levels showed a "phenomenal rise" during the last quarter of the century, and by 1900 it led all other occupations as the preferred work of college graduates, taking about 25 percent.[50] Tensions within the academic profession intensified as young men gravitated toward a field that potentially offered commitment, control over one's schedule, and a desirable life style. But the inertia and petty corruption of the established academic frustrated many, including ambitious students.

After midcentury, social pressures began pushing hard against the immature state of academic culture. Increasingly after 1840, for instance, both parents and students expected competitive written examinations. Now grades and honors placed the emphasis of an American education on personal achievement, the individual desire to succeed, and the race between students. But an effective plan of examinations, grades, merit rolls, and scholarships awarded by the college required a professionally competent faculty in which the members individually shared the values of competition, ambition, achievement, and success. No artificial structure of grading would work, as demonstrated by Harvard's way of

49 *Historical Statistics of the United States: Colonial Times to 1957: A Statistical Abstract Supplement* (Washington, D.C.: U.S. Department of Commerce, Bureau of the Census, 1960), Series H 316–17, p. 211.

50 Bailey B. Burritt, *Professional Distribution of College and University Graduates,* United States Bureau of Education Bulletin no. 19, whole number 491 (Washington, D.C.: U.S. Government Printing Office, 1912), pp. 77, 78.

distributing points and fractions of points, which not only
failed to distinguish between conduct and scholarship, but
also failed to convince students of its honesty. Instructors
could not agree on the scale of points, one critic wrote:
"Some frankly admitted that it was impossible to get within
five or ten per cent of absolute exactness; others were so
delicately constituted that they could distinguish between
fractions of one per cent. One instructor was popularly supposed to possess a marking 'machine'; another sometimes
assigned marks *less than zero*."[51] The Harvard plan was devised in the 1820s, primarily to discipline the conduct of
unruly students rather than test their mental ability or keep
insecure students in a perpetual state of intellectual preparation. It was superimposed on a college which by means of
a uniform curriculum and a uniform social routine aimed
to graduate a single model of a civilized gentleman—not a
variety of eccentric individuals who were enthusiastic about
competition and ambition.

Traditionally, graduation honors were conferred by the
faculty, which had no documentary evidence for its decision.
Examinations in a student's life, though usually lax and
oral, provoked resistance. Indeed, the possibility of any kind
of examination sent the junior and senior classes at Harvard on a rampage in 1790. They claimed that they had not
entered college with this understanding, and when their
petition was denied one student threw a stone into the
examination room. But in order to stop oral processes and
hasten anal ones other students were more calculating:

They obtained six hundred grains of tartar emetic, and early on
the morning of April 12, the day on which the examination was to
begin, emptied it into the great cooking boilers in the kitchen. At
breakfast, 150 or more students and officers being present, the
coffee was brought on, made with the water from the boilers. Its
effects were soon visible. One after another left the hall, some in

[51] Cited in Mary Lovett Smallwood, *An Historical Study of Examinations and Grading Systems in Early American Universities: A Critical
Study of the Original Records of Harvard, William and Mary, Yale,
Mount Holyoke, and Michigan from Their Founding to 1900* (Cambridge, Mass.: Harvard University Press, 1935), p. 53.

a slow, others in a hurried manner, but all plainly showing that their situation was by no means a pleasant one. Out of the whole number there assembled, only four or five escaped without being made unwell. Those who put the drug in the coffee had drank the most, in order to escape detection, and were consequently the most severely affected.[52]

Faculties gained control over the situation in the nineteenth century only when students were convinced of both the fairness and the necessity of a grading system. This transformation of attitude depended on the creation of a professional relationship between professors and students willing to compete with other students for meritorious recognition.

These developments came about slowly, in part because faculties resisted methods of student accountability based on scholarship and evaluation of the relative importance of different subjects. Harvard conducted its first written examination in 1833, and its first written entrance examination in 1851. Wayland at Brown proposed written examinations in 1842. Phi Beta Kappa first became interested in the scholastic ranking of seniors in 1854 at Harvard. In 1868, the Harvard faculty passed a resolution that "the scales of scholarship and conduct should hereafter be kept distinct." Nevertheless, in the increasingly popular metaphor of the day, professional life was a race of thoroughbreds. The academic profession, however, lacked riders willing to use whip or spur. It lagged behind.

In the years around 1870, more spirited riders entered the race—the university presidents. A persistent and exasperating paradox plagued American educators. Without professional standards Americans could neither attract nor produce competent scholars, teachers, and students; but without competent scholars, teachers, and students, Americans could not raise the standards. "Help us in the dilemma," Daniel Coit Gilman exclaimed in his inaugural address at The Johns Hopkins University in 1876; "We cannot have a great university without great professors; we

52 B. H. Hall, *A Collection of College Words and Customs*, rev. ed. (Cambridge, Mass.: John Bartlett, 1856), pp. 180–81.

cannot have great professors till we have a great university."[53]

The lament was universally heard. "It is very hard to find competent professors for the University," Eliot commented in his inaugural address at Harvard in 1869: "Very few Americans of eminent ability are attracted to this profession. The pay has been too low, and there has been no gradual rise out of drudgery, such as may reasonably be expected in other learned callings."[54] A harsh critic of his own education and professors, Andrew Dickson White observed in 1866 that college professors were a cautious group, afraid for their security and threatened by students who had not heard of—and cared little about—the eminent names of old. We must have instructors "who are what we would have our sons be," White concluded:

We must not make the mistake so common in older colleges—in selecting to govern and guide bright, high-spirited young men, tutors who do not and cannot know anything of the world and of what the world is thinking,—instructors who lead students to associate learning with boorishness or clownishness. We must make no man an instructor simply because he is poor or pious or a "squatter" on the college domain.[55]

In his inaugural address, Folwell expanded upon the condition of Yale by citing a Yale professor who in previous months had written in the columns of the *New Englander:* "The professors are not more than half paid. . . . The salaries are not more than half sufficient to support a family respectably in New Haven. . . . The Library fund is miserably inadequate. . . . The corps of instructors ought to be doubled. . . . Yale College is woefully poor. . . . She

[53] Daniel Coit Gilman, "Johns Hopkins in its Beginning," in *University Problems in the United States* (New York: The Century Company, 1898), pp. 27–28.
[54] Charles William Eliot, "Inaugural," in *Educational Reform: Essays and Addresses* (New York: The Century Company, 1898), p. 26.
[55] *Report of the Committee on Organization Presented to the Trustees of the Cornell University, 1866* (Albany, N.Y.: C. Van Benthuysen & Sons, Printers, 1867), p. 20.

has not a dollar to buy books." The prospect disheartened Folwell, who viewed Yale from the newborn University of Minnesota on the frontier: "Such is the financial condition of one of our oldest, best-managed, and most popular American colleges."[56]

The poverty of American higher education undermined even the best endowed institution in the country. Harvard awarded a Master of Arts degree "to any Bachelor of Arts who managed to 'sustain a good moral character' for three years after graduation [keeping out of jail was the more popular interpretation], and who would pay five dollars for it 'in advance.' "[57] Harvard's professional departments "could hardly be said to have entrance requirements," and examiners were notoriously lax. "If you know *that,* you know everything," Dr. Oliver Wendell Holmes retorted to William James who had correctly answered the first question of the general examination for the degree, "now tell me all about your family and the news at home." It was little wonder that Eliot called for "independent boards of examiners, appointed by professional bodies of dignity and influence." With a low opinion of his own medical education, William James was the first to agree, and Eliot announced, "It must not be supposed that every student who enters Harvard College necessarily graduates. Strict annual examinations are to be passed." Dr. Bigelow, professor of surgery, told the Board of Overseers that Eliot's reform would wreck the Medical School within a year or two. "He actually proposes," said Bigelow, "to have written examinations for the degree of doctor of medicine. I had to tell him that he knew nothing about the quality of the Harvard

[56] William Watts Folwell, "Inaugural," in *University Addresses* (Minneapolis: The H. W. Wilson Company, 1909), p. 55; Folwell cites from "Yale College and the Meeting of the Alumnae in New York," *New Englander* 28 (April 1869): 269–307; William Watts Folwell, *Autobiography and Letters of a Pioneer of Culture,* ed. Solon J. Buck (Minneapolis: The University of Minnesota Press, 1933), p. 205.

[57] Samuel Eliot Morison, *Three Centuries of Harvard, 1636–1936* (Cambridge, Mass.: Harvard University Press, 1936), p. 334; James, *Eliot,* 1:245.

medical students; more than half of them can barely write. Of course they can't pass written examinations."[58]

Although it was among the richest institutions in the country, Harvard lacked funds.[59] Eliot was refused his request for an allotment for the Harvard Herbarium required because "two such learned men as Dr. Gray and Dr. Watson ought not to be giving their precious time to the examination of the multifarious collections which are incessantly poured in upon them."[60] And Harvard lacked competent faculty. When Henry Adams came to lecture in the History Department in the early seventies, he was, to his amazement, expected to fill a gap of a thousand years which lay between Gurney's classical courses and Torrey's modern ones. Adams wrote friends: "There is a pleasing excitement in having to lecture tomorrow on a period of history which I have not even heard of till today. . . . Thus far the only merit of my instruction has been its originality, one hundred youths at any rate have learned facts and theories for which in after life they will hunt the authorities in vain, unless, as I trust, they forget all they have been told."[61] Few men, of course, could excite students with their knowledge as well as Adams could with his ignorance.

Few scholars, however, possessed either Adams's ignorance or his knowledge. In 1873, Eliot expanded upon the "alto-

[58] *Ibid.*, p. 276; Eliot, "Inaugural," *Educational Reform,* p. 11; Bigelow's statement related by Charles William Eliot, *Harvard Memories* (Cambridge, Mass.: Harvard University Press, 1923), p. 28.

[59] In 1876, Daniel Coit Gilman evaluated the property of Harvard College at more than five million dollars, and that of both Yale and the new Johns Hopkins at three and one half million dollars. Gilman estimated the income-yielding funds of Harvard at over three million dollars; those of Yale at about a million and a half. In 1874–75, Harvard's income-revenue was $387,275.02. "The college alone, not including the library, the general administration, or any of the special departments, cost $187,713.20." This was nearly the whole income of The Johns Hopkins University. "Johns Hopkins in its Beginning," in *University Problems,* pp. 4–5.

[60] Cited in A. Hunter Dupree, *Asa Gray* (Cambridge, Mass.: Harvard University Press, 1959), pp. 392–93.

[61] Cited in Ernest Samuels, *The Young Henry Adams* (Cambridge, Mass.: Harvard University Press, 1948), p. 208.

gether too significant . . . grievous fact" that cast uncertainty upon Harvard's future. The previous generation had not trained its successors.

To illustrate the failure of the system of the last 40 years to breed scholars, let us take the most unpleasant fact which I know for those who have the future of this University to care for—Asa Gray, Benjamin Peirce, Jeffries Wyman, and Louis Agassiz are all going off the stage and their places cannot be filled with Harvard men, or any other Americans that I am acquainted with. This generation cannot match them. These men have not trained their successors. This is a grievous fact which had better not be talked about—it is altogether too significant.[62]

In 1884, only 10 percent of the Harvard professors had received the Ph.D. degree. Advanced academic degrees were scarce. In 1870, American institutions awarded only one doctorate in the entire nation. The first year in which American universities awarded more than 100 academic doctorates was 1888.[63]

But there was a decisive trend in the granting of degrees, particularly the bachelor's or first professional degree. From the 1870s to the 1880s, the total number of bachelors' degrees awarded increased 28 percent, and from the 1880s to the 1890s 56 percent:[64]

*Number
of Graduates*

1871–1880:	113,131
1881–1890:	144,798
1891–1900:	226,531

Higher education gave a young man an undeniable advantage in both career mobility and social mobility. In 1893, Charles Thwing examined some fifteen thousand entries in *Appleton's Cyclopaedia of American Biography* and dis-

---

62 James, *Eliot*, 2:12–13.
63 W. H. Cowley, "European Influences upon American Higher Education," *Educational Record*, 20 (April 1939): 183; *Historical Statistics of the United States*, Series H 336, p. 212.
64 *Ibid.*, Series H 330, p. 212.

covered that an impressively high number of leaders in the major professions and occupations were college graduates. For instance, 46 percent of the physicians represented in the *Cyclopaedia* were college graduates in contrast to 5 percent in the medical profession at large.[65] American higher education was supporting an elite, and over the years that elite was expanding. In 1870, one in every sixty young men between the ages of eighteen and twenty-one was enrolled in higher education; in 1900, one in every twenty-five young men; and in 1940 one in every six and one-half young men. Before the Civil War, one in every three persons notable enough to be listed in the *Dictionary of American Biography* had attended college. By the turn of the century, the figure had risen to between one-half and three-quarters of the persons listed.[66]

The rhythm was upbeat. Increasingly, Americans appreciated the value of academic degrees for both leadership and monetary opportunities. If one takes educational achievement to be the standard of measurement, then the middle class in nineteenth-century America was numerically very small. Yet, acceptance of the cultural attitudes of this class was spreading throughout the population. From their vantage point as spokesmen for the middle class and for the cause of its institutions, the presidents accentuated and even exaggerated the failings of America's educational system. They delighted in puncturing the myths. Though Americans might be known throughout the world as a literate people, the census showed that in 1870 20 percent of the population was illiterate, including 79.9 percent of the nonwhite population. In 1890, only slightly more than half the population five to nineteen years old enrolled in school, including only 32.9 percent of the nonwhite population.[67]

[65] Charles F. Thwing, "College Men First Among . . . Successful Citizens," *Forum* 15 (June 1893): 497.

[66] George W. Pierson, *The Education of American Leaders: Comparative Contributions of U.S. Colleges and Universities* (New York: Frederick A. Praeger, Publishers, 1969), p. xxi.

[67] *Historical Statistics of the United States,* Series H 407–411, p. 214, Series H 374–376, p. 213.

Armed with the power to persuade persons who were seeking advantages in the struggle to better themselves, the presidents aggressively advocated their cause. Too few students entered freshman classes at college, the presidents argued, because the high school barely existed in America. In 1870, only 2 percent of the seventeen-year-old population was graduated from high school.[68] Proliferating colleges, calling themselves universities but undeserving of any name, partially filled the void. Inevitably, the few individuals who boasted of a college diploma could not always demonstrate secondary-school knowledge. In 1871, McCosh described America's educational system between the common schools and the college as a two-story structure without a staircase. Turning the parable with wit, McCosh spoke before the New Jersey legislature on the necessity of providing "free high schools": "Our education system is . . . like a house built at great expense by a friend of mine; it was two stories high, and commodious and elegant in every respect, but he forgot to put a stair to lead from the lower to the upper floor. So it is with our American education. . . . [Between] the highest and the lowest, there seems to be a 'great gulf fixed.' "[69]

Repeatedly, the presidents emphasized that ignorance was appalling at the highest reaches of education in America. Indulging in an "incredible luxury" in its first freshman class, Cornell in 1868 rejected fifty applicants who believed that "London is in the west of England, Havre in the south

---

68 *Ibid.*, Series H 232–233, p. 207. See also Elmer Ellsworth Brown, *The Making of Our Middle Schools: An Account of the Development of Secondary Education in the United States* (London and Bombay: Longmans, Green, and Co., 1905); Edward A. Krug, *The Shaping of the American High School*, 2 vols. (Madison: The University of Wisconsin Press, 1969–71).

69 [James McCosh], *Addresses Delivered in Reference to Free High Schools Before the Legislature of New Jersey, 1871* (Trenton, N.J.: Murphy and Bechtel, 1871), p. 8. See the address by McCosh and the response by Eliot, "Upper Schools," *Addresses and Journal of Proceedings of the National Educational Association, 1873* (Peoria, Ill.: National Education Association, 1873), 19–35, 43–44. See also Noah Porter, "Preparatory Schools for College and University Life," *Ibid.,* 1874, 42–58.

of France, Portugal the capital of Spain, Borneo the capital of Prussia, India a part of Africa, Egypt a province of Russia." The following year, Eliot wrote: "Not a few Harvard Sophomores were rather doubtful where the joke was, when one of their number announced that the Rhine is an African river. Many of the applicants for admission to the Troy Polytechnic School might be quite unable to divide by a fraction, if they should happen to forget the mechanical rule, 'invert the divisor, and proceed as in multiplication.' "[70]

Library facilities were in shocking condition. When Mc-Cosh arrived at Princeton he found the library "insufficiently supplied with books and open only once a week and for one hour." Barnard at Columbia is reported to have suffered with a librarian who became enraged when he suggested the purchase of a book. Columbia's library opened only for two hours in the afternoon, and freshmen had to obtain special permission to use it. Students turned to their literary societies for collections of books. "We have in this country scarcely any thing that can be called a library," Wayland had written about college resources in 1842. "The means do not exist among us for writing a book, which in Europe would be called learned, on almost any subject whatever." In 1870 the intolerable situation persisted. At Yale, Daniel Coit Gilman complained that "for the next two years" Yale College would be unable to purchase a book, "its scanty library income having already been expended in advance."[71]

[70] *The Inauguration of Cornell University: Reprinted from the Account of the Proceedings at Inauguration, October 7th 1868* (Ithaca, N.Y.: Cornell University Press, 1921), p. 17; Charles William Eliot, "The New Education: Its Organization, II," *Atlantic Monthly* 23 (March 1869): 363.

[71] McCosh, Reports to Board of Trustees, December 16, 1868, in Thomas Jefferson Wertenbaker, *Princeton, 1746–1896* (Princeton, N.J.: Princeton University Press, 1946), p. 310; Barnard cited in Ernest Penney Earnest, *Academic Processions: An Informal History of the American College, 1636–1953* (New York: The Bobbs-Merrill Company, 1953), p. 160; *Catalogue of the Officers and Students of Columbia College for Year 1869–1870* (New York: 1869), p. 31; Wayland, *Present Collegiate System*, p. 128; Gilman in "Yale College and Meeting of Alumnae," *New Englander*, 307.

As the presidents portrayed the American college teacher, he worked at a second-class activity that commanded slight respect. "Professor" in America could refer to a music-hall pianist, the master of a flea circus, a gymnast, a weight-lifter in a carnival. Every president commented with McCosh upon the "hard-working and under-paid professors, who should be set free from drudgery and world anxieties to give a portion of their energy to the furtherance of learning and science." Insecure and distracted, teachers were harassed. "College professors are overworked," wrote Gilman at Yale; "two of them, still in the prime of years and among the most distinguished, have broken down in health. Several whose scanty salaries are inadequate to the support of their families, are hard at work, in all their supposed hours of leisure, earning a decent living."[72]

The American college teacher appeared to be a mediocre talent seeking shelter in the chapel. In 1871, a reviewer in the *Galaxy* described him as "nondescript, a jack of all trades, equally ready to teach surveying and Latin eloquence, and thankful if his quarter's salary is not docked to whitewash the college fence."[73] Gilman commented at Johns Hopkins that "those gentlemen who are willing to teach anything or take any chair are not those we most require." The day had gone by when higher educational institutions hired "*a* professor of science or *a* professor of languages or *a* professor of history." Indeed, said Angell in his inaugural, "it seems to have dawned but recently on men's minds that teaching in the college or university is a special profession, in which as a rule a man can no more attain high usefulness without natural aptitude and appropriate training than he can in any of the other learned professions."[74]

---

72 James McCosh, *Inauguration of Rev. James McCosh as President of Princeton College, 1868* (Princeton, N.J.: Standard Office, 1868), p. 31; "Yale College . . . Alumnae," 305.

73 "The Higher Education in America," *Galaxy* 11 (March 1871): 373.

74 Gilman cited in Hugh Hawkins, *Pioneer: A History of the Johns Hopkins University, 1874–1889* (Ithaca, N.Y.: Cornell University Press, 1960), p. 40: James Burrill Angell, "Inaugural Address: University of

For instance, in 1873 when Eliot appointed James Barr Ames as an assistant professor in the law school, teaching law as a full-time profession was unknown in America. A recent graduate, Ames had never practiced law, and Eliot recalled the significance of his act:

In due course, and that in no long term of years there will be produced in this country a body of men learned in the law, who have never been on the bench or at the bar, but who nevertheless hold positions of great weight and influence as teachers of the law, as expounders, systematizers, and historians. This, I venture to predict, is one of the most far-reaching changes in the organization of the profession that has ever been made in our country.[75]

Christopher Langdell, dean of the Harvard Law School, who had quit his practice in order to teach, put the issue in his own terms. The law was not a handicraft or a trade suitable for apprenticeship. It was a "science," which required academic professors who devoted careers to analyzing, mastering, and teaching legal sources. What person was specially qualified to teach the law? Not the one who had experience in the usages of an office or courtroom, but the person who had experience in learning and investigating the law.[76]

Academic standards for professional competence in America had "confessedly fallen" to a "disreputable low." Looking forward to the Johns Hopkins school of research medicine, Gilman cited the "prevalence of quackery vaunting its diplomas" in medical practice. "In some of our very best colleges the degree of Doctor of Medicine can be obtained in half the time required to win the degree of Bachelor of Arts." McCosh, White, and Angell agreed that, as McCosh said, journalism "which exercises such influence in this

Michigan, 1871," in *Selected Addresses* (New York: Longmans, Green, and Company, 1912), p. 16.

[75] Cited in Arthur E. Sutherland, *The Law at Harvard: A History of Ideas and Men, 1817–1967* (Cambridge, Mass.: Harvard University Press, 1967), p. 184.

[76] See Langdell's statement in Roscoe Pound, "The Law School, 1817–1929," in Samuel Eliot Morison, ed., *The Development of Harvard University: Since the Inauguration of President Eliot, 1869–1929* (Cambridge, Mass.: Harvard University Press, 1930), p. 492.

country will never be elevated till those who supply it have as a rule a college education in the principles of political science."[77] Undergraduate and graduate colleges and schools within universities would help bring coherence, unity, and concentration out of what appeared to be the sloppiness, ineffectuality, and drift of a nineteenth-century American education. Middle-class individuals intended both the structure of career and specialized work in a specific subject to emerge as a source of superior character training. Regulation would not be imposed from above the individual but originate inside. In part, electives and course examinations in a content-oriented curriculum were calculated to produce this result.

Academics themselves obstructed progress toward greater professionalization and higher standards. Mediocre professors in American colleges preferred to view their efforts as administrative and supervisory rather than intellectual. Their function was to stabilize civilization, not stimulate the excesses of individual ambition. Young men, especially those who had gone to Germany, had begun to take preparatory training and vocational decisions seriously, and they advocated the pursuit of research and teaching as a lifetime career. The young men threatened the prevailing system, which rewarded seniority and personal influence, and often they provoked the irrational anger of their seniors. The established professors who received the highest recognition had made marginal if any contribution to their fields, and many attempted to discourage the better educated and more creative young men.

Consumed by its precious respectability, petty vanities, vicious politics, and religious pretensions, academic culture in America was largely fraudulent. Intellectual respect, Simon Newcomb wrote critically of higher education in 1874, "is called forth by the title, the position, and the learning, without which it is supposed the position could

[77] Folwell, "Inaugural," *University Addresses,* pp. 42, 16; Gilman, "John Hopkins in Its Beginning," *University Problems,* p. 22; McCosh, *Inauguration,* p. 25; Angell, "Inaugural," *Selected Addresses,* pp. 24–25.

not have been gained."[78] But the assumption that the position glorified the man was a lie, through which senior professors attempted to deceive both the public and themselves. Not many were gulled. The journalist writing in the *Galaxy* focused upon the "one glaring and yet deep-seated defect in our intellectual activity, it is that we are not trained to our work."[79]

In his inaugural address at the University of Minnesota in 1869, Folwell pinpointed America's problem, which was evident in Ithaca and Cambridge as well as in Minneapolis. "We are building our great national fabric according to the rule of thumb." Americans found themselves "mere empirics and journeymen at handling the terrible social problems which the war, the migration of races, and the sudden growth of great cities are thrusting upon us." What was needed was to construct a solid basis of "science not only under technical arts and learned professions but under commerce, government, and social relations."[80]

The native white Americans without capital who were aspiring to middle-class status were exacerbating America's problem. Young men were in a position to act; they were leaving the farms, moving to the cities, and pursuing managerial, white-collar, and professional occupations for which they were often unprepared. Francis Wayland had told of the sacrifices made by families of modest means which sent a boy with promise to college in order to upgrade his social status and improve his chances for success:

The labor of the household is increased. Every expense is curtailed. The table is shorn of its slender luxuries, and the wardrobe is rendered plainer and more scanty. Thus year after year of self-denial . . . is endured, that the son and brother may wear clothes such as they do not wear, eat from a table such as they do not spread, devote himself to quiet study while they are exhausted

[78] Simon Newcomb, "Exact Science in America," *North American Review* 119 (October 1874), 296.

[79] "Higher Education in America," 369.

[80] Folwell, "Inaugural," *University Addresses*, p. 17.

with toil, and enter upon a sphere of professional eminence where they know that they can never follow him.[81]

Whatever the youth's motive, the lures of a name, a home, and a respectable social position, all acquired by "head-work" and "clean hands" without initial capital, were compelling. Getting ahead in America meant, as Daniel Coit Gilman said, that "there is a difference between ability to do anything and ability to do everything."[82] And there was even a greater difference between ability to do anything and ability to do it scientifically—professionally.

Science was a word that captivated the attention of Folwell's listeners. The word embodied a set of cultural values which, as Folwell explained, distinguished the new higher education from the old. Science made men accountable for the events of their own lives and for the pursuit of knowledge that would advance the condition of mankind. "What we demand then," Folwell insisted, "is, not rules, but principles; not mere tricks of art and sleight of hand, but science; science which explains and authenticates art; which makes men masters in their work, and not mere imitators and operatives." The methods of science separated the amateur from the professional, the dilettante from the dedicated specialist. In contrast to its art or applied nature, any subject could be taught scientifically, according to its philosophic premises; methodically examined in the dry light of pure principles. Folwell was not speaking of science in a "narrow, physical, utilitarian sense. . . ."

We might, then, sum up our definition of the university in those words, already classic, of our generous countryman [Ezra Cornell],

[81] Francis Wayland and H. L. Wayland, *A Memoir of the Life and Labors of Francis Wayland Including, Selections from His Personal Reminiscences and Correspondence*, 2 vols. (New York: Sheldon and Company, 1867), 1:281. See Oscar Handlin and Mary F. Handlin, *The American College and American Culture: Socialization as a Function of Higher Education* (New York: McGraw-Hill Book Company, 1970), pp. 21–22.

[82] Gilman, "The University of California in Its Infancy: Inauguration of the President of the University, 1872," *University Problems*, p. 168.

as an "institution in which any person can find instruction in any study," it being presumed that the distinguished author of the legend intended by the words "any study" to mean *any science*.[83]

83 Folwell, "Inaugural," *University Addresses*, pp. 17, 18, 19.

8

The American University

THE HIGHER LEARNING IN AMERICA

"The age of the specialist has come," Charles Thwing wrote in a book devoted wholly to the subject of college administration in 1900.[1] Administrators in higher education had themselves emerged in the generation after 1870 as a specialized group of men who pursued their individual careers by running colleges and universities. In the early years of the twentieth century, Thorstein Veblen scorned this group as "captains of erudition," business-minded predators who corrupted the scholarly mission of a real university by packaging education in salable units, weighing scholarship in bulk and market-value, promoting the growth of a corps of bureaucratic functionaries, treating faculty as hired hands, firing controversial teachers, raiding other institutions, measuring a university by the size of its bank statement, and selling higher learning to the public by paying obeisance to the rule that the consumer always knows best.[2]

Veblen distinguished between the commercial frame of

[1] Charles F. Thwing, *College Administration* (New York: The Century Company, 1900), p. 306.

[2] Thorstein Veblen, *The Higher Learning in America: A Memorandum on the Conduct of Universities by Business Men* (New York: Sagamore Press, 1957), first published in 1918.

mind of the university administrator and the professional frame of mind of the seeker and teacher of pure knowledge. And for the past three quarters of a century, the debate about the nature of American higher education has continued to be conducted in Veblen's terms.[3] The traditional dichotomies between cynical business practices and high-minded professional ones, between the self-interest of university administrators and the creative interest of scholarly faculty members has remained intact. On the basis of the present study it would surely seem obvious that Veblen and his followers grossly overestimated the idealistic disinterestedness of professional behavior in American life, including that of the "scholarly" American professor.

The time has come to view the American university in a different light, as a vital part of the culture of professionalism in which it first emerged and matured in the years 1870 to 1900. The middle class cultivated and generously supported the American university and its distinctive character and structure. The institution provided the testing ground for the kind of world an energetic middle class sought to create for itself. And it still does so. Careerism, competition, the standardization of rules and the organization of hierarchies, the obsession with expansion and growth, professionals seeking recognition and financial rewards for their efforts, administrators in the process of building em-

[3] In a prolific literature, see within the last generation, Laurence R. Veysey, *The Emergence of the American University* (Chicago and London: The University of Chicago Press, 1965); Talcott Parsons and Gerald M. Platt, *The American University* (Cambridge, Mass.: Harvard University Press, 1973); Joseph Ben-David, *American Higher Education: Directions Old and New* (New York: McGraw-Hill Book Company, 1972); Christopher Jencks and David Riesman, *The Academic Revolution* (Garden City, N.Y.: Doubleday & Company, 1969); Walter P. Metzger, *Academic Freedom in the Age of the University* (New York: Columbia University Press, 1961). See also Frederick Rudolph, *The American College and University: A History* (New York: Alfred A. Knopf, 1962); John S. Brubacher and Willis Rudy, *Higher Education in Transition: an American History, 1636–1936* (New York: Harper & Brothers, Publishers, 1958); Richard Hofstadter and C. Dewitt Hardy, *The Development and Scope of Higher Education in the United States* (New York: Columbia University Press, 1952).

pires: basically, both the values and the arrangements within American universities have changed little since 1900. Internally, students, faculty, and administrators have used the institution in various ways as a vehicle for their ambition. Externally, a society in search of authority has located in universities a source of nonpartisan expertise and technical know-how.

Neither praise nor blame for the direction of higher education in America can be leveled at the traditional villain, the business community, because its own professional image is largely a product of business schools in American universities. Some of the evidence suggests that university presidents such as Eliot, White, and William Rainey Harper at the University of Chicago introduced businessmen to techniques of corporate promotion and exploitation unfamiliar even in the commercial world.[4] No, a far more powerful element is at work here. From the beginning the ego-satisfying pretensions of professionalism have been closer to the heart of the middle-class American than the raw profits of capitalism.

The American university has served as a primary service organization, a professional service institution which has made possible the functions of many derivative institutions serving the middle class. The university has exerted a formative influence upon society: as the matrix within which the culture of professionalism matured; as the center to which practitioners trace the theoretical basis of knowledge upon which they establish authority; as the source of a usable history, economics, political science, and sociology for individuals who in the course of rapid movement require instant ideas.

Twentieth-century institutional developments cannot be understood apart from the contribution of the American university. Not only has higher education brought coherence and uniformity to the training of individuals for careers, it has structured and formalized the instrumental techniques Americans employ in thinking about every level

4 See Metzger, *Academic Freedom,* p. 183.

of existence. As examples in this chapter will illustrate, a special relationship has developed between the kinds of training given in universities, the kinds of problems Americans can define in their lives and attempt to solve, and the kinds of people who succeed in acquiring status, power, and wealth.

In its clientele, memberships, structure, leadership, patterns of action, and service to the society, the American university takes its place in the history of the middle class as an institution first among equals. The university was a nineteenth-century creation and a twentieth-century success story, and the American public in this century generally has not required much convincing or threatening about the importance of higher education to its welfare and mobility. Perhaps this fact explains why few spokesmen have come forward in the twentieth century who were either as lucid or as concerned with the ideological weight of their remarks as the founding fathers of American university administration, such men as Eliot, White, Gilman, Angell, Folwell, Barnard, and McCosh. Twentieth-century university presidents with their managerial experience, fiscal expertise, and—frequently—figurehead status have seldom measured up to the intellectual stature of the first generation.[5] The founders set universities going in a distinct American direction. They demonstrated a skilled capacity both in interpreting the significance of their executive actions to their clientele and in explaining the legitimacy of their faith in American higher education—a faith which today many persons have begun to question.

PROFESSIONAL SERVICE ORGANIZATION

Only in the broadest general outlines has the American university conformed to major Western systems of higher learn-

[5] See "Who's Who in Higher Education," *Change* 7 (February 1975): 24–31.

ing. Education is free from church control; hereditary claims on university posts have been abolished; secondary education is distinguished from higher education; modern scientific and humanistic subjects are prominently recognized in the curriculum; and all subjects—however dependent on professional practice or applied arts—are raised to the status of theoretical studies.[6]

Moreover, dictionary definitions in nineteenth-century America usually repeated standard formulations. In 1828, Noah Webster defined *university* in two parts. First, a university was an assemblage of colleges with the legal power to confer degrees. Second, it was "properly a *universal* school," a graduate school, "in which are taught all branches of learning, or the four faculties of theology, medicine, law, and the sciences and arts." The German influence on American usage was recorded in Worcester's Dictionary in 1860. The faculty of philosophy was elevated over the professional faculties, and degrees were conferred only on "individuals who are found on examination to possess certain qualifications." The most mature definition appeared in the Century Dictionary in 1889. Universities existed to advance *theoretical* knowledge, more than merely to teach; and the *state*

[6] See Joseph Ben-David, "Universities," *International Encyclopedia of the Social Sciences*, 17 vols., ed. David L. Sills (New York: The Macmillan Company and the Free Press, 1968), 16:191–99. Ben-David defines universities as "organizations engaged in the advancement of knowledge; they teach, train, and examine students in a variety of scholarly, scientific, and professional fields. Intellectual pursuits in universities define the highest prevailing levels of competence in these fields. The universities confer degrees and provide opportunities both for members of their teaching staffs and for some of their students to do original research." For historical studies of the university system, see Abraham Flexner, *Universities: American, English, German* (New York: Oxford University Press, 1930); Joseph Ben-David, *The Scientist's Role in Society* (Englewood Cliffs, New Jersey: Prentice-Hall, 1971); Joseph Ben-David and Awraham Zloczower, "Universities and Academic Systems in Modern Societies," *Archives Européenes de Sociologie*, 3 (1962): 25–84; Margaret Clapp, ed., *The Modern University* (Ithaca, N.Y.: Cornell University Press, 1950); Walter Laqueur and George L. Mosse, eds., *Education and Social Structure in the Twentieth Century* (New York: Harper & Row, Publishers, 1967). Lawrence Stone, ed., *The University in Society*, 2 vols. (Princeton, N.J.: Princeton University Press, 1974) arrived too late to include in this study.

was actively responsible for encouraging higher learning in the nation. The university was

an association of men for the purpose of study, which confers degrees which are acknowledged as valid throughout Christendom, is endowed, and is privileged by the state in order that the theoretical problems which present themselves in the development of civilization may be resolved.

Charles Saunders Peirce participated in the editing of the Century definition, and in his own version added, "in order . . . *that the people may receive intellectual guidance.*" He associated the university with an intellectual class that would guide a nation to clear and logical ideas.[7] Gilman, an adroit administrator schooled at Yale and Berkeley, shared Peirce's bias, a common one among educated Mid-Victorians. "Civilization" was, according to Gilman, a new word introduced scarcely a century ago, and it meant the "highest welfare of mankind." At the center of any advanced civilization was a university—"the highest school."[8] To men like Gilman, schools in America were to establish objective standards for achievement by banishing partisanship in mental labor and eliminating monopolies of thought. A pragmatic professionalism typified their responses as public spokesmen for higher education.

Dictionary definitions and rhetorical excursions sounded lofty, but they inadequately reflected the idiosyncratic nature of the American university, an institution that took on its own coloration from its earliest years. Nor was this development fortuitous. In their inaugural addresses, the presidents emphasized that the university must be recognizably American, a national institution which embodied the dis-

[7] Charles S. Peirce, *Selected Writings (Values in a Universe of Chance)*, ed. Philip P. Wiener (New York: Dover Publications, 1966), p. 331. Italics mine.

[8] Daniel Coit Gilman, "The Utility of Universities: An Anniversary Discourse," in *University Problems in the United States* (New York: The Century Company, 1898), p. 46.

tinctiveness of the "national history and character." The
Scottish immigrant James McCosh agreed that institutions
of higher learning in America must be the "spontaneous
out-growth of your position and your intelligence; they are
associated with your history and have become adjusted to
your wants." The American university must bear "a stamp
and a character of its own." At Cornell, White summarized
all his formative ideas into one, "and that is the adaptation
of this University to the American people, to American
needs, and to our own times."[9] And what was that need,
as generally agreed upon?

Its client orientation emerged as the outstanding characteristic of the American university, and the clientele included the broad range of people with middle-class aspirations. "It is neither for the genius nor for the dunce,"
Gilman wrote, "but for the great middle class possessing
ordinary talents that we build colleges."[10] His remark was
accentuated by the fact that he spoke from the platform of
the privately endowed Johns Hopkins, the most research-
oriented, intellectually elitist university in America. Though
not included in the original design, an undergraduate college developed at Hopkins, in part because of Gilman's
awareness of the need for public acceptance. Higher education should be supported, Gilman argued over the years,
because of its value to the middle class: "It will happen in
nine cases out of ten, that those who go to college surpass
the others during the course of life." A man's education di-

[9] Charles W. Eliot, "Inaugural," in *Educational Reform: Essays and
Addresses* (New York: The Century Company, 1898), p. 35; James
McCosh, *Inauguration of Rev. Jas. McCosh as President of Princeton
College, 1868* (Princeton, N.J.: Standard Office, 1868), p. 16; William
Watts Folwell, "Inaugural," in *University Addresses* (Minneapolis: The
H. W. Wilson Company, 1909), p. 68; *The Inauguration of Cornell
University: Reprinted from the Account of the Proceedings at Inaugu-
ration, October 7th 1868* (Ithaca, N.Y.: Cornell University Press, 1921),
p. 22.
[10] Gilman, "The Dawn of a University," in *The Launching of a Uni-
versity and Other Papers: A Sheaf of Remembrances* (New York: Dodd,
Mead & Company, 1906), p. 262.

rectly related to his prosperity and progress, a selling point few people with ambition and even a modest stake could afford to ignore. The middle class succeeded through "brain work." Mental powers could be developed in mechanic's institutes or lyceums, Gilman conceded, but "it can be proved beyond the shadow of a doubt" that colleges served the great middle class as a "most efficient means" to its ends. An active brain constantly strived to make life more efficient. "With all their defects," Gilman wrote, "colleges are the best agencies which the world has ever devised for the training of the intellectual forces of youth."[11] By the world, Gilman meant America.

This institutional rationale for higher education in American society demanded that administrators respond to clients. The decentralization of the system reinforced the need to be responsive "to the market." American higher education, with numerous institutions, competed for students, faculty, and fiscal support. No federal commissioner of higher education existed to dispense funds, endow privileged chairs, or protect institutions that failed to perform in the eyes of the public. Even state universities were structurally independent units, both at the mercy of student-body size and administratively accountable for dispersal of their own funds received in a lump sum from state governments. Whether managing state or private establishments, university administrators were irritably sensitive to public criticism and controversy. Understandably, jealousy of competitors easily surfaced: for instance, when Eliot together with McCosh publicly opposed the creation of state universities; when Eliot privately advised the Johns Hopkins trustees against concentrating on graduate education, which would compel Harvard to compete; or when Eliot told William James, who wished to retire, that after thirty-three years James owed it to Harvard not to diminish its reputation by accepting a well-paid six-month visiting professorship at Stanford. (Not to be intimidated by an administrator

11 *Ibid.,* pp. 262–63. See also Francesco Cordasco, *Daniel Coit Gilman and the Protean Ph.D.* (Leiden: E. J. Brill, 1960).

and weary of Eliot and Harvard, James accepted the invitation.) [12]

University administrators seldom acted in a manner that risked offending the sentiments of trustees or the middle range of public opinion. For instance, after an enthusiastic White led economist Henry Carter Adams to believe that a full-time position would follow his appointment at Cornell, both White and Cornell reneged when Adams angered trustees by failing to teach economics as if the issue of free trade versus protection was central to the discipline. Because his act was controversial, Adams's professional competence was questioned.[13] But avoiding any disturbance, he quietly moved to Michigan. In the wake of the Haymarket hysteria in 1886, however, Angell hesitated to promote Adams because of negative public reaction to his book advocating moderate state regulation of industrial capitalism and the rights of working men. Only after Adams shifted his professional investigations away from the controversial subject of state action and disavowed his "socialist" views did his permanent professorship go forward at Michigan. Angell was held responsible for his faculty appointments, and he played it safe—as safe as Adams, who chose to fur-

12 Ralph Barton Perry, *The Thought and Character of William James,* 2 vols. (Boston: Little, Brown and Company, 1935), 1:440–41.

13 It was doubted further when Adams in a hastily prepared address defended the right of labor during 1886, the year of the so-called Gould railroad strike, which was a topic of discussion at Cornell: "The 'Labor Problem,'" *Scientific American Supplement* 21, no. 555 (August 21, 1886), 8861–63. According to Adams's account, trustee Henry Sage went into the president's office with clippings of the address and pronounced: "This man must go, he is sapping the foundations of our society." See S. Lawrence Bigelow, I. Leo Sharfman, R. M. Wenley, "Henry Carter Adams," *Journal of Political Economy* 30 (April 1922): 204–5; Marvin C. Rosenberry, "Henry C. Adams," in Earl D. Babst and Lewis G. Bander Velde, eds., *Michigan and the Cleveland Era: Sketches of University of Michigan Staff Members and Alumni Who Served the Cleveland Administrations, 1885–89, 1893–97* (Ann Arbor, Mich.: The University of Michigan Press, 1948), pp. 27–30; Mary O. Furner, *Advocacy and Objectivity: A Crisis in the Professionalization of American Social Science, 1865–1905* (Lexington, Ky.: The University Press of Kentucky, 1975), pp. 132–37. At a later date, Adams declined Cornell's invitation to return.

ther his career by never again taking a risky stand even in
defense of a colleague, and by accepting a cushy position
as chief statistician for the Interstate Commerce Commission. Adams then frequently went to Washington and was
welcomed into its inner circles.[14]

More than merely client oriented, American higher education was consumer oriented, as demonstrated by the exceptional number and diversity of its services. American
universities engaged in an aggressive competition for enrollments. The managers of universities equated expansion
with health; constant growth in size added up to success.
"A true instinct of university governors in a democratic
country," Eliot approvingly called this attitude toward numbers as an end in themselves, though he enormously resented
the instant universities created in the western United States
by legislative fiat and land bounty.[15] In order to boost
Princeton's sagging enrollments after the Civil War, Mc-
Cosh began actively recruiting students, and the practice

[14] Henry C. Adams, *Relation of the State to Industrial Action*, Publications of the American Economic Association, vol. 1, no. 6 (January
1887). At Michigan, Adams in his research moved away from labor
issues and became involved in the more technical questions of public
debt. See Henry C. Adams, *Public Debts: An Essay in the Science of
Finance* (New York: D. Appleton and Company, 1887); Adams, *The
Science of Finance: An Investigation of Public Revenues* (New York:
Henry Holt and Company, 1898). See also Henry C. Adams and H. T.
Newcomb, *Regulation of Railway Rates, Digest of the Hearings before
the Committee on Interstate Commerce, Senate of the United States*
(Washington, D.C.: U.S. Government Printing Office, 1906). See Furner,
Advocacy and Objectivity, pp. 138–42.

[15] Charles W. Eliot, *University Administration* (Boston and New
York: Houghton Mifflin Company, 1908), p. 79. The literature on the
land-grant colleges and state universities is inadequate: see Andrew
Ten Brook, *American State Universities, Their Origin and Progress, a
History of Congressional University Land-Grants* (Cincinnati: Robert
Clarke & Company, 1875); Earle D. Ross, *Democracy's College: The
Land-Grant Movement in the Formative Stage* (Ames, Iowa: The Iowa
State College Press, 1942); Edward Danforth Eddy, Jr., *Colleges for
our Land and Time: The Land-Grant Idea in American Education*
(New York: Harper & Row, Publishers, 1956); Allan Nevins, *The State
Universities and Democracy* (Urbana, Ill.: The University of Illinois
Press, 1962).

spread. Promotional advertising, a successful athletic program, a large list of course offerings, the acquisition of professional schools, and active alumni all proved to be valuable mechanisms in the hands of administrators as the competition between institutions intensified. The growth of American universities was unprecedented in Western civilization. In Eliot's first two decades, the number of students in the academic program alone rose from 616 to 1464. In two generations, enrollment in institutions of higher education jumped from 52,000 in 1870 to 238,000 in 1900 to 1,101,000 in 1930. The number of institutions increased from 563 in 1870 to 977 in 1900 to 1,409 in 1930.[16]

Inflation in size was matched by inflation in the variety of consumer services. As a hedge against both competition and shifting demand, American universities established themselves on as broad a base as possible. An ever-expanding assortment of functions strengthened the self-sufficiency, autonomy, and independence of the institution. Again, middle-class values explicitly informed university administrators. The undergraduate college, the graduate schools, professional schools, research institutes, agricultural stations, extension education—all were absorbed within the comprehensiveness of the American university. By the early 1900s, for instance, university-affiliated medical schools had all but driven proprietary schools out of business, and certification boards and licensing regulations reinforced the professional control of the university school. The formation of the Association of American Law Schools in 1900 represented a similar but somewhat less successful trend in legal education.

No European system resembled the American one for comprehensiveness, standardization, and responsiveness to

16 Thomas Jefferson Wertenbaker, *Princeton: 1746–1896* (Princeton, N.J.: Princeton University Press, 1946), pp. 313–15; Arthur M. Comey, "The Growth of New England Colleges," *Educational Review* 1 (March 1891): 211; *Historical Statistics of the United States: Colonial Times to 1957: A Statistical Abstract Supplement* (Washington, D.C.: U.S. Department of Commerce, Bureau of the Census, 1960), Series H 321, 316, p. 211.

clients' interests. American universities trained students at three ascending levels. The first professional degree or baccalaureate, usually awarded after a four-year general education with a focus on a major subject of study, no longer existed in Europe. The second professional degree, the master's (or the LL.B or M.D.) was granted in America in a significantly broader range of fields than in Europe. And the third degree, the Ph.D., was unfamiliar to Europeans as a professional degree awarded to a candidate who qualified in a department after formal training in an accredited institution. The Ph.D. in America tended to be a vocational degree, in its practical uses not unlike the M.D. or the various doctorates in education, divinity, and applied fields of technology. In Europe, universities did not grant educators the Ed.D., social workers the D.S.W., and only technical schools conferred the Ph.D. on engineers.

Traditionally, European professors looked down upon the career ambitions of American professors, who were disposed to sell their professional services as teacher, scholar, researcher, administrator, or recognized name to the highest bidder. But Americans attached no stigma to Angell when he held out for a higher salary and a better home before accepting the presidency at Michigan, or when John Dewey insisted upon more money to support his style of life before coming to Chicago. Indeed, such behavior enhanced both the prestige and the value of the services of these men to universities. Continually strapped for funds to support his comforts, Frederick Jackson Turner acknowledged that outside interests, including royalty offers from commercial publishers were exceedingly tempting, and even held an advantage for the university professor:

They keep the man from being a closet scholar; and, by bringing him into contact with life, they enhance his usefulness. Perhaps the main difference between the traditional college professor, supposed to be impractical, visionary, and out of touch with the world about him, and the professor of the present time, lies in just this tendency of the modern professor to mix up with the

life of his fellowmen and to do his share of the work of the world
while he does his teaching and research.[17]

American scholars functioned at a number of levels. The
temptations of popular success were difficult to resist, and
corrupting.

Because the client orientation was so overpowering, no
master plan directed the growth of American universities.
In practice, supply followed demand, though administrators
denied the relevance of the metaphor as they struggled to
diversify their institutions. Students, for instance, were given
considerable opportunities to elect subjects, transfer between
programs, and matriculate from one college to another,
without finding it necessary to leave an institution. Under
White, Cornell quickly overcame its original vocational vision and cultivated academic disciplines.[18] Like Johns Hopkins, Clark and Chicago lowered their sights as research
training institutions and introduced undergraduate education.[19] Eliot spent so much time building up the endowment, expanding the size of the student body and faculty,
and restructuring the undergraduate college around semi-

[17] Wilbur R. Jacobs, *The Historical World of Frederick Jackson
Turner: with Selections from his Correspondence* (New Haven, Conn.,
and London: Yale University Press, 1968), p. 98. For a description of
Turner's lifestyle, see Ray Allen Billington, "Frederick Jackson Turner:
the Image and the Man," *Western Historical Quarterly* 3 (April 1972):
143–50.

[18] See Carl L. Becker, *Cornell University: Founders and Founding*
(Ithaca, N.Y.: Cornell University Press, 1943), pp. 168–70 *passim;*
Walter P. Rogers, *Andrew D. White and the Modern University*
(Ithaca, N.Y.: Cornell University Press, 1942), pp. 90–140; Morris
Bishop, *A History of Cornell* (Ithaca, N.Y.: Cornell University Press,
1962), p. 25.

[19] See W. Carson Ryan, *Studies in Early Graduate Education: The
Johns Hopkins, Clark University, The University of Chicago,* The
Carnegie Foundation for the Advancement of Teaching, Bulletin no. 30
(New York: The Carnegie Foundation, 1939). See also Hugh Hawkins,
Pioneer: A History of the Johns Hopkins University, 1874–1889 (Ithaca,
N.Y.: Cornell University Press, 1960), pp. 27–28; Dorothy Ross, *G. Stan-
ley Hall: The Psychologist as Prophet* (Chicago and London: Univer-
sity of Chicago Press, 1972), pp. 186–230; Richard J. Storr, *Harper's
University: The Beginnings* (Chicago and London: The University of
Chicago Press, 1966), pp. 311–27.

autonomous professional schools and a graduate school of arts and sciences that he worried about his reputation. "I have sometimes feared," he wrote William James, "that to the next generation I should appear as nothing but a successful Philistine."[20] Eliot emphasized classroom teaching and service to the institution, and he bargained hard on promotions and salaries. In the American university, faculty members seldom became so specialized that their position depended on one category of professional service, which efficiency-minded administrators might eliminate, in the face of the fickle tastes of American consumers, for lack of demand.

INSTITUTIONAL STRUCTURE AND
INDIVIDUAL BEHAVIOR

The internal institutional structure of the American university satisfied two essential needs of its middle-class participants. It allowed for an infinite expansion in size, and it nurtured an inner discipline born of competition. The university itself was comprehensive, but all relationships within were fragmented and insecure. Individual loyalty to the institution was inspired less by affection for the corporation than by fear for the future of a career.

The basic units of the university evolved in a distinct American form. First, professionals in an area of study such as history collected in a *department* in which no one man dominated the definition of a subject. Even a senior professor with a chair monopolized only a relatively small segment of a specialized field, and his obligation extended to participation in general department affairs. Departments grew by accretion, by means of the simple addition of members who both individually represented specific areas of

[20] Henry James, *Charles W. Eliot: President of Harvard University, 1869–1909,* 2 vols. (Boston and New York: Houghton Mifflin Company, 1930), 2:87.

knowledge and individually expanded the range of a department's specialized offerings. Few departments ever willed to cease growing. By this process, departments were able to remain current with new fields of investigation, fields which often generated more student interest than traditional, well-plowed ones. A new methodology or new sphere of discovery usually dictated the hiring of a new man. By nature, the department in an American university was acquisitive.

Within the structure of the department, not only did the faculty members compete among themselves for perquisites, privileges, salary, and rank; they competed for students whose option to elect courses often reduced teaching to a popularity contest. In the history of the American university, brief assignments, histrionics, and easy grades traditionally attracted the majority of students, for whom higher education was a means to a worldly end. On the other hand, students voted with their feet by not attending the classes of arrogant and callous teachers (as well as ones with high standards). Fads swept through the American university no less than the society, and they affected the life of a department chairman, whose job as functionary could reduce itself to counting numbers and policing the behavior of individual faculty members. Not without cause did George Santayana describe academic arrangements at Harvard as a "lottery ticket or a chance at the grab-bag. . . . You had to bring a firm soul to this World's Fair."[21]

Liberal Arts and Sciences emerged as the largest college in most American universities, and it also stood out as a special American form. Europeans tended to separate the natural sciences from the studies (or sciences) of man. In England, the latter were usually found in a faculty of Art and considered to be a humanity. However, Americans bundled together sciences of every sort and separated them from the faculty of Art or Philosophy, the latter taking its place as a single department within the college of Liberal Arts

[21] George Santayana, *Persons and Places: the Background of My Life* (New York: Charles Scribner's Sons, 1944), p. 97.

and Sciences. New departments such as History, Economics, Sociology, and Political Science won their independence from Philosophy in the later nineteenth century. A humanist in nineteenth-century America often appeared to be a moral philosopher, a shallow generalist who did not legitimately belong in the university. As a member of the college of L.A.S., the physical scientist who engaged in intellectual research often felt professionally closer to the classicist pioneering in philological studies or the Shakespeare specialist than he did to the businessman scientist. Significantly, the publicized confrontation in England between Thomas Henry Huxley and Matthew Arnold on the natural sciences versus the humanities—the Two Cultures—did not attract a great deal of attention in later nineteenth-century America.[22]

The dean of Liberal Arts and Sciences presided over a vast array of departments—humanities, social sciences, physical sciences, natural sciences—which through the vehicle of department chairmen competed for his funds, favors, and endorsements. And the dean of L.A.S. represented his college in the competition with other colleges and deans for the attention of the chancellor or president of an institution. Bargaining and haggling often typified the ongoing negotiations. The combative spirit of professional college football seemed to be reflected in academic politics. Indeed, politics could be paramount, as when Frederick Jackson Turner served as a campaign manager for the selection of Charles Van Hise as president at Wisconsin. Moreover, ambitious men were known to misrepresent political decisions as professional judgments, and to accuse an academic colleague of incompetence in order to justify his unwarranted dismissal.[23]

[22] See the discussion by John Higham, "The Schism in American Scholarship," *American Historical Review* 72 (October 1966): 1–20. See also Matthew Arnold, "Literature and Science," in *The Portable Matthew Arnold*, ed. Lionel Trilling (New York: The Viking Press, 1949), pp. 405–29; Thomas Huxley, "Science and Culture," in *Science and Education* (New York: The Citadel Press, 1964), pp. 120–40.

[23] A difficult and much publicized case was Edward W. Bemis's forced resignation from the University of Chicago in 1895. Bemis was a tenured Associate Professor of Political Economy in the Lecture Study

The American university developed a sizable bureaucracy that grew in response to the professional service orientation of the institution as well as to the size of the enrollment. In fact, a professionally conscious faculty stimulated the appearance of administrators. Historically, professors had served as hired hands for the old-time college president. They began upgrading their status and asserted an independent professional identity by stressing the prior importance of their formal training and field of competence above any institutional affiliation. It was William James—psychologist, at both Harvard and Stanford. It was Frederick Jackson Turner—historian, at Wisconsin, Harvard, and then the Huntington Library. Even the graduate school a professor had attended, especially Johns Hopkins in the later nineteenth century, often took precedence in a professional identity over the university which employed him.

Academics promoted their national visibility through such forms of professional affiliation as associations, journals, editorial positions, archives, research projects, papers, prizes, government appointments, and advisory roles. The means of expression for ambitious professors proliferated in the 1880s and 1890s. Johns Hopkins, for instance, became a center for professional publications, notably the *American*

Department of the Extension Division. An advocate of municipal ownership of public services, he offended the university by criticizing commercial interests which supported the new institution. His actions served to highlight his marginal position as a lecturer in the Extension Division. Albion Small, chairman of the department of sociology, supported the charge of incompetency against Bemis and obscured the separate issues of his professional teaching, his research, and his right to public advocacy. The evidence seemed to suggest that William Rainey Harper's perception of the university's obligation to its donors, and the university's interest, was paramount in the Bemis case. None too secure themselves, many professional economists, including friends of Bemis such as Richard T. Ely, reluctantly decided that he was expendable for the sake of the public's acceptance of the profession's objectivity and respectability. Except for a brief interlude, Bemis never obtained another academic position. For various angles on the case, see Harold E. Bergquist, Jr., "The Edward W. Bemis Controversy at the University of Chicago," *AAUP Bulletin* 58 (December 1972): 384–93; Furner, *Advocacy and Objectivity*, pp. 164–98; Storr, *Harper's University*, pp. 83–85, 96–98; Metzger, *Academic Freedom*, pp. 153–61.

Journal of Philology and *The Johns Hopkins University Studies in Historical and Political Science*. The American Historical Association published its *Papers* and the American Economic Association its *Publications*. Academics filled the pages of popular magazines like the *Forum, The Populare Science Monthly,* and *The North American Review*. Entrepreneurial activities such as the publication of textbooks for a growing market of students quickly attracted the professor who wished to profit while advertising his name.

Possessed by a vertical vision and career opportunities, the new style of professor worked to establish a pragmatic relationship with the university where he taught. Legally he was employed by the corporation on contract to fulfill some vaguely defined services, such as teach for a specific number of hours for a specific number of weeks. The meaning of being a "good colleague" was nebulous. The ambitious careerist sought to maximize his income and minimize his teaching responsibilities, avoid advising students, pass on the concern with public relations to others, and apply for as much time off for professional activities as possible. For instance, moving in their isolated ways, faculty members at Harvard impressed Santayana as "an anonymous concourse of coral insects, each secreting one cell, and leaving that fossil legacy to enlarge the earth."[24]

Such men as Franklin W. Clarke, Thorstein Veblen, Joseph Jastrow, and James Cattel voiced discontent with the weakness and fragmentation of the faculty in the institution where it earned most of its bread.[25] But the majority of professors seemed to be satisfied with their indi-

[24] James Ballowe, ed., *George Santayana's America: Essays on Literature and Culture* (Urbana, Chicago, London: University of Illinois Press, 1967), p. 4.
[25] See F. W. Clarke, "The Appointment of College Officers," *Popular Science Monthly* 21 (June 1882): 171–78; Joseph Jastrow, "Academic Aspects of Administration," *Ibid.* 73 (October 1908): 326–39; Jastrow, "The Administrative Peril in Education," *Ibid.* 81 (November 1912): 495–515; J. McKeen Cattell, *University Control* (New York and Garrison, N.Y.: The Science Press, 1913); Mark Beach, "Professional versus Professorial Control of Higher Education," *Educational Record,* 49 (Summer 1968), 263–73.

vidual arrangements; this satisfaction was demonstrated in part by the fact that not until 1915 did academics establish the American Association of University Professors, a relatively ineffectual organization focused primarily on the gray area of academic freedom.[26] Academic freedom cases had been wrenching American higher education for nearly a generation with a minimal response from the majority of professors. At the turn of the century, for example, the history profession failed to either defend or help relocate George Howard, head of the Stanford history department, who was forced to resign because of his principled defense of E. A. Ross in the most notorious case of a political firing in the early history of the American university. The competitiveness of professional historians revealed itself when within a week of the Howard vacancy, the president at Stanford hired a young Ph.D. from Harvard, who accepted the position on the recommendation of Harvard's senior historians.[27]

University administrators prospered by both encouraging and taking advantage of faculty attitudes. At faculty meetings, Eliot was always looking for promising young men who might welcome the opportunity to join the administrative ranks.[28] Administrative officers assumed the tasks of

[26] See "General Report of the Committee on Academic Freedom and Academic Tenure," *Bulletin of the American Association of University Professors* 1 (December 1915): 20–39; Walter P. Metzger, "Origins of the Association: an Anniversary Address," *AAUP Bulletin* 51 (June 1965): 229–37; Metzger, *Academic Freedom*, pp. 194–232.

[27] Twenty years Ross's senior, Howard was considered to be a dignified, circumspect individual, one of the university's most dedicated professors and a founding member of the history department. The historical profession's inaction in Howard's defense has generally been ignored in the successful outcome of both Ross's own professional career and his case against Stanford. See Furner, *Advocacy and Objectivity*, pp. 251–53; Edward Alsworth Ross, *Seventy Years Of It: An Autobiography* (New York, London: D. Appleton-Century Company, 1936), pp. 77–80; Orrin Leslie Elliott, *Stanford University: The First Twenty-Five Years* (Stanford, Calif.: Stanford University Press, 1937), pp. 360–66; James C. Mohr, "Academic Turmoil and Public Opinion: The Ross Case at Stanford," *Pacific Historical Review* 39 (February 1970): 56; Metzger, Academic Freedom, pp. 167–68.

[28] Eliot, *University Administration*, p. 123.

counseling students, performing the day-to-day chores, maintaining records, relating to the trustees, assisting the alumni, and representing the institution to the public. Not only did they treat the faculty as a client, they enhanced their esteem by devising their own measures of success as professional administrators. When Frederick Jackson Turner was a powerful history department chairman at Wisconsin, he considered his efforts comparable to that of writing a book. In his capacity as an administrator, Turner found it to be both easier and more immediately rewarding to run a department than to work on his unwritten books.[29]

University administration was a career.[30] Eliot, for instance, was convinced that a young man should advance gradually through different positions, and no man should begin as an administrative officer over the age of forty-five. Eliot carried forward one of the grand myths that fostered the proliferation of administrators in the American university. They deserved higher salaries than teachers and scholars, since their work did not "offer the satisfaction of literary or scientific attainment, the long, uninterrupted vacations which teachers enjoy, or the pleasure of intimate, helpful intercourse with a stream of young men of high intellectual ambition."[31] As a professional executive, Eliot

[29] Ray Allen Billington, *Frederick Jackson Turner: Historian, Scholar, Teacher* (New York: Oxford University Press, 1973), pp. 247–48.

[30] See the proposals in Morris Llewellyn Cooke, *Academic and Industrial Efficiency, A Report to the Carnegie Foundation for the Advancement of Teaching*, Bulletin no. 5 (New York: The Carnegie Foundation, 1910). A disciple of Frederick Winslow Taylor's system of scientific management, Cooke recommended standardization of education at every level, including lecture notes. For instance, speaking of teachers as "producers," Cooke charted the time in terms of minutes teachers of physics (at four levels of rank) spent at various activities during a day. Then Cooke determined the "money value of the time" for each activity. pp. 93–95. See also Samuel Haber, *Efficiency and Uplift: Scientific Management in the Progressive Era, 1890–1920* (Chicago, London: The University of Chicago Press, 1964), pp. 65–66.

[31] Eliot, *University Administration*, p. 15. Eliot's talent for administration is described in Hugh Hawkins, *Between Harvard and America: The Educational Leadership of Charles W. Eliot* (New York: Oxford University Press, 1972), pp. 51–52, 73–74, *passim*.

presumed that his administrative subordinates were making sacrifices rather than escaping the rigors of teaching, research, and contact with high intellectual ambition. He failed to note that many more successful managers appeared within the American university than teachers.

In 1871, James Burrill Angell decided to move from the presidency of the University of Vermont to the presidency of Michigan, and already he resembled the new type of administrator. First, he satisfied the portrait drawn by the interim president and the selection committee: age in the early forties, educated, tactful, socially graceful, successfully experienced, and having a "perfect acquaintance with business and political matters." As an educator, Angell met minimal standards. More to the point, he possessed all the administrative and executive talent required by the job. Indeed, his skills were proven in his lengthy negotiations with the committee. Twice he refused the committee's offer and raised his demand for salary and perquisites. He explained that he did not want to appear to be too ambitious and leave Vermont in the lurch, and added his family was not enthusiastic about the move.[32]

Angell played the game well. During the entire negotiation, he dwelt on the issue of the personal influence, authority, and support of the president. Issues of educational policy remained peripheral. Subtly, Angell played on the feelings of inferiority and envy at Michigan of the Eastern establishment. Despite its mediocrity, Vermont was a New England institution, and since Angell was taking a risk by moving west, he required the best conditions possible. The president of the University of Michigan would have to deal with political interests at every level from local to national, and he required all the available symbols

[32] Angell's decision is documented in *From Vermont to Michigan: Correspondence of James Burrill Angell: 1869-1871*, ed. Wilfred B. Shaw (Ann Arbor, Mich.: University of Michigan Press, 1936). Angell won a salary 50 percent higher than the outgoing president's, moving expenses to Ann Arbor, and the installation of a water closet—the first in the town—in the President's House.

of status in order to enhance the prestige of the office and the reputation of the university.

Having arrived at Michigan, Angell remarked that "it is fortunate I did not attempt to teach this term. My time is fully occupied with administrative work and looking into things."[33] A division of labor between full-time administrators and faculty members was beginning to appear in the American university, and ambitious administrators increasingly viewed themselves as representing the true interests of the institution, while the faculty was merely a client. An administrator succeeded as a professional when he asserted his authority over the client just as in the outside world. Eliot, for instance, was a master at intimidating insecure, career-minded faculty members.

Eliot asserted internal institutional control by laying out the career pattern any faculty member must follow who had expectations of advancement at Harvard and in the American university. After the bachelor's degree, the young scholar should expect to spend successive periods of three to four years in professional study, in annual appointments in subordinate places, and as an instructor. Then followed five to ten years as an assistant professor. He should not expect promotion to the rank of full professor before the age of forty, and perhaps never. All this time, of course, he must behave as both a good citizen and a worthy representative of the institution. His salary increments would be modest. Instructors would not receive enough money to marry, and assistant professors only enough to support a family with few amenities. No one need complain, since the successful administrator had "no difficulty in keeping a faculty young on the average" by issuing annual contracts to a "large body" of aspiring candidates. The period of probation for promotion was lengthy, during which time a candidate was evaluated in various ways. For example, Eliot expected aspiring university teachers to marry, and before promoting an individual he observed the suitability of

[33] *Ibid.*, p. 295.

the wife. "It is a good deal safer," he said euphemistically, "to give a life office to a married man on whom marriage has proved to have a good effect, than to a single man who may shortly be married with uncertain results."[34]

It was a world of lonely, isolated, and frightened men in which Eliot held sway, a competitive world calculated to suppress warm human relationships. In the professional atmosphere of the American university, eager Americans related within themselves to their private desire for distinction, and to independence from the commonplace and the average. They related beyond themselves to the next highest rung on the vocational ladder, to the canons of the profession set forth by the elders, to the last link of the great chain stringing together a career, and to the honorary and material rewards that accompanied success. Like Eliot, professional Americans found it difficult to respond to each other as equal members of a common humanity.

EDUCATION AND SOCIAL LEADERSHIP

In every modern nation, the educational system has represented goals embedded within the expectations of the culture. A university does not survive, much less prosper, apart from a relatively broad spectrum of social interests that recognize the legitimacy of its function. The public must at least passively accept the cause of higher education, though in fact public endorsement in the Western world has tended to be active. Historians have better understood European schools than American ones in the nineteenth century, primarily because the social-class nature of the schools in those highly stratified societies was conspicuous. We can better understand the cultural vision that originally informed the American university—and continues to sustain it—when we examine American responses to the Eu-

34 Eliot, *University Administration*, pp. 93–94, 12–13, 101, 102–3.

ropean systems that many in the nineteenth century observed and admired, especially the German.

The major European institutions trained an elite. In
France, for instance, a centralized governmental agency
sponsored a specialized and fragmented system of higher
education in which only politically well-connected individuals seemed to thrive. Both in the university and in the
many private institutes, French education favored gentlemen scholars who neither encouraged the research ideal nor
built careers on scientific innovation. Bureaucratic patronage oiled the machinery. Students were required only to
pass examinations, not to attend lectures. Increasingly, the
vocationally useful degree became more a financial than an
academic matter, a privilege purchased by a worldly oligarchy.[35] In England, by contrast, Oxford and Cambridge
stood at the pinnacle of an exclusive and inbred system
that provided a gentlemanly education for the younger
generation of a snobbish governing class about to assume
its inherited position in the world of affairs. "Oxford in
particular," Charles Coulton Gillispie has written, "seems
to have been . . . almost a way of life if not a state of
grace, and an education there was not only a training of
the mind, but a social, a moral, a British, even a spiritual
experience."[36]

[35] See Theodore Zeldin, "Higher Education in France, 1848–1940," in
Laqueur & Mosse, eds., *Education and Social Structure,* pp. 53–80;
Terry Clark, *Prophets and Patrons: The French University and the
Emergence of the Social Sciences* (Cambridge, Mass.: Harvard Univer-
sity Press, 1973); C. R. Day, "Technical and Professional Education in
France: The Rise and Fall of L'Enseignement Secondaire Special, 1865–
1902," *Journal of Social History,* 6 (Winter, 1972–1973): 177–201. See
also Joseph Ben-David, "The Rise and Decline of France as a Scientific
Centre," *Minerva,* 8 (April, 1970): 160–80; Robert Fox, "Scientific En-
terprise and the Patronage of Research in France, 1800–70," *Ibid.,* 11
(October, 1973): 442–73; Maurice Crosland, "The Development of a
Professional Career in Science in France," *Ibid.,* 13 (Spring, 1975):
38–57.

[36] Charles C. Gillispie, "English Ideas of the University in the Nineteenth Century," in Clapp, ed., *Modern University,* p. 53. See also
W. R. Ward, *Victorian Oxford* (London: Frank Cass & Co. Ltd, 1965);

It was German higher education that fascinated Americans and drew them abroad to the universities of Berlin, Göttingen, Halle, Leipzig, and Heidelberg. But the reasons Americans went were not entirely clear, because so much about German society and higher education, especially after 1866, should have offended the Americans.[37]

First, the exclusive *Gymnasium*-university complex served as the hub of a bureaucratically and politically sanctioned patriciate—a mandarin class. Those who qualified for the civil service monopolized entrance into that class, but before taking the examination they needed to possess the academic credentials state supported universities conferred. However, the structure of German society arbitrarily barred industrial, commercial, and working-class persons as early as the age of five from rising into the higher civil service. Children from these classes entered the practical-oriented *Volksschulen,* from which matriculation to academic studies with the precious degrees was nearly impossible, except with regard to theological studies. The German elite drew a firm line between schooling for the herd and education for their own cultured group.[38] Describing the "representa-

Sheldon Rothblatt, *The Revolution of the Dons: Cambridge and Society in Victorian England* (London: Faber and Faber Ltd., 1968); Noel Gilroy Annan, *Leslie Stephen: His Thought and Character in Relation to his Time* (London: Macgibbon & Kee, 1951), pp. 22–48, 130–41.

[37] Apart from numerous autobiographical and biographical statements, the American experience in Germany in its intellectual dimension has been examined by Jurgen Herbst, *The German Historical School in American Scholarship: a Study in the Transfer of Culture* (Ithaca, N.Y.: Cornell University Press, 1965); Joseph Dorfman, "The Role of the German Historical School in American Economic Thought," *The American Economic Review,* 45 (May, 1955): 17–28. See also Samuel Rezneck, "The European Education of an American Chemist and Its Influence in 19th-Century America: Eben Norton Horsford," *Technology and Culture,* 11 (July, 1970): 366–88.

[38] See Fritz K. Ringer, "Higher Education in Germany in the Nineteenth Century," in Laqueur and Mosse, eds., *Education and Social Structure,* pp. 123–38; Fritz K. Ringer, *The Decline of the German Mandarins: The German Academic Community, 1890–1933* (Cambridge, Mass.: Harvard University Press, 1969), pp. 25–42; Paul Farmer, "Nine-

tives of academic culture," Frederick Paulsen, the historian
of the German university, wrote in 1895:

> We may affirm that in their entirety they form a stratum of society
> which is in the main homogeneous, and of which all the influen-
> tial and controlling circles form part. . . . Whoever possesses
> university training belongs to "society." . . . And, on the other
> hand, he who has not enjoyed a university training, or some
> academic education of equivalent value, loses infallibly a good
> deal in the eyes of many people in Germany.[39]

The mandarin class defined itself as a closed corporation,
an exclusive class that constituted a tiny elite of merit. In
contrast to America, the commercial middle classes in Germany tended to be poorly educated, socially confined, utterly selfish, and often ready to align themselves with reactionary landed interests.

Though many well-to-do Americans who visited Germany
privately sympathized with the social benefits of the class
structure, few were willing to defend it publicly, especially
once they returned to America. An aggressive middle class
in America, wishing to professionalize an increasing number of worldly occupations by establishing them upon universal scientific standards, created an atmosphere very different from Germany's. The state-supported German university purposely restricted the size of its clientele.[40] American

teenth-Century Ideas of the University: Continental Europe," in Clapp,
ed., *Modern University,* pp. 3–24.

[39] Friedrich Paulsen, *The German Universities: Their Character and
Historical Development* (New York: Macmillan and Company, 1895),
pp. 110–11. Max Weber wrote that "differences of education are one of
the strongest . . . social barriers, especially in Germany, where almost
all privileged positions inside and outside the civil service are tied to
qualifications involving not only specialized knowledge but also 'general
cultivation,' and where the whole school and university system has been
put into the service of this [ideal of] general cultivation." Cited in
Ringer, "Higher Education in Germany," p. 138. For the persistence of
this tradition, even after World War II, see Klaus Epstein, "The Bonn
Republic, 1949–1965," Chapter 23 in Koppel S. Pinson, *Modern Germany: Its History and Civilization,* 2nd ed. (New York: The Macmillan
Company, 1967), pp. 592–94.

[40] In 1880, only 21,000 students enrolled in all German universities;
116,000 enrolled in American higher education, though any parallel be-

universities, whether state institutions funded by public land grants or private institutions funded by patrons, moved in the opposite direction. Moreover, the German university offered only specialized academic training and an advanced degree, with no program comparable to the most popular degree in the American university, the Bachelor of Arts or Science. With a German Ph.D., roughly comparable to a superior American M.A., a graduate sought a teaching position in a *Gymnasium*.[41] The American with an advanced degree, more career oriented, sought a position in a university or perhaps transferred his expertise to the industrial and commercial world. Functioning in a strictly defined class society, German higher education prevented persons with practical skills, including technological and quasi-scientific ones, from broadening the scientific foundation of their knowledge. Academic disciplines imbued with professional ideals and status simply were unavailable to them.

Second, privilege not only prevailed in German society, it dominated the hierarchic arrangements in German universities.[42] The individual professor occupied a *chair* endowed by the state, and from it he dominated an entire field of study, such as history. The academic system required little accountability and tolerated more than a

tween German and American institutions must be inaccurate. In 1930, German universities and technical institutes enrolled 99,300 in twenty-two institutions; the same year American higher education enrolled 1,100,000 students in fourteen hundred nine institutions. Ringer, *German Mandarins*, p. 52; *Knaurs Konversations-Lexikon* (Berlin: Verlheag Th. Knaur, 1932), p. 1718; *Historical Statistics of the United States*, Series H 316, 321, pp. 210–11. For points of comparison between German and American universities and students, see also Charles Franklin Thwing, *The American and the German University: One Hundred Years of History* (New York: The Macmillan Company, 1928).

41 See Parsons and Platt, *American University*, pp. 111, 125 n.19; Ben-David, *American Higher Education*, pp. 102–3, 156–58, *passim*; Joseph Ben-David, "The Universities and the Growth of Science in Germany and the United States," *Minerva* 7 (Autumn–Winter 1968–1969): 1–35.

42 See Ben-David, *Scientist's Role in Society*, pp. 103–38; Hajo Holborn, *A History of Modern Germany, 1648–1840* (New York: Alfred A. Knopf, 1966), pp. 479–84.

little abuse, including incompetence. Only the full professor was a genuine professor, and the guild of senior men determined that only they could be appointed to deanships or rectorates. In alliance with the higher civil servants, the professors made up the *Kulturstaat*. In his chair the professor often controlled an institute in which he alone defined the subspecialties his assistants would pursue, and he alone sanctioned the creation of new fields worthy of recognition. Jealous of his authority, a professor could rally his colleagues to prevent fields allied to his own from coming into existence through the creation of new chairs. Personalities entered such disputes; the polemics, partisanship, and rivalries in academic circles earned notoriety.

Americans often moved from one institution to another in Germany, and they did not find themselves at the mercy of a single senior professor for years on end. They could afford to ignore the brutal patronage system that blunted the idealism of the free pursuit of knowledge for which the German university was famous. Departments did not exist in the German university, and the senior professor both privately trained and personally determined the fate of the apprentice academic who aspired to a university position. Specialized research was regarded as a creative act—a higher calling—not a professional career for which one was paid money. Hence, Germans declined to pay assistant professors as professionals at the first stage of an occupational career. During his "hungering and suffering period," the lucky apprentice might eat at the professor's table and wear his discarded clothes. By contrast, the American E. A. Ross, young and recently returned from Germany in 1891, was delighted with the prospects for an ambitious, promising economist in American universities. "To me the chief thing about a good salary is that it convinces other people about one's success," he boasted, and he could show the salary to prove his point.[43]

[43] Cited in Veysey, *Emergence of the American University*, p. 263. See also Ross, *Seventy Years*, pp. 45, 47; W. R. Harper, "The Pay of American College Professors," *Forum* 16 (September 1893): 96–109.

In the role of *Privatdozent*, assistant professors in Germany performed the drudge work of universities without any regular salary, official status, or security.[44] For instance, professors controlled the major lectures, thus depriving the *Privatdozent* of additional income from the fees. All the assistant could do was wait for possible advancement to one of the few chairs, a prospect that grew dimmer in the later part of the century. Professors were a long-lived group, and they were disposed to obstruct proposals for new chairs. Moreover, with the increasing number of students, German universities exploited the cheap labor to make expansion of the institution possible. If the *Privatdozent* failed to secure a professorship, as did many, he found his opportunities restricted for transferring to a related occupation outside the university community. He was overspecialized, overaged, and no longer suited for a teaching position in the *Gymnasium* or secondary school. Permanently trapped, he was forced into menial work in a closed universe. The agony of becoming a professor in Germany escaped most Americans, who preferred only to witness the intellectual glories of such great men as Leopold von Ranke, Wilhelm Wundt, Carl Ludwig, and Theodor Mommsen.

Third, the German professor emerged as the complete intellectual. His spiritual concern with lofty abstractions, conceptual rationality, and historical models eclipsed mere worldly concerns with empirical analysis and operational technique. The philosophical tradition in Germany was theoretical, contemplative, and introspective.[45] It was geared to a lifetime committed to basic research, and in the uni-

44 See Alexander Busch, "The Vicissitudes of the *Privatdozent:* Breakdown and Adaptation in the Recruitment of the German University Teacher," *Minerva* 1 (Spring 1963): 319–41.

45 See Ringer, *German Mandarins,* pp. 81–113; Herbst, *German Historical School,* pp. 99–128. See also Ernst Cassirer, *The Problems of Knowledge: Philosophy, Science, and History Since Hegel* (New Haven, Conn.: Yale University Press, 1950); John Theodore Merz, *A History of European Thought in the Nineteenth Century,* 4 vols. (New York: Dover Publications, 1965), 3; Herbert Marcuse, *Reason and Revolution: Hegel and the Rise of Social Theory* (New York: Oxford University Press, 1941).

versities professional interest in function, results, and practice was considered to be unworthy of the mind dedicated to creativity and the discovery of new knowledge.

An aristocrat of the spirit, the German professor pursued knowledge for its own sake; he wished to view it from the inside, not from any contemporary perspective or careerist motive. A master of the humane sciences, the academic intellectual attended to the idealistic cultivation of the objective *Geist,* the true inner man and inner society in the "culture state." In a total effort, the creative scholar contemplated the unique self-development of the whole mind and spirit of the world in its many manifestations. As one German philosopher stated the humanistic ideal; pure scholarship came into being

[w]hen, first, rational work frees itself from the mere service of life purposes . . . so that knowledge becomes a goal for its own sake, and when, secondly, the rational does not remain in isolated fragments . . . when everything rational is systematically to become a whole through being internally related.[46]

By comparison, Americans seldom displayed the intellectual patience required by the esoteric German tradition, and they found it difficult to suppress their enthusiasm for problem solving and the worldly application of scientific technique.[47]

In theory, the cultural elite in Germany won a victory for free higher learning. In practice, worldly obedience was bred into patrician professors who belonged to the civil-service bureaucracy. In the 1870s, "academic freedom"

[46] Karl Jaspers cited in Ringer, *German Mandarins,* p. 110. See also Georg G. Iggers, *The German Conception of History: The National Tradition of Historical Thought from Herder to the Present* (Middletown, Conn.: Wesleyan University Press, 1968); Carlo Antoni, *From History to Sociology: The Transition in German Historical Thinking* (Detroit: Wayne State University Press, 1959).

[47] See the contrast between the two men in Gershon George Rosenstock, *F.A. Trendelenburg: Forerunner to John Dewey* (Carbondale: Southern Illinois Press, 1964). See also Neil Coughlan, *Young John Dewey: An Essay in American Intellectual History* (Chicago and London: The University of Chicago Press, 1975), pp. 123–27, 134–37.

in Germany realistically meant the absolute right of a privileged estate to go about its abstract work without interference from outside the bureaucracy. Freedom did not include the right of a scholar to speak out as an advocate on controversial issues of public policy. For the German, freedom in the realm of the spiritual rested on submission in the realm of the political, a submission that inevitably drained the original spiritual task of its vitality.[48]

The historical approach to knowledge reflected both the academic habit of caution and the intellectual reverence for rational form which drew support from conservative bureaucrats who did not feel threatened by grand abstractions in massive books read by only a select class. The idealistic purity of the historical methodology transcended the irreconcilable conflicts of the profane world. By focusing exclusively on a historical and conceptual analysis of capitalism, for instance, German scholars neglected it as a subject of empirical social research.[49] Especially as they touched upon social problems in the contemporary world, the social sciences in Germany suffered from a lack of institutional encouragement and continuity. Political scientists were few in number, sociologists fought for recognition, and applied sciences were relegated to independent institutes such as the *Physikalisch-Technische Reichsanstalt* of Berlin.[50] Any empirical analysis that implied the need for the liberalization of the German academic world met with an authoritarian denial.

Rarified learning protected by the supreme claim for philosophic objectivity in the German university existed together with homage to nationalism and the political

[48] The historical evolution of this position is discussed in Ringer, *German Mandarins*, pp. 113–27. See also Leonard Krieger, *The German Idea of Freedom: History of a Political Tradition* (Boston: Beacon Press, 1957).

[49] See Anthony Oberschall, *Empirical Social Research in Germany, 1848–1914* (Paris, The Hague: Mouton & Company, 1965), pp. 137–45, *passim*.

[50] See Frank Pfetsch, "Scientific Organisation and Science Policy in Imperial Germany, 1871–1914: The Foundation of the Imperial Institute of Physics and Technology," *Minerva* 8 (October 1970): 557–80.

status quo in the 1870s. Nationalism harmonized the two spheres of the university and the state. Nationalism unified the whole of society, including its constitutional forms and legal structures. Nationalism served as a viable alternative to democracy, which the mandarin condemned as a system flawed by universal suffrage, disrespect for cultural authority, the upward mobility of inferior talents, inattention to the ethical and the spiritual, and the destructiveness of competition. Fearful of the ambition of aggressive Jews and the modernity they represented, German academics by and large accepted or even promoted anti-Semitism, as one mode of registering patriotic opposition to "democracy."[51] In his innermost self, his favorite place, the elitist mandarin believed that a rational destiny had specially chosen him to assume responsibility for the historical mission of the German nation. American academics might have wished for such an illustrious role, but few fooled themselves into believing anybody would stand for it.[52]

A USABLE INTELLIGENCE

Why did Americans, with their evangelical impulses, entrepreneurial habits, and suspicions of Old World privileges and central governments favor German higher education? One may conclude that what Americans selected to see and in many instances experienced in Germany served

[51] See George L. Mosse, *The Crisis of German Ideology: Intellectual Origins of the Third Reich* (New York: Grosset & Dunlap, 1964), pp. 190–203, 269–72; Ringer, *German Mandarins,* pp. 135–39, 239–40; Richard S. Levy, *The Downfall of the Anti-Semitic Political Parties in Imperial Germany* (New Haven, Conn., and London: Yale University Press, 1975), pp. 22–23.

[52] John William Burgess accommodates the model of the German university to American circumstances in the 1880s: *The American University: When Shall It Be? Where Shall It Be? What Shall It Be: An Essay* (Boston: Ginn, Heath, & Co., 1884). See also R. Gordon Hoxie, et al., *A History of the Faculty of Political Science, Columbia University* (New York: Columbia University Press, 1955), pp. 49–51.

the end of American professional careers. All other perceptions existed at the fringes of attention. The political arrangements of the German university, the arrogance of the professors, the real meaning of academic freedom, the treatment of the *Privatdozent:* these escaped the American's notice. He instead perceived those specific features of the German system that strengthened his self-confidence, making up for a serious lack in his own background. Influenced by German models, the American university cultivated in its clients a faith in the mighty power of their own "usable intelligence." Americans grew to believe that the claim to possess such an intelligence both provided the *raison d'être* of the middle class in America and justified its rising standard of living.

In brief, the German experience offered American students a way of reflecting upon the possibilities and limitations—the liberation and containment—of their own lives in the context of nineteenth-century America. Most Americans admired the capacity of the German for concentrated and thorough work, which they could translate into their own motives for professional labor. Even if the Germans were ponderous, the contrast to the slipshod manner and philistinism of the Americans was welcome. The Germans respected the significance of ideas, they knew the value of an active mind—brainwork—and they pioneered in specialized research that excavated primary sources.

Though William James was not a typical American, he was an acutely self-conscious one, the kind of individual who is torn by the deepest tensions in a culture. After a shoddy medical education at Harvard that drained his emotions, he went to Germany and experienced what many Americans felt in varying degrees. Once in Germany, James found himself in the midst of a personal crisis very much related to his identity as an American. Apparently, he derived therapeutic value from drawing comparisons between the German and the American national characters. "The impatient nature of the Americans," he wrote, "has struck me very much in the individuals I have seen here." The

Americans were rootless, ephemeral, haggard, and hungry looking; too often appearing to scrape the bottom of their resources. In contrast, the educated Germans were stable, thorough, exact, and conscientious, even to the painful extreme of appearing to be plodding, flat, dull, and unimaginative.[53]

In morbid combat with his own sense of inadequacy, James reflected approvingly on the stolid nature and "powerful construction" of the German leadership class. "It makes one repine at the way he has been brought up, to come here." From the perspective of his private self-analysis, James was suffering from an American malady:

I have been growing lately to feel that a great mistake of my past life—which has been prejudicial to my education, and by telling me which, and by making me understand it some years ago, some one might have conferred a great benefit on me—is an impatience of *results*. . . . We Americans are too greedy for *results* . . . and we think only of means of cutting short the work to reach them sooner.

James attributed this "American characteristic" in part to "inexperience of life," in part to the ease and sheer luck with which Americans had obtained material results.[54] Immaturity and childish habits in America prevented the cultivation of the inner confidence in solid mental effort and in the sacrifice of hours and hours of labor that perhaps best explained the German success.

Again and again Americans reiterated James's theme or a variant of it. Ambitious men would not go very far in the modern world without sophisticated training and the ability to organize their work. Education meant the freedom to approach one's interests as a serious scholar—professionally. The experience abroad convinced Americans that growth in one's life and work required dedicated intellectual preparation. The physicist needed to know his

53 Perry, *William James*, 1:238.

54 *Ibid.*, p. 259; *The Letters of William James*, ed. Henry James, 2 vols. (Boston: The Atlantic Monthly Press, 1920), 1:100–1, 122, 133.

higher mathematics; the mining engineer his mineralogy; the agricultural specialist his chemistry; the social scientist his facts, theories, and figures.

The sheer waste and sloppiness of American behavior appalled advocates of higher education for professional ends such as Andrew Dickson White, a student of and sympathizer with the German system. Practical Americans were engaged in a boondoggle, a charge White never tired of repeating:

No one can stand in any legislative position and not be struck with the frequent want in men otherwise strong and keen, of the simplest knowledge of principles essential to public welfare. Of technical knowledge of law, and of practical acquaintance with business, the supply is always plentiful, but it is very common that in deciding great public questions, exploded errors in political and social science are revamped, fundamental principles of law disregarded, and the plainest teachings of history ignored.[55]

Too many Americans glorified chance, the gamble, the quick return, the gold rush, the political payoff, and the unpredictable whirl of the century. Such a boom-and-bust temper of mind destroyed calculated, cerebral planning. Uneducated Americans lacked confidence in the cold light of science, and their passions disrupted social progress.

The backdrop against which White drew up the plans for Cornell University in the years immediately following the Civil War highlighted his fears. White resembled the middle-class reformer in the North who at the start of Reconstruction expressed more concern with preserving an equality of opportunity based on proven talent than with rectifying an inequality of performance based on proven deprivation. It was unacceptable to these reformers to extend legal and social guarantees to Negroes which were not extended to white persons. To do so would only eliminate the privilege of one class in favor of another,

[55] *Report of the Committee on Organization Presented to the Trustees of the Cornell University, 1866* (Albany, N.Y.: C. Van Benthuysen & Sons, Printers, 1867), p. 6.

they said, and render racial equality an artificial device. White thought that if the South was ever to recover from the war, a native middle-class educated leadership must emerge, a class that could control the region's commercial and cultural life.[56]

The Union had defeated aristocracy in the South, but it had not scotched the venomous enemy that endured within the masses of the North itself. Haste, superficiality, thoughtless passion, ignorance, fantasy, mob action, dissipation, unprofessional habits, the feint of patriotism: did these imagined shortcomings of the Irish in the North differ very much from those of lower-class Negroes in the South? This anxiety shook educators like White, especially since both the Irish and the Negroes had recently lived in aristocratic civilizations. "Observation" told the middle class that the real war for social discipline and rational consolidation had only begun. The Civil War might only be preliminary to the main event.

Between 1865 and 1875, the beginnings of the "age of the university," the irrationality of life seemed to be deep indeed to many active middle-class Americans, deeper and even less manageable than to their more passive European counterparts. The cosmic mutability of nature, the constant presence of bloodshed in America, the dread of imminent social-class warfare and labor rioting, agrarian unrest, the scandals of the Grant administration, the corruption of city bosses like Tweed, the ruthless practices of entrepreneurs like Vanderbilt and Gould: all seemed to mock authority and permanent standards in American civilization. Would any power prevail in America other than the mob or the man on horseback?

Ideological spokesmen for the American university such as Eliot justified the institution in terms of the nonpartisan professional class it would create. Democracy, according to

56 See Andrew D. White, *The Most Bitter Foe of Nations, and the Way to Its Permanent Overthrow: An Address Delivered Before the Phi Beta Kappa Society at Yale College, 1866* (New Haven, Conn.: Thomas J. Pease, 1866).

Eliot, meant rule by merit—never equality. And merit belonged to those individuals who disciplined themselves to acquire authority by concentrating on a single object. "As a people," Eliot told his inaugural audience in 1869, "we have but a halting faith in special training for high professional employments." Eliot described the "national danger":

The vulgar conceit that a Yankee can turn his hand to anything we insensibly carry into high places, where it is preposterous and criminal. We are accustomed to seeing men leap from farm or shop to court-room or pulpit, and we half believe that common men can safely use the seven-league boots of genius. What amount of knowledge and experience do we habitually demand of our lawgivers? What special training do we ordinarily think necessary for our diplomatists? [57]

Eliot concluded that without a university to select its leadership and cultivate special mental habits necessary in every special endeavor, American society was courting disaster. Eliot did not include in that leadership women, immigrants, or minorities.

The spirit that motivated Eliot's remarks touched upon the basic social reasons Americans considered in founding universities. Only the accepted authority of an elite of merit at the pinnacle of an active middle class could control the crosswinds that blew American society in opposing directions. The disorder of the Civil War era beginning in the 1840s gave impetus to the middle class in America to call for national standards just as defeats at the hands of Napoleon had given the same to the Germans earlier in the century.

Events in the 1860s proved encouraging for Americans who valued limitation, order, and consistency. The outcome of the war, for instance, immeasurably enhanced the legitimacy of the Constitution. Citizenship and due process were defined in the new amendments; secession was ruled an illegal act; and impeachment failed to assault the office of the presidency. After the debacle of the 1850s, the po-

[57] Eliot, "Inaugural," *Educational Reform*, pp. 11–12.

litical party system was strengthened when regular and open elections were held in the North during hostilities. Moreover, the collection of elaborate statistics and accurate census-taking became a regular function of the federal government. The first national income tax was enacted, the first conscription law passed, and a national banking system created to correct the abuses of the state banks.

Americans observed that among all the educational systems of Europe, only the German one came close to recruiting the best talent in the state and supporting original work of national significance. In England, for instance, leading thinkers like John Stuart Mill, Herbert Spencer, and Charles Darwin worked independently of the educational structure. Henry P. Tappan, America's most influential early exponent of the German university, wrote in 1851 that a well-ordered society required a university at its center.[58] Educators like Angell and White rationalized that with a successful university, society would need fewer regulatory institutions. The university was the hinge upon which an open society revolved. Angell succeeded Tappan as president of Michigan by eight years, and in 1871 he opened his inaugural address by saying that the "vital relation" between the State and the University "contemplates civil society as charged not merely with the negative work of repressing disorder and crime, but also with the higher positive office of promoting by all proper means the intellectual and the moral growth of the citizens."[59]

Little of the defensiveness, resentment, and suppressed hostility within the German university appeared in the American one. Public spokesmen for the American university drew the relationship between the expansion of the middle class, its prosperity, and the success of their institutions. Presidents like Gilman argued that a university education nourished free men, independent individuals who

[58] Henry P. Tappan, *University Education* (New York: George P. Putnam, 1851), pp. 69–70, 61.
[59] James Burrill Angell, "Inaugural," in *Selected Addresses* (New York: Longmans, Green, and Company, 1912), p. 3.

would emancipate themselves from mystery, ritual, and sciolistic learning. Real work was brain-work. "We must beware," Gilman said, "lest we make our schools technical instead of liberal, and impart a knowledge of methods rather than principles." Also, Folwell told his audience that the land-grant university "was made not merely for the *technical* instruction of the industrial classes, but for their liberal culture."[60] Through the educational process, significant numbers of people would be re-formed into individual characters, each a free agent pursuing his natural interest.[61] The list of the liberal vocations would expand with the advance of civilization, until the entire society corresponded to a schoolroom.

Enlightened men, the presidents envisioned the university to be a "universal" school in the new Union recently baptized by fire. As many professions as feasible would locate the center of their authority within university schools. By defining its functions comprehensively and constantly expanding its clientele, the American university would serve to enhance the public's image of a unified professional authority in the society.

The weight of that authority could not be minimized in a nation that not only lacked respect for historical tradition but which, for the most part, lacked a common past. Throughout the century middle-class Americans projected their fears of a whimsical universe into the reading of

[60] Gilman, "Johns Hopkins in its Beginning," in *University Problems,* p. 27; Folwell, "Inaugural," in *University Addresses,* p. 65.

[61] Electives in the curriculum was one device to achieve this end, and from the educator's point of view it satisfied the demand for choice and individual expression. In 1897, Albert Perry Brigham found that the existence of electives did not separate a college from a university. Such colleges as Amherst, Bowdoin, and Oberlin had more electives in the curriculum than such universities as Columbia, Chicago, and New York University. No two schools responded in the same way. Yale listed more electives than did Rutgers, which had more required courses than any other institution. "Present Status of the Elective System in American Colleges," *Educational Review* 14 (November 1897): 360–69. At Harvard, Charles Thwing found that History and Government, Philosophy, English, and Economics were the most popular subjects in an elective system. *College Administration,* pp. 269–71.

their own turbulent and scanty heritage. Most American institutions had appeared "within the memory of living men," and as autobiographies testified, living men were plagued by notoriously bad memories, especially when it came to deceiving themselves about their own earlier rascality. "We are a fiat nation," G. Stanley Hall said, echoing his suspicion about the role of historical influence in American life, "and in a very significant sense we have had neither childhood nor youth, but have lost touch with these stages of life because we lack a normal development history."[62]

Americans lacked tradition as a source of authority, but they did not lack "science." It was the primary function of American universities to render universal scientific standards credible to the public. Indeed, by means of science cultivated within the university, Americans even discovered the origins of a usable history in the German forest and on the American frontier—a scientific history now pioneered by professional scholars. To the middle-class American in the later nineteenth century, science implied more than method and procedure. Employed by Turner in his "frontier thesis" or E. A. Ross in his concept of "social control," science established a rational and orderly process of development beneath the fragmented experiences of American life. It revealed hard, documentable realities within the fluid American environment; it bolstered the self-certainty of the specialist which only the foolhardy would dare contest; it separated the professional expert who defined the limits of the possible in a given social instance from the amateur reformer who wished to make the entire

62 "Politics," in *The Complete Works of Ralph Waldo Emerson,* 12 vols. (Boston: Houghton Mifflin Company, 1903-4), 3, *Essays: Second Series,* 207; John Stuart Mill, "Tocqueville on Democracy in America (Vol. II)," in *Essays on Politics and Culture,* ed. Gertrude Himmelfarb (Garden City, N.Y.: Doubleday and Company, 1962), p. 281; G. Stanley Hall, *Adolescence: Its Psychology and its Relations to Physiology, Anthropology, Sociology, Sex, Crime, Religion, and Education,* 2 vols. (New York: D. Appleton and Company, 1904), 1:xvi. See also Perry Miller, "The Shaping of the American Character," *New England Quarterly* 28 (December 1955): 435–54.

world over by moralizing every issue. "I think then," Folwell said in 1869, "we have discovered what is that informing spirit which is to give life to the limbs and elements of the University; which can fuse, cement, and compact them into a harmonious organization. It is Science."[63]

By reducing problems to scientific and even technical terms, American universities functioned to contain within themselves controversial issues which had once ripped apart the general community. An inclusive institution, the university contained and structured the culture of ideas in American life, as college football stadiums contained and structured the culture of spectator recreation, and home economics the culture of good housekeeping. Universities quietly took divisive issues such as race, capitalism, labor, and deviant behavior out of the public domain and isolated these problems within the sphere of professionals— men who learned to know better than to air publicly their differences.

The university not only segregated ideas from the public, intellectual segregation occurred with the development of each new department in the university. A department emphasized the unique identity of its subject, its special qualities and language, its special distinction as an activity of research and investigation.[64] Any outsider who attempted

---

63 Folwell, "Inaugural," *University Addresses,* p. 18.

64 See, as examples of the professionalization of specific disciplines within American universities, Hamilton Cravens, "The Abandonment of Evolutionary Social Theory in America: The Impact of Academic Professionalization upon American Sociological Theory, 1890–1920," *American Studies* 12 (Fall 1971): 5–20; N. Ray Hiner, "Professions in Process: Changing Relations Among Social Scientists, Historians, and Educators, 1880–1920," *The History Teacher* 6 (February 1973): 201–18; Thomas M. Camfield, "The Professionalization of American Psychology, 1870–1917," *Journal of the History of the Behavioral Sciences* 9 (January 1973): 66–75; John B. Parrish, "Rise of Economics as an Academic Discipline: The Formative Years to 1900," *Southern Economic Journal* 34 (July 1967): 1–16. See also the essays in Paul Buck, ed., *Social Sciences at Harvard, 1860–1920: From Inculcation to the Open Mind* (Cambridge, Mass.: Harvard University Press, 1965); George W. Stocking, Jr., *Race, Culture, and Evolution: Essays in the History of Anthropology* (New York: The Free Press, 1968).

to pass judgment on an academic discipline contained within a department was acting presumptuously. In order to further their control over a discipline, professionals particularized and proliferated the possibilities for investigation in a field. The more technical and restricted the individual areas of investigation, the more justifiable it became to deny the public's right to know or understand the professional's mission.

Professionals who asked cosmic questions in their research, or delayed publication in order to improve the intellectual quality of their work, might easily retard the advance of a personal career. Successful careers depended upon the continual application of scientific thoroughness to limited, specific tasks at specific stages in the course of an occupational lifetime. But these limited, specific tasks easily degenerated into repetitive professional exercises which primarily served to hurdle careers upward and to distract from the serious intellectual problems at hand. In the 1880s, for instance, the recently formed profession of economists by and large cringed at Richard T. Ely's advocacy of socialism.[65] To protect his own academic career and answer the charge of unprofessional conduct, Ely in the 1890s recanted his earlier views and became a squeamish academic careerist.[66] No accusation more intimidated

[65] See Richard T. Ely, *Report of the Organization of the American Economic Association,* Publications of the American Economic Association, vol. 1, no. 1 (March 1886), pp. 21–29; A. W. Coats, "The First Two Decades of the American Economic Association," *The American Economic Review,* 50 (September 1960): 558–60; Benjamin G. Rader, *The Academic Mind and Reform: The Influence of Richard T. Ely in American Life* (Lexington, Ky.: University of Kentucky Press, 1966), pp. 28–38; Furner, *Advocacy and Objectivity,* pp. 59–80.

[66] During and after his trial at Wisconsin in 1894 on the charges of favoring strikes, assisting strikers, and teaching radical ideas, Ely took pains to emphasize his moderate conservatism. See Richard T. Ely, "Fundamental Beliefs in My Social Philosophy," *Forum* 18 (October 1894): 173–83. In contrast to his earlier support of labor, Ely now wrote that strikes could not be tolerated against "primary institutions" such as the railroads. He disavowed socialism, turned his back on the strikers at Pullman, and defended the government's use of the injunction in Chicago. In the remainder of his career, Ely avoided

the youthful, bold professional than that of being unprofessionally enthusiastic. In the process of re-establishing his scholarly credentials, Ely turned to the research topic of rural land economics, a subject that interested a select few, threatened no one, and lent itself to a vast amount of technical detail and minutiae.[67]

As Ely harshly learned, academic professionals spoke a different language from social reformers. The containment of ideas in the university placed them in a context where they could be managed in functional terms rather than radicalized in a socially demanding ideology. Universities determined the instrumental directions in which the majority of educated Americans in the twentieth century would turn their mental energies. By the early 1900s, social scientists tended to take for granted the premises of America's middle-class, competitive, capitalist society. They concentrated on the social mechanisms and techniques of communication that would make the American system less wasteful. Leading political scientists such as Frank Goodnow, John Fairlie, and William Willoughby researched the efficiency of administrative functions of local and municipal government instead of analyzing the significant conse-

academic-freedom issues, at times letting down former students and friends. He made unsuccessful bids for positions of status at Harvard and Johns Hopkins. He sought to align himself with the cautious careerists in the profession—such men as Edwin R. A. Seligman, Frank W. Taussig, Albion W. Small, Arthur T. Hadley, and the sobered Henry Carter Adams. And he moved away from the controversial topics of government and labor. His cautious views, for example, were evident in Richard T. Ely, *Studies in the Evolution of Industrial Society* (New York: The Macmillan Company, 1903). See Ely's social philosophy expressed in *Ground Under Our Feet: An Autobiography* (New York: The Macmillan Company, 1938), pp. 95–97, 185, 282. See also Rader, *Academic Mind*, pp. 130–58, 162–63; Furner, *Advocacy and Objectivity*, pp. 147–62; Metzger, *Academic Freedom*, pp. 151–62; Paul A. Samuelson, "Economic Thought and the New Industrialism," in Arthur M. Schlesinger, Jr., and Morton White, eds., *Paths of American Thought* (Boston: Houghton Mifflin Company, 1963), p. 228.

[67] See Richard T. Ely, assisted by Mary L. Shine and George S. Wehrwein, *Outlines of Land Economics*, 3 vols. (Ann Arbor, Mich.: Edwards Brothers, 1922); Richard T. Ely, Edward W. Morehouse, *Elements of Land Economics* (New York: The Macmillan Company, 1924).

quences of middle-class attitudes within government for the quality of twentieth-century urban life.[68]

Through the training provided by universities, Americans learned to engage professionally the numerous abnormalities of their middle-class society by individualizing the subject, isolating the cause, and confining the diagnosis to scientifically operative symptoms. The new public-health doctors, for example, confined themselves to the medical problems of individual cases of disease rather than write a prescription for the social causes of poverty in urban ghettos—neighborhoods owned by middle-class property interests and resented politically by middle-class taxpayers. Gynecologists and psychiatrists diagnosed female hysteria as a pathological problem with a scientific etiology related to an individual's physical history rather than anger the public by suggesting that it was a cultural problem related to dissatisfied females in the middle-class home.[69]

[68] See Frank J. Goodnow, *The Principles of the Administrative Law of the United States* (New York and London: G. P. Putnam's Sons, 1905); Goodnow, "The Work of the American Political Science Association: Presidential Address," *Proceedings of the American Political Science Association*, 1 (1905): 35–46; John Archibald Fairlie, *The Centralization of Administration in New York State* (New York: Columbia University Press, 1898); Fairlie, *Municipal Administration* (New York: The Macmillan Company, 1901); Fairlie, *Local Government in Counties, Towns and Villages* (New York: The Century Company, 1906); William Franklin Willoughby, *Territories and Dependencies of the United States: Their Government and Administration* (New York: The Century Company, 1905). In this period, the instrumental view of administrative processes was given theoretical expression by Arthur F. Bentley, *The Process of Government: A Study of Social Pressures* (Chicago: The University of Chicago Press, 1908). See also Bernard Crick, *The American Science of Politics: Its Origins and Conditions* (Berkeley and Los Angeles: University of California Press, 1964), p. 101; Hoxie, ed., *Faculty of Political Science, Columbia University*, pp. 262–63; Furner, *Advocacy and Objectivity*, pp. 284–91. The consequences of realism, relativism, scientific naturalism, and instrumentalism for twentieth-century American thought in the social sciences and jurisprudence are examined by Edward A. Purcell, Jr., in *The Crisis of Democratic Theory: Scientific Naturalism and the Problem of Value* (Lexington, Ky.: The University Press of Kentucky, 1973).

[69] See Barbara Gutmann Rosenkrantz, "Cart Before Horse: Theory Practice and Professional Image in American Public Health, 1870–1920," *Journal of the History of Medicine and Allied Sciences* 29 (Jan-

Middle-class Americans, busy with getting ahead in their own lives, acquiesced to a professional authority which both satisfied their need for individual attention and could be trusted. The first generation of university presidents—especially such men as Charles William Eliot, Daniel Coit Gilman, and Andrew Dickson White—were leaders unparalleled in the history of American higher education. As public spokesmen they were influential in expressing public attitudes sympathetic to professional habits of mind. As educators they activated the social faith in higher learning which sustained the university's expansion in the first seventy years of the twentieth century. As administrators they built the superstructure of a distinctive American institution. They made the university work for their own careers and those of other aspiring persons. They struck the tone of an American education which later generations of the middle class heard and popularized.

uary 1974): 63–64; cf. chapter 3, n. 47; Carroll Smith-Rosenberg, "The Hysterical Woman: Sex Roles and Role Conflict in 19th-Century America," *Social Research* 39 (Winter 1972): 664.

Epilogue

This book is only a beginning in understanding the ties between developments in the nineteenth century and contemporary America. The creation of higher education made a difference in American history at a crucial moment when aspiring middle-class persons were struggling to define new career patterns, establish new institutions, pursue new occupations, and forge a new self-identity. The American university was basic to this struggle. It became a central institution in the competitive, status-conscious political economy of America. It held before the society the image of the modern professional person, who committed himself to an ethic of service, was trained in scientific knowledge, and moved his career relentlessly upward.

Americans initially acted upon this image in the nineteenth century and subsequent generations have continued to refine it. All the recent controversy about the financial value of going to college notwithstanding, the positive image of the successful professional person lives on.[1] In

1 See "Is College Necessary? Caroline Bird Talks with Ernest Boyer," *Change* 7 (February 1975): 32–37; James O'Toole, "The Reserve Army of the Underemployed: I—The World of Work," *Ibid.*, (May 1975), 26–33, 63, "II—The Role of Education," *Ibid.* (June, 1975): 26–33, 62; Richard Freeman and J. Herbert Hollomon, "The Declining Value of College Going," *Ibid.* (September 1975): 24–31, 62; Caroline Bird, *The Case Against College* (New York: Bantam Books, 1975).

the future, Americans will pay considerably more for food, energy, and consumer goods—but their expectations of middle-class comforts, their excitement with careers, and their willingness to compete appear to be as keen as ever. Whatever the price of the culture of professionalism, the majority of Americans have been satisfied to pay it.

Indeed, the American middle class has come of age, and we in the later twentieth century live with the consequences of its vertical vision for everyday thought and action. Human nature has bared itself close to the bone within the culture of professionalism, a specter as fascinating as it is frightening. The many examples of both human dedication and degradation in the behavior of well-placed and well-qualified individuals, of personal nobility and pettiness, service to society and rank self-interest, discovery of great knowledge and shameless exploitation of it for profit, suggest to the historian that social idealism in middle-class America has existed only at the edge of personal cynicism and duplicity.

Perhaps never before within the last century have we as Americans been so aware of the arrogance, shallowness, and potential abuses of the vertical vision by venal individuals who justify their special treatment and betray society's trust by invoking professional privilege, confidence, and secrecy. The question for Americans is, How does society make professional behavior accountable to the public without curtailing the independence upon which creative skills and the imaginative use of knowledge depend? The culture of professionalism has allowed Americans to achieve educated expressions of freedom and self-realization, yet it has also allowed them to perfect educated techniques of fraudulence and deceit. In medicine, law, education, business, government, the ministry—all the proliferating services middle-class Americans thrive on—who shall draw the fine line between competent services and corruption?

Appendix:
Biographical Sketches

James Burrill Angell (b. near Scituate, Rhode Island, 1829; d. Ann Arbor, Michigan, 1916). Angell traced his family to old colonial stock who had lived and prospered in the same Rhode Island neighborhood for generations. He attended local academies and in 1845 entered Brown University, where he maintained an excellent academic record. Angell graduated in 1849, traveled, and was employed briefly as a civil engineer until 1851, decided against becoming a clergyman, and spent the next two years in Europe. In 1853 he accepted the chair of modern languages at Brown, a position he resigned in 1860 after dissatisfaction with educational policy. He then assumed the editorship of the *Providence Journal,* an influential daily which, under Angell's direction, consistently supported both the Republican Party and the Lincoln administration. Unable to purchase the paper, Angell in 1866 accepted the presidency of the University of Vermont, an impoverished institution with neither state support nor a clientele to sustain it. Concentrating on fund-raising, physical improvements, and publicity, he reversed the school's decline. In 1871 Angell's reputation won him the presidency of the prestigious University of Michigan, a coeducational school with a college, law and medical departments, instruction in engineering and pharmacy, and an established faculty. However, the university, which never compared favorably in material terms with private eastern institutions, fell even farther behind during Angell's administration, which lasted thirty-eight years until 1909. Angell's major innovations were professional ones: a broadened base for the student body through extension of the elective system, university certification of state high schools, permanent admission requirements for medical school, the first professorship in education and the first instruction in forestry, comprehensive examinations for the B.A., and organized graduate studies in its own school. While at Michigan, Angell accepted important diplomatic missions to China and to Turkey. He was a regent of the Smithsonian Institute and a founder of the American Historical Association, of which he was president in 1893–94.

Frederick Augustus Porter Barnard (**b. Sheffield, Massachusetts, 1809; d. New York, N.Y., 1889**). Educated in New York State academies, Barnard attended Yale College between 1824 and 1828. In the next eight years, he held a number of educational posts, at Hartford Grammar School, at Yale College (in mathemetics), and at the New York Institution for the Deaf and the Dumb. Between 1837 and 1854 he was professor of mathematics, chemistry, and natural history at the University of Alabama. In 1854 he moved to the University of Mississippi, where he served as president (1856–58) and chancellor (1858–61). When the university became involved in wartime politics, Bernard resigned, though Jefferson Davis offered him an office as investigator of the natural resources in the Confederacy. Barnard moved to Norfolk, Virginia, where under the occupation of Federal troops he wrote his famous *Letter to the President of the United States by a Refugee* (1863). His strenuous support of the Union and indictment of the Confederacy brought Barnard's name and availability to the attention of the trustees of Columbia University, where he was inaugurated as president in 1864. His tenure of office lasted twenty-five years until 1889, during which time he was best known for introducing the elective system and for establishing the School of Mines. After 1879 he advocated the admission of women to the college on an equal basis with men, a measure that was resisted until six months after his death when Barnard College opened. Barnard wrote extensively, primarily pamphlets. He was a public spokesman for rationalizing the systems of measures and weights, which affected Americans in their daily lives. He served as a president of the American Association for the Advancement of Science (1868), a member of the United States Coast Survey, and an editor of Johnson's *Cyclopaedia;* and he took orders in the Protestant Episcopal Church.

John Bascom (b. Genoa, New York, 1827; d. Williamstown, Massachusetts, 1911). The only son of a Puritan minister, who died when Bascom was an infant, he was raised in genteel poverty, with his education provided for by an older sister. He graduated from Williams College in 1849, briefly taught school and studied law, and entered Auburn Seminary in 1851. In 1852 Bascom accepted a position as tutor at Williams College, but teaching rhetoric and oratory was essentially distasteful to him. Instead he attended Andover Theological Seminary in 1854 but then returned to Williams in 1855, his vacillation between the careers of clergyman and educator resolved. During his twenty-two years at Williams he published extensively, in part to compensate for the frustrations in the classroom. Among his books were: *Political Economy* (1859), *Aesthetics or the Science of Beauty* (1862), *Philosophy of Rhetoric* (1866), *Principles of Psychology* (1869), *Science, Philosophy, and Religion* (1871), *Philosophy of English Literature* (1874). In 1874, despairing of advancement at Williams, Bascom accepted the presidency of the University of Wisconsin, which was scarcely more than a large academy, with only 407 students. After thirteen years, during which time he built up the student body, disciplined the institution, and developed the liberal arts curriculum, Bascom was forced to resign in 1887 by the politically aware trustees, who disapproved of his advocacy of prohibitionism, an unpopular measure in Wisconsin. In 1891, following some bad financial investments, he accepted a chair in political science at Williams College and retired in 1903. Thoughout his life, Bascom continued to write, with a partial bibliography listing 178 titles, including twenty books.

Charles William Eliot (b. Boston, Massachusetts, 1834; d. Northeast Harbor, Maine, 1926). Eliot's father, Samuel, was a graduate of Harvard College and Divinity School, a mayor of Boston, and a member of the state legislatures; he was elected to Congress in 1850. His mother, Mary Lyman, came from a prominent merchant family. Charles attended Boston Latin School and entered Harvard in 1849, where he showed special interest in mathematics and science. Graduating in 1853, he was appointed a tutor at Harvard in 1854 and became known as innovative because he used written examinations and laboratory exercises. In 1863 his five-year contract as Assistant Professor expired without promotion, and he left Harvard and went abroad. Then the Massachusetts Institute of Technology appointed him professor of chemistry. He resumed teaching in 1865. In 1869 he published in the *Atlantic Monthly* a two-part article, "The New Education," which brought him to the attention of the Harvard overseers. Reluctant and divided, they elected him president of the corporation, a position he retained for forty years until 1909. Eliot combined conscientious administration with effective public utterances, which almost always served to justify his actions in terms of his lucid and broad conception of an American system of values. His style succeeded. As an administrator he structured the college into a university, increasing its endowment from 2.25 million dollars to over 20 million, increasing the faculty from sixty to six hundred and the student body from one thousand to four thousand. He concentrated all undergraduate studies in the college, building around them semi-autonomous professional schools and research facilities, which subsequently drew upon the talent graduated from the college. In 1872 graduate degrees (M.A., Ph.D.) were established, followed in 1890 by a Graduate School of Arts and Sciences. In the schools of Divinity, Law, and Medicine he formalized entrance requirements, courses of study, and written examinations. Instruction in private classes for women led to the founding of Radcliffe College in 1894. Eliot raised faculty salaries and introduced sabbatical leaves, retirement pensions, and exchange professorships in France and Germany. In the college, Eliot's radical "elective" system was based on the principle that students were qualified to enter, and he naturally interested himself in admission requirements and secondary-school preparation. He became active in the National Education Association, among other groups, and chaired the report of the Committee of Ten (1892), which recommended college preparatory programs in high school and encouraged the creation of the Board of College Entrance Examinations (1901). After he retired from the Harvard presidency, Eliot remained enormously active: as an overseer at Harvard, a trustee of the Rockefeller and Carnegie Foundations, the editor of the Harvard Classics, the first president of the American Social Hygiene Association, and an architect of profit-sharing plans for American industry. He collected and published his many and varying addresses in at least fifteen separate volumes.

William Watts Folwell (b. Romulus, New York, 1833; d. 1929). Born on a farm, Folwell found his rural parents sympathetic to education, and he prepared himself for college at local academies. Interrupting his education for two years, he taught in district schools, while spending each summer working on the farm. In 1857 he graduated from Hobart College, returning there in 1858 to teach mathematics, Latin, and Greek and to study law, which he abandoned for philology within a year. In 1860 Folwell matriculated as a student of philology at the University of Berlin. Returning home after touring Europe, he enlisted and served as an officer and engineer in the Army of the Potomac during the Civil War (the only one of the presidents to wear a uniform). In 1865 he entered his farther-in-law's merchant and milling business in Ohio; in 1868 he joined the faculty at Kenyon College as a professor of mathematics and civil engineering; and in 1869 he became the first president of the University of Minnesota. During his fifteen years in office, Folwell devoted considerable effort toward establishing a comprehensive educational system in the state, with the university at the pinnacle, and including in the program junior colleges, state aid to high schools for university-bound students, and a shortened winter course for farmers. Administrative friction with the trustees eventually forced his resignation in 1884, but Folwell continued at the university as librarian and professor of political science until his retirement in 1907. He actively participated, especially in the 1880s and 1890s, in the numerous voluntary, philanthropic, and professional societies then appearing in Minnesota: Historical, Fine Arts, Geological Survey, Park Commission, Charity and Corrections. The last decade of Folwell's life, spanning nearly a century, was spent writing a comprehensive history of the state from original documents and sources.

Daniel Coit Gilman (b. Norwich, Connecticut, 1831; d. Norwich, 1908). Gilman's father was a prosperous businessman with an old colonial lineage who provided well for his son. Daniel attended Yale College (1848–52), where he studied sciences with Benjamin Silliman and James Dwight Dana. After graduation he lived at Harvard with Arnold Guyot, who influenced his emerging professional interest in geography. Between 1853 and 1855 he served together with his close college friend, A. D. White, as an attaché of the American legation at St. Petersburg. In 1856 Dana at Yale enlisted Gilman to draw up the plan for the proposed Sheffield

Scientific School, where Gilman resided for the next seventeen years as librarian, secretary, and professor of political and physical geography. He was the first administrator to take advantage of the funds which the Morrill Act of 1862 made available for the study of science and technology. Gilman refused the presidency at both the University of Wisconsin in 1867 and the University of California in 1870, accepting the latter position in 1872, after he lost out to Noah Porter in the previous year in the competition for the Yale presidency. Acrimonious state politics in California, which reduced the university to a pawn, dismayed the recently arrived Gilman. In 1874, Eliot, White, and Angell all recommended Gilman's name for the first presidency of Johns Hopkins, a genuine research and graduate institution which opened in 1876, after Gilman's extensive search for a qualified faculty in 1875. One portion of the endowment went to the university, and one to the hospital, which opened in 1889. The medical school finally opened in 1893, only after Gilman laid down the consequential principle that the university rather than the hospital would control all medical education. Moreover, asserting exceptionally high standards for the day, the medical school accepted only college graduates. After twenty-seven years, Gilman retired from the presidency in 1902, but he immediately accepted Andrew Carnegie's personal invitation to become the first president of the Carnegie Institution of Washington, which he left in frustration after three years. Gilman's many organizational activities included the American Social Science Association, the John F. Slater Fund, the Peabody Educational Fund, the Russell Sage Foundation, and the National Civil Service Reform League.

James McCosh (b. Ayrshire, Scotland, 1811; d. Princeton, New Jersey, 1894). McCosh attended Glasgow University and, after a distinguished record there, finished his studies at Edinburgh University in 1833. In 1834 he was licensed to preach in the Established Church of Scotland. Between 1835 and 1839 he held a number of pastorates, and from 1839 to 1851 served as minister in Brechin. In 1843 he joined the liberals who seceded from the state church to establish the Free Church of Scotland, thereby sacrificing their secure income. The publication of McCosh's first book, *The Method of the Divine Government, Physical and Moral* (1850), in which he embraced the intuitionism of the Scottish school and rejected John Stuart Mill, brought him to public attention and led in 1852 to a professorship of logic and metaphysics in Queens College, Belfast, where he remained until 1868. During these years, McCosh published four books which established his reputation as a formidable advocate of Scottish Realism and a severe critic of the sensational psychology, the hedonistic ethics, the empirical logic, and the religious skepticism of Mill and the British Utilitarians. In 1868 the trustees called McCosh to the presidency of Princeton, exactly one hundred years after the Scotsman John Witherspoon had filled the same position. McCosh, an efficient administrator and an effective teacher, reversed the fortunes of the ebbing institution, which suffered from the loss of southern students during and after the Civil War. He built up the faculty, established a balanced elective system, introduced graduate studies, found money for fellowships and research grants, encouraged the sciences, and expanded the physical plant. Moreover, he continued to publish prolifically, book after book, and in the early 1870s he alone among orthodox ministers dared, in *Christianity and Positivism* (1871), to reconcile both the doctrine of evolution and the existence of the Divinity. After twenty years McCosh resigned the presidency in 1888 and retired to pursue his persistent ambition of formulating a native American philosophy grounded in the tenets of Scottish Realism.

Noah Porter (b. Farmington, Connecticut, 1811; d. New Haven, Connecticut, 1892). Porter was born in a town in which his ancestor had been an original proprietor, and his father was pastor of the Congregational Church for sixty years. Educated at the local academy, Porter entered Yale College and graduated in 1831. For the next four years he taught at a grammar school, studied divinity, and tutored at Yale. In 1836 he was ordained, married the daughter of New Haven theologian Nathaniel William Taylor, and became pastor in the well-to-do rural parish at New Milford, Connecticut. In 1843 he moved to Springfield, Massachusetts, as pastor of the Second Congregational Church, and in 1846 he returned to Yale College to become Clark Professor of Moral Philosophy and Metaphysics. He spent the year 1853–54 studying at the University of Berlin. During his many years at Yale, Porter devoted considerable energy to structuring and formalizing the liberal arts curriculum. And in 1871 the trustees selected him to become the president of Yale College, a position he retained for fifteen years until 1886. His administration was controversial, with critics accusing Porter of defending the classics and the Christian college to the detriment of the overall develop-

ment of Yale as a modern university. His veto of William Graham
Sumner's adoption of Herbert Spencer's *Study of Sociology* as a
textbook brought Porter notoriety when the newspapers publicized the case. Porter's reputation mainly rests on his scholarly
achievements as a moral philosopher. His major work, *The
Human Intellect* (1868), was reissued many times and received
international recognition. The educated public acknowledged
that many of his popular essays were useful humanistic criticisms
of uncompromising positivistic sciences: *The Sciences of Nature
Versus the Science of Man* (1871), *The American Colleges and
the American Public* (1870, 1878), *Science and Sentiment* (1882).
In 1864 Porter became the editor of Noah Webster's *American
Dictionary of the English Language,* and in 1890 he edited
Webster's International Dictionary of the English Language.

Andrew Dickson White (b. Homer, New York, 1832; d. Ithaca,
New York, 1918). White's father was a banker, a man of background and wealth, and a zealous convert to Episcopalianism who
sent Andrew first to a parish school and then to Geneva College.
Rebelling against the church school after one year, White entered
Yale, the school of his choice. He earned an excellent record,
graduated in 1853, and traveled abroad to study and spend a year
as an American attaché in St. Petersburg (1854–55). In 1856 he
returned to Yale for the A.M., and in 1857 became professor of
history at the University of Michigan. With the death of his father
in 1860, White inherited considerable wealth. Since 1858 he had
been thinking about a state university for New York, a project
which his public efforts against slavery pushed into the background until 1863, when he was elected to the New York State
Senate and became chairman of the Education Committee. White
codified school laws, created new normal schools, and combined
both the Morrill Act's land grant and Ezra Cornell's large gift to
draw up a charter and a plan for Cornell University, which
opened in 1868. Ezra Cornell insisted that White resign his
Michigan position, and become president of the new university,
at which he also would be the professor of history. According to
White's plan, Cornell University would be noted for its elective
program and equality of studies leading to equal degrees, for its
use of distinguished scholars as nonresident professors, and for
its "manly" treatment of students. White's self-image was that of
a productive historian familiar with the sources, a spokesman
for educational policy, a publicist, and an expert competent to

handle important public affairs. At Cornell he generally turned administrative matters over to others, though he did not—when he could be found in residence—personally avoid confronting the financial crisis that impoverished the university in the 1870s. White left Ithaca frequently: to serve as a member of a government commission (1871), to write a report (1872), for reasons of health (1876–78), to be ambassador to Germany (1878–81). He wrote and spoke extensively; he fought for civil service reform; he was the first president and a founder of the American Historical Association (1884). He happily resigned the Cornell presidency in 1885. In the following years he lectured at many universities, refused the first presidency of Stanford, and toured the hemisphere, at times in Andrew Carnegie's private car. In 1892–94 White was minister to Russia, in 1897–1902 ambassador to Germany, in 1899 head of the American delegation to the Hague Conference. He advised Carnegie and served as a trustee for several of his big projects. White's successful books included *History of the Warfare of Science with Theology in Christendom* (1896), *Autobiography of Andrew Dickson White* (1905), and *Seven Great Statesmen in the Warfare of Humanity with Unreason* (1910).

Index